UNDER CRITICISM

UNDER CRITICISM

Essays for William H. Pritchard

Edited by

David Sofield and Herbert F. Tucker

OHIO UNIVERSITY PRESS

ATHENS

Ohio University Press, Athens, Ohio 45701
© 1998 by David Sofield and Herbert F. Tucker
Printed in the United States of America
All rights reserved

02 01 00 99 98   5 4 3 2 1

Acknowledgments

The editors thank Tom Gerety, Lisa Raskin, Ella Kusnetz, and Julie Howland in Amherst, Rob Pursley and Barbara Smith in Charlottesville, and at Ohio University Press David Sanders, Gillian Berchowitz, and Nancy Basmajian.

"Last Will and Testament of an Ex-Literary Critic" by Frank Lentricchia appeared previously in *Lingua Franca*.

Library of Congress Cataloging-in-Publication Data
Under criticism : essays for William H. Pritchard / edited by David
  Sofield and Herbert F. Tucker.
     p.   cm.
  Published on the occasion of William H. Pritchard's fortieth year
of teaching at Amherst College.
  Includes bibliographical references and index.
  ISBN 0-8214-1224-8 (cloth : alk. paper)
  1. Pritchard, William H. 2. Criticism. I. Pritchard, William H.
II. Sofield, David. III. Tucker, Herbert F.
PN85.U55   1998
809—dc21   97-37650
                                                      CIP

Theodore Baird
1901–1996

It was the obstinately gentle air
That may be clamored at by cause and sect
But it will have its moment to reflect.

Contents

II

Professions: Criticism in Question

III

Readings: Criticism in Practice

UNDER CRITICISM

Herbert F. Tucker

Introduction

Counter-Love, Original Response

T HE ESSAYS THAT follow were sought out on account of their authors'
relation to William H. Pritchard, and they are published on the occasion of his fortieth year of teaching at Amherst College, his alma mater.
In a career that spans five decades Bill Pritchard has built up the many
kinds of relation that array a teacher-critic with his catholicity and charm,
a literary reviewer with his stamina, a colleague and friend with his un-
failing interest in what can be said about what books can say. These traits
of Bill's have drawn into our collection essays from a remarkable spec-
trum of contributors: distinguished and emeritus professors' work appears here, and so does a current graduate student's; writing by Bill's
former pupils adjoins that of his own peers in study at Amherst and Harvard. The collection also boasts a literary-historical sweep that outgoes
even Pritchard's. While addressing particularly his areas of expertise in
transatlantic modern literature and criticism, our contributors reach
all the way back to the Gilgamesh epic and pay respects on the home
stretch to Plutarch, to Chaucer, and several times to a figure who, given
Bill's *Lives of the Modern Poets*, has a special tutelary status here: Samuel
Johnson.

Contributors were encouraged from the outset to submit essays of a personal rather than academic kind: a distinction that our authors have construed in a variety of ways. As a result the reader will find strongly represented in this book writing that approaches pedagogical topics by means of anecdote, memoir, and confession (sometimes by that name, oftener by implication). These tales out of school, mostly grouped in part I under the rubric "Criticism in Training," share as a point of departure the memoir Bill Pritchard published as *English Papers* in 1995. That volume, together with Robin Varnum's account the next year of Amherst's extraordinary record of composition instruction in the time of Theodore Baird, *Fencing with Words,* and with the discerning 1997 review Bill published in *Raritan,* constitutes a veritable archive for the study of a signal episode in the development of English as a discipline. So the testimonial essays on teaching and learning that are gathered in our first section possess, independently of other and more obvious virtues, documentary value as materials for the history of American liberal education in the twentieth century.

Another result of the editors' invitation to write personally for *Under Criticism* is that its contents exhibit a degree of ideological divergence that is seldom seen today in an academic book, and that is the more noteworthy in view of what might have been reckoned the trimming pressure that a one-man, one-college occasion would exert. Marxist, humanist, phenomenologist, deconstructionist, feminist, classicist, postmodernist, revanchist positions are all aired in these pages—now for broadcast, now for fumigation. A well-tempered spirit of decency breathes through the whole, the editors trust, yet not so pacifically as to lull the reader into mistaking courtesy for temporizing. Most prominently in part II, "Criticism in Question," but actually right across the book, our contributors leave small doubt that the personal kindles the polemical, and that frank, crisp judgment is something criticism needs if it is to prosper.

The clarity of candor and the grace of strong views are merits long familiar to students whose encounters with Lewis or Frost or Jarrell have been sharpened on Bill Pritchard's books, and more familiar still to followers of his steady output of periodical essays and reviews. As lately anthologized in *Playing It by Ear* (1994), these writings constitute the most cogent proof—maybe the only possible proof—for the thesis propounded in that collection's keynote essay, "Ear Training." In this his critical manifesto, Pritchard of Amherst maintains in theory (and with the understated authority of the lapsed philosophy student he is) a position resolutely anti-theoretical: The whole of criticism is less than the sum of its parts. In class or out, criticism dies once it loses touch with the practical experience of the specific instance. Ideas and facts are things criticism must work with, but the moment it starts working *for* them it has ceased to be criticism and become something else. In order to have a hearing the critic needs to keep listening. This prescription of Bill's seems in one sense amiably modest, yet in another sense its ambition is breathtaking. For it throws the whole burden of proof onto the unbeholden, unaccommodated act of critical response. It leaves the critic nothing to go on, or turn to, but nerve—senses, sympathies, wits trained on a lifetime's reading —in a fresh confrontation with writing whose weight or beauty or interest only that confrontation, and certainly no hearsay, can disclose. This is the species of high challenge that summons the essays comprised by part III of our book, "Criticism in Practice," an ensemble of independent interpretations that bear out a Pritchard principle: The best revenge is reading well.

It has been a lively concern of the editors all along to keep our invitation to *contribute* clear of the Brahmsy, festschriftlich bunting of *tribute*; from the first we have had in mind a book that would honor its Amherst occasion by exceeding it. Yet despite our vigilance the range of contributors, literary works, critical topics, and perspectives gathered for discussion here does constitute a tribute, and by reason of their very range. At a pitch beyond the skill of editors to coax or inhibit, this book renders tribute to the breadth of Bill Pritchard's circle of literary acquaintance, and also to a fine persistence in certain manners of approach and habits of focus that go, among that circle, under the name of criticism. Since it is these manners and habits that give our book what unity it may claim, let me conclude with a word about them and about the shared disposition of response they evince. And since the invitation to write personally applies here across the board, let me have my say in a mode of commentary and appreciation that is now, for me, second nature.

〜

Criticism may stop at nothing, but it has to start at something. It lives by the provocation of what Frost memorably named *original response:*

> Some morning from the boulder-broken beach
> He would cry out on life, that what it wants
> Is not its own love back in copy speech,
> But counter-love, original response.

Some poet before Frost must have seen how in American English the match between *wants* and *response* might renew an old figure of thought by rhyming it into a figure of sound. But seldom can the call-and-reply of rhyme have answered so fully to the purpose as here in "The Most of It." The whole quatrain being about repetition with a difference, it is rightly clinched a little awry: the rhyme stands for love, and does so the more firmly thanks to the syntactic and etymological unlikeness between the parts of speech it does not copy but couples. The same goes for the reverberation that brings the consonants in *cry out on life* back with overtones in *counter-love*—a cry broken yet mended, altered yet recognized—much as the rhythmic urging of the spondee *cry out* is mated, rather than echoed, with the iambic promise of *response*.

Whether the emergence and transit of the "great buck" that soon engrosses "The Most of It" represents an answer to this outcry, or just a sequel, is a point the poem spectacularly moots ("—and that was all"), leaving us to return and see how our quatrain has anticipated the riddling of the whole. *Cry out on life* is that odd Frostian thing a nonce idiom, a turn of phrase that sounds homier at a distance than it proves close up. The phrase summons to mind the invocatives "cry out to life" and "call on life," but it's not these exactly. And the utterance it describes will prove less than satisfactory as either an invocation of anything so numinous as Life, or an evocation of anything so phenomenal as the buck. That the cry can conjure phenomena at all, much less sort out what they mean, is as far from certain as *cry out on life* is far from the rigor of challenge ("call life out") or judgment ("declaim on life"). What Frost's nonce idiom does instead declare is a state of *provocation*: a state of mind that half observes, and half invents, what it cries out on; better yet, that makes of observation a type of invention.

The hard, spare, diagrammatic quality of circumstance that grounds "The Most of It" sets off the provoking "He" of the poem as a man elementally provoked into his calling. He is, let us say, a first critic. His very call for original response is an original response *avant la lettre:* a drawing up of conditions within a frame of things that is given, yet that his outcry, by reframing, unsettles. To hear that desirous, contrary outcry as a paradigm of the *counter-love* it solicits in return—an articulate restoration to life of what life mutely wants—is to understand how much the prosodic link between *wants* and *response* has to say about the antiphonal implication of the answer in the question, and of the satisfaction in the need. The counter-love of original response performs within Frost's quatrain, across the figural tradition of echo writing with which it resonates, and in the practice of reading that learns to attend to both, a criticism of life.

That criticism might be at once responsively and originally practiced is something I learned at Amherst College under the example and tutelage of William H. Pritchard. His was the first voice I ever heard read out "The Most of It," one of many poems he showed students it was possible to render in an understated but engaged way that took life from the text and rendered something back. Class time on either side of these vocal readings would be given to interpretation, though even this more ordinarily academic kind of "reading" took the form less of exegesis (what a passage might mean) than of replay and reply (how it sounded or felt, and what *that* might mean). Even by an Amherst standard this teaching was remarkable, I realized long afterwards, for its habit of keeping interpretation-as-commentary responsible to interpretation-as-performance. Neither priestly possession of the text nor rhapsodic possession by it—indeed, anything but—Bill's recitations had instead to do with an intelligence playing in and off the contours of language as they shaped forth an attitude. And to this attitude criticism paid its respects, with interest, by the candor of a praise or dispraise whose currency lay in vocal attentiveness. Here was counter-love, original response in the lingua franca of what another Frost poem calls "oversound," a medium that made difficulty interesting and that invited emulation. After a class of Professor Pritchard's on Eliot or Hardy or Yeats, never again would words' song be the same.

About what I once learned to emulate I have since come to understand that it draws on the odd, virtually bottomless fund of critical desire, which is the desire to hail creative power by responding to it as if for the first time. What criticism wants is to *rejoin:* not to make the initial move itself, and not to second somebody else's motion either; but to get back to authentic originality by getting back *at* it, in a sense, and framing a rejoinder that answers one provocation with another. As counter-love, the desire of criticism puts up that loyal opposition which Blake called truest friendship; as scholarly or teacherly care, it complements an essential curatorial duty to get things right with a quite different and no less essential duty, which Arnold called curiosity, to find things wrong, or at least enough out of line to stay in play. Because criticism may stop at nothing, original response means taking even the hallowed classic or finished masterpiece as an open question that needs to be talked back to. And this constitutive openness entails, in turn, putting off whatever conclusive authority the critic seems to be putting on. Join this game and you find yourself under criticism.

I

LESSONS
Criticism in Training

William J. Pritchard

Hearing Voices

I<small>N</small> 1994, <small>PREPARING</small> to study for my Ph.D. qualifying exams, I got the idea that I could hear rather than read some of the works on my lists. *Clarissa* and *The Life of Johnson* I would take in through my eyes, but the poetry, I thought, might be better ingested aurally. As someone who knows hundreds of songs but only a handful of poems, I figured I might be more likely to remember, say, "Alexander's Feast" or "The Garden" if I experienced them as sounds rather than sights. My plan was that each day, on my twenty-minute walks to and from the library, I would listen not to my usual tapes of assorted popular music but to tapes of poetry. On a visit to my parents, I announced this plan and asked my father (whom this volume honors) if he would make me a tape of his reading of some seventeenth- and eighteenth-century poems. He agreed to do so, and later that summer he sent me a ninety-minute cassette entitled "Poems, 1600–1780."

Like much about my exam preparation, such as my plan to set aside the final two weeks for reviewing and reflecting on what I had read, the poems-on-tape scheme was not realized as I had imagined it. For one thing, I discovered that I quite badly needed a shot of rhythm and blues both before and after a day of reading in the library; unknown poems proved no match for the easy gratification of familiar tunes. Also, I never got around to recording any poetry tapes of my own. My sole tape was the one my father made, and that, because my instructions to him had been entirely vague, turned out to contain only a few poems that I needed to know for the exam. Still, although the tape played no role in my exam preparation, it did become valuable to me both as an anthology of poems that matter to my father and as a document of his voice speaking through those poems (and those poems speaking through his voice). In the pages that follow, I want to describe what is on the tape, to characterize the difficulties and pleasures of listening to it, and to consider the tape in relation to some of the ideas in my father's essay "Ear Training," which he has termed his "Credo."[1]

Side A begins with some short lyrics by minor poets (Ralegh, Davies, Nashe, Shirley) and then serves up larger helpings of Jonson, Donne, and Herbert (and a tentative few of Shakespeare sonnets). Side B closes out the seventeenth century with Carew, Marvell, and Dryden (forgoing Milton), and then, as the tape grows full, hurries through a truncated eighteenth century that contains only Pope and a bit of Cowper. The preference, for obvious reasons, is for shorter, lyric poems; the major poems of Dryden and Pope appear only in excerpts. The poems are read always with care, though not always flawlessly; mistakes are corrected but not erased. The cassette itself is of low quality, suitable for recording an interview or board meeting or other occasion upon which the musical qualities of the human voice are not of interest. So there is a substantial amount of hiss on the tape, and my father's voice, already somewhat narrow in its range, is further compressed and flattened. His upstate New York accent can be detected at times, pushing "God" towards "Gawd," and the vocal style tends to be percussive and staccato rather than sonorous and legato. Monosyllables such as "wit" and "what" and "yet" are pronounced almost without vowels, and moments of pure vowel, such as the interjection "O!," are rendered not with full-throated ease but more as a kind of groan. (At one point on the tape, he describes his voice as "lugubrious.") There are occasional glimmers of irony in his voice, when he comes across a phrase that he himself uses ironically ("dear boy") or when (as in these lines from "Windsor Forest") there is a wide discrepancy between the diction of the verse and that of his own normal speech: "GRANVILLE commands; your aid, O Muses bring! / What Muse for GRANVILLE can refuse to sing?"

Still, whatever the limitations of the human and electronic equipment, together they produce moments of remarkable elegance and poise, even passion. The delicate ending of Jonson's poem on the death of his daughter ("This grave partakes the fleshly birth; / Which cover lightly, gentle earth") is handled with admirable restraint; the reading of Donne's "Good Friday, 1613. Riding Westward," perhaps the high point of the tape, is quite gripping in its sustained intensity. Many of the readings betray a deep inwardness with the poems; these are, as he remarks at one point, poems he has lived with for a long time. The voice moves confidently and steadily, though not effortlessly, from line to line.

For there is always effort. Throughout the tape, a slight strain is audible, as he navigates these demanding vocal passages and attempts to perform what they seem to require of the voice. Sometimes he follows a poem with an apology for not getting it quite right; sometimes a poet is introduced as being especially unreadable, as in this worried preamble: "Herbert. A problem. What to read of Herbert, and how to read Herbert? My voice not right for Herbert. *Whose* voice is right for Herbert?"

That sense of an unattainable "rightness" of performance, I want to suggest, is an important corollary to the argument of my father's essay "Ear Training." There he develops Robert Frost's distinction between "eye readers" and "ear readers," characterizing and championing the latter. The ear reader, Frost says, is the sort who reads slowly and attentively enough to hear "the sentence sounds." Keeping this reader in mind, a writer will "[n]ever . . . write down a sentence in which the voice will not know how to posture *specially*," since "[t]he reader must be at no loss to give his voice the posture proper to the sentence."[2] Frost insists, for instance, upon "the very special tone with which you must say" the second sentence of his poem, "A Patch of Old Snow": "You must be able to say Oh yes one knows how that goes." But in further examples Frost admits, "I can hear it better than I can say it. And by oral practice I get further and further away from it."[3]

Ear reading, then, differs from reading aloud and may not facilitate it. The ear reader can hear, in the mind's ear, the "right" version of a poem, its Platonic ideal, but will find his or her voice unable to realize that ideal in performance ("oral practice"). An awareness of this inability can be frustrating but perhaps also liberating. I recently heard my father tell a class of freshmen not to bother saying they were no good at reading poetry aloud; he reassured them that, in attempting that activity, "we're all inadequate in different ways." But he might have added, in a more discriminating vein, that an ability to perceive one's own inadequacy, to hear and to try to correct the ways in which one's reading falls short, is the mark of a trained ear.

It is in the moments when he corrects himself that my father's ear training reveals itself most obviously on the tape. For example, he begins Ralegh's poem to his son as follows:

> Three things there be that prosper up apace
> And flourish, whilst they grow asunder far.
> But on a day they meet all in one place,
> And when they meet . . . And *when* they meet, they one another mar.

The first time he lands with too much force upon the "meet" of line four, a word which, having been spoken in the previous line, does not require such emphasis. The corrected reading brings out instead the poem's progress from the vague "on a day they meet" to the more ominous "And when they meet . . . ." Of course, one might also wish to emphasize the second "meet," so as to underscore the line's alliterative pairing of "meet" and "mar." Or one might seek a compromise solution and attempt to emphasize both "when" and "meet," but one's voice will probably prove incapable of such refinement and precision.

On the tape, my father rereads not only to correct mistakes but also to handle moments when the voice cannot, in one reading, convey the complexities of a word or line. The pun at the end of Jonson's sonnet "To William Roe" requires, on the tape, two different pronunciations:

> This is that good Aeneas, passed through fire,
> Through seas, storms, tempests; and embarked for hell,
> Came back untouched. This man hath traveled well . . . travailed well.

Similarly, my father feels the need to offer two versions of the final line of Marvell's "richly ambiguous and ironic" poem "Mourning":

> I yet my silent judgment keep,
> Disputing not what they believe;
> But sure, as oft as women weep,
> It is to be supposed, they grieve . . .
> It is to be sup*posed* they grieve.

A final line such as this one may be likened to the famous duck/rabbit optical illusion, which can be seen as either a duck or a rabbit, but never as both at once. On the page, the line conveys perhaps trust in, perhaps skepticism of women's tears; read aloud, the voice must choose.

"My voice not right for Herbert. *Whose* voice is right for Herbert?" One possible answer to the question would be, "Herbert's voice." The enduring institution of the poetry reading suggests that the author is fittest reader of the poem, the one most keenly attentive to its technical and emotional intricacies. Marvell, perhaps, could perfectly capture the appropriate "posture" required for the last line of "Mourning." And yet it often happens that poets read their works idiosyncratically, or self-indulgently, or just plain badly. F. R. Leavis has this to say of T. S. Eliot's rendition of his *Four Quartets*:

> Mr Eliot, if a great composer, is not a great, or good, or even a tolerable executant. His voice, as he uses it, is disconcertingly lacking in body. One wouldn't wish him to elocute in the manner of Mr Robert Speaight (whose *actor's* declamation of Mr Eliot's verse empties it), but a capacity for some strength of tone is clearly desirable. Mr Eliot's reading is of course not un-intelligent and insensitive in the actor's way, but it is not positively intelligent and sensitive in the way one would have expected of the poet himself. Judged by that standard it *is* unintelligent. His command of inflexion, intonation and tempo—his *intention*, as performer, under these heads—is astonishingly inadequate.[4]

The poet's "astonishingly inadequate" way of reading is redeemed only in contrast with "the actor's way," which is to elocute and declaim and empty the verse. Thus another possible answer to the question "Whose voice is right for Herbert?" is rejected. Geoffrey Hutchings, in an essay entitled "Reading Poetry Aloud," seconds this rejection: "With few exceptions, professional actors are not inclined to permit a poem to do its own work, and consequently read poetry poorly."[5] Hutchings advocates allowing the poem "to speak for itself," but he later suggests that poems lack clues as to how the voice should, in Frost's words, "posture specially." The reader aloud, Hutchings says, must "impose upon the perceived grammatical structure a dimension lacking from the visual code—that is, appropriate intonation patterns." For Hutchings, the printed poem lacks something that the voice must supply; for Frost and Pritchard, the poem contains sounds and senses that the voice can never entirely capture or convey.

Another point of difference between Hutchings and Pritchard is Hutchings's pious insistence that "the reader aloud is a performer who operates between the original message and the recipient and he has a grave responsibility not to obscure that message. Thus he must arrive at a thorough comprehension himself before projecting the poem" (38). In contrast, my father bluntly declares, "I don't have to understand these poems.

In fact, I don't." To prove his point, he proceeds to read Shakespeare's bewildering Sonnet 94 ("They that have power to hurt and will do none"). My father would certainly scoff at the idea that one could *ever* "arrive at a thorough comprehension" of the "original message" of any poem worth "projecting." In "Ear Training" he expresses a desire to forgo the search for meanings and messages and to stay instead at the level of language, or perhaps technique: "[A]ggressive and all-too-confident ways of understanding . . . get in the way of good reading. They do so by providing crude and hasty ways for us to avoid what we should be engaged in; namely, with *listening* to the rhythms and manner of presentation, the 'feel' of the scene" (Hemingway's "Indian Camp" is the text under criticism here).[6] A reader who is not concerned to figure out the poem's (or the story's) Meaning will conceivably be more receptive, more alive to felicities or peculiarities of language that might mean as much or more than the poem's "original message." Thus on the tape, before reading the anonymous "Weep No More," my father admits, "I don't know what this means," but after it he singles out the poem's ninth line for praise: "I think old Anon. did well there, especially with 'Sleep is a reconciling.'"

When listening to the tape, I find I have no choice but to stay at the level of language. Many a poem on the tape has washed over my ears without my even being certain of its topic, let alone its message. For a variety of reasons, it is almost impossible for me to follow even the shortest of the poems on the tape from beginning to end. Often my mind gets stuck on an intriguing phrase, such as "Sleep is a reconciling" or (in "Good Friday, 1613. Riding Westward") the couplet, "There I should see a sun by rising set, / And by that setting endless day beget." My mind pauses to untangle the conceit—sun/son, rising/setting—and when I rejoin the poem, I find it has ridden a good deal further westward without me. The listener, of course, does not control the pace at which a poem is read (most of the poems on the tape go along at a moderate clip). With the page before my eyes, I can pause or reread in order to refocus my wandering attention; pausing or rewinding the tape is a more cumbersome and inexact business.

When I do manage to keep pace with a poem, it is not usually by following its train of thought but rather by counting its syllables. Meter and rhyme scheme and stanzaic form are relatively simple matters to the eye reader, but they are much harder for the ear to detect alone. I was surprised to find, when transcribing poems from the tape, how quickly they "took shape"—that is, how readily form became visible where it had not been audible. My difficulty in hearing poetic form on tape is partly a condition of my father's reading, which tends to make the most of enjambments and irregularities in meter. His reading of Thomas Carew's heavily enjambed "The Spring" faithfully follows the poem's "sentence sounds" and hides the fact—immediately evident to the eye—that it was written in heroic couplets. Here is how the poem's opening lines look to the ear:

> Now that the winter's gone,
> The earth hath lost her snow-white robes;
> And now no more the frost candies the grass,
> Or casts an icy cream upon the silver lake or crystal stream;
> But the warm sun thaws the benumbed earth and makes it tender,
> Gives a second birth to the dead swallow,
> Wakes in hollow tree the drowsy cuckoo and the humble bee;
> Now do a choir of chirping minstrels sing
> In triumph to the world, the youthful spring.
> The valleys, hills and woods in rich array
> Welcome the coming of the longed-for May.
> Now all things smile; only my love doth lower.
> Nor hath the scalding noonday sun the power to melt that marble ice
> Which still doth hold her heart congealed
> And makes her pity cold.

Hearing it as I have transcribed it above and not seeing it properly written out, one misses much of the play between sentence sounds and couplet sounds that—to the eye reader, who can see the text—makes the poem. It may be that, despite Hutchings's insistence "that all poetry is meant to be heard and that hearing it read aloud adds a dimension to its enjoyment and appreciation," some poems should be seen and not heard, or at least seen as well as heard. "Speech alone," says Herbert, "Doth vanish like a flaring thing / And in the ear, not conscience, ring."

Another potential distraction from the poems on the tape is my father's prefatory remarks about them. Carew's "The Spring," for instance, when it arrives halfway through the tape, is introduced by these words:

> OK, now I've been waiting to read this poem. This is my most beloved
> poem, or at least I've made it into that—what I memorized in the summer
> of 1953, out there in Lake Geneva, Wisconsin, as I was reading the Viking
> Portable Library *Poets of the English Language*, just came across this poem
> by Thomas Carew, called "The Spring." And, as you can see, this is, this is
> the perfect poem, I think.

Such an introduction creates interest, certainly, but also complications. Whereas my father "just came across this poem," I encounter it as a thing already perfect and beloved. I listen to the poem, try to hear for myself its perfection and, inevitably, do not recognize it. (I think of this as the *Citizen Kane* syndrome: you go to see the greatest film ever made, and sit through it wondering what's so "greatest" about it.) Besides, what was more immediately compelling to me than the rather conventional dramatic situation of the poem was the image of my father, fresh out of college, in Wisconsin for some strange reason, acquainting himself with the canon, testing his mettle on the poets of the English language. The romance of this scenario, and its analogy to my own exam preparation, gave me much to think about while I failed to attend to the poem ringing in my ears. Jonson's "To Lucy, Countess of Bedford, with Mr. Donne's Satires" is preceded on the tape by a similarly diverting anecdote:

> [This] is a memorable poem to me because I heard it first when Paul Alpers, my friend, quoted it in a seminar by Reuben Brower on Pope, in a report about Pope, and I'd never heard this poem before, never heard of Alpers before, but he read it with such warmth that it's always stayed in my mind as a favorite poem, favorite Jonson poem.

The twin constellations of distinguished poets (Donne, Jonson, and Pope) and critics (Brower, Alpers, and Pritchard) tend, for me, to outshine "Lucy, you brightness of our sphere, who are / The Muses' evening, as their morning star."

It is misleading, however, to suggest that these prefatory remarks only obstruct access to the poems. They also provide a way in, by detailing some of the ways in which seventeenth-century poetry might matter to someone today. Interestingly, the way in which many of these poems began to matter to my father, what first made him want to live with them, was (as with "To Lucy") the experience of hearing them read aloud. Frost, Brower, Theodore Baird, and G. Armour Craig are all invoked, in addition to Alpers, as previous, memorable readers of poems on the tape. The critical voices, also, of Leavis, Eliot, and Yvor Winters are remembered as having provided invitations to individual poems. In that sense, then, Carew's "The Spring"—the fortuitous discovery in a mute anthology—is something of an anomaly. When my father encountered most of these poems, they already belonged to other voices, and it was in part his allegiance to and respect for those voices that made the encounter significant.

At one moment in the tape, he half-jokingly requires similar allegiance of me. He introduces "Good Friday, 1613. Riding Westward" as a poem "which Armour Craig read aloud and it made an impression on me and I memorized it." He then adds, "So, Will, promise to memorize this." This adjuration, like the present of Pound's *Cantos* which I received one Christmas, could be seen as asking too much of a son. But the poem which Alpers read so warmly suggests, more subtly, not only the obligation but also the honor that a gift of (difficult) poems can confer:

> Lucy, you brightness of our sphere, who are
>> Life of the Muses' day, their morning star!
> If works, not the authors, their own grace should look,
>> Whose poems would not wish to be your book?
> But these, desired by you, the maker's ends
>> Crown with their own. Rare poems ask rare friends.
> Yet *Satires*, since the most of mankind be
>> Their unavoided subject, fewest see;
> For none e'er took that pleasure in sin's sense,
>> But, when they heard it taxed, took more offense.
> They, then, that living where the matter's bred
>> Dare for these poems yet both ask, and read,
> And like them too, must needfully, though few,
>> Be of the best, and 'mongst those best are you,
> Lucy, you brightness of our sphere, who are
>> The Muses' evening, as their morning star.

The poem's stern, somewhat discouraging aphorism—"Rare poems ask rare friends"—seems to require of the recipient an extraordinary, perhaps unattainable excellence. But this discriminating admonition is balanced by the more inviting promise of the later lines, the promise that by daring to ask for, read, and like these poems one can take one's place among "the best." And though I don't necessarily believe this flattering promise, I still like to hear it spoken.

Notes

1. William H. Pritchard, "Ear Training," in *Playing It by Ear* (Amherst: University of Massachusetts Press, 1994), 3–18.

2. Robert Frost, *Selected Letters*, ed. Lawrance Thompson (New York: Holt, Rinehart, and Winston, 1964), 81, 80 (July 4, 1913).

3. Ibid., 112 (February 22, 1914).

4. F. R. Leavis, "Poet as Executant," in *A Selection from Scrutiny*, ed. F. R. Leavis, 2 vols. (Cambridge: Cambridge University Press, 1968), 1:88.

5. Geoffrey Hutchings, "Reading Poetry Aloud," in *English Studies in Africa* 23:1 (1980): 31–39 (further citations will be noted parenthetically in the text). The prejudice in favor of actors remains strong, however. Penguin's new English Verse audio anthology is advertised as "featuring acclaimed British actors."

6. Pritchard, "Ear Training," 9.

Roger Sale

On Not Teaching at Amherst College

IN 1995 RICHARD MCCORMICK (Amherst '74) became president of the University of Washington, where I have taught since 1962. I had taught before that at Amherst, so I wrote McCormick. I said I was not sure his Amherst resembled mine, but the Amherst I'd known, though chockablock with faults, was a serious school. Also that Washington, where I had happily taught for over thirty years, is not a serious school.

Subsequently McCormick and I had a good conversation in which he proved himself to be as good a listener as I'd been told he was. Washington is not a serious school, I told him, because no one gets paid a dollar more or a dime less for teaching well or ill; I have many friends who have taught hard at Washington almost as long as I have who make a bit more than the hiring-in rate for beginning assistant professors. A scandalous situation, made worse because many—including McCormick?—who know about it see nothing much wrong with it.

Before coming to Washington I had thought little about what my colleagues would be like. I soon saw that most had left a graduate program at one university to come to another university, and so quite often they continued to think like graduate students: their task was "research," their

19

mode of writing was the "scholarly article," they preferred teaching graduate students to undergraduates and saw their being excused from teaching 100- and 200-level courses as their first step up the ladder toward success. Fitting right in with the university's values, most of them were not among those who, many years later, make a bit more than the beginners. I was flabbergasted, frequently and uncharacteristically tongue-tied. It was years before I stopped feeling that my five years at Amherst had created a gap between me and everyone else, and even now I trace much of what I do as a teacher to my Amherst experience of 1957–62.

I make two cameo appearances in Bill Pritchard's *English Papers*. In the fall of 1958 I was starting my second year at Amherst, Bill his first. We both played down, or did not know how to assess, my being a year his senior on the faculty and his having been much more to the manor born. The manor had two names, Amherst and Harvard, and Bill had been to both. I'd gone to Swarthmore and Cornell, and since I'd barely heard of Amherst at those places, I assumed, I think rightly, that people at Amherst only politely acknowledged my comefrom.

As a result, I did not know I was, as Bill describes me, "the most outspoken . . . certainly the most provocative" of the junior members of the English Department. I knew I had ground to make up, because I was always playing an away game, and because I felt from the beginning that teaching at Amherst involved something more serious than anything I'd encountered at Swarthmore or Cornell. Friends at Swarthmore once described me as a "puppy with mature bark." At Amherst I was outspoken, provocative, the maturely barking puppy.

One morning, Bill's account continues, this pup "suddenly turned and asked 'Had I had a good class yet with the freshmen?'":

> I said my class on Assignment 5 had been OK. "I haven't," Sale responded, immediately making me feel like the sort of insufficiently critical horse's ass who thought he'd had a "good class."

At some level of awareness, we were playing poker. I was speaking as though I had two not very good pair in a draw game, hoping an early bet might convince Bill I had better cards than I had:

> He then described how, the other morning in his class, he had talked about Ted Williams to make some point about the matter of paying attention. Ted Williams! Why hadn't I thought of that. . . .

I had the shabby two pair still, but I'd bluffed successfully. With Roger for a friend, one needed fewer enemies.

Later Bill writes that my being fired at Amherst was a "complicated piece of injustice." Whatever created the injustice, in fact I had been outspoken and provocative enough to offend a number of people. Whatever his sense of the injustice, Bill added he too had been offended one morning when he, just waking up, heard me loudly whistling "Haunted Heart" as, a few yards away, I walked to my car. Surely, the whistling implied, I was off to teach a better class than he would.

At some point in those five years I moved from being someone who was hoping, or indicating, that he might someday belong at Amherst, to someone who seemed challenging, daring his elders to fire him: "If I am given tenure here I will take it, and the person I will become is someone I do not want to be, but I haven't the strength, will, or insight to see that, so I will make you get rid of me instead." After tenure was denied, the president of the college assured me I could stay another year if I wished. Theodore Baird told me he was on leave the following year and hoped I'd stay to teach his Shakespeare course. This was early December in 1961, and I knew even as these offers were made that I'd go to the MLA after Christmas to look for a job and that I'd be out of Amherst the following summer.

Occasionally at Amherst I had a conversation with colleagues about where we'd go if looking for a new job. Pittsburgh, I remember, had been one choice, but when I applied for jobs it was as though Pittsburgh wasn't far enough away. I wanted a big school in a city; I knew sufficiently little that, after picking Minnesota and Washington, I also named two that weren't really in cities, California at Berkeley and at Riverside. Clearly, I wasn't so much going someplace as leaving someplace, the farther away the better. Minnesota and Riverside did not want me, Washington and Cal did. I picked Washington, maybe a bit because everyone assumed I should pick Berkeley, but mostly because Washington was in Seattle and Cal was not in San Francisco. Having said I wanted a city, I was sensible enough to choose one. I have no idea why I never considered UCLA.

Amherst was a serious school because its finest minds were centrally involved in the teaching life of the college, and because many of these devoted themselves to teaching first- and second-year students. Few teachers at Swarthmore had any interest in teaching such students, and Freshman Comp at Cornell was boilerplate, indistinguishable from comp classes taught throughout America. The introductory English classes at Amherst were taught by most of the staff of the department, and two or three staff meetings in each course were enough to show me I was not in Kansas anymore.

At the outset the sophomore introduction to literature, English 21, was more exciting because less dismaying and overwhelming. It was assumed I could teach, that first fall, *Leaves of Grass, Pygmalion, Pride and Prejudice* and *King Lear*, and perhaps I could, but I was very grateful for the staff meetings and for the pages a member of the staff would write for each work about how he was going to teach it, and how his proposed writing assignment grew out of the classes. The best journals of the time could not better the care and subtlety with which some of this "poop," as it was nonchalantly called, was written. The audience was good and no one wanted to look bad. When I wrote my first poop, on *Othello* in my second year, I spent weeks working it up, and I feel grateful that in ensuing years I had opportunities to write on *Macbeth, Juno and the Paycock, Don Juan, Lord Jim, Women in Love, Four Quartets, The Alchemist* and Ben Jonson's lyrics, and Iris Murdoch's *The Bell*. I cite this to show the range it was assumed we all could command. Write for colleagues as though how we taught these works was as engaging an intellectual challenge as we knew, write as though jargon and footnotes and scholarly apparatus were enemies rather than handmaids of understanding, and you better write well.

The freshman composition course, English 1, was something my past left me totally unprepared for, and to which I could respond only with awe and panic. It was Ted Baird's invention. It was, he said, the heart of his intellectual life, and on the whole he is the most formidable person I've ever met. He had read everything, apparently, and the learning emerged as a question, or a joke, and never as a display. He wrote only a handful of essays, but all had wonderful titles: "The World Turned Upside Down" (on Defoe), "Corn Grows in the Night" (on Thoreau), "Darwin and the Tangled Bank," "Sympathy: The Broken Mirror," "A Dry and Thirsty Land" (on Congregational ministers and the founding of Amherst College). A student had written that Richard III screams he will give his kingdom for a horse. "Tell me," Ted asked, "When did the scream come into English literature?"—which silenced the student and sent me off speculating both as to the question's answer and how one came to formulate such questions.

And here was this composition course at the heart of his intellectual life, a course like no other:

Assignment X: Describe an experience in which you became lost. Then, on the basis of this description, define "lost." Assignment Y: Having described the experience of becoming lost, describe what you did to become found again. On the basis of your description, define "found."

The assignments required no breadth of knowledge, no intellectual or literary life at all. Amherst students arrived with their combined 1400 SAT scores, convinced their admission ushered them into man's estate, willing to sit at the feet of teachers if they would act like Olympian gods, and here they were faced with questions that could seriously be asked of nine- or ten-year-olds. They huffed and puffed on their papers, and instead of receiving Olympian comments got sharp, slashing, ironic, funny responses designed to say to them, "The day you wake up or show up, I will be there."

I was dazzled. I dazzled students, partly by imitating my elders, partly because I much preferred thinking of Ted Williams as a great example of paying attention to teaching Levels of Diction and the Term Paper. The on-the-job training had to be done quickly. English 1 had no text other than samples of student papers, but since the student wrote three times a week, it had plenty of these: 2 sections x 3 papers/week x 25 students/class = 150 papers/week, plus frequent papers for English 21. You had to learn to read papers fast, and one major creator of the gap between me and most colleagues at Washington is that I did learn this and they never had. Also, with assignments that asked questions anyone could ask and answer, all sense of specialist or expert goes out the window, to be replaced by the conviction that in reading and writing one's response must be personal or it is nothing.

In the spring of my first two years at Amherst, I team taught with Bill Heath a course called Introduction to Literary Scholarship, and one day we agreed I would write a memo to the students. I did, showed it to Bill, and he said "That's a first-rate piece of writing." The memo itself disappeared into the students' hands, and I'm sure it only gave memo-like directions or suggestions, but that's what made his comment important for me: a carefully crafted memo could be a first-rate piece of writing; comments on papers could be too. I wrote a couple of articles that were published, a couple more that weren't, but the writing I did there was only slightly different from, and was never more important than, the writing I did on a memo, an assignment, a comment, English 21 poop. It made literary, intellectual, and academic life seamless.

I grew fast, ungainly, powerful, someone ripe for a complicated piece of injustice. "What I wanted, who can say? How can *I* say, when I never knew?" Thus Pip describes his life with Joe Gargery at the forge in *Great Expectations*. We may think we know what Pip wants, but in Pip's case as well as my own I think it's best to say we did not know, and the answer would emerge only in action. What I did was to inquire about teaching jobs in Africa, and stopped only when I learned jobs there lasted eighteen months or longer, and I was unready to resign and take off for Ghana or Nigeria with my wife, and children aged four and one. What I did was to say, with great vehemence as I dug through snow to ice, trying to wedge cardboard under a rear tire, "If I can go where I don't have to do this, I will." What I did was alienate two senior people in the department without calculation or craft but with pleasure. In the autumn of my fifth year, when I knew some decision about tenure had to be made, I ignored that and poured my energies into my first set of English 1 assignments on which I'd spent the entire previous summer and which raveled and unraveled a number of times during the term. When told I was to be let go, I was no Coriolanus, but I knew there was a world elsewhere. Washington first stood out for me when Robert Heilman, the UW chair, said in our interview that it rained a lot during a Seattle winter, but seldom snowed.

What made Amherst a serious school was part of why I wanted to leave. Amherst now is somewhat larger than it was then, half its students are women, there is no core curriculum to absorb the energies of its finest minds, and it does a lot to bring the other schools in the Connecticut valley into its life. Amherst then had around 1,025 students and 120 male faculty. The entire freshman class was doing the same assignments in four courses. It was almost unheard of for students not to come to class, do their homework, or get written work in on time. The place felt hermetically sealed. The students always faced their teachers for their learning, and what they learned they learned in classes. Much as I loved the power I could exert over a class under these conditions, I didn't *like* it.

Even as all this was happening, the times were changing. For as long as I had been a student or a teacher in college, the implicit stance of most teachers, the explicit stance of some, was against the prevailing middle-brow culture of the Eisenhower years, and classrooms were the best place to learn that stance. By the early '60s students were as much inclined to take their cue for rebellion from Martin Luther King, Jack Kerouac, Che Guevara, John Kennedy, or Allen Ginsberg as from any well-paid academic in a well-heeled academy. During spring vacation of 1961 one Amherst student visited Fidel Castro in the mountains of eastern Cuba, and another compiled evidence of racial discrimination in housing in St. Louis. I had no desire as yet to join these people or groups, but I didn't live in a vacuum and I'm sure these changes played their role in my desire to leave and go west. By the time I left, Amherst was no longer the place I'd gone to leave father and mother to cleave unto my wife and help start a family, no longer the amazing English department and college that flushed me out of the refuge of graduate school and urged me to fly. It had come to resemble Swarthmore and Cornell in my head, as schools, small towns and cities, as places that seemed to know only themselves and others like them.

In 1993, for a questionnaire at the fortieth anniversary of my Swarthmore class, when asked what was the most surprising change in my life, I answered, "That I am no longer an easterner." I carried a lot of baggage west. Concerning cities, knowing no better, I could think Seattle would look like the rows of high-rise apartments along the Bronx River Parkway in New York. Concerning large universities I could only hope students at Washington were better than those I taught at Massachusetts to defray moving expenses. Concerning the United States, I had never been west of Louisville, and so, starting with long rolling rises in the cornfields of Iowa, the scales were dropping from my eyes: a river as wide and as decisive as the Missouri, silver dollars and the big sky of Montana, deep mountain experiences going through the Cascades in Washington, turning right on red and Mt. Rainier visible from a hundred miles away in Seattle. I'd hoped it would be a major event in my life, and so it has proven to be, but it took years of adjusting.

Since I want my emphasis to fall on teaching at Washington and not at Amherst, I want here only to mention some things, not directly related to teaching, that have at times played as important a role as any teaching in making me feel well and truly settled into my life, at the university, in Seattle, in the west.

I came to be in a city, and when I saw that Seattle is a city of wooden framed houses, looking nothing like the Bronx River Parkway, I wasn't sure I was in a city at all. Two things happened to help me feel less puzzled and dismayed. First, Jane Jacobs's *Death and Life of Great American Cities.* Jacobs's eyes, like mine, were those of an easterner, but I was so entranced by her that I determinedly set out to translate her terms into others more appropriate in describing Seattle. That I eventually could do this emboldened me some years later to start a history of Seattle. Second, we bought a house, better than any I thought I could afford, partly because of a loan from my wife's father, partly because its price had lowered since black families had begun moving into what had been an all-white neighborhood. The school our children went to was mostly black, the church we joined was mostly black. We became integrationists and, for a few years, felt we were in a limited way as much part of civil rights activism and the War on Poverty as anyone.

This for me culminated when I directed the university's first Upward Bound project in 1966–67, eighteen months of work as exhilarating and exhausting as any I've ever done: start with poverty's children, high school juniors doing poorly in school who were in some way "promising," bring them to school on the university campus for a summer, see them through their senior year, come back for a second summer and hope they could attempt college seriously. It culminated a second time in *Seattle Past to Present* a few years later, a work I never would have attempted had I not been at Amherst to learn that a response is personal or it is nothing. Eventually there was a guidebook to Seattle and a lot of writing about local matters—the Sonics, the zoo, the racetracks, city streets, small shopping areas and, to come back to that, teaching at the University of Washington.

I could only intuit that I wanted to live in a city. But, except for the intuition that I wanted to marry the woman I married, I know no other that proved truer or mattered more.

Leaving Amherst, I said I was leaving a place whose ideal was the creation of a whole man and going to where the ideal was of a whole society. I was reaching. I knew neither if anyone at Washington cared about a whole society nor just what I meant by the phrase. I believed it, though, and still do, even if I know what it means only in instances and examples.

The way the University of Washington is "a great research institution" is directly responsible for its being not a serious school. No member of the faculty can be rewarded in the way academies reward—in salary, secure employment, reduced teaching loads—except by writing and publishing something called "research." It is neither confident enough in its own judgments that it can make its own rules for how it will reward its faculty nor modest enough that it can be flexible about the relation of publishing to perishing. The university has no interest in "the whole society." Students are a necessary nuisance. So, to accept the university's values is to be dead meat as a teacher.

Lord knows what I would have done had I arrived at Washington directly from Cornell. Fortunately, I hadn't, and Amherst had given me ways and means to proceed on my own. The students were clearly better than those at Massachusetts, since Washington is not surrounded by prestigious private schools skimming the cream of the area's students off the top, and at their best are as good as any I could imagine. But they were different from Amherst students, and I had to learn simultaneously to insist that I was not interested in instructing them or telling them what to do and to deal with their genuine difficulties when I thus insisted. I said earlier that the comments I learned to write at Amherst were "sharp, slashing, ironic, and funny, designed to say 'The day you wake up or show up, I will be there.'" When I did the same at Washington almost everyone ran as if escaping an onrushing threshing machine. Students came into the office and cried. They dropped, they complained to advisors. Chastised for writing cautiously, they retreated into greater caution.

An Amherst teacher's stance often had to be antagonistic because the superbly trained students would see no reason not to go on acting like successful high school students if the teacher let them. Students at Washington have no such level of confidence and so frequently have little resiliency when they feel attacked. Most have gotten where they are by being obedient, and assuming obedience will take them where they think they want to go. Give an Amherst lad "On the basis of your description, define 'lost,'" and he might be annoyed, mystified, or challenged, but he would assume the path to his education went through giving the task his best effort. Give a Washington student that assignment and whatever annoyance, mystification, and challenge might result, there would also be a sense that this is an unpleasant detour from the path to education, and even a best effort might yield only paralysis.

It took me some years to see this, and it has taken all the time since to find ways to respond to it. Students at Washington are not sealed off from their surroundings. The campus is in the middle of the city, students live off campus, mostly, at their parents' homes, in shared apartments, or in homes they have made with a mate. They work at jobs from fifteen to thirty hours a week. Many come to the university not to be there but to get the required number of credits, the "required" GPA needed for admission to graduate work, and to move on. Any appeal to leave their society for the little community of the classroom mostly does not compute for them.

Bill Pritchard once invited Julian Symons, the English critic and mystery novelist, to teach at Amherst for a year. Later he came west and, stopping in Seattle, had lunch with us. He had no sooner seated himself than he asked, "Why do you want to teach C students?" It had been so long since I had thought in such terms that I could not give a good answer. I might have asked why a good Leftist like Julian wanted to ask such a question, but I didn't think in those terms either. Had I fumbled with the phrase "whole society," he could easily ask what in hell I meant by that, but I would have done better had I tried.

Washington students are a synecdoche, a part standing for a whole. A class is a Representative Anecdote. If the students "stand" in my course or at the university, their "sub-stance" is outside there; their scene is seldom marked off from their society. Individuals of course are individuals, but a class of students, to say nothing of the whole class of being called "students," is representative. Their scene can seem at times almost to dictate their acts, and thus reduce them to passivity as agents.

These are terms we all associate with the name of Kenneth Burke. I have twice devoted an entire course to Burke. One might think, given my description of Washington students, that Burke would not only be too difficult—as he might be for any class—but defeatingly so: can you expect us to get *that?* While each time many students did say that, a surprisingly large number were not defeated. "You were right," one told me after the course was over, "to say we might find ourselves standing on a street-corner waiting for a bus and thinking Burke-thoughts. Sometimes I'd call Matt up and ask him to talk some Burke with me." I gradually realized that Burke did not seek to take them out of their world, as Dickens, Melville, and Faulkner do, but to make their world differently intelligible.

Hold on to that example while I offer another. At the suggestion of a colleague, I ordered Bartholomae and Petrosky's *Ways of Reading* for an advanced composition course. I was dismayed when I saw it, an anthology of the politically and intellectually up-to-date: Foucault, Anzaldua, Geertz, Percy, Pratt, Patricia Williams. The back of the book has sequences of assignments, but loose ones, not tight like Amherst English 1 assignments. But there was one on Difficulty that I could use. Not only were the students going to find the reading difficult—as I frequently did myself—but they were scared to be shown what they did whenever they found a piece of reading difficult. Halfway through the course I felt we were coming close to the DNA of bullshit. The closer we got, the more scared many became, but I think almost all saw that what we were talking about was what they did, in their daily school lives. Paolo Freire or Klaus Theweleit might remain "over there" for them, but the question of what you do when something stays "over there" is of real practical importance. And this kept them going when it seemed that all else was defeating them.

Both these examples come from recent years. I would not have seen the possibilities for either in my early Washington years. It simply has taken a huge amount of time and energy to find out what will and won't "work." Being used to being obedient, students usually think their best energies are employed when they're doing as they're told with something that takes a fair amount of time. Since I don't think these are their best energies, our relations frequently are frustrating. Being pretty much rooted in their world, they usually aren't curious or imaginative, especially on their own, as something good to be. So I keep saying that what we want is hard work that leads to a sense of fun and play, because this is work that leads to learning you can take with you after the course is over.

Here's a list of authors and works that "work" (I exclude the likes of *Pride and Prejudice* and *Great Expectations* which seem to work universally): the New Testament gospels, Chaucer, especially *Troilus and Criseyde*, *Paradise Lost*, *The Rape of the Lock* and *Moral Essay II*, *Clarissa*, Hardy's poetry, *The Wind in the Willows*, *Ulysses*, Burke, especially *Attitudes towards History*, Frost. Here is a list of works that don't "work": most of the Hebrew scriptures, *Sir Gawain and the Green Knight*, *The Faerie Queene*, Ben Jonson, Marvell's poetry, *The Dunciad*, *Emma*, Wordsworth's *The Prelude*, most Byron, Shelley, most Trollope, *Alice in Wonderland*, Beatrix Potter, *Parade's End*, *Four Quartets*. If Bill Pritchard were to draw up the same list after teaching forty years at Amherst, then my point is meaningless, but I rather suspect he wouldn't. Students at Washington enjoy working hard at a text under two conditions: when the imagination of the author is not alien, and when the work shows visible results. Perhaps most difficult for them are texts where everything is on the surface and the surface is subtly and delicately conceived, like *Gawain*, Jonson, and Potter. *Paradise Lost* can work where *The Faerie Queene* usually does not because Milton clearly is facing problems and difficulties students can understand and Spenser is not. *Ulysses*, though everything is on the surface there too, is always a pleasure because hard work with it is rewarding, first just in comprehension but then in an appreciation of how sad and funny a book it is, our century's greatest comedy. It helps, incidentally, that in a large university one can teach almost anything, so, in a sense, in my thirty-odd years at Washington I have been perpetually teaching a version of English 21, Introduction to Literature, with this or that as theme or focus, the range being the result of constantly trying to find something that interests me that can also interest them.

When "getting an education" means getting credits, fulfilling requirements, worrying about grades and a GPA, and ending with a degree, it can sometimes seem that it's miraculous that any student gains a different, more personal, and more engaged sense of education. When the majority of the students have some kind of job in order to be able to go to school, that work can easily become a tail that wags the dog, since not showing up for work can get you fired, while not showing up for class may not carry any penalty at all. When teachers are all "professors," when all classes are "lectures," it's hard for any student, and especially hard for a class of students, to feel they are major players here, that they create if not control the chemistry of the group. They are, and remain for the most part, strangers to each other throughout. They take comments personally since they are so used to distant impersonal ones; they don't *prefer* quizzes and exams to papers, but they frequently speak as though what they'd most like is an exam that could be called a paper, where all they have to do is what they've been told to do.

The situation, then, that I perpetually face is one where the antagonism is built in, and where any statement or enactment of that antagonism is almost certainly going to be counter-productive. They need to be derailed, to have their writing challenged, to be given assignments that do not tell them what to do, to be made unhappy and to write less well at least for awhile, to feel they have resources they may never have used before in a school setting. Frequently, then, students feel they are getting double messages: you are a very "positive" teacher, I "enjoy" the class, but all your comments on my papers are "negative." I then try to tell them the difference between high standards—a term I seek to avoid because in their heads it's already got a 4.0 scale built into it—and high expectations—which I do have, insist on having if they'll let me.

In working it out there are allies: the authors, mainly, but also those students who, for whatever reason, want to come to class, want to enter into conversation, and enjoy the sense of liberation that comes through discipline. There's also an odd ally in the size of our classes, almost all of which are limited to fifty students. That may seem like much too large a group—and teaching two such classes in a term, with the proper amount of writing assigned, is always hard—but fifty enrolled usually ends up meaning about thirty to thirty-five coming to class, and if mostly they are the same thirty to thirty-five every day, then there are some good talkers and some good listeners, and school can feel energizing. Granted, in order to learn how to lead a discussion with groups that size, I practically disqualified myself for working well with any group under twenty. But there aren't enough groups of under twenty to make that terribly worrisome.

Earlier I spoke of the '50s ideal with which I started teaching, that of the class as an outpost, a space station above the ruck of postwar American glut. What seems to have replaced it is a community of strangers standing as a synecdoche of possibility for the society as a whole. In this community, when it's at its best, people talk with each other as well as at me, and at its very best the students are talking about our current reading as I come into class and after I leave it. They know each other only well enough to do this talking. They're for me, or against me, or both, but even those against me will say the possibility for such a community does not exist in many of their classes; it is not, after all, a serious school. What have I done? I've learned their names early on, I've read their papers hard, I've done a lot of reading aloud, I've tried to enjoy myself as much as possible in class, all signs of English 1 and English 21 being done again and again.

Living in a city. A community of strangers. A whole society.

William Youngren

Pritchard, English 1, and Me

DURING A CLOSE FRIENDSHIP that has now lasted almost a half century, Bill Pritchard and I have argued about many things. But there is nothing we have argued about so often (and so enjoyably) as the required English course we both took as freshmen at Amherst, the course officially titled English 1–2 but that we always refer to simply as "English 1."

Many others have shared our continuing interest in this course, which ceased to exist in the late 1960s. There have been articles about it in educational journals, memoirs by those who taught it, at least one doctoral dissertation about it, and now an excellent book devoted to it, Robin Varnum's *Fencing with Words*.[1] I gather that the course is also a popular subject of conversation and debate at the reunions of classes like ours, whose members were subjected to it.

I

We arrived at Amherst as freshmen in the fall of 1949, at the beginning of what we soon learned was the third year of the college's "new curriculum." Since we had no idea what the old curriculum had been like, we didn't know what was new about the new one. Most of our courses were required, and they seemed merely later installments of what had been available in high school: history, humanities, math, physics. But the English course was something else again. For one thing, there were no assigned texts. For another, we had to write a short paper for every single class in the term. Most important, we had no idea what the course was about, and our instructors wouldn't tell us.

Our year—we later learned that a whole new set of English 1 assignments was written for each academic year—we were first given a brief statement entitled "What an Apprentice Does." We were then asked, in a series of assignments, to recall situations in which we had been apprentices, and to explain how we had learnt what we had learnt, how we had expressed ourselves, what difficulties we had encountered. This led to papers in which we had to talk specifically about difficulties of communication, and finally to our being asked to define such terms as "Understand," "Meaning," and "Vocabulary." It was all very puzzling. The only thing that seemed clear was that we should not run to the dictionary for definitions: each term had to be defined by reference to actions we performed in the actual communication situation.

This was of course very far from what most of us were accustomed to: those high school English courses in which bored old-maid teachers exuded a genteel, vaporous "appreciation" of literature that they had, long ago, absorbed from similar teachers, and that it was impossible either to agree or argue with. We therefore assumed that English 1 was what was new about the new curriculum. But in this we were wrong. Only much later did I read the true story of the new curriculum, and of English 1's rather troubled relation to it, in Gail Kennedy's 1955 book, *Education at Amherst: The New Program.*[2]

Kennedy vividly explains how, from the late nineteenth century on, pressures were exerted upon American liberal arts colleges that seemed, by about 1940, very likely to squeeze them out of existence altogether. These pressures came from two directions, from below and from above (as Kennedy puts it). On the one hand there were demands for technical and vocational instruction; on the other, the influence of the German universities, which was already turning many colleges into mini-graduate schools. By 1940, one gathers, things looked pretty chaotic to concerned teachers in all fields. There was no longer any agreement on an indispensable body of knowledge that a liberal arts college should transmit through specific course requirements, and even colleges like Amherst were offering a "smorgasbord" of courses, unplanned and uncoordinated. That, in effect, was the old curriculum; the new curriculum was Amherst's response to this perceived crisis in education.

Kennedy, a professor of philosophy at the college who was also chairman of the committee that devised the new curriculum, had earned his graduate degrees at Columbia, the American university that had most conspicuously and most famously pioneered "great books" or "Western Civilization" courses in the understandable burst of cultural chauvinism that followed World War I.[3] It is thus no surprise that the committee recommended for freshmen and sophomores a required two-year humanities sequence, the first year of which would be a course "essentially of the 'Columbia type,' in which a series of books, chosen by common agreement among the teachers of the course and from a variety of historical and cultural backgrounds, would be read in chronological order" (Kennedy, 58). But in English 1, as I have said, no books at all were read—on principle. Far from being the prime representative of the new curriculum, English 1 was in fact a holdover from the old one.

It had begun life in 1938 as English 1c, a composition course offered as one of three options for freshmen, the others being a survey course (1a), and an introduction to poetry and prose fiction (1b). All entering freshmen were required to take what the course catalogue called "an objective placement test in English composition."[4] Those who ranked in the upper third on this test could choose between English 1a and 1b, while the others were consigned to English 1c. At first a few books were used in English 1c, usage texts and literary works such as *Walden* and *The Education of Henry Adams*. But the only begetter of the course, the late Professor Theodore Baird, soon decided that he could accomplish his aims more effectively by having students write solely about their own experience.

This three-option arrangement continued through the academic year 1941–42. In the fall of 1942 all three courses were still offered, but their numbers had been changed: English 1c, Baird's composition course, had now become English 1–2, with English 1a and 1b trailing behind it as English 3–4 and 5–6—though still available to only a limited number of students. How did the composition course achieve this rise in status? These of course were the war years, when Amherst College was largely occupied by servicemen. English 1–2, the 1942–43 catalogue noted, while still only an elective, was now "Required by the Navy, recommended by the Army." By the next year, English 1–2, though still termed an elective, was the only English elective offered for freshmen; by the year following, 1944–45, it was required of all freshmen.

One way or another, then—and one would love to know the political ins and outs—Baird had managed to make his bookless composition course the English course required of all Amherst freshmen, and thus the course that came closest to occupying the role of the freshman humanities course envisaged, at just about this time, by the committee designing the new curriculum. Quite understandably, he did not take kindly to the committee's recommendations: he was not about to see his carefully nurtured brainchild swept aside in favor of an old-fashioned great books course of the "Columbia type."

The committee's attempted way out of this impasse was to propose a compromise, "a humanities course in the freshman year which would run parallel to the existing course in English composition" (Kennedy, 183–84). Two key words in the ongoing discussion were "orientation" and "integration." In an angry rejection of the committee's proposal that was signed by the English 1 staff (but that sounds very much like Baird's characteristic prose), these two words were mockingly thrown back in the committee's face:

> We, the instructors in English 1–2, have worked out an "orientation" of the Freshman mind and an "integration" of Freshman knowledge which we believe is a workable, teachable answer to the needs which the Humanities Course proposes to fill. We have developed our methods of orientation and integration by actual class-room teaching, and we use these methods every day that we teach. English 1–2, therefore, might well be officially designated as the Introduction to the Liberal Arts which it in fact is for those who take it now. (Kennedy, 184)

All those great books, in other words, were unnecessary: you could give students an Introduction to the Liberal Arts without having them read anything at all!

It was Reuben Brower, at that time part of the English 1 staff, who broke the deadlock by proposing an alternative freshman humanities course, the introduction to critical reading that would become English 21–22 in our time at Amherst and Humanities 6 in 1954, after Brower had moved on to Harvard. While all freshmen would be required to take English 1–2, they could choose which humanities course to take along with it, the originally proposed great books course or Brower's new option. This apparently appeased Baird—perhaps because his course, though now to be taken in tandem with a humanities course, would still be required of all freshmen while that would not be true of either humanities course, a mark of their inferior status. In the event, Brower's proposed course "proved to present difficulties of staffing which led to its being withdrawn from consideration" (Kennedy, 229). But the stratagem—if that's what it was—worked. The great books stayed. Each freshman would take English 1 three hours a week and Humanities 1 two hours a week first semester, and English 2 two hours a week and Humanities 2 three hours a week second semester.

II

I was most interested to learn all this. For as I stumbled through my first two years of college, I grew to feel that English 1 lay somehow outside the new curriculum. Our other courses required lots of reading and were firmly and traditionally goal-oriented, while English 1 was not only bookless but also a mystery. And once I decided, in my junior year, to major in English, English 1 increasingly seemed at odds with the aims and methods of the other English courses I took. To speak frankly, I hated English 1 whereas Pritchard and my other friends all seemed to love it. And what I objected to was precisely the lack of any specified content, the absence of any reading or in-class instruction that might have given point and direction to the endlessly confusing, seemingly pointless assignments.

Moreover, while there was nothing to read, nowhere to go for any notion of what the course might really be about, a heavy, portentous air hung over the whole endeavor. One got the teasing sense that a Great Secret—something about the true relation of language to reality, most likely—was behind it all, and would finally be revealed, when we, the initiates, were sufficiently prepared. But nothing was ever revealed. My section-man for English 1 was a historian of science named Bill Stahlmann, who a decade later was my colleague in the M.I.T. Department of Humanities—and who confessed to me, in a convivial moment, that he had never known what the damned course was about either. In my senior year, determined to give English 1—this famous course that apparently everyone but me thought was so wonderful—another chance, I asked Baird if I might audit his section. Permission was duly granted, but no illumination ensued.

I came to feel that the simultaneous creation of mystery and coy refusal to clear it up was Baird's conscious program and for many—though certainly not for me—the source of his power and attraction as a teacher. In the fall of 1961 I wrote a letter to Pritchard in which I spoke of the air

Baird constantly gave off of "withholding knowledge"—which I declared, rather melodramatically perhaps, was, in a teacher, "the sin against the light." I then mentioned something Pritchard had told me about Baird's condemnation of other places such as Cornell and Harvard because there you couldn't "speak your mind"—as you could, presumably, at Amherst:

> Precisely what TB has never done, it seems to me, is to speak *his* mind. In my experience at least, whatever comes comes as an attitude, a parry to an unexpected quarter, a thing-in-itself framed by the moment and self-suffi-cient, not at all felt as Part of an interesting and educated sensibility.

By way of illustration I recounted an incident that had taken place some-time earlier at the house of Armour Craig, Baird's unofficial English 1 sec-ond-in-command. A classmate of ours had mentioned Humanities 1, "in response to which TB stopped, furrowed, pouted and delivered: 'I don't under*stand* what they do in that course.' This is plainly nonsense—and representative nonsense."

My sense of how Baird operated, both in and out of the classroom, is repeatedly borne out in Ms. Varnum's book, by the testimony of col-leagues and former students, and also by his own staff memos and public pronouncements. "Teaching is a mystery," he wrote in a 1990 letter to Ms. Varnum. "Nobody knows how to teach. Nobody knows how to learn" (Varnum, 55). And in a description of English 1 written in the late 1950s he warned students: "You may feel at times that you are not being taught what you ought to be taught, that your teacher does not seem to give you the answers you seek, but you actually are in a situation where no one knows the answers" (Varnum, 250). Here (one was meant to feel) was the last just man on earth, the new Socrates, the only teacher honest enough to admit—and in such simple, unacademic language, too—that he knew nothing about his profession.

Yet Dale Peterson, who taught the course as an intern when he was a graduate student at Yale, told Ms. Varnum: "You had the sense that this man knew what he was doing, but would never let on quite what he was doing" (Varnum, 209). And Jack Cameron, a member of the Amherst Eng-lish Department who is a friend of many years' standing but with whom I have never discussed English 1, remarked of his first years teaching the course: "You always felt as if there was something to be understood there which you didn't understand" (Varnum, 144). "English 1 was, in my view," Cameron concluded, "very much an authoritarian enterprise." The au-thority of course emanated from Baird, whom Cameron saw as "classically the embodiment . . . of a tribal chief, a patriarch, a powerful father figure" who, however, "refused to take true responsibility" for his authoritarian role and was "disingenuous in not acknowledging the force of his own presence" (Varnum, 146–47).

Ms. Varnum also cites a 1947 memo by either Baird or Walker Gibson, at that time a member of the English 1 staff, that says, of an accompanying assignment in which the students were asked to compare two brief passages of prose: "With proper secrecy, and ambiguous passages, two-thirds of the boys ought to get this wrong." Ms. Varnum then reports:

> Years later, when I asked Gibson about this observation, he didn't remember ever having written such a thing, but he conceded, "That sounds like an English 1 instruction." He then suggested sarcastically that it might be used as a "little frontispiece remark for your whole thesis: 'With any luck two-thirds of them will get it wrong.' If two-thirds of them got it right," he added, "we would have to give up." (Varnum, 122–23)

Even Ms. Varnum, who strives to remain neutral about the course, is impelled by her own extensive experience as a composition teacher "to register my distaste for the way its staff undertook to disorient students or trip them up. . . . The notion of setting traps . . . bothered me. So did Baird's refusal to reveal his objectives to students" (Varnum, 130).

The experience of reading Ms. Varnum's book was, for me, something like attending a support group. I had always thought I was the only one who disliked (and saw through) English 1. But now I discovered that our numbers are legion. Finally, however, and somewhat to my surprise, it was Pritchard who, of all Ms. Varnum's informants, most clearly and tellingly expressed what I found intellectually dishonest about the course:

> At the best moments, and there were such moments, you felt as if you were exploring and as if you were thinking about very important matters, that is the relationship of words to reality, silence to speech, order to chaos, and all those oppositions that provided so much of the rhetoric here. And that is why people thought there must be a philosophy behind this, there must be a secret, if you could only find out the secret. (Varnum, 133)

What particularly drew me to these sentences was the repeated "as if." Pritchard, careful and accomplished writer that he is, very pointedly does not say that at those best moments, which he goes out of his way to assure us did indeed exist, the staff and students of English 1 actually were thinking about those large philosophical issues framed by the oppositions he enumerates. He only says "you felt as if" you were doing so. Nor does he say that there actually was a "philosophy" or a "secret" behind the course, but only that "people thought there must be" one. For those large, philosophical-sounding oppositions did not in fact embody the results of any real thinking or understanding but only provided what Pritchard, once again very pointedly, calls the "rhetoric" with which the course was surrounded.

Reading this, I was reminded of Helen Deutsch's chapter on what she calls the "as if personality" in her book *Neuroses and Character Types.* Though such a person at first seems outwardly normal, the observer soon gets "the inescapable impression that the individual's whole relationship to life has something about it which is lacking in genuineness." Such a person may be "intellectually intact," and yet may see "no difference between his empty forms and what others actually experience." "Further consequences of such a relation to life," Deutsch tells us, include "a highly plastic readiness to pick up signals from the outer world and to mold oneself and one's behavior accordingly."[5] This seems to me an accurate description of the relation in which English 1 stood to the intellectual world it pretended, often with considerable grandiosity, to explore with earnest rigor.

III

Those who have written about English 1 have expended considerable energy in the attempt to trace its intellectual roots. The famous names of Wittgenstein and I. A. Richards have often been invoked. Yet Baird told Ms. Varnum that he "never, I think ever, read a word of Wittgenstein," and that he thought that "Richards was a fake" (Varnum, 49, 67). He did, from time to time, distribute reading lists to his staff—though never, so far as I know, to his students—and Richards's name turns up regularly, along with those of such philosophers as Whitehead, William James, and R. G. Collingwood. Yet Baird also told Ms. Varnum that the course "was homemade; that's the truth of the matter," and he added: "I was no philosopher. I never have been able to keep my mind on a piece of philosophical writing; I have tried" (Varnum, 49).

The seemingly contradictory nature of the evidence derives, I believe, precisely from the "as if" character of English 1. It pretended to be a course that dealt seriously (though obscurely) with ideas, but in fact it was no such thing. The instructors were virtually forbidden to give out any

substantive answers to questions raised by the assignments, and so nothing ever had to be thought out clearly or in detail. Aside from generalities
and tag-phrases, it is hard to imagine what such writers as Whitehead,
James, and Collingwood (let alone Wittgenstein) could have contributed
to such an enterprise. The writers who really helped to shape English 1,
whose names also appeared on Baird's lists, were rather different. The
most important seem to have been Percy W. Bridgman, Henry Adams,
and Count Alfred Korzybski, founder of "general semantics."

Bridgman was a Harvard physicist who, like many physicists of the
1920s, tried his hand at popular philosophy. Near the beginning of his
best-known book, *The Logic of Modern Physics* (1927), Bridgman proposes
that in future all physicists agree to define their concepts in terms of the
operations by which these concepts are applied to phenomena: "the true
meaning of a term is to be found by observing what a man does with it,
not by what he says about it."[6] To Baird this meant, roughly, that a word
means whatever you use it to mean. He was fond of entering his classroom
through a window, then pointing to it and asking his students what it was.
When they replied that it was a window, he would correct them, insisting
it was a door. It was this central concept of "operational definition" that
was responsible for the stress, in English 1 assignments, on defining all
terms by reference to actions performed in the relevant situation, not by
reference to the dictionary.

The Education of Henry Adams, which Baird began teaching to Amherst
freshmen in 1927, the year he arrived at the college, was a book that he regarded almost with reverence. Harold Laski, writing to Adams's lifelong
friend Mr. Justice Holmes, called the *Education* "a sophomore performance,
full of the false profundities of which one ought to cease to be capable at
twenty-five";[7] yet I think it was precisely Adams's melodramatic cultural
pessimism that drew Baird to his book. He was fond of quoting Adams's
dour dictum: "Chaos was the law of nature; Order was the dream of
man."

Yet Baird, who also made great play with the terms "chaos" and "order,"
was mistaken in assuming that he and Adams meant approximately the
same thing by them. The chaos Baird was fond of invoking was simply the
surrounding world and our experience of it—before we begin to use words
to talk about either. In a 1959 assignment he wrote:

> The existence of chaos is a fact of experience. We encounter it daily, hourly.
> We know it is, even though when we begin to talk about it we make some
> kind of order. (Varnum, 37)

It was this process of turning chaos into order through the use of language that fascinated Baird. "The keyword of this course is thus 'order,'" he wrote on a 1947 exam, and in a 1991 letter he told Ms. Varnum that "We were interested in the way LANGUAGE makes order out of chaos" (Varnum, 109, 85). In another 1959 assignment he explained that this process of making order was essentially one of sorting or classifying: "When we write or talk and use words and symbols and signs, what we are doing is making sets, composing, organizing, ordering similarities" (Varnum, 37).

Adams meant something quite different by chaos and order. The order that he sought, unsuccessfully, all his life could only have been attained if science had provided decisive confirmation of the ultimate philosophical principles he had grown up with. His early reading of Darwin had led him to be optimistic that this might indeed occur, but his hopes were dashed in 1903, when he read the second (1900) edition of Karl Pearson's 1892 *The Grammar of Science*. In the chapter of the *Education* that bears as its title the title of Pearson's book, Adams cites the following brief passages from *The Grammar of Science*:

> Order and reason, beauty and benevolence, are characteristics and conceptions which we find solely associated with the mind of man.
>
> In the chaos behind sensations, in the "beyond" of sense-impressions, we cannot infer necessity, order or routine, for these are concepts formed by the mind of man on this side of sense-impressions.
>
> Briefly chaos is all that science can logically assert of the supersensuous.

Adams's famous comment directly follows: "In plain words, Chaos was the law of nature; Order was the dream of man."[8]

Adams is not talking, as Baird was, about the chaos of sense-impressions and external events that surrounds us until we start to make order out of it by utilizing the classificatory or sorting powers of language. That chaos, though potentially ever-present, we can at least do something about; Adams's chaos, on the other hand, is an ineradicable permanent condition we must learn to live with. To confuse matters still further, Pearson did not regard his chaos as the dire occasion for hand-wringing that Adams took it to be. Like his contemporaries Mach and Poincaré, Pearson was a phenomenonalist philosopher of science. He believed that all scientific laws are merely "constructs," derived by interpreting the correlations among our sense-impressions. Such laws, therefore, can tell us nothing about that ultimate reality that so concerned Adams. But this belief in no way dampened Pearson's optimism about the future of science, which he unquestioningly regarded as our most reliable source of knowledge.[9]

Baird was especially attached to the phrase "running orders through chaos," which he thought he had read in Adams's *Education*. Early in his book, Adams does use a similar phrase in defining "the task of education," and it was this passage that Baird singled out, in conversation with Ms. Varnum, as "the classic passage; that's what we had in mind when we put together a lot of our assignments" (Varnum, 37). Ms. Varnum, who uses the phrase "running orders through chaos" as one of her chapter titles, writes: "I think it was Adams's use of 'orders' in the plural that specifically appealed to Baird. Your order, the plural form indicates, is not the same as my order" (Varnum, 37). But the relevant passage from *The Education of Henry Adams* reads as follows: "From cradle to grave this problem of running order through chaos, direction through space, discipline through freedom, unity through multiplicity, has always been, and must always be, the task of education, as it is the moral of religion, philosophy, science, art, politics, and economy" (Adams, 12). The order sought by Adams, depending as it did on scientific confirmation of philosophical principles that he had been raised to believe were universally true, would, if attained, be the same for all mankind. Hence the singular form: "order."[10]

Something closer to what Baird meant by order and chaos—though they do not often use those terms—can be found in the writings of Korzybski and his followers. Korzybski begins his 1933 book *Science and Sanity*, the Bible of general semantics, by insisting on an absolute distinction between two levels, or groups of levels, of reality: first, there are the nonverbal or objective or (as Korzybski sometimes calls them) "un-speakable" levels, comprising the basic submicroscopic flux, known to physics but not experienced directly by us, and ordinary objects, events, and feelings as we experience them; then there are the verbal levels, comprising the words we use to talk about the nonverbal ones. Korzybski was something of a kook, and *Science and Sanity* is an almost unreadable book, filled with fanciful, totally unfollowable recommendations as to how we must revise our language to avoid confusing these levels with one another. For this state of confusion was Korzybski's version of chaos. But these recommendations, in the form in which they are given by Korzybski, need not concern us here.[11]

The rough places in Korzybski's thought are made plain, more or less, in the writings of his two best-known followers, S. I. Hayakawa and Stuart Chase. It is they, rather than their master, who had a powerful direct influence on teachers of English during the 1940s and 1950s. Hayakawa and Chase made sense out of Korzybski's recommendations for linguistic reform by translating them into terms that have to do with knowledge or awareness rather than with language. What they principally inherited from Korzybski (and passed on to their readers) was his hierarchical view of reality, as embodied in his scheme of nonverbal and verbal levels.

What distinguishes each of Korzybski's levels from the one just beneath it is that the higher level omits, through a process of abstraction, certain characteristics or attributes found on the lower one. Thus the pencil we see is derived from the submicroscopic flux underlying it, and thus too the word "pencil" is derived from the pencil itself: the fact that the actual pencil is made of wood (or metal), or that it is red (or yellow), is not included in the meaning of the word "pencil." Similarly, as we move up the "abstraction ladder" (as it was called): the phrase "object to write with" omits reference to still more characteristics of the actual pencil—that is why we can also use it to refer to a pen or a piece of chalk. And the phrase "physical object" omits still more.

As we move up the ladder, from submicroscopic flux to ordinary objects to the various verbal levels, reality thus gets progressively thinned out, so to speak. This is, however, not necessarily a bad thing, but simply a fact about language and its relation to the world. In *Language in Thought and Action* Hayakawa writes:

> The test of abstractions then is not whether they are "high-" or "low-level" abstractions, but *whether they are referrable [sic] to lower levels*. If one makes a statement about "culinary arts in America," one should be able to refer the statement down the abstraction ladder to particulars of American restaurants, American domestic science, American techniques of food preservation, down to Mrs. Levin in her kitchen.[12]

Korzybski's grand design of linguistic reform thus boils down in practice to the helpful (if obvious) rule of thumb that we should always know what we are talking about and be able to furnish appropriate and convincing examples.

Yet despite Hayakawa's disclaimer in the passage just cited, what many readers took away from their study of general semantics was precisely the sense that the primary task of language—indeed, perhaps its sole task, apart from the direct expression of emotion or sensation—is to furnish descriptions of reality that make reality more manageable but inevitably reduce its complexity and diminish its richness. Though words may help us make sense of the world, they yield only a rather attenuated image of the world. (Korzybski's favorite analogy for the relation of language to the world was the relation of a map to the territory it maps.) Moreover, the metaphor of the abstraction ladder gave readers the impression that verbal descriptions of reality, at best a poor substitute for the thing itself, become (or at least are liable to become) still poorer as they become more general.

To insist as strongly as Korzybski, Hayakawa, and Chase did on the absolute separation of language from reality, and on the superior richness and complexity of reality, quite naturally led them to regard the preverbal natural world with sentimental reverence. In *The Tyranny of Words* Chase writes eloquently of our relation to this world:

> This contact comes before language and cannot be spoken. The eye receives light-waves from the apple, but says nothing. This apple, any apple, any object or act, is on the nonverbal level. Here we see it as a cat sees it, quietly and without words. . . . Here is the base from which all our proud words rise—every last one of them—and to it they must constantly return and be refreshed.[13]

While Korzybski seems to be offering us a science of meaning that will help us to use language better than we do now, he and his followers end up by giving us what Kenneth Burke once perceptively called "glimpses into an almost mystical cult of silence."[14]

IV

From Adams, then, Baird seems to have borrowed almost nothing of substance. He simply liked the air of melodrama evoked by the terms "chaos" and "order." English 1–2 assumed that the average freshman arrived at Amherst in a mental (and perhaps spiritual) state that could fairly be termed chaos—though of course he didn't know this. Under the sway of a belief that language—his language, of course—and reality were pretty much the same, he badly needed to be jolted into recognizing that words are very slippery, that everyone uses them differently from everyone else, that communication is difficult, a rare occurrence in fact. English 1–2 would provide that jolt.

This is where general semantics came in. In a twenty-four-page memo of August 5, 1946, "English 1–2: History and Content," Baird insists at the outset:

English 1–2 is not a body of metaphysical propositions, a system of logic and epistemology, complete, final and known as the truth. It is not a content course in which teachers transmit the laws, rules, principles of writing, as part of the heritage of the past, to be added to that store of information which every well educated man is supposed to carry about with him.

In Baird's tone we can hear, perhaps, the anger recently aroused by the curriculum committee's desire for a freshman humanities course that would, in effect, celebrate "the heritage of the past." A little further on, he tells why he eliminated all books from the course:

There was too much writing about writing. . . . Every page, every chapter, was an invitation to do the half dozen things that every English teacher knows how to do—to talk about style or the history of English Literature or the history of ideas or to describe the literary type or to refine the student's emotional life and cultivate his aesthetic sensibilities, and so on.

And a few pages later, after repeating that "English 1–2 is not a collection of propositions or a body of information to be transferred to the student's mind," he writes: "It is an instrument, created by purposeful effort, to do a particular thing, a means to an end, a force to motivate action."[15]

What is significant here is Baird's strong desire—his yearning, even—to break out of what he sees as a vicious cycle of words begetting more words, a cycle that he believes is necessarily perpetuated by "writing about writing"—that is, by papers that students write about assigned texts rather than about their own experience. He wants instead to get in touch with Chase's silent, wordless world. The concept of action, the problem of how to get physical action directly into words (insofar as this is possible), the need to make writing itself as close as possible to nonverbal action—all these were central to Baird's thought. As early as 1939 he characterized the course's subject as "the writing of English—not a state of emotion, nor a body of information, but an action."[16]

It is thus no surprise that Baird followed Korzybski's lead in creating something of a mystique about the area of experience that lay (or seemed to lie) beyond the reach of words, the area he was fond of referring to as "the inexpressible." In a 1952 essay about the course he thus explained why the first half of English 1–2 was devoted to having students describe their (mostly) physical actions:

A student who is a good tennis player sets out to write a paper on what he does when he serves a tennis ball. He knows he knows what he is writing about, yet as he begins to address himself to his subject he immediately encounters the inescapable fact that his consciousness of his own action contains a large area of experience quite beyond his powers of expression.

As a result, the poor student is "rendered almost speechless," and so "produces a mess." While he knows he can perform the action, he has learned that he "does not know in the sense that he can communicate this action to a reader. At this point the teacher tries to get him to distinguish between these two levels of experience"—which are, of course, the inner, psychological or experiential, correlates of Korzybski's nonverbal and verbal levels. The student is then led to recognize that at least "a part or an element of his experience can be communicated to another person when he isolates the order in which he throws the ball into the air, raises his racket, and so on, and that the order of his action as distinguished from the action itself is the subject of his writing."[17]

The clear implication is that everything about the student's tennis serve except the order in which the various actions constituting it were performed belongs to the nonverbal level of his experience, and therefore remains—perhaps forever?—beyond his reach as a writer, inexpressible. Surely this is not only flatly untrue—any decent sportswriter can capture in writing far more than that about the serving of a tennis ball—but hopelessly (and puzzlingly) arbitrary: why, out of all the possible "elements" of a tennis serve, should the order in which the server's various actions were performed be singled out as the one that is not inexpressible?

It was most important to Baird to maintain, and to inculcate in his colleagues and students, his belief in and reverence for the inexpressible. In a 1990 letter to Ms. Varnum he asked the following series of provocative questions:

> How much of experience anyway, can be expressed in language? 5%? What abt in music? in other symbols? What then was the 95% unexpressed? Can you be aware of that while talking and writing? What does the awareness of the inexpressible do to your own conviction in what you are saying? (Varnum, 261–62)

Is language really so limited as all that? And what do we mean when we say that something is inexpressible? The very form of the question would seem to defeat all possible attempts to answer it.

Yet the concept of the inexpressible is hardly unexaminable. When we are young and naive, I think we often say that what we are feeling, and trying to communicate to another person, is inexpressible when (and simply because) we cannot get the other person to agree with us. If he really knew what we meant, agreement would automatically follow. When we are older, more experienced, and a little more sophisticated about language, we take a somewhat different view of the inexpressible. What sorts of thing are most often said to be inexpressible? The feeling of being in love for the first time. The taste of a 1952 Château Margaux. The majesty of Beethoven's Ninth. But surely all we mean when we call these, and similar, experiences inexpressible is that there is nothing we can say that will perfectly replicate any of them, that will make another person have them, then and there. Yet this fact is due not to any limitation or failure of language. The widespread popular idea that it is can be traced to what Max Black has called "the muddled notion that the function of speech is to *reinstate* reality." Black adds: "the best recipe for apple pie can't be eaten—but it would be odd to regard that as an inadequacy."[18]

The more one thinks about it, the odder it seems for a college English department to spend its time impressing upon its students the limitations of language and the vastness of the realm of the inexpressible. For surely the job of an English department is precisely the opposite: to make its students aware of the enormous resources of language—as used by great writers, of course, but also as the rest of us can learn to use it, to describe and to evaluate critically what we read, and to share our experience of literature (and the other arts) with others. This, of course, is just what the Amherst English Department did so superbly in our time—after one had somehow blundered through the unnecessary obfuscations of English 1.

As a sophomore, I was so disgusted with English 1 that I vowed never to take another English course as long as I lived. But during the summer of 1951, between sophomore and junior years, I traveled around Europe with a small jazz group—which, incidentally, included Pritchard. He and our clarinetist, Frank Chace, talked about literature a good deal, and somehow got me into reading Joyce. During our travels I devoured *Dubliners, Portrait,* and *Ulysses,* and composed songs to a couple of the poems in *Chamber Music.* That did it. Though I understood precious little of *Ulysses,* it gave me the feeling that I have since discovered it often gives to adolescent readers: literature suddenly seemed of vital importance, and it suddenly seemed to have been written just for me.

I had been rather halfheartedly pursuing a German major. But I had gradually realized that between the medieval poets, whom I had read freshman year with a retired professor named Eastman—who lived at 86 Northampton Road, in a house later occupied by various Pritchards—and Rilke, I liked only Goethe and some bits of Heine and Hölderlin. When we returned to Amherst that fall of 1951, Pritchard, who had decided to major in philosophy, began sitting in on the English junior honors seminar. He brought back thrilling reports of what went on there, and I suddenly got the idea that if you wanted to learn how to tell good works of art from bad, the English Department was the place to be. So a few weeks into term I became an English major.

From John Moore and Ben Brower, my instructors in English 21–22, the introduction to critical reading required of majors, I heard nothing whatever about the limitations of language but learned a great deal about its resources. And as I went on, taking almost every English course in sight, it occurred to me that the dynamics of an English major at Amherst was oddly like that of an old-time revival meeting. Like the fire-and-brimstone preacher who denounced you for your sins until you were thoroughly depressed, Baird and Company intimidated and perplexed you with their gloomy nonsense about encroaching chaos and the virtually insurmountable difficulties of communication. But then, when you were on the mat, beaten, it was suddenly announced that all you had to do was to come down front and make your decision for Christ (or, in this case, English literature), and the kingdom of heaven could be yours after all.

V

It should not have been this way. I don't know that English 1 did anyone any great harm. But it did waste a lot of important time, and it pretentiously concocted and peddled spurious mysteries—which I guess I do believe is the intellectual sin against the light. Actually, I am grateful to the course because the questions it raised (and refused to answer) led me to do a great deal of reading in philosophy. Still, I would submit that Baird's view of what a beginning writing course should be and do, and of its relation to the literature courses that are the principal work of an English department, was dead wrong.

It is simply not true that having students read books and then write about them is a bad way to teach writing because it produces "writing about writing," and thus steers you in the wrong direction, away from your proper goal, the nonverbal world of action. Writing about one's own physical actions is not somehow more basic, a more natural place to begin, than writing about other people's words. We do not have to learn to do the former before we attempt the latter, as we must all learn to walk before we try to run. This is pure mythology, extrapolated by Baird from Korzybski and his disciples. Indeed, writing about one's own tennis serve is both harder and less interesting, less productive of real thought, than writing about, say, the *Iliad* or Montaigne or a novel by Henry James.

Baird thought that assignments that led to talk, between teacher and student, about "style or the history of English Literature or the history of ideas," talk that might help the student "cultivate his aesthetic sensibilities," had no place in a writing course. In his 1939 essay on the course in its early stages, he made it clear that he wanted to strip away all such cultural excess baggage in order "to reduce reading and writing to their simplest terms" ("English 1 C," 332). So he had students start with their own actions and work outwards: after a first term spent describing tennis serves and the like, they were asked to describe what they did in their other courses at Amherst.

In the second term of our freshman year, the spring of 1950, we were asked to take some barometer readings and then, a few assignments down the line, to define "Science"; later in the term we were given some population statistics for the Connecticut Valley in the nineteenth century and then, eventually, asked to define "Historian." What real knowledge could possibly be expected to result from charades of this sort? None, it seems to me. The aim, I suppose, was to show us that words mean different things at different times to different people, that the dictionary does not hold the solutions to all one's problems, that a window becomes a door when you enter a room through it, that (in short) words mean whatever you make them mean by your actions. If you think communication is difficult now, just try actually basing your use of language on your own private "operational definitions"!

In over forty years of teaching literature—and along with it, inevitably, writing—I have only once tried to base a freshman course on autobiography, and I found it to be a mistake. Not only is writing about oneself more difficult, and generally less enlightening, than writing about a first-rate assigned text; what a student reports about his own experience is, technically, incorrigible. Faced with a stale, boring, cliché-ridden account of what my neighborhood is like or how I fell in love last summer or how I serve a tennis ball, a well-trained English teacher naturally wants to insist that it must all have been more complex, more ambivalent, more interesting—more like literature, in a word—than the student has made it out to be. And often this will work. But if, as sometimes happens, the student says, simply, "No—that's exactly what I did, exactly how the scene looked, exactly how I felt," then the teacher is in no position to argue. Of course he can always sneer or bully—and Ms. Varnum's book makes clear that a lot of that went on in English 1. But if the student is unintimidated, and sufficiently aware of his rights to demand evidence, there is really nothing the teacher can say. How then to justify that C-minus?

On the other hand, if you have a text, there between you and the student, a neutrally placed object that you both are in a position to regard disinterestedly, then you have something to argue from. Of course you will not always get the student to agree with you—nor should you want that always to happen. But if he is to disagree effectively, he will have to come up with arguments of his own, based, just like yours, on the text open before you both. Either way he will learn something about how critical arguments proceed, and thus how critical thought takes place. And, I would add, if the text happens to be a great book, one rich enough to have been enjoyed and argued about for centuries, such discussions will be all the more likely to be very interesting indeed. The advocacy of great books courses therefore has a strong empirical justification, and is not founded merely on a slavish veneration for "the canon," or on a snobbish desire to teach only books by "dead white males."

No one learns to write in a vacuum. Writing is not just another skill that can be taught as one teaches baseball or skating. I am of course speaking of the kind of writing that it is the business of a liberal arts college to teach. This is, I take it, neither "creative writing" (poems, short stories, and the like) nor the quasi-formulaic journalistic writing (the basic sports story, the basic police story) that is presumably taught in schools of journalism. It is, rather, expository prose that is clear, solidly based on relevant evidence, coherently argued, unpretentious in tone and diction, appropriately expressive, and finally persuasive. This sort of writing is always writing about something, never simply writing in a vacuum. Therefore it is most effectively taught, and most efficiently learnt, not in an intellectual vacuum, as in English 1, but in a course with an intellectually demanding content that is of some interest to the student.

Learning to do this sort of writing is not merely learning a skill or a technique because it is learning to think in a new way: more clearly and consecutively, and at greater length, than one can do without putting one's thoughts into writing. Human thought realizes or actualizes itself only in language. Moreover, all discursive thought of any complexity—as distinguished from the genius's sudden flash of inspiration, which can have enormously complex implications—can only take place in written language. We can all improvise—in class, say—arguments of a certain depth and complexity, but our mental storage capacity is severely limited and soon runs out. Beyond a certain point, we simply have to start putting words on paper, forming them into sentences and paragraphs, seeing how they look when we have got them outside of our heads and have made them stand still on the page for critical inspection.

Now one of the oddest things about English 1, as Ms. Varnum's book makes amply clear, is that the two men most responsible for planning and carrying on the course, Baird and Armour Craig, did very little writing after completing their doctoral dissertations, and published almost nothing. Pritchard noted, of the senior professors who taught English 1, that "with the exception of Brower, and even he not until he went to Harvard, nobody published" (Varnum, 140). Ms. Varnum also points out that many of the junior staff who did not get tenure began to publish immediately upon leaving Amherst. Walker Gibson, who did get tenure but chose to leave anyway, remarked that "the best thing that ever happened to me as a young teacher was to land a job at Amherst College in 1946, and the next best thing was to leave it when I did" (Varnum, 224)—that is, in 1957, two years before Gibson published the first in a series of successful writing texts.

I remember vividly the sense we all had, as undergraduates, that to write and publish was slightly *infra dig*. If your thought could actually be fixed, frozen in words, then it must be a bit crude—not infinitely complex, subtle, ever-changing, playfully and ironically alive to every twist and turn of the ongoing dialectic that formed our intellectual life. Of course this came mostly from Baird—and perhaps also from Robert Frost, who was an occasional though vital presence on the campus during the early 1950s (but who, it should be noted, seemed to have no trouble publishing).

In the 1961 letter to Pritchard that I cited earlier, I tried to describe the effect such an attitude might have had on Baird's younger, tenure-hungry colleagues: "I can well imagine what it must have been like to be made to feel, by this older and obviously very bright fellow, that if you wrote, if you, in effect, spoke your mind in a sustained utterance that Committed you to a certain position and a certain argument (necessarily ignoring other positions and arguments which you weren't against but which weren't strictly Relevant), you were somehow being dishonest, not sincere, not English 1."

That letter was written just after the summer during which both Pritchard and I wrote what would be our first published pieces, for a book called *In Defense of Reading*, Ben Brower's collection of essays by those of us who had taught Humanities 6 with him. Some years earlier Pritchard and I had made a sort of pact that we would not succumb to the Amherst anti-publishing pressure. We talked about this often, but I particularly remember one late Sunday hungover breakfast at Cronin's in Harvard Square, sometime in the late 1950s, in the course of which we promised ourselves and each other that we would write and publish a lot, that we would become—the half-humorous, half-defensive phrase has stuck in my memory—prolific "critical hacks."

I have come to believe firmly that writing should be taught by teachers who regularly write, revise, and publish, for they are surely better able to show students how the process of writing actually goes on than are teachers who write nothing but assignment sheets. Indeed, I think that the general air of deliberate mystification surrounding English 1 was a direct result of the fact that Baird and Craig did not often attempt to give clear and extended written expression to their thoughts. If one is not accustomed to the discipline of writing, it is easy to slip into the bad habit of forever ducking behind the provocative question, of repeating, over and over, as a sort of mantra, that "there are no easy answers" in order to justify one's failure to give one's students any answers whatever, only questions and more questions.

In his 1946 memo Baird cites a number of the questions asked in English 1 assignment sheets: "What *is* a technique?", "What is the difference, what is the similarity, between a bodily and a mental technique?", "Is this mind-body distinction (which students accept as a basic fact) a sound one?", and so on. He then assures us that "In order to mark and grade a theme in a composition course we had to think through these large issues for ourselves" ("English 1–2: History and Content," 7–8). Are we then to believe that the English 1 staff actually did "think through" the mind-body dualism? Perhaps so; but we can be sure that the results of their thought were never transmitted to the students in the course.

VI

How then, in view of all the terrible things I have been saying about English 1, do I account for its immense popularity with a good share of those who took it? I am not sure. Certainly the endless, thinky questions that so irritated me did help many students cultivate a skeptical habit of mind.

And I am sure that the constant analysis, in class discussion, of recently submitted papers did a lot to discourage the fancy writing most of us had brought with us from high school. Also, Baird had made himself into a prominent and attractive "campus character," just the sort of colorful old duffer you expected to encounter if you went to a famous New England college, Mr. Chips got up as Foxy Grandpa. And he was intimately associated with the course in everyone's mind, whether or not they had had him as a section-man. Several of Ms. Varnum's informants said that it was their experience of English 1 that made them want to major in English, and this I am utterly at a loss to understand, my own experience having been precisely the opposite. On the other hand, most of the people I recall speaking most fondly, in later years, of English 1 were history or political science or economics majors who never took another English course. For them, English 1, with its strange puzzles and enigmatic challenges, was the spice of their college years, a quirky wake-up call to adulthood. Many of Ms. Varnum's informants compared the course, and often quite affectionately, to boot camp.

But where does this leave Pritchard? The reader will have noticed that he figures prominently in the title of this essay and has popped up from time to time during its progress. I was led to think about English 1 once again by reading, in his excellent memoir *English Papers*, the following sentence: "I'm convinced that an important reason why the deconstructive turn (with its emphasis on aporias, slippages, dangerously floating signifiers) had the effect on me of being very old news indeed, was the skeptical attitude toward language cultivated in the English classroom decades previously."[19] Since this remark occurs in the midst of a discussion of English 1, I take it that the phrase "English classroom" means (or may even be a slip for) "English 1 classroom."

I think Pritchard is absolutely right in seeing important similarities between English 1 and "the deconstructive turn" in literary studies. Deconstructionists too fret ponderously about the slipperiness of language and the consequent "indeterminacy of meaning"; and they too are fond of stirring up big questions—everything is "problematical"—yet are mostly ignorant of philosophy and incapable of coherent argument. Once again the air is thick with pointless mystery-mongering. But the present situation is of course much worse: English 1, an against-the-current operation if there ever was one, was taught by a small number of men at one small college; deconstruction (or whatever it's calling itself this week) is a genuine (and genuinely destructive) movement.[20]

From many conversations I know that Pritchard shares my low opinion of deconstruction. Heretofore he has certainly not shared my opinion of English 1. I am therefore pleased to present this essay to him as an affectionate challenge: if you and I agree about the worthlessness of deconstruction, and about the similarities between English 1 and deconstruction, why don't we agree about English 1?

Notes

1. Robin Varnum, *Fencing with Words: A History of Writing Instruction at Amherst College during the Era of Theodore Baird, 1938–1966* (Urbana, Ill.: National Council of Teachers of English, 1996). Though I did not hear of Ms. Varnum's book until after I had begun work on this essay, it proved of enormous help to me—as will be obvious to any reader. I am therefore most grateful for it. See also: James H. Broderick, "A Study of the Freshman Composition Course at Amherst: Action, Order, and Language," *Harvard Educational Review* 28 (1958): 44–57; Walker Gibson, "Theodore Baird," in *Traditions of Inquiry*, ed. John Brereton (New York: Oxford University Press, 1985), 136–52; and John Carpenter Louis, "English 1–2 at Amherst College: Composition and the Unity of Knowledge" (Ed.D. diss., Harvard University, 1971).

2. Gail Kennedy, ed., *Education at Amherst: The New Program* (New York: Harper, 1955). Later references to this work, as "Kennedy," will appear in parentheses in the body of the text.

3. See Timothy P. Cross, *An Oasis of Order: The Core Curriculum at Columbia College* (New York: The Trustees of Columbia University, 1996).

4. The information in this and the following paragraphs is taken from the Amherst College course catalogues, 1938–39 through 1947–48, relevant portions of which were provided, in photocopies, by the staff of the Amherst College Archives. Throughout the preparation of this essay I have been greatly indebted to Archivist Daria D'Arienzo and her associates for their generous help.

5. Helene Deutsch, "Some Forms of Emotional Disturbance and Their Relationship to Schizophrenia" (1942), in *Neuroses and Character Types: Clinical Psychoanalytic Studies* (New York: International Universities Press, 1965), 262–81; see especially 262–66.

6. Percy W. Bridgman, *The Logic of Modern Physics* (New York: Macmillan, 1927), 7. For historical background see L. Susan Stebbing, *Philosophy and the Physicists* (London: Methuen, 1937).

7. *Holmes-Laski Letters*, ed. Mark DeWolfe Howe, 2 vols. (Cambridge: Harvard University Press, 1953), 1457.

8. The passages cited from Pearson and Adams's comment on them may be found in *The Education of Henry Adams* (New York: Modern Library, 1931), 450–51. The Pearson passages may be read in context in *The Grammar of Science* (London: J. M. Dent and Sons, 1937), 94–97 and 118–20. This "Everyman's Library" volume, though now out of print, is the edition of Pearson's work that is most readily acces-

sible in libraries. It also has a valuable introduction that recounts the tangled textual history of *The Grammar of Science.*

9. For a detailed (and amusing) account of Adams's encounter with Pearson's work see William H. Jordy, *Henry Adams: Scientific Historian* (New Haven: Yale University Press, 1952), 228–36.

10. In his review of *Fencing with Words,* Pritchard follows Ms. Varnum in this error, citing the passage from Adams with "orders" for "order." See "Amherst English," *Raritan* 16 (Winter 1997): 143–57.

11. For a fuller account of general semantics, see my essay "General Semantics and the Science of Meaning," *College English* 29 (January 1968): 253–85; and Chapter 1 of my book *Semantics, Linguistics, and Criticism* (New York: Random House, 1972). For more on Hayakawa, see my review of his *Symbol, Status, and Personality,* in *Partisan Review* 31 (Summer 1964): 462–68.

12. S. I. Hayakawa, *Language in Thought and Action,* 2nd ed. (New York: Harcourt, Brace & World, 1964), 187–88.

13. Stuart Chase, *The Tyranny of Words* (New York: Harcourt, Brace, 1938), 39.

14. Kenneth Burke, *A Grammar of Motives* (New York: Prentice-Hall, 1945), 239.

15. "English 1–2: History and Content," 1, 5, 8. A copy of this document may be found in Box 1, English 1–2 Collection, Amherst College Archives. Later references to it, as "English 1–2: History and Content," will appear in parentheses in the body of the text.

16. "English 1 C," *Amherst Graduates Quarterly,* August 1939, 328. Later references to this essay, as "English 1 C," will appear in parentheses in the body of the text.

17. "The Freshman English Course," *Amherst Alumni News,* May 1952, 195.

18. Max Black, "Linguistic Relativity: The Views of Benjamin Lee Whorf," in *Models and Metaphors* (Ithaca: Cornell University Press, 1962), 248. On "the inexpressible," see also Wittgenstein, *Philosophical Investigations,* trans. G. E. M. Anscombe (New York: Macmillan, 1953), Part I, para. 610, p. 159ᵉ.

19. William H. Pritchard, *English Papers: A Teaching Life* (St. Paul, Minn.: Graywolf Press, 1995), 24.

20. I should like to make it clear that I am not "against theory." This blanket accusation is commonly directed by deconstructionists at anyone who is against deconstruction because he believes it to be bad theory—that is, because he believes it does not explain the facts it presumes to explain. The assumption of course is that before Derrida and de Man no one had ever tried to theorize about literature or literary criticism. We can also see this assumption in the title of Richard Poirier''s well-known essay on Humanities 6, "Hum 6, or Reading before Theory," *Raritan* 9 (Spring 1990): 14–31. In the glory years of Humanities 6, beginning in the mid-1950s, there was in fact a lot of very interesting (and helpful) literary theory being written by English and American analytic philosophers—a body of work that American students of literature might explore with profit. For details and bibliography, see my essay-review "What Is Literary Theory?" in *The Hudson Review* 26 (Autumn 1973): 562–71; and the entry "Semantics and Poetry" in *The New Princeton Encyclopedia of Poetry and Poetics,* ed. Alex Preminger and T. V. F. Brogan (Princeton: Princeton University Press, 1993), 1135–38.

Fred Pfeil

The Passing of the Ice Ball;
or, Appreciating Bill

IT COMES AS SOMETHING of a surprise to have been asked to contribute
an essay to this volume in honor of Bill Pritchard. After all, at the college where I work, aside from my fiction workshops I regularly teach
courses in film and popular culture; while my critical reputation, if indeed
one exists, would have to be based on the work I have done on such sub-
or non-literary topics as the "male rampage" films of Bruce Willis and
Mel Gibson, the "soft-boiled" detective fiction of Robert Parker, James
Lee Burke, and K. C. Constantine, and even the phenomenon of Robert
Bly's *Iron John* and the mythopoetic "men's movement" of a few years
back. In the course of these errant pursuits, moreover, I have frequently
set the issue of aesthetic valuation at least momentarily aside in favor of
questions of cultural significance and ideological implication, and invited
my students and readers to do the same; just as I have both made use of
various theoretical concepts and perspectives from critics and theorists
from Barthes and Lacan to Jameson and Haraway, and attempted to make
those same concepts and perspectives more accessible to and useful for my
students and readers alike.

All this, as any reader of Bill's lucid memoir knows—let alone any for-

mer student—seems guaranteed to elicit from someone of his temperament a mixture of horror and contempt. Likewise, *English Papers* makes it
quite clear that Bill feels his own perspective and values have been jeer-
ingly dismissed by the younger, theoretically hip, racially and sexually
different colleagues with whom he must share Johnson Chapel now that
so many of his white male elders and peers have, in one way or another,
moved on. So let me too be clear, first about my disinclination to link arms
with either side against the other in this dispute, and secondly about my
intention to pay homage to the example of his professional life, if only by
responding to it with that "ambiguity," "complexity," and "disinclination
toward rallying round the cause" that he tells us characterized his own reaction to the upheavals he and I both witnessed from our curiously similar standpoints during the time I was a student at the College on the Hill.[1]

I refer, of course, to the years 1967–71, smack dab in the middle of the
time Bill declares was that of "the dismantling of a college in preparation
for reconstituting itself in another"—and, it must be said, for Bill, lesser
—"style" (153). And I say "curiously similar" because for me, too, those
adrenalized days of all-college meetings, teach-ins, building seizures, and
moratoria were fraught with ironies that even now continue to resound.
While full of doubts as to the value and appropriateness of his actions,
Pritchard continued to hold his class in modern poetry during the "campus strike" of 1970 in the wake of the deaths at Kent State; and had I been
a student of his at the time, I would have been there, full of doubts as I
was, not about the justice of the cause but about the depth and sincerity of
my classmates' fervent actions, and full of appetite as I was, like the
younger Pritchard himself, for any literary work held to be a part of the
(yes, white, Western, male-dominated) cultural treasure trove to which it
seemed only Amherst offered me full admission, and then only for a scant
four years.

Put simply, my standpoint during most if not all of my Amherst years
was that of a bedazzled and resentful peasant. Having left, but not entirely
left behind, the tiny factory town not only I but both my mother's and
father's families were from to arrive at Amherst in the fall of '67, I soon
contracted there a chronic case of Nietzschean *ressentiment*, that chronic,
maddening and delicious discomfort composed of the hopeless longing to
join the club of the highborn combined with the equally strong desire to
throw all its members down the nearest well. So I stared over the top of
my buscart at my putatively revolutionary classmates in the dining halls
of Valentine, arguing wording and strategy as I scraped the remaining

food off their plates and savored my sour doubts as to how long their commitment to Serving the People would actually last in the presence of working-class folks of whatever race or gender, from whom, in my observation at least, even most of the SDS crowd tended to recoil in fear or contempt. Or, for that matter, how long they would hold out against the threat that their own, to my eyes unlimited, stash of admission tickets to such parklands of high culture and class privilege as this one, with its many lovely shaded pathways to good jobs, secure careers, and settled reputations, might be curtailed.

Yet more than I cared to admit to myself at the time, I myself loved the parkland of highmindedness that was Amherst—loved it more and better, I felt, than its natural inheritors ever could. For how could all those ruling-class radicals around me possibly prize at its worth such a lovely, enchanted space of art and thought in which, moreover, every step was taken to ensure the physical comfort of those of us engaged in the strenuous exercise of our intellects and the rigorous cultivation of our sensibilities? Those other guys, I figured, had been disporting themselves on some such landscape ever since they were old enough to speak, while I, nerd and bookworm of my factory town, had spent most of my conscious life yearning without much hope for such a kingdom. In this respect, of course, my own social and intellectual history makes a slant rhyme with Bill's, growing up nearly twenty years earlier in another, somewhat larger but still provincial company town a hundred fifty miles away from my own. His family and upbringing seem, from the account given in *English Papers*, to have been more professionally oriented and "respectable" than my own scruffily petit-bourgeois hearth and home—as were, and apparently remain, the constancy and dependability of his impulse to "be sincere but not embarrassing, controlled but not stuffy" (15). But we both came to Amherst hungry for a kind of food we couldn't get much of where we were from—hungry for big ideas, great works, and for others as interested in taking them seriously as we liked to think we were.

In those days, though, a proper Amherst man was encouraged to trade in his gourmand's capacity for a gourmet's palate, and learn some table manners from his peers and his professorial elders. For Bill Pritchard this gentlemanly declension from the urge to find in the works of the great Western philosophers and writers the wisdom "to fill the void that a Christian faith had once filled" to the more decorous desire merely to emulate the example of those critics and "favorite teachers" who "held the keys to help me unlock the cultural hoard" (34) seems to have been executed far more easily, quickly, and comprehensively than it was in my case. Before finishing up his undergraduate years at Amherst, this young man so temperamentally concerned with taking the middle way between sincerity and stuffiness had already realized that "An ability to discriminate was exactly what I wanted to possess" (35). It would take some further stretch of time before he finally abandoned the path he had been desultorily treading down Philosophy Lane, renounced an interest in ideas as such, and declared himself for literary studies. But the glow that radiates from Bill's descriptions of his own time with Amherst English as an undergraduate makes it clear that all the fires—steadily warming, neither too wild nor too hot—had already been kindled and lit long before he consciously recognized this campground as home:

> English 1 had a heady flavor. Those of us who flattered ourselves that we eventually "caught on," and who were at least rewarded with respectable grades, caught on to something we took to be an all-important crucial difference between words and things, language and reality—between mind and the world-out-there. That world we now understood to be chaos, without pattern or design, awaiting only our human strategies—verbal ones—for running lines of order through it (23).
>
> In discouraging . . . talk about biography or "ideas" or other larger contextual possibilities, the course [Introduction to Literature] may have too confidently advised us to think small . . . , and my own future reluctance to talk about contexts rather than texts was probably encouraged by this sort of critical training. Yet the materials presented for our attention—Wordsworth and Frost, *Lear* and Ben Jonson—surely demanded a strenuous engagement with words on the page (29).

"That world out there we now understood to be chaos"—but how many possible designations of what and where the chaos is supposed to be might we understand the phrase "out there" to mean? Out beyond the seminar room in Johnson Chapel? Beyond Amherst College? Beyond the class-based, class-promoting gentlemanly sensitivity Amherst training was intended to inculcate and/or reinforce? Or, both more narrowly and broadly, out beyond the realm of literary language itself? For most of Bill Pritchard's happy life as teacher, scholar, and critic, there has been no reason to discriminate among these optional readings, much less to seize on and stick with any particular one. Once he has found the echo of his temperament in the ethos of the English Department in the great age of Baird and Brower, the rest of the story *English Papers* tells consists of variations on the theme of his satisfaction until the late 1960s and their aftermath showed up to spoil, or at least taint and diminish, all the serious, "strenuous" fun of "thinking small." The year of grad school at Columbia, nominally to study philosophy, is something of a misstep, but while there at least he gets to check out Lionel Trilling's spellbinding performances. The graduate faculty at Harvard turns out to be chockablock with desiccated literary antiquarians; but Reuben Brower is there, too, to help him get aboard, and take the young man under his pedagogical wing as a member of the section-teaching cadre of Brower's "Hum. 6," a course in which, as you might easily have guessed, "inquiry was specifically directed at language rather than at ideas" (87). Plus there's the crowd of other recent Amherst grads with whom he can hang out, such exemplary older brothers as Richard Poirier, Thomas Edwards, and David Ferry, each of them heroically "unafraid to speak, in the first person, of his responses" to works which invited the kind of "largeness of focus and originality of concern" such young, toughminded critics could in turn bring to bear on them (71). Small wonder that, when the call comes from the Amherst network he has hardly left inviting him to return for a brief interview, with what all concerned assume will be a job offer waiting at the close, Bill feels there is "only one way to go" (105). Indeed, it would seem that for all the admirable range of his subsequent scholarship and writing, since his undergraduate years at Amherst Bill has hardly felt the need, as an intellectual, to go much of anywhere else.

And small wonder that by the time I was there in the late 1960s, this Seventh Son of Amherst, or perhaps more precisely, of Amherst English in the era of Theodore Baird, had come to seem the embodiment of that very performative aesthetics of strenuous engagement and sensitive discrimination which he and most of his colleagues both practiced and, with more or less Zen-like obliqueness, preached. Ultimately Baird himself was, of course, still the chief and most terrifying eminence atop this particular hill; but Bill Pritchard, with his gentler, less scathing contempt and his somewhat hipper, more contemporary literary taste, was assumed to be his understudy and successor. Likewise, as Pritchard was to Baird, so we ourselves—that is, the most sincere yet least stuffy, most passionately engaged yet least partisan among us, those most committed to verbal precision and grace yet least hung up on simple meaning or mere ideas—might hope to become to Pritchard himself. To get in this game, though, you would have to learn not only to pay well-nigh exclusive attention to the words on the page, but also, and at least as importantly, to perform your own responses to those words in such a way as to escape the "combative teasing, frequently inflected with sarcasm" that would be your lot the second you fell into what the critic of *your* performance—that is, your professor—perceived to be dullness or error. All this, plus learning to accept the risk of "relatively low grades," all as "part," Pritchard tells us, "of becoming a man" (118).

Of course *everything* about Amherst College—the old stuff Pritchard clung to as well as the new styles he distrusted or despised—was in the late 1960s still by definition "part of becoming a man." The question is what type of masculinity he had, and, on the evidence of *English Papers*, still quite clearly has, in mind. For starters, it seems to be one that involves and requires a lot of complicated dances back and forth between submission to authority on the one hand and assertions of unabashedly defiant individuality on the other, both in terms of the epigone's (or junior faculty member's) relation to the senior professor and the reader's relationship to the literary text. In either case, the game consists of yielding oneself up to the potent yet runic signals thrown off by professor or poem, but then responding to this experience of submissive attention and reception with a corresponding but independent, sensitive yet toughminded, verbal performance of one's own—a performance which, it must immediately be added, is intended neither to supplant nor to explicate, neither to overthrow the primary text or pedagogical patriarch, nor to grovel before the throne, but to stand, in its properly modest but wholly personal way, more or less without a wobble on its own.

"The style I cultivated in reviewing and encouraged in my students," Bill tells us in his memoir, "put a high premium on literary performance as something to admire both in works of art and in the critic's sentences about those works" (163). Consider the acquisition and display of such skill as a mode of masculinity—as the touchstone, that is, of a particular style of performance of gender itself—and you will at once perceive and be able to measure its distance from the far more widespread, even arguably hegemonic form of masculine self-construction called Professionalism, admirably defined by R. W. Connell as that "combination of theoretical knowledge with technical expertise . . . central to a profession's claim to competence and to a monopoly of practice . . . emotionally flat, centered on a specialized skill, insistent on professional esteem and technically based dominance over other workers, and requiring for its highest (specialist) development the complete freedom from child care and domestic work provided by having wives and maids do it."[2] The expertise Bill prizes and displays is, after all, ultimately far more a kind of sensitivity than it is a science. Thus his disdain for the formalist New Criticism emanating from the likes of Brooks, Warren, and Wellek at Yale throughout the 1950s, with its rather too readily articulated standards and mechanically learnable skills; and thus his admiration for a critic like Leavis, who "knew his mind and seemed to live in order to perform the acts of valuing and discriminating" and for whom "being a literary critic didn't necessitate the elaboration of a theoretical statement in which one disclosed one's principles" (75).

Setting the Amherst English style of masculinity against that of its professionalist cousin in this way helps us understand something of the genealogy and internal complexity of the former precisely insofar as it constitutes itself in distinction from and defense against the latter's values and tendencies. Both, it goes without saying (and therefore must be pointed out), require for their "highest (specialist) development the complete freedom from child care and domestic work provided by having wives and maids do it." Yet where professionalism is—or claims to be— neutral and objective, even in Connell's terms "emotionally flat," the Amherst English style was to be unabashedly explicit, and even passionate, about one's preferences. Where professionalism bestows its highest honors on those who achieve "technical dominance," Amherst English, in what Bill thinks of as the golden years at least, awarded its laurels to those who attended most sensitively and most artfully enacted their response. If such norms, qualities, and standards ultimately derive from those of the English gentry whose last social hurrah was in the mid-eighteenth century and whose last bastion was until recently in the British university system (and if le Carré is accurate, its intelligence services, MI5 and the like), they have come down to us today together with an ever-increasing risk of appearing simply insufficiently masculine, especially when viewed from a professional's or (Lord knows) workingman's perspective.[3] Thus, within and outside the classrooms of Amherst and in Bill's memoir alike, the repeated emphasis on "fierce" argument, "strenuous" engagement, and "rigorous" or even "toughminded" response; and thus too the figuration of this aesthetic's subjectivism as the ultimate, no-net test of one's worth. Are you tough enough to take Baird's lashing sneers, or Pritchard's lighter flickings of contempt, and make something out of them? Tough enough to yield yourself up to their obscure direction and to the endlessly wonderful elaborations of the verbal surface of the text, yet still come back articulately alive?

Sensitive yet toughminded, submissive yet distinct: Baird's and

Pritchard's was a hard act to follow, and by the late 1960s a somewhat contested one as well. But for me, and I dare say for most of my cohorts in English, it was really still the main if not the only game in town. At one point a small group of majors asked for and got a meeting with the English faculty, at which a few of them made so bold as to complain that they were not being treated with the respect due to them as human beings. As I recall it, though—for I was there, albeit characteristically on the sidelines—once Baird rose up to tell them they were not human beings, but students, just as he was not a human being but a professor, their feeble protest was done, and we were all back in place and role, playing the game. Yet something of the cost of that game, it seems to me, registers even in the quotation Bill approvingly provides of his mentor's own written description of that event. "'I vehemently denied,'" Baird wrote to Bill on leave in London, "'that I was a Human Bean [sic], that he had any claim to this. . . . Are you or are you not a Human Bean [sic], etc., all with as much bitterness as I could control . . . .'" So much vehemence, so much bitterness is indeed still carried and conveyed in this writing that it might well make us wonder: does its snarling energy not perhaps contain within itself something close to that same "Pure Whine" Baird claims in this same letter to have heard as an entirely "new note" in a protest which continues to upset him despite his quite effective squelching of the resistance it expressed? Could it not be, at least to some extent, in this scenario as in the ones Freud discusses in his famous essay, that the child who is being beaten and the man doing the beating are one and the same, both deriving in their turn from some now virtually unrecoverable shaming wound?

This is, of course, intended to be an essay about Bill Pritchard and his example; but to be about Bill it has also had to become about the transmission of a certain modality or style of Amherst-based masculinity from one generation of men to the next, from Baird to Bill and from each and both of them to younger men like me. In my days at Amherst, however, that style was offered up for emulation at least as often and effectively outside the epicenter of Johnson Chapel's seminar rooms as within their compass. For those of us smitten with the bug, there were endless opportunities to hone one's skills in Valentine Hall or down in the social dorms, just as Bill himself had done years earlier at Amherst and Harvard, performing our enthusiasms for this novel or piece of music or, for that matter, this professor and/or course. And, hopefully with the same brio, performing our evaluations of our classmates' performances in class and out. Was So-and-So a "good man," that is, was he possessed of a "good mind"? "Good mind," of course, had nothing to do with the depth or nature of the candidate's commitments or values outside of his commitment to the game—though this last obviously precluded any too cloyingly sincere attachment to a particular religious, philosophical, or political perspective. What it meant was that mind's ability first to discriminate, then to perform its justification of its own discriminations, with a blend of grace and rigor that was up to the standards we flattered ourselves we had sufficiently internalized as to be able to impose on our peers.

On one side lay "facile" and "glib"—which was where, as I recall, most of the candidates who failed this snotty peer review smashed up; while those who ran off the other side of this Demolition Derby dirt-track were condemned at best to be patronized as "earnest" or declared DOA as simply "dull." So, too, were these the Scylla and Charybdis of those occasions when a few of the most promising "good men" were invited to hang out with one of their English profs outside of class. Or so I remember them, anyhow—including that evening in the spring of my final semester at Amherst in 1971, when thanks no doubt to my performance in his course on eighteenth-century poetry, I myself was invited to a dinner at Bill Pritchard's house. In the course of that typically decorous yet excruciating high-wire-act evening, I was introduced to, and urged with (and against?) the other guys there to appreciate, the musical performances of Fred Astaire and the rapid-fire satire of Lenny Bruce. And I guess I must have felt I was doing all right—getting through it well enough, anyhow, to have plunked down beside Bill on the couch, somewhere towards the end of the evening, and asked what was, for me anyhow, a daringly personal question. What, I wanted to know, was it like for him to have taught with Baird after having, as a student, first been subject himself to that brilliant curmudgeon? What had it been like (Baird had retired two years before) to have had that terrifying eminence as a colleague?

Bill's gracious response to my question was a story, which as I recall it went like this. At the end of one of his early years on the Amherst faculty, he and Baird and another few colleagues were sitting next to one another on the same side of a table up on the second floor of what was then still the Octagon, questioning a senior English major there to defend his dull thesis on Chaucer. Listless, perfunctory questions from the members of the committee; plodding responses from the lackluster student; outside the room, the torpid air of the inside of a pressure cooker; here inside, a soporific stale sweat bath. Despite his own best efforts, Bill himself was close to nodding off by the time the freak hailstorm blustered up out of nowhere, prompting Baird as the one sitting closest to the second-floor exit door to rise and step out to the fire escape, unleash the door from the landing rails to which it had been lashed and so shut out the worst of the hullabaloo outside. The thesis defense then resumed, without comment; but a moment later Bill, sitting next to Baird, felt the back of the older man's hand press against his leg beneath the table. Reading and responding to this signal as best as he could, Bill slid one of his own hands underneath the table surface, held it palm open, and in the next moment felt the weight and sheer intensity of a stone of ice somewhere between a golfball's and a baseball's size plopped in his hand. In the midst of his attempt to keep the shock off his face, he heard Baird's voice: "Pass it on," the older man had just whispered beneath the student's dull droning and the storm's muffled crashing, with nary the slightest movement of his thin lips.

Now, nearly forty years later, Bill is still passing that ice ball along, and looking to see how the new and different folks down and across the table from him deal with it. It is the game he lives to play, and has indeed played most of his life; and, assuming the account he gives of the Amherst English Department and the students it now serves in *English Papers* is at least subjectively accurate, it is as sad to think of him having so few colleagues and students to play it with nowadays as it is to note how little respect or understanding he has for any other game or playing field. The subject must be literature, defined in quite narrowly canonical terms; the act, a performative appreciation of the literary text's own self-performance. How odd, then, to feel such gratitude to the Amherst English game and its demands, and even such agreement with Bill as I do, given the renegade and turncoat anyone like me must appear to be when viewed from his coign of vantage! For at least in my own mind, sound critical work in contemporary popular culture must absolutely be grounded in just such precise, deep, and comprehensive attentiveness to the immediate surfaces and patterns presented by this or that example of its present workings, as well as to the precise texture and nuance of one's own responses to this or that film, rock album, or mass-mediated phenomenon, as Bill Pritchard, Theodore O. Baird, G. Armour Craig, and Amherst English taught me to pay to the words on the page—even if the aim of such critical practice in cultural studies has less to do with aesthetic discrimination than with social and ideological symptomology. There are good reasons, after all, for paying close attention to cultural texts, literary and otherwise, aside from simply or, for that matter, complexly *liking* them, just as there are good reasons for seeking to comprehend the social location, affiliations, and historical genealogy of one's own and others' pleasures. But that every valid act of literary and cultural criticism must include as at least one of its central moments the most unmediated (albeit always overdetermined) encounter possible between critic as reader and object as text, and that that interchange should be taken in as directly on the pulses and viewed as intently through the mind's eye as I was encouraged, browbeaten, and bullied into doing with literary texts at Amherst—these remain defining principles of my own work, and defining standards by which I judge both my students' and my peers'.

In fact, at the risk of perturbing both "conservatives" and "radicals" in today's vexatious and depressing "culture wars," including perhaps Bill himself and those colleagues in Amherst's present-day English Department from whom he feels so estranged, I will venture to close by asserting my own, no doubt Amherst-influenced, cultural conservatism more aggressively still. For it seems to me that the greatest threat that an ever more corporately funded and controlled, and ever more amnesiacally consumerist culture poses to us all—of whatever class, race, sexuality, or gender—lies in the pressures and inducements such a culture offers us to stop paying close, sustained, or conscious attention to much of anything: to words, or musical notes, or the play of images, or for that matter even to the specificities of our own states of mind. Certainly my students at Trinity College by and large have a harder time and less skill at paying close attention to any and all cultural texts or practices than they did, say, ten years ago; as, given the account Bill gives in *English Papers*, do his present-day students at Amherst, whether they are writing about Milton or *Mean Streets*. One of our greatest American poets of this century, Muriel Rukeyser, advised us to "Pay attention to what they tell you to forget"; and the great American poet of the last one, Walt Whitman, insisted that "To have great art, you must have great audiences." The first piece of advice is political and/or psychological in focus, the second cultural; but to me, in this land at this time, they both come down to the same insistence on the supreme and endangered value of critical attentiveness itself. Bill Pritchard may disdain those who seek to cultivate that attentiveness within English departments but outside of traditional literary studies. But I honor him nonetheless for continuing to insist on its indispensability for the study of literature, and beg his pardon for thinking it relevant out beyond the literary ballpark as well, where we are called on both to appreciate the felicities and to deplore the depredations of all the culture that comes our way, and to regard ourselves and others as human beings, not as Beans, cultivating such judgments and such respect alike as part of the larger labor of creating the democratic culture of which Whitman and Rukeyser continue to invite us to dream.

Notes

1. William H. Pritchard, *English Papers: A Teaching Life* (Saint Paul, Minn.: Graywolf Press, 1995), 148. Page numbers of all subsequent quotations from this volume will be cited in parentheses within the main text.

2. R. W. Connell, *Gender and Power: Society, the Person, and Sexual Politics* (Stanford, Calif.: Stanford University Press, 1987), 181.

3. R. W. Connell, *Masculinities* (Berkeley, Calif.: University of California Press, 1995), 214.

Rand Richards Cooper

Living in the Gap

Teaching is something I've done rarely in my writing career, and always nervously. A fiction writer experiences a kind of semiconscious knowledge through the day-to-day practice of art; but teaching, because it involves that mysterious other participant, the student, requires a further, tricky formalizing. The effort can fall spectacularly flat. And yet when it's working, teaching reminds you of things you need to keep knowing. A successful class—to cadge a famous line from Flannery O'Connor—leaves you feeling you'd be a good writer, if only you had somebody to teach every day of your life.

One such moment came my way a couple of years ago. The scene was a fiction-writing seminar I taught to students in an MFA program. I'd had them read "A Telephone Call" by Dorothy Parker—six pages of interior monologue in which an unnamed narrator agonizes while waiting for her boyfriend to follow through on a promised call. Parker leads her through a series of breathless reversals, from worshipping the inattentive lover to loathing him ("I wish he were dead, dead, dead . . ."); and from beseeching God ("Oh God, in the name of Thine only beloved Son, Jesus Christ, our

Lord, let him telephone now") to chastising Him ("You see, You don't know how it feels"). It's a slight piece, but a lively one; the invitation is to snoop into a mind that believes it is parading its own foibles in private:

> It would be so easy to telephone him. Then I'd know. Maybe it wouldn't be such a foolish thing to do. Maybe he wouldn't mind. Maybe he'd like it. Maybe he has been trying to get me. Sometimes people try and try to get you on the telephone, and they say the number doesn't answer. I'm not just saying that to help myself; that really happens. You know that really happens, God. Oh, God, keep me away from that telephone. Keep me away. Let me still have just a little bit of pride. I think I'm going to need it, God. I think it will be all I'll have.
>
> Oh, what does pride matter, when I can't stand it if I don't talk to him? Pride like that is such a silly, shabby little thing. The real pride, the big pride, is in having no pride. I'm not saying that just because I want to call him. I am not. That's true, I know that's true. I will be big. I will be beyond little prides.
>
> Please, God, keep me from telephoning him. Please, God.

And so on.

It was the beginning of the semester, and my dozen student writers were itching to discuss the story. One pronounced it a "brilliant take on the infantilization of women in a patriarchal era." Another was fascinated by the "religious impulse" of the story; we live in a secular era in which religion is "practically a taboo," he said, and Parker was "playing with that." A third student, noting that the story had been written in the 1920s, said she thought it amazing how much foresight Parker had had in seeing how enslaved we would become to technology, and in presenting the telephone as a "fetishized object."

When they were finished, I praised the resourcefulness of their remarks, then asked: was there anything else one might want to say about the story—any other *kind* of response? Blank stares. "Are you satisfied we've done justice to Parker's accomplishment in writing *these* six pages?" More blank stares. I tried to help. Did it strike anyone that to talk about "A Telephone Call" in terms of infantilization and the fetishizing of technology was to leave something about Parker's story unsaid—or perhaps unheard? What was it like to read the story? Did anyone find it funny? Feel tempted to chuckle a little?

Doubtful frowns and fingers paging through the text. Finally one student spoke up. "It was funny how she would sort of build herself up and then suddenly, boom, it would all come crashing down." She hesitated. "I mean, it was kind of pathetic, but it was funny at the same time."

I thought that was something, and said so; a comment like that brought us closer to the story. I explained that what left me less than satisfied with talking about infantilization and fetishized technology was a disjunction between these ideas and the feel of Parker's story itself. Yes, you could say those things about the story, and say them coherently, staking out a territory of large meanings in which the story fit. But wasn't it troubling that you could say the *exact same things* about the story if it had been written, say, as a third-person narrative with a lot of distance and a somber tone? Framing a response to Parker's story in such large terms had the curious effect of neutralizing it, of bypassing the very qualities that made it *this* story and not some other, "equivalent" one.

I read some of Parker's sentences out loud. Wasn't there something playful in the impertinence of invoking God to intervene in the telephone system, then berating him for not doing so? Or in the lurch from adoration of the beloved to scattershot vituperation, that chanting wish that he were dead, dead, dead? What to do with the excessiveness of it? (Someone had commented, helpfully, that it seemed so "excessive.") Didn't that very excess indicate sentiments in the writer other than indignation, or interest in the "issues"—an appreciation, a pleasure in a predicament so nervously sketched in?

I wasn't trying to make any great claim for the story. In fact, I told them, I wanted them to open themselves up to the possibility of *smaller* claims. The claims of the words—for instance, words like "I wish he were dead, dead, dead."

A student broke in. "But you're *reading* it that way."

I asked her how she would read it. Soon she was reading aloud, trying out different ways of saying Parker's words, other students pitching in with their own performances, trying to convince me—and themselves— that I had pushed the humor too far, that there was a note of anguish in Parker's narrator more penetrating than what I had heard. Maybe so. In either case, an important move had been made in our reading. The students had altered the stance they took, complicating the configuration of elements so that instead of the text and its meaning, now there was the writer, her words, and they themselves, the readers. Yes, the story meant something only because we were "reading it that way." And what it meant depended on how we read it, including how we *heard* it, trying out lines and words and hearing how they sounded, much as writers do when they dream them up in the first place. Meaning was not an answer but an event, a happening; a performance and its reception.

Tracing the lineage of this class takes me back two decades to my freshman year at Amherst College. I was on the other side then, a big-ideas reader; but I was about to encounter the Amherst English Department.

High school had taught us to write about books with an impartial rigor. There was a high quotient of what someone would later wittily call "science envy" in those papers; the hallmarks of the style were objectivity and self-effacement, clarity of argument and solemnity of tone. These were theme-and-support papers, the big idea bolstered by evidentiary quotation. I had performed obediently, producing sentences such as these: "In *The Grapes of Wrath*, John Steinbeck portrays a family whose experiences mirror the economic hardship of the 1930s and delineate a universal theme: the spiritual dislocation of man." "*The Great Gatsby* depicts a romantic figure whose life and death illuminate our need for illusions and the fragility of hope in a heartless world."

If my way of writing about books had the side effect of making *The Great Gatsby* and *The Grapes of Wrath* sound like much the *same* book, well, no one pointed that out to me, and if they had I wouldn't have minded— for I wasn't entirely sure what it was that writers did (though there always seemed to be a good deal of depicting and delineating going on); and anyway, reducing a book's scratchy particularity was part of the basic challenge of English. When you entered a novel in order to write a paper about it, you found a mass of unruly scenes and language, much of it irrelevant or even hostile to your purposes; mightily you turned the crank of your Main Idea until finally you had transformed the chaos into those rock-like sentences. There was something presidential about sentences like that, I thought. They sat atop your paragraphs one after another, A,B,C,D, a miniature Rushmore. They sounded *official*.

Bit by bit, Amherst chiseled away at my Rushmore. It began with English 11, where my teacher, John Cameron, had a low-key intensity I found elusive. The points he wanted to make about books—and about our responses to them—were knottier than I was used to, less certain-sounding. More troubling, however, was his take on my writing. It was the practice in English 11 to use photocopied excerpts of student papers in class discussion. The first round included something from my paper, and I recall how my delight churned into hot horror as it dawned on me that Cameron intended not to praise and ratify what I'd written, but rather to prod it a little. This was going to be a steady theme, because the thrust of English at Amherst was to get us to do three things I distinctly hadn't been doing in high school: 1) Read locally rather than globally, slowing down to spend time in this scene, that passage; 2) Begin our sentences with "Joyce wants ..." rather than "Stephen Dedalus wants ..."; and 3) Focus our attention on "the experience of reading" the passage/story/writer in question.

Bafflement, annoyance, panic, and occasionally a saving mirth shared with fellow sufferers formed my response to English 11. We yukked it up a good deal over the touchy-feeliness of *What is the experience of reading this passage?* What were we supposed to say? "I'm sitting on a train reading *Dubliners* and hey, I'm having a great time!"? I tried to be less presidential and Rushmore-like, more tentative-sounding, and waited to see if anything sank in, even as inwardly I vented my frustration. Clearly there was some other kind of reading "they" wanted me to do, some other kind of reader "they" wanted me to be. But what kind?

As it turned out, another kind of reading had existed in my life all along. Hiding behind that Official Reader who scoured novels for topic sentences was another reader, who loved books in an unarticulated and private, even furtive way. Years before, in early grade school, I had started reading every night in bed. I had a miniature flex-necked Tensor reading lamp, impressively high-tech-looking for the late '60s, which cast a cone of white light just wide enough to contain my book, leaving the rest of the room dark enough so that my parents had no idea (so I thought) that night after night I was stretching the allotted half hour into an hour, two hours, reading until my wrist and hand cramped up from supporting my head, and the lines on the page began to swim.

I read mostly boys' books. There were the Hardy Boys and Alfred Hitchcock's Jupiter Jones series, and the Chip Hilton sports stories, then Tom Sawyer and Huck Finn; in sixth grade I plowed through the historical novels of Kenneth Roberts. Adjacent to my room was a storage room containing boxes of books my father had read as a kid, and I read those—adventures like *Tom Swift and His Big Dirigible* or *Across the Pacific!* or *Toby Tyler*, by James Otis, about a boy at a carnival who loves and loses a pet monkey, a novel that reduced me over and over to helpless, shamed tears. Or a curious genre of sports mysteries with titles like *Death on the Diamond* and *70,000 Witnesses*—the latter featuring a football game in which, at the bottom of a terrific pileup of players, the star halfback lay dead (the ref did it, with a syringe.)

The pleasure I took from these books surpassed description; and I wouldn't have wanted to describe it. Reading wasn't something you talked about with your pals at school, like sports or bikes. Its pleasures existed on a dim but deeply familiar level of self where one was, for better and for worse, alone. Even now it is challenging to write about experiences which trail back into the shadows of early childhood. I'm talking about the almost subliminal level of self on which impressions and stray thoughts associate freely, where sounds grow shapes and colors flavors. The brilliant, blooming patterns of green and yellow lights I could produce on the darkened skyscape of my mind by pressing thumb and forefinger into my closed eyelids as I lay in bed at night; or the mysterious comfortingness of my orange night light, which I somehow could almost taste, sweet like orange-flavored aspirin. The strange satisfaction of running the sidewalk and matching your stride against its sectioned lengths, but just a little out of phase, so that with each leap the space between your foot and the next crack grew smaller, smaller, until whump!—you flew over the crack to the next square completely, and started the cycle all over again. Or the games you played with teachers' names (Teeny Weeny Mrs. Sweeney!); or how the days of the week had colors—Tuesday yellow, Wednesday black, Saturday blue; or the steady syncopation of nonsense notions chanted just under your mind's breath, *LET'S go home let's GO home let's go HOME!!*

The reader lost in books night after night in the light of the Tensor lamp was doing something related to all that. Much attention gets paid to the role of the visual in writing (Conrad's pledge "before all, to make you see"); but there's more than that going on in the mind of a reader, who hears and hefts words as much as he sees pictures. Literature is a spatial and textural phenomenon, a thing of shapes and surfaces. The magic of reading, William H. Gass has observed, is that when we do it, "thought seems to grow a body"; and the child reader, fresh from a time when letters presented a strange and formidable geography, and the relations between sounds and words and words and objects seemed anything but obvious, understands this. If the stories I liked at age ten were realistic ones (no science fiction for me!), it was because the act of reading *itself* was magical, and showed its magic most dazzlingly when played against the recognizable and real. Reading wasn't real life, but an improvement on it, the sounds of words adding extra meaning to the innocuous. In real life, when someone walked into a room, he just . . . well, walked into the room, and who cared? But in books people strode in, skipped in, slipped in, sauntered in. The novels I read under the Tensor lamp worked like music, they went for your whole body, carrying total effects of joy and sorrow. They gave you real life intensified through words that thrummed like rain on the roof or dry-scratched you like boredom.

And what was that, after all, but an experience of reading?

English 11 had knocked the Official Reader in me back a step. But it was left to Bill Pritchard and his Modern Satire and Fiction class, in the fall of 1978, my junior year, to finish him off.

I came to Pritchard's class with curiosity, a survey of friends having disclosed starkly divergent views—the yeas smiling conspiratorially, the nays shrugging him off with a baffled What's-the-big-deal? The class was held in a crowded Red Room in Converse Hall, and that proved an awkward size and setting for Pritchard's procedures. I sat high up in the rows with Michael Gorra (later to become an English professor at Smith), and the two of us tried to get a grasp on things. Here was a lecture run by someone who refused to lecture. Pritchard's classes presented no extended argument, but rather a series of noticings, pointings-to, and questions. It proved almost impossible to take notes on something so essentially off-the-cuff. Looking at a passage, Pritchard would toss out a kind of conventional-wisdom reading. Then he'd ask, Is there more to it than that? The "more" was an invitation for us to comment on a writer's style, which meant his (or her) characteristic relation to his characters, to language, and to us. Is Hemingway's performance in the story "Soldier's Home" all bluff and bluster, or is there something there to admire? If so, what? Norman Mailer accused Bellow of pouring sympathy like cream all over his characters. Is that what Bellow does to Tommy Wilhelm in *Seize the Day*? How would *we* describe what he does? How might we compare it with what Flannery O'Connor does to Mrs. Turpin in the waiting room in "Revelation"? Paper assignments worked the same way. Using a quotation from some critic to get us going, Pritchard would ask different questions that were really all one question—what is interesting to you in this writer? And this meant: Where does he or she end up taking you, and what is it in the words that gets you there?

My pleasure in writing those papers verged on the illicit. Quickly I intuited that while in person Pritchard seemed stern, what he "wanted" in papers was rather the opposite. You could do anything in a Pritchard paper, bring in anything. Jokes, parodies, strange comparisons, song lyrics, advice your mother gave you: the lid was off. Could I get away with saying that reading Bellow was like being at a lecture, or in church, where the sense of being *improved* was strong? Or write a personal intro to my paper on Flannery O'Connor telling how during spring break I had argued with my high school girlfriend, now attending a Catholic university, about the meaning of O'Connor's work, my girlfriend shoving her Jesuit professor's interpretations of Christian symbolism at me as I complained that she was missing the point? Could I use *that?*

Apparently so. Paper after paper came back graced with approving exclamation marks in precisely those places I felt I had pushed the limits. I'd show the paper to Gorra—look, he even went for *this!* This was great, I thought. This was like getting paid to have fun.

Breakthroughs in life (in love, in work, or in art) often function through just this kind of loosening of the rules. Obstacles have been removed, some part of yourself brought into play in a way you hadn't imagined before, turning chores into delights and making for a sudden and dizzying enlargement of the possible. I thought I was getting away with something. But really I was learning something. What Pritchard taught—by example—was a way of reading that made literature personal. His guiding concepts ranged from the sacred to the whimsical: Frost's feats of association, Arnold's touchstones, and the Taxicab Driver's Test, in which the first paragraph of any story or novel had to be engaging enough to make the literary cabbie (who could read only one paragraph per stoplight) read on. Taken together they created a kind of readers' schoolyard where the meaning—and merit—of a particular writer or book or poem could be argued out, no holds barred. And for that you needed any tool that came to hand: contentious assessments, extravagant comparisons, whatever. All good literature, Pritchard taught, was a performance that captivated and surprised; the challenge in responding to it was not to squash that performance with the steamroller of what he would elsewhere call "grad school English," but rather to keep it in play a little longer, to rise to the occasion. Good writers were never boring, never dull; why should *you* be? You had to meet style with style.

Those of us who thrived in Pritchard's classes were intrigued by *his* style. My friend Mark Hinrichs and I distilled what we decided were the essential Pritchardian gestures, then went around emulating them. There was the grimacing shrug, eyebrows and shoulders rising, one hand floating out in front; the thoughtful nod of agreement, eyes averted, mouth turning down at the corners; the sudden unexpected laugh and raised finger—"Well said! Well said!"; the fabulous contortions in front of the class, one knee gymnastically lifted to perch on the table as a point was delivered, stork-like. One whole semester Hinrichs and I paraded around campus, curious grimacing clones. We thought we were doing a number on Pritchard. But imitation, as John Updike has noted, is praise. What we sensed in these gestures was intensity, moreover a specifically literary intensity. It seemed a physical struggle to express—or, even better, be impressed *by*—the right word.

A way of reading based on listening to words and being impressed or moved by the right one made sense to me; and beyond that it allowed the reader in me to speak encouragingly to the would-be writer. When I recalled a novel I cared about, it was usually a certain sound I recalled. In *Lolita*, for instance, the stifled sob of Humbert Humbert's "—every night, every night—." In Russell Banks's *Continental Drift*, the ominous, thudding rhythm of three sentences introducing us to Bob Dubois: "He loves his wife and children. He has a girlfriend. He hates his life." One could talk fruitfully about Banks's novel in any number of broad contexts—class, ethnicity, the myth of American social mobility—but whatever claim the novel made to a place in *my* memory was contained in the sound of those three sentences. Similarly, as I began writing fiction myself, I found that what would get me going on a story was rarely an idea as such but rather a tone, a voice, an angle of view. These things *were* the story, at least as far as its inspiration and composition were concerned. Not the what, but the how. And if I couldn't hear it, it wasn't there.

Some years ago a very bright student of mine, a perceptive reader but a newcomer to fiction writing, burst out one day in class: "*Now* I see! It isn't *about* something—it *is* something!" I owe this most basic of writerly operating principles to my teachers at Amherst: Cameron, David Sofield, Armour Craig, Robert Stone, and above all Bill Pritchard. He pushed me on toward being the kind of reader I needed to be in order to be a writer— one who for better or for worse was going to be seduced, to quote Pritchard quoting Wordsworth, by the "grand elementary principle of pleasure . . . a pure organic pleasure in the lines."

Pritchard's way of teaching, which places style and voice center stage, is out of favor on campuses these days. The advent of cultural criticism has opened the gate to the stuff of everyday life, making the enterprise of discerning "good literature" seem fusty and irrelevant, even as arguments over canonical issues have made it seem reactionary—a way of covertly enforcing a particular literary value or type. (Yes, Pritchard would say: *good* literature!) The buzz these days is elsewhere, surrounding teachers and approaches more easily identifiable with social, historical, or political concerns. Twenty-year-olds, by and large, want answers, the bigger the better; and the kind of literature class that supplies them plays to a catchy and compelling music. A student makes an observation about a book, the professor picks it up and runs with it, showing how it ties in with this political theme or that social reality way over here, and what Theorist X said about the historical development of Phenomenon Y (the infantilization of women, the fetishizing of technology), and another student tosses in how that meshes with what he has seen in his own life, and bing bang bop . . . it all fits! This is the text-and-context music of things snapping into place; the satisfaction of the Yes!

Pritchard's classes never had that kind of flow. Pauses abounded. In fact, you could say that a certain kind of pause was the essence. In his memoir, *English Papers*, he discusses how his best classes take him to a point where he isn't entirely sure any more about a poem or a passage. He gets his students to help him unsettle it, and that unsettling makes it new again, makes it happen. "The trouble with most books about teaching," he writes, "is that . . . they put themselves behind some big idea that, if carried into practice, would alleviate or resolve crisis." Pritchard, on the other hand, provokes small crises, opening up an area of doubt where meaning is up for grabs, and an interested, teetering uncertainty is the norm.

There is a state of mind I aim at when I write—I am tempted to say it *is* writing—in which something is always *about* to happen: an unarticulated feeling about to be formed by a word or phrase (if only I can *get* it!) into something I didn't even know I knew. A writer pauses in this gap, and focuses all his or her attention to *listen*. Some small part of the world is about to yield itself up in words whose particular shape, sound, and cadence will connect him to those intimations of charity, longing, laughter, and fear that are the stuff of art. Nabokov calls this state of heightened awareness "aesthetic bliss." Finding one's way into it is the daily requirement—and reward—of a writer's life.

Bill's teaching takes place in that gap. In those pauses of his he is doing what writers do—listening to find out what happens next, and inviting his students to listen too. "The ear," Frost once wrote, "is the only true writer and the only true reader." That might not be the whole story, but I think it goes pretty far. In *The Writing Life*, Annie Dillard tells of a student anxiously asking his writing teacher whether she thinks he has what it takes to be a writer. *I don't know*, the teacher responds. *Do you like sentences?*

Helen Deutsch

"Since Our Knowledge Is Historical"[1]

Homage to William H. Pritchard

I'LL BEGIN WITH the story I can still hear. In Bill Pritchard's classroom, on the second floor of Johnson Chapel, in the fall of 1979, in a course on nineteenth-century poetry, we were reading "Tintern Abbey"—in my case, for the first time. On the first day, which might have been the first day of our acquaintance, Bill told us that he was teaching the course because his family had gotten tired of hearing him talk about Wordsworth. That modest self-irony, along with the generosity of his confession's tacit invitation, opened what has been for me a lifetime of conversation. Thanks to Bill, Wordsworth's egotistical sublime had no competitors, and I was able to encounter his voice free of precept or preconceptions. As we read through the poem in class, I heard something in "Once again I see / These hedge-rows, hardly hedge-rows, little lines / Of sportive wood grown wild,"[2] that struck a chord in me, so much so that although, unlike Bill, I'm not a ready quoter, I've memorized the lines.

I couldn't analyze the resonance I heard then, but to hear it was enough. Now I would say what I heard was a looking and a looking again that was also a rhythmic phrasing and a rephrasing, a focusing of the gaze in precise words, a fusion of the printed page (gestured toward by the play on "lines") with the speaking voice, of artificial nature, the hedge-rows sportively resisting their limits, with natural art. This ordered deliberation, its music of hesitation, repetition, and final correction, united seeing with describing with remembering ("once again") in a way that demanded my own performance of auditory re-vision, while also provoking my memory. I heard in that rhythm another poet I'd read in my first course in Johnson Chapel, English 11 (I'd read backwards when it came to poetry, starting with modern American poets and ending with the Renaissance, and a great deal of that reading was done with Bill)—Elizabeth Bishop, characteristically looking, looking again, and ultimately recognizing the particular place portrayed in "this little painting (a sketch for a larger one?)," "a minor family relic" in which "life and the memory of it cramped, / dim, on a piece of Bristol board," in "Poem": "Elm trees, low hills, a thin church steeple / —that gray-blue wisp—or is it?" I told Bill about the connection, a bit nervously, never having made that sort of comment in class before, and what I learned from his affirming response was not so much what I'd gotten right but that this moment of auditory intuition was how literary study began.

Four years later, a graduate student at Berkeley, I introduced myself to Neil Hertz, visiting for the spring, whose course on George Eliot I had signed up for at Bill's urging. I confessed that I was nervous: how could one write about 900-page-long novels with any kind of confidence? I preferred poetry, because you could see it all at once, keep an entire sonnet in your mind's eye. Hertz's response: What makes you think you can say everything there is to say about a sonnet? Hertz too, it seemed, was willing to forgo definitive seeing for limitless saying. The Pritchard/Hertz connection opened up not only the moment of reading but also a history of reading, at once alien and personal, that I imagined as a past Amherst.

Transforming that moment into presage and unconscious parody of the kind of sublime blockage Hertz spoke of and wrote about, I took my only incomplete in his course. But I found that incompleteness rich and inspiring, and my inheritance of it more liberating than silencing. If you can never say it all, you might as well enjoy saying what you can, you might as well play. You might as well, to put it another way, enjoy the freedom of not knowing. "If it's never any fun," as Reuben Brower once quoted D. H. Lawrence in defense of what he called "the play of the whole being" that is serious reading, "don't do it."[3] Such freedom, I was learning, was still time-bound.

Paul de Man, in an essay I read years later on Brower's famous Harvard close reading course, Hum. 6, in which Hertz, Pritchard, and de Man him-self all taught, remarked in an oddly material locution that "the profession is littered with the books that the students of Reuben Brower failed to write."[4] Brower's embodied presence as reader and teacher was memorial-ized for me in the story of the "A for life" Robert Frost gave him after lis-tening to the Amherst student read an obscure Elizabethan poem in class,[5] while his written presence (acknowledged by many who'd heard him teach to be, in all its power, no substitute for the man himself in the classroom) gave me a model for thinking about the way English poets read and revised the classics. The book I eventually did write, a study of Pope begun with my Amherst honors thesis on revisions of epic similes from the *Iliad* through the *Aeneid* through Dryden to Pope, indebted to all three of his former students, was haunted by Reuben Brower.

Much later, while on a postdoc at UCLA's Clark Library finishing the Pope book, I was, appropriately enough for the locale, on the phone "pitch-ing" my book to Harvard's humanities editor, a friend of and authority on de Man. I was already discouraged, since others I'd talked to had rejected out of hand the idea of a "single author book" on, even worse, a poet, con-cerned about sales in an anti-monograph age of cultural studies. I ex-plained that my interest in Pope began with an interest in literary imitation of the classics, specifically in the British Augustan canon's embattled em-ulation of their Roman models, and that the book was about deformity. "I see," he responded excitedly, "a kind of Reuben Brower for the nineties!" and the book had a home.

For me, however, his acknowledgment was profoundly dislocating. The last and most important in a series of similar recognitions, that telephonic exclamation provoked a strong sense of déjà-vu and self-doubling, an un-easy mixture of pride and distress. My uncanny wobble of ambivalence in response to yet another assessment of myself as a known quantity with someone else's name gave me a personal stake in the anxieties of original-ity and authorship I continue to write about. It was as if I had, unknow-ingly, been marked by the debt I owe to and share with Bill, had been far too good a girl, and too good a student.

These stories of mine share a common theme: great teachers haunt their students, as they teach them to bring poetry to life and living speech. Good students learn to remember and to forget as they listen, to hear as if for the first time. What does it mean to train someone's ear if not to haunt the act of hearing? The Amherst I attended was not the place where my teachers had studied or where Brower, Baird, and others taught the "slow reading" that would change my life. But precisely for that reason Amherst was for me a haunted place.

For a young Jewish woman fresh from a large public high school in Queens, who had little idea of how to synthesize those facts of origin into a name, much less an identity, Amherst was at first a statistic in the Barron's guide—"the hardest school to get into in the country"—and a fantasy of the view from Memorial Hill. That view's pastoral idyll framed an equally foreign reality. Coeducation at Amherst, barely begun when I arrived, was for many either a sign of a lost paradise (the bathos of fraternity boys lamenting, at an all-college forum on the subject, the intrusion of woman into an existence one characterized as "like a monastery"), or a harbinger of harmony still to come (the president's slightly kinder but equally vexing description of Amherst women as a "civilizing influence"). But this dissonance, while it didn't at first make me a feminist, helped me to understand that pastoral Amherst, and pastoral in general, as at least in part an ahistorical fantasy of a past meant to obscure the present. "Hedge-rows, hardly hedge-rows": the way in which I at once knew and didn't know this provided the impetus for my first knowledge of poetry as my own version of pastoral, free from theory, free from history, free to be heard.

Education after Amherst came to mean incorporating into my life as a teacher and scholar what I'd had to learn, sometimes painfully, outside the classroom. But such a process began with the freedom to play. "The Groves of *Eden*, vanished now so long, / Live in Description, and look green in Song":[6] outside the classroom I might have been the cause of the fall, but in class the gates of Eden, that "Earthly Paradise" which Bill recalls, echoing a phrase of Brower's farewell speech to Amherst in *English Papers*, were open, and poetry was revived in the present tense. But the poetry led me outside that classroom, too, to the classics, and the merging of literary with personal history.

I first learned Latin not from the great John Moore, another of my Amherst ghosts, nor at my high school where there wasn't enough demand to justify the expense, but from my grandmother, the first one in her family of Russian immigrant steelworkers in Youngstown, Ohio, to go to college and the only one to finish, nicknamed the Ivory Girl for her 99.4% average, a classics major with dreams of archeology who stayed home to raise four children and two grandchildren. We went through Wheelock one summer on the front porch of our house in Flushing. My grandparents required Latin of all their children: my grandmother's sole province and the bedrock of her absolute intellectual sovereignty in our family, the classics were invaluable educational capital. But as personified by my grandmother they had little to do with social capital. For me they had everything to do with desire and frustration, with lives half-lived and languages half-alive. The incompleteness of my grandmother's ambition echoed the semi-audible remnants of ancient tongues and foreign meters preserved only in print. Latin, and the Greek I soon afterward learned at Amherst, provided me with a counterpoint to the ear's present.

That painstaking labor which never fully brings a dead language to life provided Brower with the model for slow reading, which he once described as designed to replicate the experience of line-by-line translation of the classics for students of English poetry.[7] My classics courses were ordered for communal humility: the first, longer section a patient unpacking of a set of lines, the last few minutes ironically announced as "meaning time." Built into the encounter with Latin or Greek was a self-effacing skepticism about our attempts at mastery. In Bill's class the form of that defamiliarization, what he calls "critical modesty,"[8] remained the same, but literal translation was itself translated into auditory performance.

How can a feminist scholar working on that shibboleth of fashionability, "the body," be perceived—by herself and others—as a kind of "imitation" of Reuben Brower? Or to rewrite the question from within, how did I come to write a book about Pope's personal deformity and perfect form?[9] If the translator learns to appreciate failure, the imitator is forced to reckon with difference. Grappling with both, just as Pope, from the *Iliad* that "tuned the English tongue," to that Horatian poem without an original, the *Epistle to Dr. Arbuthnot*, excelled at both, I came to appreciate the innovative impossibility of originality. While Pope civilized Homer for the ladies, his Horatian imitations are embattled emulations, positing a polite, moderate, and playfully elusive Horace against whom to perform a final version of heroically aberrant satire. Augustan imitation made me curious about what the present tense of poetry, the playing on its surface Bill had exemplified, at once promised and withheld.

Bill gave me free entrance into the British canon, and he provided me with a model of reading flexible enough to appreciate Pope's theatricality and, most importantly, auditory enough to hear the shifts of tone that make his poems cohere. How else to figure out what it was like to read Pope, how first to understand the shift from the vitriol of the attack in the *Epistle to Dr. Arbuthnot* on that androgynous "vile Antithesis" Sporus to the self-celebratory negatives culminating in "Not proud, nor servile, be one Poet's praise, / That, if he pleased, he pleased by manly ways" (336–37) if not as musical in its emotional crescendos? But while Bill, the ideal reviewer who made Leavis's *Revaluation* required reading, also emphasized evaluation and discrimination, a faculty I equate with what the eighteenth century called judgment, in emulating him I listened for connections, aspiring to another eighteenth-century faculty, wit. The sensitivity to echo and allusion that made me hear Bishop in Wordsworth from this perspective became a mode of paradox, a way of hearing literary history. The couplet itself, and Bill and I read lots of them, in its negotiation of literary oxymorons of particularity and generality, ear and eye, came to order my own habits of mind, connecting what I could hear with what I could, by its means, begin to envision.

With the couplet form I could frame Pope's physical deformity. I first encountered the poet's image as I sat reading in Amherst's library, not in the form of the famous rat-man hybrid that graced the frontispiece of the Twickenham edition of the *Dunciad*, but in the sonorous prose of another of Bill's favorite critics, Samuel Johnson, whose *Lives of the Poets* surprised me with the strange familiarity of their unruly details:

> The person of Pope is well known not to have been formed by the nicest model. He has, in his account of the "Little Club," compared himself to a spider, and by another is described as protuberant behind and before. He is said to have been beautiful in his infancy; but he was of a constitution originally feeble and weak, and as bodies of a tender frame are easily distorted his deformity was probably in part the effect of his application. His stature was so low that, to bring him to a level with common tables, it was necessary to raise his seat. But his face was not displeasing, and his eyes were animated and vivid. . . .
>
> Most of what can be told concerning his petty peculiarities was communicated by a female domestic of the Earl of Oxford, who knew him perhaps after the middle of his life. He was then so weak as to stand in perpetual need of female attendance: extremely sensible of cold, so that he wore a kind of fur doublet under a shirt of very coarse warm linen with fine sleeves. When he rose he was invested in bodice made of stiff canvas, being scarce able to hold himself erect till they were laced, and then put on a flannel waistcoat. One side was contracted. His legs were so slender that he enlarged their bulk with three pair of stockings, which were drawn on and off by the maid; for he was not able to dress or undress himself, and neither went to bed nor rose without help. His weakness made it very difficult for him to be clean.[10]

The question here became (and it took years to formulate properly) not what was it like to read this passage but how was a good close reader to situate this passage? What kind of reader of Pope was Johnson? What did this description of Pope's "person," which evoked Pope's own self-description, or story of his "petty peculiarities" have to do with his poetry? Why was Johnson, whose sadistic fascination here is contagious, so intent on embodying the powerful voice that (so he concludes his *Life*) constitutes the place where, if nowhere else, poetry is to be found? If Pope's deformity was "the effect of his application," did that mean that reading and writing had literally left their mark on his body, making him a child in a highchair, an enervated lady, cosseted, corseted, and "in perpetual need of female attendance"? Was deformity being portrayed here as a symptom, a punishment, or merely a fact of prurient interest to eighteenth-century readers? When I encountered William Empson, another favorite reader of Bill's and then of mine, writing two hundred years later with less grudge to bear than any angry contemporary or embattled heir, on the gorgeous lines with which Pope sees "laughing Ceres reassume the land," toward the end of the *Epistle to Burlington*, "the relief with which the cripple for a moment identifies himself with something so strong and generous gives these couplets an extraordinary scale," I knew I'd come up against the limits of reading.[11] In these vexed juxtapositions of extraordinary literary scale with aberrant authorial form, I'd found Pope's ultimate couplet.

In my narrative of Pope's career, those limits are transformed into opportunities for inimitability, self-possession, and originality. Johnson's interest in Pope's body turned out to be symptomatic of a larger cultural fascination that made the image of the great author and ground-breaking literary entrepreneur a joint creation of poet and public. By moving the hyper-visible fact of the poet's body from the margins of scholarly curiosity to the center of his poetry, I was able to envision Pope's poetics as a productive confounding, through allegiance to the untranslatable particular and the historical embodied detail, of fantasies of transparent presence, a canny transformation of his compromised originality into inimitability. Poetry extended from Pope's couplet outward, prompting me to connect whatever I could use—Horace, de Man, Foucault, Freud, Benjamin, Adorno, Maynard Mack, Pope's portraits, caricatures and lampoons, the feminist and Marxist work of Laura Brown, Ellen Pollak, and Carole Fabricant, and of course, Reuben Brower's classicism, even bits of my Amherst thesis—in my own act of creative imitation, governed by what Brower would call "the imaginative design" of the original. To do this I needed theory, I needed history, but most of all I needed the freedom to play from within Pope's poetry that I'd learned in my own particular situation in Johnson Chapel.

The narrative I've constructed here is of a scholar's coming of age; I've focused on my own indebted difference, on an inheritance at once alienating and enabling. Yet I've left out in the process so many of the particulars of Bill's generosity: his gift of unlimited time for independent study and office chat when a beautiful afternoon, or I surmise now, his own work must have beckoned; his love of good conversation, in the classroom, on his long daily walks, at his parties for visiting celebrities which I attended with awe, later, when I'd graduated, over meals at his kitchen table (where we'd smoke Trues), or at the Town House in Belchertown or Kippy's Seafood Pier in New York or the Berghoff in Chicago; his praise for my hubristic review (appreciative with a modicum of criticism, the formula I'd learned from reading him) of his own *Lives of the Modern Poets* in the Amherst Student; his piano performances and lectures on jazz demonstrating that professors need not be bound to and by one brand of expertise; his unabashed relish for his daily soap opera and the Celtics (thanks to him I discuss *Melrose Place* with students and colleagues without shame); his letters over the years, full of the details of daily life and reading, often enclosing his latest review, a memoir about Brower, a convocation lecture, sometimes, best of all, a book. Small wonder, with a teacher who from the beginning made me feel like a colleague, and who provided me with a model for a joyful life of conversation with books, with students, with friends, that I brought to other classrooms in different schools a sense of ease and engaged pleasure in the world of texts and the world at large which was profoundly social. On Eve's side from the beginning, for both of us, paradise alone was no paradise at all.

Bill taught me that a good teacher passes on neither right answers nor specific interpretations but the music and freedom of thought. And recently he has come to haunt my teaching life more than ever. This past winter, I decided to organize a graduate seminar not, as I usually do, around an ongoing research topic or theme and across a variety of genres—"Early Modern Masculinities" would wait until next year—but simply to read "British Poetry after Pope." I worried at first: would my enrollment drop? (It did slightly; so much the better.) Would the students resist so much close reading? (Yes, at first, but they got used to it.) Did I have sufficient handle on the material to teach it without having fully mastered it? (What did good teaching, which is all about not knowing, ever have to do with mastery?) Could I possibly get students to erase from their brains the term "Preromantic" and appreciate this poetry on its own terms? (Three weeks of Cowper and no Wordsworth helped.) Such worries prove what I've always suspected, that teachers constantly vacillate between remembering and forgetting what they know, and that at their best they remain students.

As class progressed, I kept remembering what I'd first learned with Bill: what is good reading if not to hear as if for the first time? Yet what we heard were voices that, despite the received wisdom about their "flight from history," lamented, performed, and transformed their belatedness into solitary inwardness, voices whose power seemed to come from the impossibility of speaking first or without the mediation of print. Gray's *Elegy*, haunted by commonplace, its retired attempts at distinction paradoxically popular; Collins's "Ode on the Popular Superstitions of the Highlands of Scotland," imagining, at a politely Horatian distance, past voices of Bardic prophecy and a vision of second sight; the rhetorical fireworks of Young's *Night Thoughts* evoking, simultaneously, Milton, Hamlet's soliloquies, and the monitory voice of the pulpit; Charlotte Smith's *Elegiac Sonnets*, claiming authentic emotion while performing the voices of Petrarch, Werther, and her own fictional characters, displaying, in quotation marks, the plundered platitudes of loss; Cowper's movement in Book III of *The Task* from an imagined epitaph for a protected pet hare to a Christianized mock-georgic celebration of cucumber farming: all of them voicing, as if for the first time, the enabling burdens of literary inheritance. To hear these poets anew, we found, necessitated the ongoing translation of whatever we called history—be it the literary history necessary to hear allusion's innovation, to understand the deployment of sapphic stanzas or ballad measure, or to articulate the aesthetic debates about sublimity; the religious history required to understand the Graveyard School didacticism, Elizabeth Carter's melancholy transcendence, or Cowper's evangelical conversion and subsequent despair; the social and economic history implicit in Goldsmith's nostalgia in *The Deserted Village*, or Cowper's anxiety about the value of poetic labor in *The Task*; the history of sexuality involved in considering Gray's epitaphic use of amatory form in the "Sonnet on the Death of Richard West"—into our collective present.

When the level of generality in the room rose too high, or the background noise of our analysis became deafening, or when such labor ceased to amuse and we just wanted to enjoy ourselves, we read "not sullenly perus[ing] / In selfish silence,"[12] but together and out loud. In the process of shifting conversational gears, in listening to voices not our own, we often found ourselves productively baffled, silenced, and struck by the audible details solitary reading had obscured. We remembered, as if for the first time, how much can be learned by giving up, at least for a while, and at least for oneself, the desire to know. The joke Bill remembers that went around Harvard in the early '60s, which renamed Hum. 6 "How to Write about Literature without Actually Knowing Anything,"[13] may have been more true, and surely more profound, than the joker intended.

I began with an anecdote of such reading in Bill's classroom, and I'd like to end with another from the more distant past. Doctor Johnson, for the most part impatient with Gray's poetry—"the mind of the writer seems to work with unnatural violence," he remarked of the *Odes*—concludes his *Life of Gray* by "rejoic[ing] to concur with the common reader" in the "character of his Elegy":

> The *Church-yard* abounds with images which find a mirrour in every mind, and with sentiments to which every bosom returns an echo. The four stanzas beginning *Yet even these bones*, are to me original: I have never seen the notions in any other place; yet he that reads them here, persuades himself that he has always felt them. Had Gray written often thus, it had been vain to blame, and useless to praise him.[14]

Neil Hertz has written eloquently, in an essay our class also read, about Johnson's own forgetfulness in his praise of Gray's lines about forgetfulness:

> For who to dumb Forgetfulness a prey,
> This pleasing anxious being e'er resigned,
> Left the warm precincts of the cheerful day,
> Nor cast one longing lingering look behind. (85–88)

Hertz reminds us of Arthur Murphy's observation of Johnson in semi-solitude:

> the contemplation of his own approaching end was constantly before [Johnson's] eyes; and the prospect of death, he declared, was terrible. For many years, when he was not disposed to enter into the conversation going forward, whoever sat near his chair, might hear him repeating, from Shakespeare,
>
>> Ay, but to die and go we know not where;
>> To lie in cold obstruction and to rot;

This sensible warm motion to become
A kneaded clod, and the delighted spirit
To bathe in fiery floods.

And from Milton,

for who would lose,
For fear of pain, this intellectual being?[15]

I can't do justice to the subtleties of Hertz's argument here as it covers a range of "intimate and rhetorical" tableaus from Johnson, to Descartes, to "actual" fleas, to Robert Lowell, but I do want to touch on his conclusion in order to reach my own.[16] For Hertz, Johnson's oral repetition of Milton and Shakespeare facilitates "the forgetting of those lines as poetry—as plangent phrasing—and their internalization as nature or truth." The work of such forgetting enables Johnson to imagine a collective "common reader" with whom he can concur "because he has also forgotten what differentiates him from them—for example, his knowing those lines from Shakespeare and Milton, among other refinements of subtlety and dogmatisms of learning," with whom he can concur, in other words, because he is not Gray. For Hertz "the position of the common reader" is "inconceivable without that forgetfulness."[17]

What Johnson forgets in Hertz's narrative, it seems to me, is what I'd like to call, with my own brand of pathos, the loneliness of scholarly authority. Withdrawn from conversation but with company close by, Johnson repeats and obliterates from thought both death and the poetry about it. Reading the retiring Gray, whose "art and . . . struggle are too visible,"[18] he rejoices to see art disappear in the *Elegy*, and with it the boundary between reader and poem, as its "images find a mirrour in every mind," and "every bosom returns an echo" to the sound of its sentiments. Eye and ear unite in an originality that erases authorial distinction. That these lines should be at once unique and familiar—never seen elsewhere but always felt here, on Gray's page and in Johnson's heart—speaks to the social impulse at work, an impulse allied here with pleasure, in Johnson's practice of reading and writing.

Johnson's relieved return to common reading works as a kind of allegory for what I emulate in Bill as a teacher, what I inherit from him with a difference. Teaching, like poetry, involves a kind of willing suspension of disbelief, a conscious forgetting (as we consider the difference between Johnson's oblivion and our own) of what one knows in order to listen to others. In my version of that Amherst classroom, at a large public university in southern California, we may revive a common reader whom we murder to dissect, or reconsider what oft was thought in true Wit's nature, but in doing so we converse with each other, asking not what does it mean but how, translating and transforming ourselves in the process and in the time-bound present. Each, at his or her best, together and apart, like Elizabeth Bishop, in the waiting room in Worcester, Massachusetts, looking at pictures of an alien place in *National Geographic*, hearing a cry of pain, and becoming aware—all at once—of her own body, her own humanity, her own mortality, and her own name, forgetting and finally remembering the date.

Notes

1. My title refers to the closing lines of Elizabeth Bishop's poem "At the Fishhouses": "and since / our knowledge is historical, flowing, and flown." All quotations from Bishop are taken from *The Complete Poems, 1927–1979* (New York: Farrar, Straus, Giroux, 1983).

2. William Wordsworth, "Lines Composed a Few Miles above Tintern Abbey," lines 15–16.

3. Reuben A. Brower, "Reading in Slow Motion," in *In Defense of Reading: A Reader's Approach to Literary Criticism*, ed. Reuben A. Brower and Richard Poirier (New York: E. P. Dutton & Co., 1962), 4.

4. Paul de Man, "The Return to Philology," in *The Resistance to Theory* (Minneapolis: University of Minnesota Press, 1986), 24. De Man's description of Brower's method echoes what I'm trying to convey about Pritchard's: "They were asked, in other words, to begin by reading texts closely as texts and not to move at once into the general context of human experience or history. Much more humbly or modestly, they were to start out from the bafflement that such singular turns of tone, phrase, and figure were bound to produce in readers attentive enough to notice them and honest enough not to hide their non-understanding behind the screen of received ideas that often passes, in literary instruction, for humanistic knowledge. . . . I have never known a course by which students were so transformed" (p. 23).

5. See William H. Pritchard, *English Papers: A Teaching Life* (Saint Paul, Minn.: Graywolf Press, 1995), 90.

6. Alexander Pope, *Windsor Forest*, lines 7–8.

7. Brower, "Reading in Slow Motion," 6. For Brower such a translation of the labor of close reading from classics to English carries over not just technical or formal principles but also a kind of moral "guardianship" of language, "once performed by teachers of the ancient Latin and Greek classics, [which] now falls to the teachers of English and other modern literatures. Why is this so? Because they are committed to the principle that the study of letters is inseparable from the study of language" (19).

8. Pritchard, *English Papers*, 104.

9. Helen Deutsch, *Resemblance and Disgrace: Alexander Pope and the Deformation of Culture* (Cambridge: Harvard University Press, 1996).

10. Samuel Johnson, *Life of Pope*, in *Selected Poetry and Prose*, ed. Frank Brady and W. K. Wimsatt (Berkeley and Los Angeles: University of California Press, 1977), 531–32.

11. William Empson, *Seven Types of Ambiguity* (New York: New Directions, 1947), 128.

12. William Cowper, *The Task*, Book III, lines 393–94.

13. Pritchard, *English Papers*, 91.

14. Johnson, *Life of Gray*, in *Selected Poetry and Prose*, 641–42.

15. Arthur Murphy, *Essay on the Life and Genius of Samuel Johnson*, in George Birkbeck Hill, ed., *Johnsonian Miscellanies*, 2 vols. (Oxford: Clarendon Press, 1897), 1:439, cited in Hertz, "Dr. Johnson's Forgetfulness, Descartes' Piece of Wax," *Eighteenth-Century Life* 16 (November 1992): 168. Hertz notices, in the same vein as Gray's editors, that "this pleasing anxious being" "rehearse[s] the beat, the theme, and the feel of Claudio's 'this sensible warm motion' (*Measure for Measure*, 3.1.118–121) and Belial's 'this intellectual being' (*Paradise Lost*, 2.146–151)" (168).

16. Hertz, "Johnson's Forgetfulness," 168. Hertz refers specifically here to "the gesture implicit in the pronoun *this*, a gesture at once intimate and rhetorical, like placing one's hand on one's heart," a paradox I align with my own interest in the author's body.

17. Hertz, "Johnson's Forgetfulness," 179.

18. Johnson, *Life of Gray*, 642.

Howell Chickering

Chaucer by Heart

WHEN TEACHING POETRY, I often discover I have gotten a poem by heart without meaning to. This first happened to me during the spring of 1966, my first year teaching at Amherst College, in my section of English 2. The beginning of that semester's syllabus had been designed by G. Armour Craig to move the freshmen away from reading "for the message" to paying close attention to wit, tone of voice, the sound of sense. We had already completed three weeks and six writing assignments when we came to Robert Frost's "Neither Out Far Nor In Deep." The syllabus first called for a paper describing the student's own initial response. It asked only one deceptively simple question, "How do you read this poem?" Then, after a class on the papers, the students were asked to consider two opposing interpretations and to respond again:

> Reader A says of this poem that it praises the ongoing life of watchful wait-
> ing of the common people: they may not be gifted intellects who see deeply
> into everything, but the poet sympathetically praises them because they
> keep trying.
>
> BUT
>
> Reader B says that this is a poem about dullness and even stupidity; it is a

91

gesture of scorn towards those who gaze indolently at a life in which nothing happens, nothing can be seen. Now how do you read this poem? How would you convince another person of your reading?

The two readings were of course irreconcilable and asked for two entirely different auditions of the tone of voice in the final quatrain:

> They cannot look out far.
> They cannot look in deep.
> But when was that ever a bar
> To any watch they keep?

Did the final question testify to the nobility, however futile, of human yearning, as Reader A thought, or was it only the sour cynical scorn heard by Reader B? The minimalist details of the poem could be read so as to support either interpretation. In our staff meeting, Bill Pritchard was of the opinion that you couldn't really know how to read the tone of the poem, because Frost had deliberately made its tone opaque, equivocal. In this, though I did not know it, he was echoing Randall Jarrell's 1952 essay "To the Laodiceans," in which Jarrell described the tone of the last lines as a "careful suspension between several tones, as a piece of iron can be held in the air between powerful enough magnets."

It was not a tone that freshmen could be expected to get right, even on the second try. Most of them were still looking for the metaphysical mooring of the poem, "Frost's point." Armour observed that, in a way, the poem was *about* such people who must "read things in." As a first-year teacher, I found myself thoroughly engrossed in all this, and I decided to slow my class down to half speed and ask the students to read aloud, dramatizing their own interpretations. I also asked them what they saw in their mind's eye when Frost says:

> The people along the sand
> All turn and look one way.
> They turn their back on the land.
> They look at the sea all day.

Who were the people? How many? How were they dressed? Where was the land, to the left or right? On which side was the sea? Was it the Atlantic or Pacific? (I had Frost's "Once by the Pacific" in mind.) What did they see when Frost says "The wetter ground like glass / Reflects a standing gull"? How did the beach slope, to give that image? Should they be thinking of "ground glass"? Did "a standing gull" play upon "a standing joke"? All this took time, and we spent a first fifty-minute class on the first eight lines, and a second fifty-minute class on the second eight lines. When I began the second class, I said casually, "Now, how does it go?" and surprised myself by reciting the whole poem by heart. I was delighted to have it so thoroughly in mind.

We went on to read some poems by George Herbert, a few more by Emily Dickinson, and even a whole book, *Walden,* and then the semester was over. We read them very slowly, though not as slowly as "Neither Out Far," and I frequently found myself walking down the hall saying things like "I made a posie as the day ran by: / Here will I smell my remnant out," or "Tell all the Truth but tell it slant— / Success in Circuit lies"—often, in fact, quoting entire poems by Dickinson. I did not know it at the time, but I and my section were continuing the activities that Bill had practiced as a sophomore at Amherst in the "Introduction to Literature" course designed by Reuben Brower:

> We were invited to try the poem out by performing it orally; adjustments and modifications could be made in the speaking voice to provide an invaluable check on interpretive overeagerness, indeed on abstraction of any sort. I now think that this emphasis on sound was a good deal more important than anything we figured out about metaphor or attitude. Tone, tone of voice, was the key to realizing the poem; if we could get that right—whatever "right" meant—the rest would follow in due course. But the practice of reading aloud, whenever possible, before the interpretive argument began—although, of course, it had already begun in the decisions made about how to read aloud—was also a way of promoting the sense of freshness of response essential to the good critic. (*English Papers,* 27)

It is one thing to read a poem so intently that you memorize it involuntarily. More usually, instead of intensive study, an affinity of sentiment or diction has already touched us at a primary level when we realize that we already know a poem by heart. At times, it is inexplicable, what Wallace Stevens in "Table Talk" calls "largely a thing / Of happens to like, not should"—a formulation Bill used some years ago in asking freshmen to confront their own predilections. Most often, it is the poem's verbal "tune," just as it is with catchy songs on the radio that we can't get out of our heads. The idea of "the catchy" is not a very dignified critical concept, but it testifies importantly to poetry's primary appeal to the ear. Many students whom I have queried on their memorizations make an explicit analogy between popular songs and poems with regular meter and rhyme. What we "catch" is the pattern of repetitions, both phonemic and formal. I myself have found that the flat hard *aaa bbb ccc* rhyme scheme of Frost's "Provide, Provide" is as much a mnemonic device as a tonal value. Certain especially musical forms, like the villanelle, in the hands of a good poet, fuse sound and sense so firmly that they need only a little help beyond rereading to enter memory. This is particularly true of two villanelles of passionate grief, Elizabeth Bishop's "One Art" and Dylan Thomas's "Do not go gentle into that good night." It is almost impossible *not* to memorize the first tercet of "Do not go gentle" as soon as you read it, due to the repetitions of its sounds:

> Do not go gentle into that good night.
> Old age should burn and rave at close of day;
> Rage, rage, against the dying of the light.

The texture of sound is so elaborately self-echoing, and so focused on the doubled meta-word "(R)AGE," that when I first wrote it out from memory for this essay, I misremembered "rave" in the second line as "rage." It is, of course, harder to memorize the rest of Thomas's poem, even with its regular rhyme scheme, because the emotional development of the poem is essentially complete by the end of the first tercet. Not so with Bishop, who keeps the full significance of her deliberately tinny *a*-rhymes on "-aster" veiled until the wrenching revelation of her last stanza. As for Chaucer, mainly a narrative poet, colleagues and students alike testify to having individual lines in mind from the first reading. I think of "He was a verray, parfit gentil knyght," "And al was conscience and tendre herte," or "O martir sowded to virginitee," which Matthew Arnold regarded as a prime example of Chaucer's "virtue of manner and movement." These, and many other lines and couplets, are memorable mainly as auditory landmarks in our perception of Chaucer's narrative and descriptive techniques. If we have them by heart, it is because they help us map Chaucer's poetic imagination rather than because of their overplus of verbal music. This is also true of those lines that we have by heart from novels.

It is a rather different matter to decide consciously to memorize a poem. Usually one wants to appropriate it as one's own words. I have collected a wide range of student testimony on this score. Lisa H. Cooper (Amherst '93) says, "Once it's in your head, it somehow *belongs* to you, and the act of memorization creates a personal relationship that's not there when you just underline the words on the page, even when the book belongs to you. In fact, I think that's why I underline and write in books when I'm not memorizing—it is the same kind of appropriative act on a lesser scale." Reena Sastri (Amherst '94) finds satisfaction in "making it my own, not necessarily as a way of analyzing it, in fact rather the opposite—instead of maintaining a critical distance, you (at least for the time you are actively memorizing it) try to absorb it whole." In addition to the pleasures of possession, students also claim a deeper personal understanding of those poems they have got by heart. Toby King (Amherst '94) says, "To truly understand a poem (whatever that means) you must be able to look around the poet's universe from the inside, not into it from the outside, through a dirty window of paper. You must transcend the print and paper, which is merely a vehicle of transportation: the sooner it is tossed aside, the better."

A similar view is expressed by Helen Vendler in her recent account of living with, and within, Shakespeare's sonnets for the last forty years.[1] At this stage, having many of them already by heart, she has undertaken to memorize them all. She has achieved "an internalization so complete that the word 'reading' is not the right one for what happens when a text is on your mind. The text is part of what has made you who you are." The sonnets in her head now seem to be her own speech. For Vendler this deep personal possession is an aspect of enhanced critical understanding: "When I cannot remember a word, it means I have not understood its function in the poem. As soon as I grasp its function, the word does not leave me. This is instructive." But she also finds value in that dirty window of paper upon which a poem first appears, noting that her visual reading of the sonnets, especially in the Quarto version, has shown her "things that uttering the sonnets as my own speech had not revealed," such as orthographical symmetries lost in modern printing.

What sort of poems do we get by heart? Most people, even Vendler in her astonishingly ambitious project, memorize relatively short poems. They tend to be lyrics, and usually not more than forty or fifty lines long. Bill tells me that the longest poem he ever got by heart was Robert Lowell's "A Quaker Graveyard in Nantucket," which is one hundred and twenty-five lines. It was during the summer following his first year as a teacher at Amherst, and he and his family were vacationing on an island off the coast of Maine, in a cottage where he could hear the surf in the distance (what better mnemonic aid?). My own freshman English teacher at Dartmouth in 1955, James Dow McCallum, told our class that, now that he was getting older (he was then sixty-three), he was wakeful at night and wanted something to do, and so he had memorized some two thousand lines of *Paradise Lost* to recite in the dark. We freshmen, who were deep in bewildered delight at Milton's sonorities and symbolism (we spent half the semester just on Milton), were not sure whether this was humanly possible, but he did quote from memory many of the passages we discussed in class. Clearly, McCallum and Vendler are exceptions in their prodigious feats of memory. In the best sense, they are professional memorizers, and their activities point up by contrast why most poems willingly got by heart are relatively brief: they are *shaped* sayings that stick deep, skeins of words that we take into ourselves as our own, and then put to personal purposes. My friend Bonnie Wheeler, a medievalist at Southern Methodist University, names her own reasons exuberantly: "For the sheer pleasure of knowing, for holding on to something that doesn't go away in the dark, for the physical delight of the new places your tongue finds in your mouth, for the brain exercise of a newly atrophied part of the Western person's mind: all these and more are reasons I memorize poems and make my students do also. I have never cared if they hate it or love it; I only care that they own it."

To own a poem in this way is different from just remembering it. "Getting it by heart" is different from "knowing it by rote," I tell my Chaucer students every fall: it is possessing the words *in cuore*, inside your physical body, where the rhythms of poetry have their origin and their first effect. "By rote" is merely mechanical recall (the *OED* finds no clear etymology, but I suspect the term comes from Latin *rota* "wheel" and the idea of repetitive turning). From the start, I urge them to put their memorized stanzas in some other place than their rational brains. They elect a first course in Chaucer whose stated objectives are "to read *Troilus and Criseyde* aloud in Middle English for personal enjoyment and, while doing so, to develop a sharp ear and eye for its best poetic effects." For many of them, it is their first college course in poetry, and they learn about English prosody by reading John Hollander's *Rhyme's Reason* at the same time they are studying Kökeritz's *Guide to Chaucer's Pronunciation*. They read aloud in Middle English on the first day, and every day thereafter. Long ago I borrowed the approach of Emerson Brown at Vanderbilt: he walks into the first class meeting with a Middle English photocopy and begins by reciting it aloud. "With a gesture or two, I have the students repeating after me, until they are speaking Chaucer's lines in the way we like to think Chaucer might have wished them to sound. All this happens before anybody has said a word of modern English."[2] This acts out a value that I pursue throughout my own course, and make explicit in my syllabus:

Course Rationale. Declamation, quizzes, memory work: this is an unusual way to conduct an introductory English course at Amherst College. It may seem a primitive method, but if you do the daily work you will find it efficient and fun. You will learn to read Chaucer's language, and to hear his poetry as lines, by speaking as you read. Learning by doing: there is no other way. In addition, it is historically pertinent: most classical and medieval poetry was "published" by being read aloud, and had its being in the mouth and ear before it entered the eye and mind.

Most undergraduate courses in Chaucer in the United States focus on the *Canterbury Tales*, and most do not ask for much more than the first eighteen or forty-two lines of the *General Prologue* by heart (according to an informal survey I have conducted on the Internet). I have always felt that the language of the *General Prologue* is too rich and varied for beginning students—it changes with each new pilgrim's occupation and costume. At the outset I want a certain redundancy of vocabulary and stylistic gestures. I also want the students to encounter complete poems as soon as possible. So during the first three weeks of intensive language study (they use the Language Lab and I listen to their tapes) we read the "Envoy to Bukton," the "Envoy to Scogan," and "To Rosamounde," and then they write a few sentences describing the poet's tone in "To Rosamounde." Is he heartsick, or is he happy to be unrequited in love? Is it even really love? Good students can already begin to get it right. Then we read the *Parliament of Fowls* for the next two weeks, and they start writing short critical papers and memorizing one or more rhyme royal stanzas per week. After the *Parliament*, they spend the rest of the semester on *Troilus*, with Boethius's *Consolation of Philosophy* as ancillary reading. The final exam is, naturally, on the complex and problematic ending of *Troilus*: what are its different tones, what do they mean, what is its relationship to the rest of the poem?

Much of Chaucer's poetry is unmemorizable, and some of it is unmemorable. It would be both Herculean and pointless to get by heart, say, the *Man of Law's Tale*. Even as brilliant a piece as the *Miller's Tale* is nearly impossible to memorize in its entirety. In fact, in my second-semester course on the *Canterbury Tales*, I ask for no memory work, though the first sentence of the *General Prologue* remains a fetish for many students. All the poems in the first-semester course, however, are in stanzas. I require the students to get by heart the first stanza of the *Parliament* and, after that, they select their own stanzas, as a matter of "happens to like," from our current reading. All told, they get by heart a minimum of ten stanzas, or seventy lines. Many learn extra stanzas, for no extra credit. I begin by telling them that Chaucer almost always capitalizes on the rhyme royal form, and that they will find it easier to memorize stanzas if they think about how the poet had to lay his sentences out in five-beat lines that rhyme *ababbcc*. That first stanza is an excellent example, and also stands as an emblem for the subject matter of all the poetry in the course:

> The lyf so short, the craft so long to lerne,
> Th'assay so hard, so sharp the conquerynge,
> The dredful joye alwey that slit so yerne: [fearful; slides; quickly]
> Al this mene I by Love, that my felynge   [understanding]
> Astonyith with his wonderful werkynge
> So sore, iwis, that whan I on hym thynke
> Nat wot I wel wher that I flete or synke.[3]   [whether; float]

There is high metrical drama here. The fluid rush of astonishment that enjambs the *bb* couplet in the center of the stanza is a sharp and pleasing shift, both lyrical and comical, that overturns the heavy balance of the antitheses in the first three lines, with their Horatian tag and Petrarchan oxymoron. The speaker regains a precarious balance only in the puzzlement of the last line, firmly closing off the *cc* couplet. Various ideas of love, and different ways of writing about it, will continue to delight and puzzle Chaucer, and us, for the rest of the semester.

Virtually all of Chaucer's rhyme royal stanzas, both in these two poems and the four stanzaic poems of the *Canterbury Tales*, are complete units of thought. His sentences rarely carry over to the next stanza, though often his topic does. This raises interesting theoretical questions about the narrative strategies of a poetic form that keeps ending and beginning every seven lines,[4] but in class we focus mainly on the audible texture of the poetry. On Fridays, usually, at the start of the hour each student stands up in turn and recites a stanza to the class. I then ask the other students to identify it, to say where it comes in the poem, and what its poetic force is in context. If most of the hour passes while we are doing this, at the expense of the day's reading assignment, I consider it time well spent. I often ask the reciter why he or she chose the stanza. The reasons given are usually literary, but sometimes personal, comically replicating the attitudes Chaucer imputes to young lovers in the imagined audience of *Troilus*. Many of the same stanzas are chosen year after year, perhaps thirty or forty out of the more than twelve hundred that we read during the course. This I ascribe not to student taste, but to Chaucer's power in shaping his poetic utterance.

He creates certain high moments where narrative and dramatic meanings are concentrated in the musical structure of the stanzas.

One might therefore expect that in between these moments of high intensity there would be unmemorable gray areas. However, at the end of the course, I play a game with the students in which we each take a turn reading a stanza aloud from anywhere in *Troilus*, and the class has to identify who is speaking at what point in the poem. If you can stump the experts with your one stanza, you then give them the next seven lines. Ninety percent of the time it takes only the one stanza for someone to identify it correctly. Any stretch of fourteen lines is always identified by one or more students. That is not what you would expect of a poem over eight thousand lines long, especially one organized more by the rules of medieval rhetoric than by any naturalistic premise. Though readers return more frequently to favorite nodal passages, Chaucer's entire poetic integument is closely woven. Each stanza adds its minute particulars to the web of narrative, and hence is easily recognizable. The only exceptions are Pandarus's prolix speeches of advice; their interchangeable *sententiae* make them hard to identify immediately.

Chaucer's power of utterance also has inspired spontaneous student imitations over the years. Sometimes they are burlesques in ersatz Middle English, with Prof. Chickering cast as Pandarus. Occasionally they are begging stanzas (compare Chaucer's *Complaint to His Purse*) aimed at gaining extensions for overdue papers. To write an imitation, you need to internalize the stanza pattern as a way of making sentences. Getting by heart does the same thing. Students tell me that they notice more about how Chaucer's syntax fits the structure of the rhyme scheme, and, in turn, they use the rhymes to remember the sentence structure. They also say they have a fuller awareness of poetic nuance in the stanzas they get by heart. Looking back on the course, Andrew Krull (Amherst '96) says, "Plot, for me, ultimately took a back seat to poetry, and I think the memorizing helped me stay in touch with the ambiguity in word-play and theme."

These are undeniable benefits for students of poetry, but there is a potential downside to memorizing and declaiming. Despite readers' claims that they hold a poem more complexly in mind when they have it by heart, I suspect that most of us memorize a poem with a particular "scripting." To fully appropriate its tones as your own speech, you have to hear it in your mind's ear with a particular dramatic enactment, one which you are not likely to change. The danger is that this internal vocalization of the text will magnify one set of reading responses and will shut down others that are present in the text, as in the case of "Neither Out Far." The problem occurs not only in memorizing but also in reading aloud from the text, as Alan T. Gaylord has demonstrated at length for Chaucer.[5] To declaim well, you must have a "take" on your stanza, you must think you know the sound it makes as dramatic speech, lyrical gesture, narratorial head-wagging. This can make for lively classes, and students give plausible dramatic interpretations of, for instance, Criseyde at the moment in Book II when from her window she first sees Troilus ride down the street and says, "Who yaf me drynke?" But there are always several readings of such an emotionally dense moment, and, as Gaylord rightly says, to select only one such reading for declamation flattens out the meaning of the text considerably. In all first-rate poetry, too, there are meanings that are understood mentally more than they are heard, silent explosions of significance in the reader's mind. Gaylord argues, and I would concur, that the pleasures and benefits of reading Chaucer's poetry aloud outweigh these limitations, especially if one declaims or recites as a *reader*, and not as an actor giving a performance. As a reader "one *says* the verse in order to find those places that *will not be said*"—he gives as illustration the "morning after" scene between Pandarus and Criseyde at III.1555–82, particularly the evasive stanza that begins "I passe al that which chargeth nought to seye." Declamation will also "rehearse for one's imagination the breadth and body" of what *can* be said. It is valuable because you "participate physically" in Chaucer's prosody, "punctuate linguistically (prosodically) the syntactic contours of Chaucer's verse," and "foreground the texture" of those patterns of sound that support the sense.

Whether getting a stanza by heart codifies one internal audition to the exclusion of others or whether it creates a fuller understanding of multiple meanings, we still begin by reading the stanza and figuring out how we think it goes. This usually means entertaining several possible vocalizations while performing the activities Gaylord describes. Playing around with such possibilities in class, my students have to balance the regularity of a predominantly iambic pentameter line against the intonations and cadences of an imagined speaking voice. They also have to decide at what pace the poet wants the stanza said. And then, a particularly delicate question: how much to emphasize the rhyme words, particularly when a line is half enjambed, that is, when you hear a pause at the line-end but you don't quite come to a stop. Figuring these things out will alert any reader to the tonal and textural aspects of a stanza. No one could do it for every stanza of *Troilus*, of course; it would become a killing drudgery, not live reading. But I have done it enough during my annual rereadings over the last thirty years, and have been enough enlivened by it, that I think I can describe what one knows better about Chaucer's poetry for having got many of his stanzas by heart.

It is not necessarily anything new about the imagery, themes, symbols, characters, or plot. Rather, first and last, the memorizing reader becomes more aware of the verbal texture, the stanza pattern itself, and how the syntax fits the meter and rhyme. As Frost says, "The possibilities for tune from the dramatic tones of meaning struck across the rigidity of a limited meter are endless" ("The Figure a Poem Makes"). Exactly how those possibilities are realized in individual instances is what you know better once you can say them aloud at will. Put abstractly, this sounds quite simple and obvious but, for most readers of Chaucer, recognizing these poetic features is a learned skill, infrequently acquired. In fact, noticing how the sense fits the form is a special pleasure not usually enjoyed in print by most professional critics of Chaucer.[6] I hope the close reading of a few more stanzas from the *Parliament of Fowls* will make that pleasure more available, perhaps even repeatable with stanzas of one's own choosing.

A stanza well into the poem exemplifies what Arnold called Chaucer's "divine fluidity of movement." Having fallen asleep, Chaucer as the narrator has been moving through a series of literary dreamscapes all concerned with love and its proper ordering. Emerging from a long description of the interior of the Temple of Venus, he returns to a garden resembling the terrestrial paradise, in which, upon a hill of flowers, the goddess Nature will convene the parliament in which birds of all species choose their mates on St. Valentine's Day. Later called "the vicaire of the almyghty Lord," she is the chief allegorical figure who orders human love, though she will have difficulty controlling the clamorous fowls. The stanza is his first moment of recognition, in which he identifies her as a queen fairer than any created being:

> Whan I was come ayeyn into the place
> That I of spak, that was so sote and grene,   [sweet]
> Forth welk I tho myselven to solace.   [walked I then]
> Tho was I war wher that ther sat a queene   [aware]
> That, as of lyght the somer sonne shene
> Passeth the sterre, right so over mesure
> She fayrer was than any creature. (295–301)

The movement of these lines is remarkable. The iambic swing of the first line runs on in natural word order with no inversion for meter until the second foot of the second line. There is an easy, unemphatic significance in the associations of the rhyme words: the green "place" gives Chaucer some "solace" (it was both steamy and doleful in the Temple of Venus), while the "queene" governs the "grene" of springtime, and is then linked to the "shene" of the sun (the heat and light of God's love?) in the following simile. Most rhyme royal stanzas break into two syntactic units within the rhyme scheme (*aba bbcc*, for instance, or *abab bcc*—there are roughly five types), and here the proportion is 3:4 with the *bbcc* lines warmly and rapidly enjambed, one right after the other, even as Chaucer develops the poised simile comparing the superlative beauty of Nature to the light of the summer sun surpassing the stars. He moves with audible swiftness through this hierarchical medieval comparison to arrive at a complex stroke of wit in the *cc* couplet: Nature, as the near and efficient cause of all created beings, *must* be fairer "than any creature," and is also "over mesure" in the Boethian sense that no created being can measure its creator, while her still unsaid name is immanent in the very rhyme-sounds of the couplet. ("Nature" and "mesure" become the *a*-rhymes of the next stanza.) The rush of discovery past the line-ends is balanced by the caesuras at "I of spak," "welk I tho," and "was I war," metrical gestures that halt the observer, giving him pause at what he sees in his vision. In addition, the parity of "war" and "sterre," both in the same metrical position and ringing in the ear as a half-rhyme in Middle English, shows that Chaucer already understands the value of this great queen. These properties of the stanza, both pausing and running forward, are a poetic "enactment," as F. R. Leavis would call it, of the narrator's mental rhythm of recognition and evaluation.

There are other ways that stanzas act out the sense in the *Parliament*—musically, for instance. But first I should point out that the poem's overall design is highly self-reflexive. To dream his vision, Chaucer must first read an old book, for "out of olde bokes, in good feyth, / Cometh al this newe science that man lere" (24–25)—just as students now read Chaucer's old book itself. Exhausted at the end of the day by reading and by certain unnamed cares, he falls asleep and dreams about his reading, which has been Cicero's *Somnium Scipionis*, the Dream of Scipio the Younger, in which the Roman general dreams he meets his grandfather Scipio Africanus, who shows him Carthage "from a sterry place," an exalted vantage point, and gives him moral instruction *sub specie aeternitatis*. Africanus will soon appear to Chaucer in his own dream (the very work *we* are reading, or dreaming), where he will treat Chaucer with a comic lack of ceremony. But in the *Somnium* Africanus ponderously describes the music of the spheres to Scipio, going on at professorial length.[7] Chaucer not only abbreviates Cicero brilliantly; he casts the description itself in the form of verbal music:

> Thanne shewede he hym the lytel erthe that here is,
> At regard of the hevenes quantite;   [compared to]
> And after shewede he hym the nyne speres;   [spheres]
> And after that the melodye herde he
> That cometh of thilke speres thryes thre,   [the same; thrice]
> That welle is of musik and melodye
> In this world here and cause of armonye. (57–63)

In the first two lines Africanus and Scipio remain among the stars, as in Cicero, but instead of looking down upon "the lytel erthe" as they do, Chaucer and his readers are positioned "here" in both the first and last lines. The link between the *a*-rhymes "here is" and "speres" points up the contrast of locales. Chaucer emphasizes the actions of showing and hearing by the three inversions of verb and subject in the first quatrain, with the subject "he" internally echoing the *b*-rhymes of "quantite," "herde he," and "thryes thre" in an overplus of sound beyond the demands of rhyme. The cascade of "er" sounds ("erthe," "here is," "speres," "herde he," "speres" again, "here" again in the last line) becomes the dominant internal rhyme in the whole stanza. It is a dominant that is resolved by the liquid alliterations in the closing couplet ("welle," "world," "musik and melodye," the last word being repeated from line four). While the first and third grammatically inverted lines have clear caesuras, the lines about the magnitude of the heavens and the melody of the nine spheres flow without interior pauses. Perhaps it is not too much to say they are simulacra of that music, especially when heard together with the half-enjambments of "herde he" and "melodye"—exquisitely sweet almost-pauses on long vowels.

What makes the stanza truly musical, however, is the playful numerical conceit (not in Cicero) within the central *bb*-rhyme, where Chaucer names the nine spheres as the square of three. One needn't be a medieval Christian to see the significance of this. It is a stroke of wit worthy of George Herbert, and very likely the idea that generated the verbal music of the stanza. "Music" in medieval times meant "number" and "proportion" even more fundamentally than it meant "melody" (thus Boethius's *De institutione musica*, the basic treatise on the subject), and "armonye" results here on earth when all the elements of the universe are proportioned in their correct degree ("Take but degree away, untune that string, / And hark what discord follows," says Shakespeare's Ulysses within the same world-view). Such *musica* is more easily heard above and beyond us, but at times we humans can hear it down "here," as when "instruments of strenges" are "in acord" later, in the paradisal garden, where their "ravyshyng swet-nesse" is "Acordaunt to the foules song alofte," which is like the "voys of aungel in here armonye" (190–203). But nowhere do we hear that music more clearly, as poetry, than in this "thryes thre" stanza.[8]

The stanza form can also act as a set of stage directions for a comic turn. The word "acord" in the *Parliament* means not only "chordal har-mony" but also "agreement," legal or otherwise, and Chaucer puns on the word several times, since disagreement is the order of the day. The initial love-debate between three noble eagles about which of them should re-ceive the hand of the virginal "formel egle," Nature's "gentillest" creation (373), is anything but harmonious, and eventually the entire parliament degenerates into squabbling: not only do the three suitors quarrel among themselves, but the lower classes of birds (goose, cuckoo, water-fowls) are quite annoyed at having to wait during the courtly filibuster before choos-ing their species-specific mates and getting on with the "engendrure" (305) that pricks their hearts in the spring. The resulting cacophony may parody London parliaments that Chaucer knew. God's love is what makes the spheres go round and produce their music, but the human varieties of love are less perfect, be they erotic choices or societal agreements made for the common good ("commune profyt" in Chaucer, *res publica* in Cicero). The debate reaches its nadir after the female turtle dove has blushingly averred that a lover should be true even to a dead mate. The next stanza gives a firm shape to silliness:

> "Well bourded," quod the doke, "by myn hat! [jested]
> That men shulde loven alwey causeles!
> Who can a resoun fynde or wit in that?
> Daunseth he murye that is myrtheles?
> Who shulde recche of that is recheles?" [care; careless]
> "Ye queke," seyde the goos, "full wel and fayre!
> There been mo sterres, God wot, than a payre!" (589–95) [more]

What type of hat does the duck wear? Humanized bird-debates were not new in Chaucer's day—*The Owl and the Nightingale* antedates the *Parlia-*

ment by two centuries—but the insouciant aplomb with which the poet
mimics human speech and its foibles makes us frequently forget that the
characters have only avian identities. "Causeles" of course is grossly
twisted in meaning: the duck scorns the turtle dove's fidelity in widow-
hood as merely unrequited love, and his barrage of three questions, each
complete within a line, assumes that the only possible reason for loving is
to be loved in return. Chaucer probably discovered the duck's "hat" in
thinking ahead to the derogatory pronoun "that." The duck's utter scorn
is utterly ignoble, given the alternative causes of love already alive in the
poem, such as the altruism of a noble heart. Having got the duck through
five lines of indignation, Chaucer hits upon the happy idea of having the
goose chime in, to fill the final couplet. (This proportion of 5:2 occurs in
about twenty percent of all his stanzas.) She has already been called "a fol"
who "can not be stille" by the sparrow-hawk (574), and here she has to put
her two cents in again: "You quack very well indeed!" She has heard his
human sense as duckly quacking, which reduces her own approval to the
barnyard level. There are more stars in the sky than just a pair (more than
one pebble on the beach), she says, adding to the duck's quasi-proverbial
rhetorical questions. In the next stanza, such a low view of love will be
ridiculed by one of the male eagles—"Out of the donghil cam that word
ful right!" (597). The construction of this stanza is a good example of
Chaucer's freedom of choice, and his supple exploitation of dramatic opportunity. To compose the whole stanza with seven abruptly end-stopped
lines adds a delicious formal flatness to the water-fowls' view of love,
which comically self-destructs upon audition, especially with the hard,
flat, and totally unexpected words "hat" and "queke."

Further acrimonious exchanges soon reach a peak, and Nature steps in,
commanding silence. She gives the young bird-maiden the chance to
choose whom she likes, and the "formel egle" in embarrassed and edgy
tones tells her that, as yet, she "wol nat serve Venus ne Cupide" (652); she
chooses not to choose. So much for finding a harmonious mate amongst
the avian aristocracy under the benign gaze of Nature. Yet, having told
the three suitors to try again next year, Nature then gives each of the
lower birds its mate "by evene acord" (not in harmony, just by mutual
agreement) and happy they are, embracing each other with their wings.
Then, in honor of Nature and their own bird natures, and hardly cancel-
ing out the many ambiguities about "right love," higher and lower, that
Chaucer has created in the poem, a chorus of birds sings a French roundel,

welcoming summer and saying good-bye to the long nights of winter. Finally comes perhaps the most interesting and memorable stanza of the poem:

> And with the shoutyng, whan the song was do,   [done]
> That foules maden at here flyght awey,   [their]
> I wok, and othere bokes tok me to,
> To reede upon, and yit I rede alwey.
> I hope, ywis, to rede so som day
> That I shal mete some thyng for to fare   [dream, or meet]
> The bet, and thus to rede I nyl nat spare. (693–99)

Here poised wordplay and surefooted rhythms play against the rhymes to create a richly mixed tone that recapitulates many of the poem's concerns without resolving them. It is a brilliantly inconclusive conclusion. The first point I always clarify for students is that "the shoutyng" does not mean that the roundel was inharmonious, but refers to the birds' huzzahs at the roundel's conclusion. This loud signal of glad desire wakes the poet up, and he immediately goes back to his books, a comic touch in itself, to continue looking for something morally "improving," or perhaps simply something that will help him since he has lost his taste for love (as Africanus observes in line 160).

The stanza means to waffle intelligently about the act of reading for personal instruction, incarnating the rhythms of a strong but as yet unfulfilled expectation. The fowls seem to have quite flown away by the end of the second line, due to its smooth iambic lope, with no caesura or only a very light one after "maden." Fled is that music:—Do I wake or sleep? The internal rhymes in the next line ("wok," "bokes," and "tok") reinforce the idea that to wake up is to be impelled to read anew, out of a curiosity unsatisfied by either the dream or prior reading, yet Chaucer also says that to read is to hope to "mete" (which means both "meet" and "dream") something more helpful. Dreaming is like reading, then, and reading is like dreaming. In addition to the double meaning of "mete," we can see this equivalence in the *a*-rhymes, only one letter away from being rime riche—"awey," "alwey"—which produces an opaque equivalence between the dream-reality of the birds' disappearance and the poet's obsession with reading. His obsession is pointed up not only by the fourfold internal repetition of "rede" but also by a second off-the-page meaning of that word, a sort of overtone: although syntactically here it can only mean the verb "to read," it also means "to counsel, advise," or as a noun, "counsel, advice," which is surely part of what the poet is seeking.

The final tercet supplies a yearning motive for this Constant Reader, but does not fulfill it. To read "so" as to "mete" something that will make you fare "the bet" (the consonance is a further index of yearning): how to do that? How to read *so* that it will happen? The whole poem has been a grand try at dreaming up an interpretation of Chaucer's reading that will clarify and focus a right attitude toward sexual love, and a right place for it in the social order (it is a disruptive force everywhere in secular medieval literature). At the same time, in its patchy, sequential, inconclusive construction, the poem has been leading the reader on a goose chase for definitive answers. In the final lines, Chaucer counterpoises his present lack against the forward motion of the lines opening out toward future possibility: the prior quatrain ends with a full stop at "alwey," then "some day" half enjambs the next line, and then "for to fare / The bet" accelerates to a full run-on into the last line, coming up sharply at the heavily stopped "bet," and then closing with the fourth and final repetition of "rede." It is a profoundly satisfying tonal performance, inflected by the rhythm, the swing, of the lines. Reading may be a fruitless activity, but we still can't stop doing it. So, too, loving, with all its "dredful joye."[9]

Notes

1. Helen Vendler, "Reading, Stage by Stage: Shakespeare's *Sonnets*," in *Shakespeare Reread: The Texts in New Contexts*, ed. Russ McDonald (Ithaca and London: Cornell University Press, 1994), 24–41; quotations pp. 25, 24, 27.

2. Emerson Brown, Jr., "Diverse Folk Diversely They Teach," in *Approaches to Teaching Chaucer's "Canterbury Tales,"* ed. Joseph Gibaldi (New York: The Modern Language Association of America, 1980), 70.

3. Citations of Chaucer's poetry are from Larry D. Benson, gen. ed., *The Riverside Chaucer*, 3d ed. (Boston: Houghton Mifflin, 1987). At a few points I have silently altered punctuation to give the sense or cadence as I hear it.

4. See Clare Regan Kinney, *Strategies of Poetic Narrative: Chaucer, Spenser, Milton, Eliot* (Cambridge: Cambridge University Press, 1992), 31–69, 182–83.

5. Alan T. Gaylord, "Reading Chaucer: What's Allowed in 'Aloud'?" *Chaucer Yearbook* 1 (1992): 87–107; quotations pp. 106–7.

6. Notable exceptions to this generalization include, among others, Charles A. Owen, Jr., "'Thy Drasty Rhyming . . . ,'" *Studies in Philology* 63 (1966): 533–64; Stephen Knight, *Rhyming Craftily: Meaning in Chaucer's Poetry* (Sydney: Angus and Robertson, 1973); Alan T. Gaylord, "Chaucer's Dainty 'Dogerel': The 'Elvyssh'

Prosody of *Sir Thopas*," *Studies in the Age of Chaucer* 1 (1979): 83–104; Mark Lambert, "Telling the Story in *Troilus and Criseyde*," in *The Cambridge Chaucer Companion*, ed. Piero Boitani and Jill Mann (Cambridge: Cambridge University Press, 1986), 59–73; Jay Ruud, "'In Meetre in Many a Sondry Wyse': Fortune's Wheel and the *Monk's Tale*," *English Language Notes* 26 (1989): 6–11; Clare Kinney, loc. cit.; Barry Windeatt, "To rym wel this book til I have do," in his *Oxford Guides to Chaucer: Troilus and Criseyde* (Oxford: Clarendon Press, 1992), 354–590; and Jahan Ramazani, "Chaucer's Monk: The Poetics of Abbreviation, Aggression, and Tragedy," *Chaucer Review* 27 (1993): 260–76.

7. "I [Scipio] gazed in astonishment, and when I came to myself I said, 'What is this, this great sound which so fills my ears and is so sweet?' 'That,' he [Africanus] said, 'is produced by the onward rush and motion of the sphere themselves; their separation into unequal but carefully proportioned intervals, blending high notes with low, produces various harmonies; for such mighty motions cannot be so swiftly carried on in silence; and Nature brings it about that the spheres at one extreme sound with a low note, and at the other with a high. Therefore, that highest sphere of heaven, the star-bearer, whose turning is faster, is moved with a high, loud note, while the lowest, lunar, sphere has the deepest note; for the ninth sphere, the Earth, remaining motionless, fixed in one position, always clings to the middle place of the universe. But the other eight spheres, two of which (Mercury and Venus) move at the same speed, produce seven distinct notes—a number which is the key to almost everything.'"—trans. D. S. Brewer in his edition of *The Parlement of Foulys* (London: Thomas Nelson and Sons, 1960), 135.

8. See further John P. McCall, "The Harmony of Chaucer's *Parliament*," *Chaucer Review* 5 (1970): 22–31; David Chamberlain, "The Music of the Spheres and *The Parlement of Foules*," *Chaucer Review* 5 (1970): 32–56.

9. In addition to those mentioned in the body of this essay, I wish to thank the following, who answered queries or otherwise contributed to its conception: Jonathan Blake, Jack Cameron, Anne Johnson Cody, Erica Edell, Peter Elliott, Terrence Holekamp, Julia Kent, Leslie Lockett, Kim Townsend, and Carol Trabulsi. I also thank all respondents to my informal survey on the electronic Chaucernet. I am grateful to Nancy Mason Bradbury, Carolyn Collette, Arlyn Diamond, and Sara Jane Moss for helpful comments on a penultimate draft.

Joseph Epstein

Is God Dead, Frosty?

Reflections on Teaching

I BEGAN TEACHING fairly late—at the untender age of thirty-seven—and without especially generous motives. I had worked at various editorial jobs and had begun the economically precarious life of a free-lance writer when the chance to teach at Northwestern University was offered to me. I took it straightaway. I had no great regard for academics, but one thing about them I did incontestably envy: their leisure. Apart from the acquisition of learning, which was reportedly a full-time job for anyone who had taken up the life of the mind, teaching struck me as a seven-month job. When one subtracted the long summers, the Christmas and Spring breaks, the orientation, reading, and final examination weeks, it was perhaps less than seven months. Piece, it looked to me, of bloomin' cake.

As everyone knows, there is no training for university teaching. What anyone who teaches in a university invariably does is imitate the teachers one most admired when oneself a university student. I never went to graduate school, and had finished only a B.A., fifteen years before, at the University of Chicago. Many great men—I remember no women of important reputation in those days—taught at Chicago, but the few who were among my teachers I saw, from the middle distance, as lecturers. Most of these, moreover, tended to have German or Dutch or English accents, which to me, a boy of the American middle west quite gone on the notion of the superiority of European culture, greatly added to their intellectual glamor. In short, I had no models worthy of imitation in my own teaching, unless I was prepared to teach in a foreign accent, which I didn't feel I could quite bring off.

Before I began, I asked a friend, a contemporary who had been teaching for a decade or so, if he had any advice for me. "Never let them go outside," he said, grimly. "No matter how nice the day, never attempt to teach a class out on the lawn."

I made a note of it. What I didn't ask this friend was whether or not to teach in a necktie. He, a man who enjoyed the tumult and loosening of formalities of the 1960s, did not. He also taught in jeans as did a number of other men of my age in the English Department at Northwestern at the time (1974). One fellow taught in jeans, boots, and a denim jacket—the perfect type, or so I thought, of the academic cowboy. Because I owned no jeans—being myself a tan washpants man—I decided to teach in a tie and jacket. For reasons I shall make clear presently, it was, I felt, the correct decision.

In my first class, in a course for freshmen called Novels of the 1920s, I read the roll, a perfunctory act that went smoothly enough until I came to the name—a Czech name, I believe—of Pipal, Faustin. An amiable red-haired young man, raised his hand, then said: "I wonder, sir, if instead of Faustin you could call me Frosty." Emiliano Zapata, I thought, I'm not going to call this kid Frosty. I imagined myself fashioning questions about Nietzsche confronting the abyss, then asking, Well, what do you think about the death of God, Frosty? "I think," I replied, after a slight pause, "I shall call you Mr. Pipal." And so I did—and so I called everyone else in that class and in every other class I taught over the next twenty-odd years Mr. and Miss and, occasionally, Mrs. Once, an ardent feminist asked that I call her Ms., and so, henceforth, for a full quarter I hissed out Ms. Lovelady, for that was her name.

Two decisions—to wear a necktie and to call students by their last names—and a good portion of my teaching style was fixed. As a teacher, I was not to be chummy, a pal, a great guy. I was instead to be, by deliberate decision, a square, an older man, a bit of a stiffo. What I could not control was my own humor, which kept (and keeps) leaking out. Humor in the form of no doubt turgid little ironies, rather pathetic jokes, and fairly wild whimsy, these are also part of my protocol in front of a class, there, I suspect, quite as much to entertain the teacher as his students. Not long ago to illustrate an example of a rhetorical question, I explained that such a question involved a foregone conclusion and offered the example, "Does a male teacher check his fly?" On another occasion, I asked if anyone knew how to split an infinitive. When no one answered, I found myself leaping into the air and delivering a mock karate chop to the words, written on the blackboard, "to run."

I have been teaching now for more than twenty years, all of them at Northwestern, but I have an uncertain notion about my quality as a teacher or, what is perhaps the same thing, about the efficacy of my teaching. For many years, I have taught a course in writing called Fundamentals in Prose Style to would-be poets and novelists; and in recent years I have been teaching courses in Henry James, Joseph Conrad, and Willa Cather; more recently still, after having published a collection of my own short stories, I have been drafted to teach a course called Reading and Writing Fiction. Are any of these courses—I won't go so far as to ask worth the money—any good?

As a legacy from the 1960s, Northwestern, like many another school, asks teachers to have their students evaluate them and their courses. My student evaluations have not been very helpful. In them, I am often cited as nice, or amusing, or entertaining, or interesting. Occasionally, some quietly resentful student slips the stiletto beneath my heart with a dark insult. I seem to have blocked all these out or I would provide an example or two. The only truly helpful bit of practical criticism I have received from all these years of teaching came in a four-word sentence: "He jiggles his change." Now there is a criticism one can do something about; my change and keys now go into my briefcase before each class. The only memorable remark ever to turn up on one of my student evaluations is this: "I did well in this course; I would have been ashamed not to." I wish I knew what lovely chord I struck in the student who wrote it.

For the truth is, one of my secret agendas, my subtexts as we say nowadays, has to do with making my students hate that part in themselves that is ready to live quite comfortably with the sloppy, the faulty, the fifth-rate. I want them to feel guilty as hell when they turn in poor work or have read a great work superficially. When they do so, I want them to feel they have let not only me but, more important, themselves down. As a teacher,

I don't in the least mind invoking guilt or using, when it seems appropriate, gentle, stabbing touches of fear; my only complaint is that too many students are impervious to either.

I have always taught under the burden of thinking myself something of a fraud. My own so-called higher education didn't really take place in the classroom. At the University of Chicago I encountered teachers whose intellectual styles I admired. But I never took more than one course from any single teacher. Nor did any teacher see anything in me worth encouraging, let alone cultivating. What's more, I think they were right. I was never in any way a superior student. What I learned, I tended to learn alone, in my own, quirky, entirely individual way. What I did get from a few teachers was a sense that the world of art and intellect, of higher learning generally, was one in which passion could count for a great deal. In my own teaching, I attempt to convey my own passion for the things I teach. This is doubtless one of the reasons that I do less well teaching books that I don't really love and have therefore ceased to teach them.

Teaching has led me to believe that one of the best ways to gain education is to go to school not as a student but as a teacher. I know that I read books that I teach much more intensely, much less dreamily, than I ever used to read for other people's classes, however much I was impressed with the books there. Although I am in my late fifties, and although I am almost certain that I know more than my students, I still teach with a fair amount of nervousness about embarrassing myself through ignorance before my students. This doesn't mean never saying that I don't know what something means or why something is as it is—I admit to this kind of ignorance often enough. But it does mean knowing everything that, with a bit of work, is knowable about any book I teach.

Alan Bennett, the English playwright, in recounting his failed career as a university teacher, remarks that he "could never find sufficient comments to fill the necessary hour, and nor could my students." I, too, have always worried about filling the time. "I am really best," wrote Elizabeth Bishop, apropos of teaching, which she also came to later in life, "when I talk about what I think. That's the only way to teach. If you prepare too much, you just talk artificially." Something to that. Yet I am one of those teachers who tend to over-prepare; I go into a class scheduled for ninety minutes with enough material to last a Labor Day weekend, and then usually discard the material in favor of saying what I think.

When I began teaching, I did so with considerable trepidation. Over the years this has lessened but not disappeared. I no longer take my students' ignorance, or even stupidity, personally. I used to be a bit offended when a student would drop off to sleep in one of my classes; now, for some perverse reason, I am rather amused by it. If he cannot arise inspired, I tell myself, at least he will awake refreshed. But I remain upset at the prospect of boring my students. I have been exquisitely bored on so many occasions, many of them lectures or other putatively educational events, that I dislike the notion of myself contributing to the gross national boredom.

All these things make for a certain anxiety connected with my teaching. When I was a student and for a number of years afterward, I would have infrequent but memorable student nightmares. Fear of failure owing to educational delinquency was the theme of most of them. In such nightmares I am on my way to take a final for which I am not only unprepared but have scarcely attended class throughout the term; usually the course is in a subject such as Persian or Boolean Algebra—a subject, in any case, that I cannot hope to fake my way through by brilliant writing.

I have now traded in these student nightmares for teaching ones. In my teaching nightmares, I have agreed to give a lecture on a subject I know nothing about—Hungarian literature, say—or I have lost my notes, or I cannot find the building in which I am to teach. As anyone in the head trades would be pleased to tell me, these dreams exhibit sheer anxiety.

I hope it doesn't show, but I never go into any class without at least a slight edge of nervousness. (I take solace from anecdotes about brilliant teachers who, over a forty-year career, turn out to have vomited before every class they ever taught.) Although I occasionally lecture to my classes, my courses all entail discussion. My classes at Northwestern tend to be of between twenty-five and forty students; the writing courses are given to between fifteen and twenty students. I teach on Tuesdays and Thursdays, which means eighty- as opposed to fifty-minute sessions. I tell my students that I reserve the right to mark them down for poor attendance, and I also tell them that I expect them to contribute to classroom discussion, usually adding, in a movie Nazi accent, "We 'ave vays of making you talk!"

And here I must interject a word about my students and about Northwestern University, where I have done all my teaching. I am, I realize, lucky in this, for Northwestern is fairly highly regarded, as the world, shaky in its confidence, reckons institutions of high education. Many of its teachers themselves went to Harvard-Yale-Princeton-Stanford-Berkeley, and would doubtless like to return to those little valhallas of academic snobbery. Many of my students probably just missed being accepted at these same schools, though by the time they walk into my classes, most of them in their junior or senior years, they appear to have gotten over it. (It is said that intellectual serenity in this country consists of not giving a damn about Harvard; and if this is true, then I can claim to have achieved it.)

The great thing about these students, for me, is that on their way to Northwestern they seem, almost all of them, to have acquired what I call the habits of achievement. They read the book, they write the essay, they show up for class. Demands can be made of them. They are, for the most part, good students, and some are extraordinarily good—certainly more talented, more penetrating, generally a good deal brighter and livelier than their teacher was at their age.

Most of the students who take my classes are also self-selecting; they have chosen the classes I teach. They either aspire to write or, by becoming English majors, have declared a serious interest in literature. Yet, even after having said all this, I have to go on to say that only a small percentage of my students feel the excitement about literature and writing that ignites the flame of true passion. This is to be found, to use a phrase of John Calvin's, in only "a select minority."

About this minority generalizations are not easy. When I first began teaching, in the middle 1970s, my best students were almost invariably kids who had gone to Catholic schools, most of whom were none too happy about their past education, which, enlightenment figures now, they thought they had shaken off. In fact, their past education, which in those days had given them a good grounding in fundamentals and in argument, was easily the most impressive thing about them. These were kids still taught by priests and nuns.

Now I cannot make any such easy socio-religious distinctions. Certain of my students, Calvin's select minority, owing to magical and quite indecipherable combinations of education, experience, the old polluted gene pool, and odd good luck, just turn out to be considerably brighter than others: they may come from broken homes in Colorado, from happy homes in Southern California, or for all I know from lesbian homes on the West Side of Manhattan, they may have gone to expensive private or slightly menacing public schools, but for some unexplainable reason they have caught the flame, and in so doing make my job as a teacher vastly easier.

Whether I am correct to do so or not, I teach to the smartest students in the class. I don't know any other way of doing it. The less smart students may resent it. When I condescend, it shows badly. Fortunately, in a

class of, say, thirty students, six or seven of them turn out to be able to sustain serious discussion; in a class of fifteen, the number is often, but not inevitably, fewer. I have had some classes—I am thinking of a Henry James course I taught four or so years ago—in which intelligence seemed to radiate out of every chair in the room. I suspect that Henry James himself may have had something to do with this, calling forth, as his writing does, the best efforts of all his readers. I was frequently surprised how quickly the eighty minutes seemed to fly by.

I once taught a course in the sociology of literature that was dominated by seven or eight militant feminists, whose politics seemed to poison the air. I felt as if the pronoun police were scrutinizing my every sentence. I spent a considerable amount of time batting down the sad clichés they had learned in the classes before mine and would go on to learn in the classes after mine. In this course I realized, for the first time, how much teaching depends on the good faith of all parties—or at any rate how much my own teaching does. If you think your teacher is essentially trying to cheat you by foisting his corrupt ideas on you, then the spirit of learning cannot long survive in the room. From a teacher's point of view, if you sense you are viewed as the enemy, that is no good goad to the learning transaction either.

After sixteen years in school as a student, and now twenty-three years in school as a teacher, I am still more than a bit unclear about what goes on in that transaction. I know that I did not take much more from my teachers than bits and hints having to do with what thinking is like, which are the important books, who the indispensable writers. The University of Chicago, when I went there, was good at all this. Perhaps a few among my teachers showed an example of mental elegance in action. Do I do this much? Ought I to hope to be able to accomplish more?

I sometimes feel more than a touch of envy for those who teach more solid subjects than I: calculus, say, or beginning French. Students come to them knowing nothing of their subjects, and they depart—most of them—able to solve problems or conjugate irregular verbs. But what do students take from a course I give in the novels and stories of Joseph Conrad? What is the benefit to them from having been in the company of a great mind (Conrad's, not mine) for ten weeks? What help do they derive from the explanatory aids given them by a less than great mind (mine, not Conrad's)? I do not like to dwell overlong on these matters. "The horror!" as a certain businessman traveling in the Congo once noted. "The horror!"

One gray winter's morning, I asked a roomful of students if they thought Joseph Conrad believed in evil. They allowed as how Conrad, otherwise clever fellow that he was, might possibly have believed in evil. But, as I came to discover, for themselves, not a man- or womanjack among them did. When I pressed them, they wanted to know what exactly I meant by evil. Begging their pardon for name-dropping, I said I meant the work of the Devil—motiveless malignity, badness for badness's sake, pure freakin' flamin' evil.

Evil, it soon became plain, was an altogether foreign, not to say outrageous, conception. Goodness, sweet altruism, a mother's love, the handsome heroism of a Marine jumping on a grenade to save his comrades, this they could accept. But evil, no, not now, not ever, not a bit of it: all bad actions could ultimately be explained by background, psychology, the absence of love. I told my students that, if they could not believe in evil, then they might just have a little problem with literature generally, for the problem of evil was often at the heart of serious literature. But, then, as so regularly happens in pedagogy, if not in life, the hour—or, rather, hour and a half—was up and the problem of evil could be forgotten for the weekend.

Much of my work as a teacher, it sometimes seems to me, has to do with bringing my students troubling news. I tell would-be writers that art is not for weaklings and that in the end desire weighs more heavily than early talent. I have just finished teaching a course about Willa Cather, who, as anyone who has read her knows, is a marvelous writer but who, as many who have read her may have forgotten, is also a dark writer. No happy marriages in Willa Cather; romantic love in Cather's fiction is a bit of a shuck. "Art and religion (they are the same thing in the end, of course)," says Godfrey St. Peter in *The Professor's House*, "have given man the only happiness he has ever had." If you are twenty, beautiful, and flush with life's possibilities, do you really want to hear this? Can you, in any case, really believe it? Try to be a young man or woman on whom nothing is lost, I tell my students, invoking Henry James, but sometimes, I suspect, they shouldn't mind their teacher himself getting lost.

Complaint—about one's school, one's colleagues, one's students— seems to be integral to teaching. I know I do my fair share, though I confine almost all of it to my wife and to my journal. In search of something else, I recently had recourse to my journal for 1982, in which three entries in a row have to do with my teaching and which demonstrate, I think, something of the complexity, at least for me, of being a teacher. I quote myself:

February 10, 1982: *Yesterday I was informed—mistakenly—that two students had dropped out of my writing tutorial. I thought this might have been a reaction to my roughing up their first papers with my marginal comments. More interesting, though, I found myself resentful and a little hurt. Odd that I can still be affected in this way; odd that it remains important to me to be well thought of even by children. Perhaps odd isn't the word.*

February 12, 1982: *Spent six straight hours with students yesterday, which left me groggy. It is no good to be so long with, and doing most of the talking to, people who haven't the authority to call you down, let alone to call you a bullshitter, which after gassing away pretty much ex cathedra for six hours is what you feel yourself to be.*

February 19, 1982: *Teaching of late takes up all of my time, which leaves me less than ecstatic. Not scribbling enough. Grey Chicago weather no help. I grow dull.*

Part of my problem as a teacher is that teaching is only one of three things I do: the other two are editing a magazine and writing essays and stories. Taken together the three jobs keep me off the street. But they also make me aware how much more time I could give to teaching, meeting more with students, cultivating the best among them more carefully than I now do. Yet at the same time I am not at all sure that, if I were only to teach and do nothing more, I would have such authority as a teacher as I now have. The fact that I am a practicing writer, I am reasonably sure, means something to my students, even if many of them have never read a word I have written. Though they may not ever have heard George Bernard Shaw's mischievous aphorism—"Those who can't, teach"—I suspect that many are ready to subscribe to it. The word academic, after all, didn't get its pejorative sense out of nowhere. Yet, paradoxically, I have myself sometimes thought that the reverse of that aphorism is quite as true: Those who can, can't teach, or at any rate would rather, given a choice, be doing.

Perhaps all this is really no more than dancing around the truism that no one of any quality ever really believes he is a good teacher? One may be consistently entertaining, but entertaining, though sometimes a help, isn't the same as educating. The longer I'm in it, the less I am sure what education is supposed to provide. My journal entry for September 23, 1980 (the beginning of a new autumn term), reads: *"Must retain perspective on what teaching is supposed to be about—getting other people excited about the things I love."* But it is ridiculous to think one can sustain such excitement. Journal entry for January 1, 1981: *"I have yet to teach a dead class this quar-*

ter; one cannot be very far off, surely." Journal, January 8, 1982: *"Taught what I thought were two fine classes yesterday, then came out, the weekend ahead of me, to a flat tire. A parable therein?"*

A much used metaphor, I know, but teaching is best regarded as a roller coaster: all ups and downs and very little straightaway. Journal, June 7, 1981: *"Spent the past three days reading students' papers—always a disheartening experience. One realizes that fully a third of one's class is too coarse-minded to have possibly understood what one was all quarter long saying. Then one usually discovers one or two students—usually girls—who, though too shy to speak, turn out to be extremely intelligent and whom, because they never spoke up, I have had no awareness of."*

When I sense my teaching going badly, it feels ghastly, a kind of death by talking. Sometimes, sitting at my desk, a fifty-nine-year-old man, I find myself inditing "imprecise" in the margin of a student's paper, or instructing another student that "lifestyle" is a word "best avoided," and a powerful wave of hopelessness passes over me.

Yet there are also the exhilarating moments. I have had students who have written brilliant things for me. I'm not one of those teachers who claims that he has learned so much from his students, but I have sat in the middle of some fairly scintillating conversation about writing and writers. And, let me confess it, I have fallen in love with a number of my students. Before the sexual harassment suits come pouring in, let me quickly add that my love has been of a Socratic kind and has been divided between male and female students. (I am a registered heterosexual; but please don't ask me where you go to register.) Sometimes, usually as a result of spending an hour or two a week with students working on an independent tutorial, I find my heart going out to these students, watching them as they begin to sound their own intellectual depths.

At the end of each quarter's teaching, I usually mark down, in my journals, the names of the three or four students who have made a favorable impression on me. But I am regularly amazed at how quickly I forget so many of the names of my students. Journal, March 4, 1983: *"Last day of teaching yesterday—pleasure at finishing does not diminish. A few memorable students: a shy, intelligent boy named John Swagert, an artistically passionate girl with an intelligent smile named Sandrine Shoen, a more conventionally pretty girl of strong philistine intelligence named Sharon Silverstein."* Mr. Swagert and Miss Silverstein are lost in the swamp of my memory—they may have been memorable, but not for long. Where are you now? How many jobs, children, disappointments have they accrued since last they sat in my

class, looking up at me, not yet twenty-one, wanting, wanting, wanting, unmarked faces saying, give me knowledge, approval, anything else you happen to have on you.

Over the more than twenty years that I have been teaching, I have stayed in touch with, perhaps, forty or so students. They work at various jobs: in publishing, journalism, advertising, law, business, educational publishing, teaching. Those who have stayed in Chicago I meet for lunch or late afternoon coffee once or twice a year. Some I don't see for years at a time, but then will get from them a letter, sometimes with a request for a recommendation for a grant or a testimonial for a job in a line of work utterly different than the one they have been working at. When we meet, we speak with comfortable candor, and I feel a good deal less the comedy of teaching. I have students who are now themselves older than forty.

Some of my most memorable teaching experiences have been one-on-one, in what at Northwestern are known as "independent studies." In these tutorials a student reads and writes a paper or story with a professor, often for honors in English. I have had some fine independent studies sessions, chiefly with young women. One such student wrote a paper in which she showed that, in his fiction, F. Scott Fitzgerald had rendered all the evidence for what is today the most up-to-date information we have about alcoholism; the paper was so good that, with a bit of editing, I ran it in *The American Scholar*, the magazine I edit. Another student wrote brilliantly for me about her own almost staggering shyness. Yet another wrote a charming essay called "Memoir of a Half-Catholic Girlhood," in which she described her life before two cataclysmic events in her family life: Vatican Two, which threw her very Catholic mother, and her family's move to Southern California, which finished the family's Catholicism off. Both events effectively ended her Catholic childhood, and the essay ends with her recounting her inability to return to the Church yet trying all other churches in an attempt to fill a hole she suspects will never be refilled. And then, a year or so ago, I supervised a sweet story written by a student of strong Russian Orthodox faith, about a Russian Orthodox woman who, in the midst of a pregnancy, is discovered to have cancer but refuses, lest she offend God, to have an abortion. Pretty impressive stuff, let me tell you.

The other day, walking into a class, I thought that, over twenty years, the faces of my students haven't much changed. The only face that has changed has, of course, been mine. Teacher, I ask myself, have you become any wiser over the past few decades? It's not altogether clear that I have.

I have learned to talk about books and writing more efficiently than I once did. But does my talk bring any useful insight into the lives of many of my students? I wish I could say more confidently than I can that it has.

In many an Oxbridge memoir that I have read I seem to remember coming across a passage about some tutor of whom it is said that he was thought to be a bully but his students generally earned firsts. At Oxford and Cambridge, teachers do not grade their own students, so that teaching is, quite literally, put to the test. Since I grade my students, as do most teachers in most American universities, my own quality as a teacher is far from evident—and in this miasma of uncertainty it is likely to remain.

I know that, during certain magical moments in classrooms, I have sensed the sort of genuine excitement going on that feels suspiciously like education. This is the splendor that one awaits and yet knows cannot be permanently sustained. Along with the possibility of delight, the inevitability of dubiety, I fear, is built into teaching. Did Socrates, or Maimonides, or Saint Thomas sense he was getting the message across? Being supremely good teachers, they, my guess is, probably had their own superior doubts. Meanwhile, speaking for myself, I am quite pleased that the notion of malpractice suits against teachers has yet to catch on in a big way.

Helen Vendler

Harvard Graduate School, 1956–60

PERHAPS I CAN best respond to Bill Pritchard's *English Papers* by re-calling the rather different graduate school experience I found at Har-vard. One memoir deserves another, and one of my most unclouded memories of the four years I spent in graduate school is of happy congru-ence with the Amherst contingent—Bill Pritchard, Neil Hertz, Bill Youn-gren, and, by extension, Bill Youngren's wife Mary Ann Miller Youngren. They were smart, they were "real," and they gave themselves to literature. They had opinions, forceful ones, but they also knew how to laugh. I shared with them an affection for Ben Brower, with whom I studied, and who be-came one of the readers of my dissertation on Yeats. He too loved poetry (as many of our teachers did not), and I felt reassured in his presence.

What was Harvard like in those years? (The following account is some-what expurgated, but not much.) It has to be said that a young woman did not have the same experience at Harvard as a young man had. Harvard was still a men's school in legal fact, though the classes had been co-educational since the time of World War II. Women (undergraduate and graduate alike) belonged to Radcliffe College, which was a free-standing institution in terms of scholarships and fellowships, which came from its own endowment. The Harvard endowment, being much bigger, could support the male graduate students in some luxury; women graduate students lived on next to nothing.

I was glad to receive my admittance form from "Radcliffe Graduate School" (a nonexistent institution, in one sense, since all instruction was provided by Harvard). But my fellowship consisted of tuition remission and a yearly stipend of $600.00; and I knew from the admission materials that the room charge for a shared double was itself $330.00 for the year. That left me $270.00 to live on, not enough. My parents disapproved of my going to graduate school and living away from home; a decent girl, in their estimate of things, did not leave her parents' roof except to be married. I could not expect, nor did I want to take, money from them.

I decided to throw my dilemma into the lap of Radcliffe. I went to the administrative offices and said, "You've given me a fellowship; now you have to give me a job so that I can come." A little surprised, they gave me a job; I was to be a girl Friday, substituting during the summer for anyone who went on vacation. I moved from office to office; I even ran the switchboard. In the Business Office, I learned to read a double-entry ledger and use an adding-machine, and I typed the entire college budget for the year. I worked in the Registrar's office typing up transcripts (no photocopies in those days). That was the best office: Ruth Davenport, the Registrar, was a woman of cultivation and discretion and literary taste. She outlined what had to be done each day: telephone, mail, filing. And she added, "When the day's work is done, if you have any extra time between phone calls, you have my permission to read." I read Virgil and Ovid for the Ph.D. Latin exam, and was perfectly content. At the end of the summer, Miss Davenport gave me a copy of Adrienne Rich's first volume, *A Change of World*, which she had had Adrienne inscribe for me. (I treasured it; it was later stolen from my house during an English Institute party to which people brought other people.) I worked for Miss Davenport during my four years of graduate school, both every summer and whenever the workloads peaked in the Registrar's office (mostly, the opening of terms and exam periods). I don't know of any other graduate student who worked, though perhaps some did.

My prospective pay from Radcliffe, in the summer of 1956, meant I could sign the forms accepting graduate student status. It remained to find a place to live. Most first-year men lived in the men's graduate dorms, where they quickly made the acquaintance of many of their fellow graduate students in their field. Women had the choice of living in the new women's Graduate Center on Ash St. (nowhere near the men's dorms) or, if they recoiled in horror as I did from that arrangement, in a small co-op house. The Graduate Center (later named the Cronkhite Center in honor of Bernice Brown Cronkhite, then Dean of the Radcliffe Graduate School), was—and still is—constructed in a preposterous way. The student rooms —all on the upper floor—were small cells, and could in no way be construed as bed-sitters. Men, of course, were not allowed to visit in the student rooms. Down below, on the first floor, several absurd rooms were available in which one could see one's gentlemen-callers (or other visitors): these were called "The Morning Room," "The Music Room," "The Writing Room," and "The Map Room," as I recall. And the *pièce de résistance* on this lower floor was "The Ballroom," for all those balls graduate women were doubtless going to give.

Probably the Graduate Center was an improvement on whatever warrens had served graduate women as lodgings before its construction. But it was insufferably genteel in its decor and wholly unsuited to adult living, not only in its nunlike cells but also in its cafeteria meals. And—the killer fact for me, since I am a night person—the telephone switchboard went off at 10 P.M. (when a normal graduate student day, as far as I was concerned, was just beginning). Of course, one could not have a private phone. So I investigated the little co-op house at 77 Brattle St.; it was a pleasant old house, and I could share the top front bedroom (luckily with Barbara, a roommate both sane and nice, a physicist). There were two other graduate students in English in the house, and one of them, Grace, a year ahead of me, became a close friend. We did our own cooking, we could make phone calls at all hours, and we could feel unencumbered by a ballroom.

Well, I was all set: I had my room, I had my job, now I could choose my courses. One had to have one's program card signed by the chairman of the English Department once one had filled it out; and so, bearing my program card—on which I had inscribed, among others, a course by I. A. Richards, whose work I knew—I went to the chairman's office. He looked at me coldly, once I had given him the card, and said, "You know, we don't want you here, Miss Hennessy; we don't want any women here." I was so deeply shocked I couldn't speak. He went on to say, "You can't take this course with I. A. Richards: he's not even a member of the department." (Richards's appointment—not that I knew this then—was in the School of Education; he was supported by Carnegie Funds to do research on

Basic English; nonetheless, his course was listed among the English Department offerings.) The chairman crossed out Richards's course on my card, saying, "Have you had Chaucer?" To my silent head-shake, he said, "Well, then, you'll take Chaucer." And he ushered me out.

I went back to my dormitory trembling in body and mind. When I got to 77 Brattle St., my friend Grace was being visited by Mary Ann Miller, another second-year student, not yet married to Bill Youngren. I said, close to tears, "Do you know what he said to me? He said, 'We don't want you here, Miss Hennessy. We don't want any women here.'" Mary Ann snorted and said, "Oh, don't pay any attention to him! When I came here last year, he said to me, 'Miss Miller, you'd better get all A's, or you'll be out of here after one semester.' And then of course I discovered that there were people getting all B's who'd been here for ten years!" I felt better after that, but still shaken to my pins, and confused. I thought they had wanted me: after all, it was the English Department that did graduate admissions, and they had after all given me a fellowship.

(Years later, a friend who was acquainted with that chairman told him I was still unable to forget his words to me that day. I then ran into the chairman at the MLA in 1969: he said to me, "Helen, So-and-So told me that you still remember what I said to you when you came to Harvard." "Yes," I said, flustered, "but he shouldn't have told you, it's all water under the bridge." "No," he said in his southern drawl, "I was wrong. I apologize.")

In 1956, I could imagine no reason for the chairman's words; later, I saw that many men of his generation had become disillusioned with their women graduate students, who dropped out to get married, or finished their degree and never taught, or taught for a while and took part-time work after having children, or rarely published even if they taught full-time. Men such as the chairman blamed the women, not realizing how structural and social conditions militated against a successful academic career for women, who were discouraged—by their parents and often by their husbands, not to speak of administrators in higher education—from conceiving of themselves as scholars. I was dejected, looking around me, to see that all the women academics whose books I knew—Marjorie Nicolson, Rosemond Tuve, Ruth Wallerstein, Helen White, Helen Gardner, Muriel Bradbrook—were single. I wanted to marry and have children, but I also wanted, just as much, to read and write. There seemed no example of anyone doing both.

At last, into my courses I went. I was lucky: Harvard was having two notable visitors. Rosemond Tuve was substituting for Harry Levin while he was on sabbatical, and I entered her seminar "Romance, Allegory, and Pastoral, with special reference to Spenser," where she tumbled books onto the table and referred to "Christine" and "Chrétien" and other authors of whom we had barely heard, but made us feel, with her limitless interest in the thought-forms of the past, that the inviting mystery of Spenser was a gate into the central genres of his age. And Northrop Frye was giving two courses, one on Criticism (which meant that we heard the *Anatomy of Criticism* just before publication spellbindingly delivered *à haute voix*) and one on Myth (given in the bowels of the Fogg, and thrillingly accompanied by slides of Blake's prophetic art). I was auditing the Frye courses, along with half of Harvard, it seemed; a long serpentine queue would wend its way from Harvard Hall to the Fogg between the two courses, given back to back at 10 and 11; I was given to saying that Frye was the only man I would get up at 9 o'clock for.

(Later, when I was 2d vice-president of the MLA, Norrie was president. By that time, after meeting over the years, we knew each other in a cordial way. There was a moment which forever marked his blunt virtue for me. The subject of discussion at the Executive Council meeting was whether the Gay Caucus could "fly up" to Division status. The Caucus had fulfilled all the provisions in the by-laws for doing so, but several members of the Executive Council were determined to prevent this institutionalizing of gay studies, arguing that there was no such thing as "gay literature," that such an action would set a bad precedent, that there was no telling what "they" would do if given "their" own division, and so on. I was annoyed enough to say—mainly to offend the officious pieties of the opposing group—that I could easily imagine a course in modern gay literature starting with Whitman and Cardinal Newman and going on through Gerard Manley Hopkins and Oscar Wilde and Henry James to James Merrill, but that argument didn't get us anywhere. Our one lesbian sat silent; she told me afterwards that she felt unable to argue for the motion because people would have thought it, coming from her, a variety of special pleading. The discussion stormed on, till finally Norrie stepped in, saying, "I don't believe in any of these categories—women's literature, gay literature, black literature—since I think there is only literature. But I have been so scandalized by the attitudes exhibited here towards our colleagues in the Gay Caucus—hearing them referred to as 'those people' and 'them' as if they weren't part of us—that I want to announce that I will vote for the motion as a matter of ethical principle." The others fell silent, and the motion passed. It was this sort of intellectual dignity that one felt as a student, listening to Norrie. He believed literature was worthy of the highest respect and the deepest inquiry, and that belief made his classes enthralling.)

Of course, being barred from officially taking Richards's class didn't keep me away from it; I audited it. For the first time I encountered a teacher who thought a single poem worth two hours of class time. To be taught a Keats ode, or a Marvell poem, by Richards was to see how much a poem contained, and how complex a set of interrelations arose from its internal imaginative syntax. Many of my teachers, the literary historians among them, tended to think that the poem could be taken for granted (hadn't we all read it at home?) and that class time should be spent on historical and philosophical contexts. I used to sit in such classes silently seething: "But why don't they ever mention. . . . But why don't they ever say. . . . But why don't they ever look. . . ." I imagine there are students who sit in my classes feeling the same, if they are hungry for an approach other than mine. But for me, Richards filled my need for an example of criticism that centered on the poem, that went deep into the powers of words, and that saw the poem as a radiant exfoliation from a glowing center. After dedicating my first book, in a conventional way, to my parents, I dedicated my second book, in a heartfelt way, to Richards.

Yes, and there was the Chaucer class, a full year of it, in which I became rapidly disaffected during the first term, during which we (a mixture of graduates and undergraduates, mostly the latter) read the minor poems. The *Troilus* was taught as one long dirty joke, with many sniggering remarks directed at the male eighteen-year-olds. Granted, I was a priggish girl, but I don't think it was simply my straight-laced upbringing that made me hate the teacher's ways; it was that all the delicacy of apprehension and sophisticated humor of the poem was lost in his vulgarizing of its effects. In the second semester the teacher dwelt, predictably, on the coarser elements of the *Canterbury Tales*. Of course, he had been teaching all-male audiences for many pre-war years. Perhaps he had once taught Chaucer more faithfully, and had gradually broadened his approach in an attempt to reach his undergraduates over the obstacle of Middle English. But for me it was a torture to sit through that class (and an added smart that I was there because of the will of the chairman). The Chaucerian was more bearable in his seminar on Arthurian material (which I took because one needed two classes to skip the medieval section of the oral examination). Still, his dictatorial method was to hand out, the first day of class, face down, an index card to each one of us which, turned over, gave us our topic for the semester. I lucked out; I got the Holy Grail. Since I was already a confirmed Wagnerite, I settled into the legends with good will. I ingested so much alliterative verse, between the medieval alliterative tradition and Spenser, that I got my paper back with silent loops drawn by the professor joining all the alliterations in my own sentences, of which I had been utterly unconscious. At last, the Chaucerian's sense of humor amused me when I was its object.

I had, as a relief from Chaucer, a year-long course in modern Irish prose and poetry with John Kelleher, which I signed up for because the year before (at Boston University, where I was a special student) I had found, at the tail end of a Victorian literature course, William Butler Yeats. I had known all the poets before Yeats through my mother's books; and I had known all the poets from Eliot on through the first book I ever bought for myself, Oscar Williams's *Little Anthology of Modern Poetry*. But Yeats had fallen between the cracks; and so, when I came to him after the Rossettis and Wilde, I thought "WHO is THIS?" The Kelleher course—taught by an incomparable reader with a writer's understanding of literature and an intuitive historian's understanding of human affairs—put Yeats in context for me, and led me to Kelleher's seminar in Yeats, where I wrote a paper that became my dissertation. But before that happened, I had come, in Kelleher's course, to my first graduate-school pitfall; I had entirely misinterpreted a story by Frank O'Connor in my first paper, reading "straight" what was to be taken ironically. Without a word of criticism (except for the appended "B"), Kelleher simply wrote, "Try looking at it this way," and sketched the ironic reading. I blushed for shame, it was so obvious once it was pointed out. But I appreciated his kindness—as I've had occasion to do, all my life. (He gave me his Trinity College, Dublin, gown—a "woolly bathrobe," he called it—when, many years after him, I was given a Trinity honorary degree.)

And I encountered Douglas Bush through a seminar in Newman and Arnold, where I discovered the joys of contextualizing through reading such things as *St. Paul and Protestantism*. Bush's minuscule handwriting introduced me—a largely self-taught writer, since I had done my undergraduate degree in chemistry—to the joys of purism: "There are no degrees of uniqueness," the tiny marginal comment would say to my use of the phrase "more unique," and I would be delighted with the truth of the observation. He, too, like Kelleher, had the art of setting you straight without making you feel stupid. And, like Kelleher, he made no distinction between men students and women students; they both recommended me and supported me as eagerly as they did the men under their care. A few years after I left graduate school, before I had even published my dissertation, when I was teaching at Cornell and taking care of my small son, I was astonished to find in my mail a letter from the Guggenheim Foundation saying that Douglas Bush had recommended me to them. I wrote to Mr. Bush saying that at the moment I had no expectation of constructing a Guggenheim project, but that I was very grateful to him, the more so since I had not been his dissertation advisee and he had no particular responsibility for my future. He wrote back, saying he knew it was probably premature, but he just wanted to be sure that they knew about me so that when I did apply, the recommendation would be there. It was through such actions that I came to realize that any crude notion that men as such oppressed women as such was untrue; there were only unprejudiced men and prejudiced men, and one could tell them apart.

I should not let Perry Miller's large class in the American Renaissance go without mention. It was in many ways a wonderful class; Miller had torrential energy and a capacious memory, and to hear him talk about almost anything was to be well entertained and well instructed. He was responsible for my first publication; when he gave our papers back, I found written on mine, "Can I give this to the *New England Quarterly?*" I wasn't quite sure what he meant, so I went up and asked him; he explained that he wanted to give it to them for publication. "Well I guess so, of course," I said, rather taken aback. And so it was published: I was surprised; it was so easy. Yet Miller's class had begun very badly. It was the first day; the room was mobbed with about two hundred students. Miller came in harrumphing, and then he noticed that prominently seated in the front row was a nun, her face framed in the large halo of her starched headdress. He growled, "I don't like talking when I know there's somebody in front of me disagreeing with my point of view, so I would be obliged if all Roman Catholics left this course." Naturally, nobody was identifiable as a Roman Catholic but the nun (who was a graduate student in English). These days, there would be a storm of protest; but in those days professorial authority was such that no one said a word. The nun, in a very dignified way, picked up her books and began to rise. One of the male graduate students, also a Roman Catholic, escorted her out of the room (he, of course, returned at the next meeting, since nothing in his dress identified him as one of the proscribed). Once again, I was shocked as I had been a few days earlier by the chairman's words to me. What sort of men were these?

And what else was going on in my life besides courses and work at

Radcliffe? There was the making of friends. With one exception, all the other women who had been admitted to the English graduate program in my year had dropped out; and the exception was someone with whom I had nothing in common. Grace, a year ahead of me, left after her orals, unsure that she wanted the theatricality of teaching; Mary Ann married Bill and moved to Boston. My friends were consequently men; but aside from some parties, and falling unhappily in love, I was not a very social person. I had come from an asocial house, and didn't really know how to connect with my contemporaries in any easy way. My upbringing had been significantly unlike theirs (Catholic schools from the sixth grade through college) and my life had been an entirely sheltered one, without trips or vacations; they had mostly been in upper-class schools and colleges, came from well-off families, were already possessed, in some cases, of stocks and bonds, and didn't have to work to earn their keep. From the third year of graduate school on, the successful men could be house tutors; their room and board (and even maid service) were provided, and they had the easy social access to faculty and other tutors that house lunches and dinners offered. And the English Department furnished them with Dexter Fellowships in the summer, of which the purpose was "to see the cathedral towns of England." Women graduate students could not be house tutors; they had to pay for their own room and board and be their own cooks and maids in their frugal and shared apartments. They had no access (Radcliffe and Harvard still being separate economic institutions) to Dexters. Their numbers were few, their social isolation extreme. Yet, in spite of the pangs of unhappy love, I was intensely absorbed in my reading and writing; even though, in the spring of my first year, I composed my Yeats seminar paper (which became my dissertation) with tears of romantic despair running down my cheeks, I could feel the exhilaration of coming to a real understanding of Yeats's strange metaphorical prose in *A Vision*, and putting what I saw into words. Really, to make myself happy, I had only to walk into Widener Library and sit on the floor of the stacks and let books drop into my lap.

I've run together the first two years of graduate school in my mind, but I do know that it wasn't until the second year that I encountered Ben Brower, in a course on Pope. Pope was not, for all his brilliance, quite my cup of tea (my closest friend used to deplore what she regarded as my lugubrious taste in poetry and mournful lieder, having herself far more of the comic spirit than I; she liked Pope better than I knew how to). Besides, I had just undergone the most profound literary experience of my life; I had found Wallace Stevens (a taste shared by only one other graduate student, my friend Frank Murphy—the student who rescued the nun, now a professor of English at Smith). All I wanted to do was write on Stevens: and there I was, stuck with Pope. What was delightful about the Pope seminar was Brower's intimate acquaintance with Pope's Latin models; I had never before heard anyone talk easily about Virgil and Horace. Brower's pleasure in the allusive fit between one language and another, and in the translation of genres over centuries, communicated itself to his students; but the best thing he did for me was let me write my seminar paper on didactic poetry as exemplified in Pope's *Essay on Criticism* and Stevens's *Notes toward a Supreme Fiction*. That paper gave me the beginnings of my book on Stevens's longer poems. I can imagine that some other teacher of Pope might feel it within his rights to exclude Stevens from a Pope paper; Brower's tenderness toward the intellectual bent of a student is still, to me, an exemplary act of a teacher's not standing in a student's way.

I didn't talk in graduate school seminars. I truly didn't know how to. I had read most of the English poets for many years before I entered graduate school at twenty-three, and I had seen a fair amount of poetry in French, Spanish, Italian, and Latin (my father had taught my sister and me languages from the time we were born, and in addition to my three years of high school Latin, the schools I went to had us sing the liturgy in Latin—including such things as *Tenebrae*, the Holy Week services, and the Psalms). The conversation of my peers often seemed to me to be on an awfully low level. I couldn't enter at that level, and yet it felt impertinent to enunciate another level altogether. Besides, since I hadn't done literature in college, I had no idea what conventions governed the discussion of literature in a classroom. I didn't suppose that anyone was noticing my silence; but years later, a friend who had seen my dossier said that there was a most peculiar item in it—one of my Harvard professors had said that I had done very well on my papers, but that he couldn't predict what sort of a teacher I would be since he had never heard me utter a word in class. The friend telling me this could hardly believe I had *ever* been a silent presence.

Only twice did I run into academic difficulty because of being female. I wanted to take Perry Miller's seminar in Melville, and expected no difficulty: hadn't he, after all, liked the paper I had done in his class? But when I asked him, he said no, and added, roughly, as I recall: "I can't have girls in my seminar: we meet at my house, and the boys and I talk and drink, and I couldn't talk the way I want to in front of girls." There were other professors in other departments (Professor Hooton of anthropology being one, if I remember correctly) who also refused to let women enter their seminars. I was disappointed, but I never thought of complaining. Anyway, supposing I did complain, what sort of future would I have in a seminar into which I had forced my way?

The other difficulty concerned the Poetry Room, then, as now, located in Lamont Library. Because of the administrative separation of Harvard and Radcliffe, there were two separate undergraduate libraries, and women were not allowed to enter Harvard's Lamont Library except in the summer, when it was open to both sexes to serve the Summer School. The Radcliffe Library was located in the building now housing the Schlesinger Library. Graduate students of both sexes could of course use Widener (the research library) and Houghton (the rare book library). I was writing a dissertation on Yeats's *Vision* and his later plays. The *Vision* was first published in 1925; later, Yeats revised it heavily and republished it. It was easy enough to buy the final version, but the 1925 version—the one essential to me—was a Lamont Poetry Room book. I could not enter Lamont. What to do?

I took my problem to John Kelleher, who assured me he'd straighten it out and find a way to transfer the book somewhere I could use it daily— perhaps to Houghton, since it was a rare book and did not circulate. Well, it was not so simple. The *Vision* belonged to the undergraduate collections, he was told, and could be used only within the purview of an undergraduate library. I could, they said, use it in the Radcliffe Library, but since it was a rare book, I had to use it in the office of Miss Porrit, the Librarian, an office open only 9–5 Monday through Friday (not the most convenient hours for a teaching fellow). It would be sent to Miss Porrit's office by a bonded runner; and I had to request it, for any day I wanted it, twenty-four hours in advance. "But I need it every day," I said helplessly— it was a constant point of reference both in itself and for the plays I was writing on. Well, then, it was explained, I would have to telephone every day for the bonded runner. For months, I telephoned Monday for Tuesday, and Tuesday for Wednesday, and Wednesday for Thursday, and Thursday for Friday, and Friday for Monday. I can't imagine what it cost the libraries to allow me to do my dissertation. And I don't understand, to this day, why it couldn't simply have been put on a shelf for me at Houghton. Without John Kelleher's intervention, I might have had to abandon the thesis I wanted to write. Whenever I walk past Lamont these days, I am fiercely glad that the Poetry Room is open to everyone, town as well as gown.

I haven't said much about teaching. No one, of course, taught us anything about teaching. I became a tutor the second year women were allowed that status, in 1958–59. We had soporific tutorial meetings, of which I remember only Stephen Orgel (now a professor at Stanford) convulsed with silent laughter at the pompous things being said up front by the head tutor. I was assigned a non-honors junior tutorial, in which the students were, for reasons I forget, to read the metaphysical poets. It was my first experience of teaching, and I had a group of four: three were debutantes and clubbies (as they were known in those days) who were coasting through college with gentlemanly C's, and one was an earnest student, trained in a Yeshiva, who wanted to scrutinize texts with a microscopic eye. The elegant three trailed in with no preparation; the fourth came in with learned Biblical references. I hovered impotently, not knowing what to do. It was my worst teaching term in graduate school. After that, I never had such a heterogeneous group, nor such an unprepared clutch of people as my languid three. I never taught more than "one fifth" (in Harvard parlance, the smallest possible teaching load, generally two honors seniors doing theses), because I wanted to spend my time reading and writing; consequently (I think one fifth paid $800.00 a term at that point) I was as poor as a church mouse. I made my own clothes, and watched enviously as the male house tutors bought records and went to concerts. Nonetheless, I wanted to get through in four years and become a grown-up; I was appalled to discover that there were people at Harvard who were G-10 and even G-13. My two most strenuous and pleasurable tutorials are still memorable: I read all of Shakespeare with Julius Novick, now a professor of drama at SUNY Purchase, who even then knew immensely more about the drama, and about Shakespeare, than I; and I directed a senior honors thesis on Spenser and the Nicomachean Ethics by Ann Chalmers (who knew Greek, as I did not, and had exquisite taste); she (now Ann Watts) has become a professor of medieval literature at Rutgers-Newark.

In the fall of my fourth and last year at Harvard, I was offered an instructorship in English for the following year, and accepted. In the event, I later had to decline it, since I was getting married and going to Cornell with my husband. I was the first woman the department had ever offered an instructorship to, and the chairman (a different one from the one who had seen me in) gave way to a tremendous anger, and to an outburst to the effect that women were no good, that I had ruined everything for any woman coming after me, etc., all the while hurling books at me from his shelves. I backed out of his office, and left. Many years later, we made peace.

If this account does not resemble Bill Pritchard's, it signifies only how little we, as friends and fellow graduate students, knew of each other's lives. Many names have gone unmentioned here: the other women in my co-op house, both congenial and uncongenial; Audra Browman, with whom I shared an apartment during my third year; my friends Paul Alpers and Donald Friedman (both professors at Berkeley), Martin Wine (recently retired from his professorship at the University of Illinois at Chicago), Joel Porte and Bob Kiely (both my colleagues at Harvard till Joel left for Cornell), and David Kalstone, who has died. They, and others I knew more glancingly, gave me a great deal through their intelligence and spirit and learning. Mostly, I felt that we were in this enterprise together, and that we had a love of books in common. It was the first time that I had been in surroundings where I felt at home, for all the loneliness and singularity of being a young woman in that place, at that time.

II

PROFESSIONS
Criticism in Question

Frank Lentricchia

Last Will and Testament of
an Ex-Literary Critic

I ONCE MANAGED to live for a long time, and with no apparent stress, a secret life with literature. Publicly, in the books I'd written and in the classroom, I worked as an historian and polemicist of literary theory, who could speak with passion, and without noticeable impediment, about literature as a political instrument. I once wrote that the literary word was like a knife, a hammer, a gun. I became a known and somewhat colorfully controversial figure, regularly excoriated in neo-conservative laments about the academy.

The secret me was me-the-reader, in the act of reading: an experience in which the words of someone else filled me up and made it irrelevant to talk about my reading; an experience that I'd had for as long as I can remember being a reader. This secret life implicitly denied that any talk about what I had undergone could ever be authentic. My silent encounters with literature are ravishingly pleasurable, like erotic transport.

In private, I was tranquillity personified; in public, an actor in the endless strife and divisiveness of argument, the "Dirty Harry of literary theory," as one reviewer put it. My secret life eventually was to be shared with students in my undergraduate classroom, while my public life as lit-

erary intellectual continued to be played out in the graduate classroom.
Two types of classroom; two selves unhappy with one another.

◈

Once, and only once, I posed the following question to undergraduate majors in a course I teach at Duke University on modern literature: "Anybody here like literature?" Looks of puzzlement and concern: *is he stoned?*
I like my undergraduates, with whom I share a bond of stubborn naiveté.
We believe that literature is pleasurable and important, as literature, and
not as an illustration of something else. I've posed the same question in
graduate seminars. The response never varies: knowing laughs, disturbing nods of recognition, a few stares of impatience and hostility. They assume I'm one of them. They say, "You don't believe that literature is
important as literature." Then they point to the damaging evidence of
some of my work in the field, usually to a book called *Criticism and Social
Change.* I want to reply, "You need to understand the context." I say nothing. They believe that the book is clear, that no context can modify its
essential meaning, and they're right. When *Criticism and Social Change* appeared in 1983, I was convinced that a literary critic, *as a literary critic,*
could be an agent of social transformation, an activist who would show his
students that, in its very form and style, literature had a strategic role to
play in the world's various arrangements of power; that literature wasn't
to be relegated to the Arts and Leisure supplement of the Sunday paper,
as if it were a thing for weekend amusement only. I would show my students that what is called "literature" is nothing but the most devious of
rhetorical discourses (writing with political designs upon us all), either in
opposition to or complicity with the power in place. In either case, novels,
poems, and plays deserved to be included in the Sunday section called
News of the Week in Review.

Over the last ten years, I've pretty much stopped reading literary criticism, because most of it isn't literary. But criticism it is of a sort—the
sort that stems from the sense that one is morally superior to the writers
that one is supposedly describing. This posture of superiority is assumed
when those writers represent the major islands of Western literary tradition, the central cultural engine—so it goes—of racism, poverty, sexism,
homophobia, and imperialism: a cesspool that literary critics would ex-
pose for mankind's benefit. Just what it would avail us to learn that
Flaubert was a sexist is not clear. It is impossible, this much is clear, to exaggerate the heroic self-inflation of academic literary criticism.

To be certified as an academic literary critic, you need to believe, and be willing to assert, that Ezra Pound's *Cantos*, a work twice the length of *Paradise Lost*, and which ninety-nine percent of all serious students of literature find too difficult to read, actually forwards the cause of worldwide anti-Semitism. You need to tell your students that, despite what almost a century's worth of smart readers have concluded, Joseph Conrad's *Heart of Darkness* is a subtle celebration of the desolations of imperialism. My objection is not that literary study has been politicized, but that it proceeds in happy indifference to, often in unconscionable innocence of, the protocols of literary competence. Only ten to fifteen years ago, the views I've cited on Pound and Conrad would have received barely passing grades had they been submitted as essays in an undergraduate course. Now, such views circulate at the highest levels of my profession in the essays of distinguished literary critics.

I've never believed that writers had to be superior in anything, except writing. The fundamental, if only implied, message of much literary criticism is self-righteous, and it takes this form: "T. S. Eliot is a homophobe and I am not. Therefore, I am a better person than Eliot. Imitate me, not Eliot." To which the proper response is: "But T. S. Eliot could really write, and you can't. Tell us truly, is there no filth in your soul?"

✑

When it's the real thing, literature enlarges us; strips the film of familiarity from the world; creates bonds of sympathy with all kinds, even with evil characters, who we learn are all in the family. Each of these points has been made long ago in response to the question, What is literature for? With no regrets, I tell you that I have nothing new to offer to the field of literary theory.

I confess to never having been able to get enough of the real thing. I worry incessantly about using up my stash and spending the last years of my life in gloom, having long ago mainlined all the great, veil-piercing books. Great *because* veil-piercing. Books propelling me out of the narrow life that I lead in my own little world, offering me revelations of strangers, who turn out not to be totally strange; a variety of real worlds, unveiled for me, for the first time.

If you should happen to enjoy the literary experience of liberation, it's not likely that you do so because you're able to take apart the formal resources of literature. All that you know is that you live where you live and that you are who you are, and not someone else. Then you submit to the text, you relinquish yourself, because you need to be transported. You know with complete certitude that, when you are yourself, you are only, at best, half alive. Even if you can't say what it is, you know when you're in the thrall of real literature. You can't get your fix from reading the Op-Ed page or, for that matter, any other pages in discourses you think of as *not literary*. If asked to define "literary," you could not do it. If pressed, you'd say, "I'm not interested in the question." It's like asking me who God is. You might say, as I would, "The question 'What is literature?' is a question for those who secretly hate literature." If you put a gun to my head, I'll say, "All literature is travel literature; all true readers shut-ins."

The first time that I traveled it was 1956 and I was sixteen. I was in bed. Ever since, I have to do it in a bed, or reclining on a couch, or on the floor, with my knees drawn up—just like the first time, the book leaning against my thighs, nestled in my groin. The first booking was arranged by a high school teacher named (honest) LaBella, who said to me out of the blue: "Live fast, die young, and have a good-looking corpse." He told me that he was quoting a line from a novel that I should read, *Knock on Any Door* by Willard Motley. I tried to take out the book from my hometown public library but was informed that I could have it only if I brought them a letter from my mother saying that it was okay, which my indulgent mother was happy to write.

After supper, I withdrew to my room, shut the door, and read deep into the night. Next morning, I didn't bother with breakfast. My mother looked in to ask if I was sick. I kept on going into the early afternoon, when I finished, still in my pajamas, unwashed and unshaven. Too bad I couldn't have hooked up a catheter.

I was living in the world of Nick Romano, a good Italian-American Catholic, an altar boy, who through a terrible unfairness is cast down into the mean streets of Chicago's West Side and, eventually, at twenty-one, into the electric chair for a murder that he in fact committed and that I wanted him to get away with. Live fast, die young, and have a good-looking corpse was Nick's motto. He loved a girl named Rosemary, who loved him back passionately. They actually did it.

I was also a good Italian-American Catholic, crazy for a girl named Rosemary, but whom I never talked to, never mind the other thing, which almost nobody in my teen world did. I lived in Utica, New York, a small ethnic town, where parents were strict, where the streets were not mean. I had (and have) a dramatic life in books, not on the streets.

A couple of years ago, I learned that the late Willard Motley was gay and black, and that he only rarely wrote about blacks. Occasionally I try to factor Motley's race and sexual orientation into what I experienced when I read his novel. I can't do it. Recently, I learned that Motley said, in response to an obvious question, that he considered himself to be a member of the human race. In the current academy, there's no possibility of accepting that statement as anything but a pathetic dodge.

When I grew up and became a literary critic, I learned to keep silent about the reading experiences of liberation that I'd enjoyed since childhood. With many of my generation, I believed that my ability to say the words "politics" and "literature" in the same breath was the only socially responsible way to affirm the value of literary study.

Then, seven years ago, I lost my professional bearing and composure. The actual crisis occurred in a graduate class, just as I was about to begin a lecture on Faulkner. Before I could get a word out, a student said: "The first thing we have to understand is that Faulkner is a racist." I responded with a stare, but he was not intimidated. I was. He wanted to subvert me with what I thought crude versions of ideas that had made my academic reputation, and that had (as he told me before the semester began) drawn him to my class. And now I was refusing to be the critic he had had every right to think I was. And I felt subverted. Later in the course, another student attacked Don DeLillo's *White Noise* for what he called its insensitivity to the Third World. I said, "But the novel doesn't concern the Third World. It's set in a small town in middle America. It concerns the technological catastrophes of the First World." The student replied: "That's the problem. It's ethnocentric and elitist." I had been, before that class, working hard to be generous. After that class, I didn't want to be generous anymore and tried to communicate how unspeakably stupid I found these views, but had trouble staying fully rational. There was an explosion or two of operatic dimension. I wasn't the tenor hero; I was the baritone villain.

So I gave up teaching graduate students. I escaped into the undergraduate classroom—in other words, slipped happily underground in order to talk to people who, like me, need to read great literature just as much as they need to eat.

❧

I'm a teacher who believes that literature can't be taught, if by teaching we mean being in lucid possession of a discipline, a method, and rules for the engagement of the object of study. I believe that the finest examples of the object of study cannot be ruled and that, therefore, professional literary study is a contradiction in terms. Great writing is a literally *unruly*, one-of-a-kind thing, something new and original in the world of literature, which (like all cultural worlds) is dominated by the conventional and the rule-driven: the boringly second rate. Where then is the teacher? In my classroom, I assume, but cannot prove, that there can be illuminating conversation about the peaks of unruly originality, from Homer and Dante to Joyce and Proust. I assume that such conversation cannot be replaced by what goes on in the sociology or the economics classroom.

We do not, after all, tell economists that all economic data and systems are actually disguised examples of novels, poems, and plays. Yet this is precisely the form of absurdity that the professional study of literature has taken. The sad situation in the literary wing of the academy is that those who spent (when teenagers) the days and nights of their lives with their noses happily buried in imaginative literature now believe that they must look elsewhere, to academic disciplines, for the understanding and values of their happiness. And look elsewhere they do, with holy zeal. They embark upon a course and leave their happiness far behind.

I believe that what is now called literary criticism is a form of Xeroxing. Tell me your theory and I'll tell you in advance what you'll say about any work of literature, especially those you haven't read. Texts are not read; they are preread. All of literature is x and nothing but x, and literary study is the naming (exposure) of x. For x, read imperialism, sexism, homophobia, and so on. All of literary history is said to be a display of x, because human history is nothing but the structure of x. By naming x, we supposedly name the social order (ordure) as it is, and always has been. The point of naming it? Presumably to produce a contagion of true understanding (the critic as social interventionist), from which would follow appropriate social change in wholesome directions, though it has to be noted that the literary academy has long been staffed by people with righteous understanding, who assiduously disseminate that understanding in the classroom, and still the world remains governed by sexism and so on. In the hearts of those who study literature lies the repressed but unshakable conviction that the study of literature serves no socially valued purpose. Too bad academic literary artists can't accept their amateur status—that is, their status as lovers.

If the authority of a contemporary literary critic lies in his *theory* of x, then wherein lies the authority of the theory itself? In disciplines in which he has little experience and less training. The typical literary critic who wields a theory is not himself a sociologist, historian, or economist, as well as a student of literature. A scandal of professional impersonation? No, because the impersonators speak only into the mirror of other impersonators and rarely to those in a position to test their theories for fraudulence. An advanced literature department is the place where you can write a dissertation on Wittgenstein and never have to face an examiner from the philosophy department. An advanced literary department is the place where you may speak endlessly about gender and never have to face the scrutiny of a biologist, because gender is just a social construction, and nature doesn't exist.

My reader has the right to pose some questions: You say that literature of original character can't be taught. So what is it that you do in your classroom? And you are obviously weary of the pounding chatter about sexism and so on. Are you saying that those subjects of academic literary criticism are not important just because they are fashionable? Is not literature significantly about such subjects, whether or not literary critics take them up? My answers: Literature is about homophobia and so on, but only because literature is about everything real and imaginable under the sun, including man as a political animal. Imperialism and so on are subjects for imagination, not agendas or ideas to be illustrated. Imaginative writers have but one agenda: to write beautifully, rivetingly, unforgettably.

What I see in the academy is an eager flight from literature by those who refuse to take the *literary* measure of the subject, whatever the subject may be. The literature student sees the objects that historians and sociologists see, but he ought to see them through the special lens of literature as objects in stylized and imaginative landscapes. The authentic literary type believes with Oscar Wilde that life is an imitation of art. Sociologists don't believe that; philosophers don't either. Why should they? They're sociologists and philosophers, who know that life is an imitation of sociology and philosophy.

I would take it as a sign of renewed health in literary studies if critics would recognize the value and authority of other disciplines, in which they have (for the most part) but cocktail party acquaintance, disciplines practiced by serious people, many of whom do not take literature seriously, but perhaps more seriously than they take literary critics, whom they think of as charlatans deluxe. I would take it as a miraculous sign of full recovery if contemporary literary critics would recognize the impious comedic dimension of the most serious and weighty works of the literary tradition.

❧

The first thing that I do in my classroom is shut the door and then make sure it's shut tight. (Unfortunately, on the windows of my classroom there are no shades.) Since I do not believe that, as a literary critic, I can have honest recourse to method, theory, and discipline—original writing being, by my definition, the antithesis of those things—I'm uneasy about what I do on university grounds, where those in charge have every right to expect that professors convey knowledge in systematic fashion, so that students might come away with an "education"—rules of investigation that they might apply to texts that I haven't taught them. The academy doth make scientific impersonators of literary critics, who should rather be anarchists.

Behind closed doors, with only undergraduates in attendance, I become something of a rhapsode. As Plato says in the *Ion*, rhapsodes are enthusiasts. We're out of our minds. Like all rhapsodes, I like to recite from the text. I tell my students that in true recitation, we're possessed, we are the medium for the writer's voice. I speak the text as the writer would speak it—this is my radical and unverifiable claim—and the phrases and sentences flow out of me as they flowed from him in the process of creating the text. The writer flows into me and out of me: my mouth his exit into our world.

My listener-students, in the moment of recitation, are infused, taken over by the writer's original voice embodied in me. They too become possessed. Rhapsode and audience assume a single strange consciousness, not their own: "living," not "knowing" the text. We are simply, and collectively, mad.

Because I am an imperfect rhapsode, I bring to my students what I know about literary history, the author's life and times, literary forms, types, and styles: real knowledge, slowly and sometimes painfully gained over a lifetime, which takes me to the brink of the text itself. My doctorate in literature helps, but it does not take me inside. I share this knowledge with my students, but it doesn't substitute for an honest act of reading. Then we face, let us say, James Joyce's *Ulysses*, and quickly learn that, when we confront the page itself, calling *Ulysses* a novel, or a comic epic in prose, or an odd instance of satire, or a modernist experiment, doesn't do us much good, even if we have sophisticated understanding of what these things mean. At the level of the page itself, all I have is my relatively informed sensibility and a number of years of reading, as I fumble in the dark of originality. We try to describe what is on the page. That's all.

In my classes we creep along (a whole semester, for example, on *Ulysses*). We tend to have difficulty getting through reading lists. I am a slow reader. We tend not to come to large conclusions. We don't know, at the end of a semester, what *Ulysses* means. We even have a hard time with the question, What is *Ulysses* about? A harder time, I'm pleased to say, at the end of the semester than at the beginning. I'm not comfortable with questions about meaning or subject matter. I am a man flying from ideas, including his own.

Most of all, we get lost in the particulars of Joyce's writing. We like to wallow. We try to see "characters," "Dublin," "narrative," but what we only see is writing. Again and again we make the reader's equivalent of the discovery that Marcel Proust made when he finally knew that he was a writer. The young Proust was burdened with a sense that a mystery lay concealed behind certain objects of the world which he could not get out of his mind. His sense of concealed significance coincided with his despair of finding a literary vocation. Then one fine day the rind of things peeled away and he saw that the mysterious significance was a phrase, perhaps a word, maybe a fragment of a sentence. And these were *his* words, first fruits of his wanting to write. Proust found his own writing as the secret concealed behind things. So the reader of Joyce, or of any writer of force, looking for the big things behind the text, will in the end find the only big thing, the writing in its specific shape and texture, and all that the writing incarnates, thanks to its specific shape and texture. The reader stays happily, then, at the surface of the text, where all the deep stuff resides, trying to describe the surface—feeling about in the dark, then reporting back from the dark in words that would describe the encounter with strange combinations of words.

My classes are an attempt to share a text in this way. The text so shared is memorable, we remember it long, because we hover over the surface untiringly; low-flying readers we are. We would memorize *Ulysses*. Teacher and students textually bonded for about fifteen weeks; becoming something cohesive and intimate, an enworded community. Later, when we must part our ways (they graduate and go away for good, only a few return) we will occasionally (in our privacy) see our lives through the world-bearing words of *Ulysses*, and we'll recall each other and ourselves in that classroom, and we'll be united again in a way, in Joyce's writing, as we travel again together in a world made by Joyce. I think that's a good enough reason to teach literature, in any classroom.

Alan Lelchuk

The End of the Art of Reading?

A Modest Polemic

I n a March 1997 essay in the *New York Times Magazine*, James Atlas, an editor of the magazine and a literary biographer, made the case that great "modernist" literature was really a "fraud," and that the real truth, or his secret revelation, was that most of the twentieth century's greatest writers were "boring" to read. In particular Mr. Atlas cited five novelists—James, Proust, Joyce, Woolf, Faulkner—and chided them for the difficulties their work presented to the general (intelligent) reader, like himself. In other words, "modernism," via these writers, introduced a level of "abstruseness" into fiction that precluded easy reading. Why couldn't they be like the older, traditional writers of the previous century, Mr. Atlas mused, who wrote straightforward novels in the realistic mode?

"So what's the problem here? Is it me or is it literature?" Mr. Atlas put the matter, in the sort of breezy rhetoric that marked the tone of his demolition, "I don't have any trouble reading nineteenth-century fiction: the Brontës and George Eliot and Balzac and the Russians. Or a lot of 20th, for that matter. I greatly admire Conrad and Lawrence and Forster. The smoking gun, I submit, is modernism—that moment when literature retreated from the accessible style that had made it such a popular form and turned inward, to the exploration of consciousness. In the hands of James, Joyce, Proust and Virginia Woolf, literature became a means of registering states of mind rather than telling a story."

Immediately it should be said of course that writers write novels, while critics invent and name literary movements. Modernism was not invented by Proust or Joyce; what they created were *Swann's Way* and *Ulysses*. Second, let's not mistake rhetorical hyperbole for reality; there never existed a Big Bang literary "moment" when a critical edict was issued, demanding that "literature retreat from the accessible," or else! Indeed, as Atlas acknowledges, at the same time that James and Joyce were producing their complicated texts, other writers were still writing more straightforward novels. Third, is it really true that all novels before the modernists were so readily accessible to the reading public? Works of Sterne, Melville, George Eliot? Hardly. Finally, and perhaps most important, that last damning complaint aired by Mr. Atlas, concerning absence of storytelling, is deeply misguided. That a tale is told in a new way, or an action is rendered in an innovative fashion, does not necessarily mean that a writer is giving up on story. The great twentieth-century writers were not after all minimalist technicians or experimental theorists like many of our contemporaries, who care little about the actual story, or are determinedly anti-story, believing that this is the next step of the avant-garde.

On the contrary, the stories narrated by James, Joyce, and Proust are among the most memorable in the history of fiction. Who does not remember the deep betrayals and jealousies of Swann, the comic but poignant Dublin wanderings of cuckolded Leopold Bloom, the bloodcurdling "civilized" cruelties inflicted on James's Isabel Archer or Maggie Verver? The fact that those novelists exhibited literary voices of unique sensibility did not deter them from "storytelling," in their own manner. Seeing a story from a whole new perspective, registering a familiar action by means of an intensified use of language, producing intricate singular sentences that demand a fully alerted mind, all this could only freshen a reader's interest in story, not deaden it. And besides, was not all the new heightened attention to language and *to the way the story was rendered* an inevitable development from the great realist himself, Flaubert?

And is it not noteworthy that the one great European modernist omitted from the journalist's critique is Franz Kafka? (In his place is Virginia Woolf, who frequently failed in her experiments with language and the novel, creating a confusing maze rather than a refocused clarity.) The reason for the omission of Kafka is obvious: his prose style is simple, straightforward, easy to understand. No problem of inaccessibility there, on the surface, and therefore that master didn't fit Mr. Atlas's narrow dogma. Of course difficulty exists in Kafka, but it resides elsewhere, at the heart of the matter, in the novel's meaning. A "traditional" story becomes in his hands a seductive and terrifying enigma of resonance and beauty, a Liszt sonata in the hands of Horowitz. In other words, the refreshening crafted here has less to do with prose style, and more to do with story and interpretation. Ambiguity, rather than certitude; open-endedness, rather than closure; narrator bewilderment, rather than authority. These qualities formed the mindset of his protagonists, and also the responses of his readers. The result was a new drama of fear and nightmare, accessible on the surface, puzzling at the depths.

The early-twentieth-century novelists were indeed telling a story, but that story involved the history of intimacy and progress of authenticity as much as anything external. That is, unlike the nineteenth-century writers who sought to paint a broad social and political canvas, covering public manners and morals, these modernists concentrated on a more inward rendering of events, the candid tale of how the individual registers the familiar or bizarre in his inner life. The reason for this, to my mind, had to do with authenticity; more and more the writer wanted to do away with publicly received wisdom and pious platitudes, and get at a more personal and honest response. What does it *feel like* to wander about your beloved Dublin, in the space of twenty-four hours, and wonder about your wife at home with another man? What exactly does it *feel like* to enter into a living nightmare, an authoritarian court which has no exits and has issued no charges, but which prosecutes you nevertheless for some awful act of wrongdoing? In order for those modern stories to be felt with new force and persuasive power, the reader had to feel, along with the protagonist, the intensity of the moment, the palpability of the event; authenticity was all. Each sentence, each paragraph, each thought carried a new weight now for the novelist. Once again, the footprints of Flaubert can be seen.

Plots often became paragraphs, in which small circles of thought and bits of action percolated, steamed; story was now borne along in two parallel lines, you might say, in this microactivity as well as the more conventional macrodevelopment. Did this mean a more focused concentration incumbent upon the reader? Yes. Was there more going on now, more textured activity within a smaller unit of space and time? Absolutely. But rapt attention, tenacious reading, could bring richer reward. A page of Proust, a paragraph of Joyce or James—or one of Bellow in our time— would afford large pleasure, sudden insight. Hence the lesser attention paid to plot as we knew it, and the keener interest in "seeing" and "hear- ing" the smaller units. Obviously the burden upon the reader, and the critic, grew under the new writerly vision.

But it is not surprising after all that the journalist here would protest against these writers, as impatient or closed-minded readers have protested for years. Or that Mr. Atlas did not want to take the old masters along for his "airline" or "vacation" reading. Why work hard, as a reader, when you could more easily castigate the writer for making you work so hard? This latest "Philistine Manifesto," as Philip Roth called it, is one that appears every few years in the popular press, but, coming from the Bellow biogra- pher, is all the more depressing for its source, and symbolism.

If the Atlas essay is just another sign of the anti-intellectualism that lingers in the popular American mind, it is also a sign of how far removed the journalist is from the actual reading of a literary text and the serious desire to understand the creative artist. In this regard he rather surpris- ingly joins some academicians, for example certain deconstructionists, certain feminists, who too frequently remove themselves from the real lit- erary demands and pleasures of dealing seriously with contemporary lit- erature in the cause of pursuing such higher realms as theory and politics. By "seriously" I mean with an open-minded intelligence, literary knowl- edge and flexibility, a training in taste and love of literature, and a crucial desire to know and understand the creative artist and his or her aims in a particular work. That is, the true critic wants to be part of a tacit part- nership with the writer, not forsaking his critical sense but not abandon- ing the writer either. Without the one where would the other be—if we think, along with Virginia Woolf, that the best critic was also the ideal reader?

Among the very small group of contemporary critics who have kept that unique partnership alive and well in their work (and person) is William Pritchard. When you read him on poetry or prose, you feel al- ways the activity of wanting to understand Frost or Larkin, Updike or Powell, as much as the activity of the critical act itself, measuring and crit- icizing the text in question. For in Pritchard we have a critic who listens in to the frequencies of the writer first and foremost, alert and attentive to the literary voice he is hearing, rather than a critic who is using the writer and his poem or novel as a launching pad for his own self-interested agenda. And that "listening" is crucial, for it implies Pritchard's belief in a creative partnership: the critic becomes a kind of helpful co-pilot to the author (and reader), rather than a cocksure stunt pilot flying solo in his own stratosphere of private theory, leaving the author (and work) below on the tarmac, alone and wondering. Listening in, reading closely, hearing a writer's voice, takes a cultivated patience, a trained ear and eye, common sense, and an underrated mettle—especially in this era of critical narcissism. In sum, listening in means placing the highest value on the writer and his words, on giving full due to *his or her* creative play, not the critic's.

Listening in means making observations like this, from "Larkin's Presence": "Along with sex, the richest 'elsewhere' in Larkin's experience was American jazz, even as he listened to plenty of it. . . . Larkin and Amis may have had better ears than any other recent English writers (or is it just that my own ear is tuned to them?) and I can't believe it had nothing to do with how much jazz, Pee Wee Russell and the rest, they listened to."

Or this, from "Ear Training": "With Hemingway, who—unlike Shakespeare—leaves out rather than puts in, aggressive and all-too-confident ways of understanding . . . get in the way of good reading. They do so by providing crude and hasty ways for us to avoid what we should be engaged in; namely, with *listening* to the rhythms and manner of presentation, the 'feel' of the scene. 'A bass jumped, making a circle in the water. . . . It felt warm in the sharp chill of the morning': how could anyone who really listens to those sentences want to go on and talk about rejection of the father or retreating from reality? Why would they not want instead to talk about the beautiful sequence Hemingway has created here, from the father rowing, to the sun coming up over the hills, to the jumping bass, to Nick trailing his hand in the water and feeling it 'warm in the sharp chill in the morning.' Why would they not want to engage with what Frost says all poetry is about—'Performance and prowess and feats of association.'"

Would that all writers received such a close hearing from a critic. (Or such a warm welcome from an academician, in an English department, when one is a visiting writer. Unlike many professors, Pritchard actually likes hanging around writers, engaging them in literary conversation and befriending them. Perhaps this accounts in part for his delicate critical sense, and deep respect for the creative act.) Naturally a good deal of this tuning in comes, I think—apart from his training at Amherst (with Theodore Baird) and Harvard (with Reuben Brower) and his tuning in to Frost's shrewd ideas about poetry—from the same basic love of literature that has always motivated the creative artist. For is it not true that in all the splendid critics of recent times, figures like Edmund Wilson, Philip Rahv, Randall Jarrell, T. S. Eliot, one senses a hand reaching out to the writer, an attempt to ascend, by means of the critical act, to the poet's or novelist's level of creative passion? Interestingly, you will not sense this aspiration in some other notable critics, such as Irving Howe or Lionel Trilling, who are more on the lookout for a political idea or ideological position lurking in a book. Political reading, so popular at the moment, did not invent itself *ex nihilo*, though the sophisticated versions of it practiced by Howe and Trilling were very different from current dogmatic examples.

We are talking here about a serious devotion to the study of literature, not a dabbling judgment of it in order to determine whether you can take it along on vacations or whether you can dust off generalizations about Modernist Movements. Now "devotion" to literature may sound like a term of religious hyperbole, but I take it as a simple truth. Serious readers are devoted fans of real books; otherwise you cannot come to terms with the likes of Joyce and Proust and Faulkner. Instead you will find them "abstruse," too difficult, and condemn them as "boring." Could one really conceive of Wilson or Jarrell, Kermode or Rahv being anything less than devoted, sacredly devoted, to the great writers?

But especially in this day and age, in this America—our Giant Discount Store of pop magazine reading and pulp fiction, PBS and NPR "culture," mindless movies and endless movie chat, TV numbing and bestseller dumbing (not merely the mass adulation of Stephen King or John Grisham, but, worse, their adoption in some college courses and the reviews of them in the *New York Times* or *New York Review of Books*)—in such an era of vulgarity and entertainment distractions, it takes devotion, not anything less, to continue serious reading. Devotion, to preserve the tight circle of fellowship between reader and writer. Devotion, to keep literary culture alive. Right now it is barely flickering.

As I have implied earlier, it has been of little help that numerous teachers of literature have abandoned that ambition. Instead they have sought an agenda which, while not unworthy in itself, has been overtly politicized: to expand the canon, to teach courses in minority literature and literature by women, to instruct the young in theory. Unfortunately, while performing all this historical revision, they have insinuated into young minds a serious mistrust and devaluation of many major male authors, introducing a new way of reading their works—always searching for the subversive subtexts beneath the slippery surface. In short, they have exchanged literary goals for political goals, more or less writing off "mainstream" general literature as dangerously outdated, male-prejudiced, furtively ideological. Rather than promoting a full appreciation and discipline of serious reading, their mission has turned—in various courses, in tenure appointments or new hirings—to point out the wrongs of white males (dead authors or living profs). Democracy, not excellence; uncovering subtexts rather than understanding surfaces; employing coded jargon for basic English; reevaluating classic male writers and branding them with demonizing marks (chauvinist, racist); all this has gone into creating a new atmosphere in departments of English, one in which too often the attraction of reading great works has been replaced by the mission of reading correct works.

So too with book journalism, just a few decades ago a high arbiter of literary taste. Where once the likes of Howe, Wilson, Macdonald, Rahv—critic-reviewers and polemicists who argued out of a passion for literature—formed a varied but consensual literary ground, now literary journalism has fallen into the hands of such avowedly middlebrow readers as Mr. Atlas who complain of difficult reading and boring modernists like Joyce or Proust. Certainly we still have exceptions to the rule, but for the most part that public ground of sound judgment and able direction has given way to an intellectual quagmire. No wonder that the good general magazines—like the *Atlantic*, the *New Republic*, the *New Yorker*—are sometimes read less for their literary muscle than for other reasons. Just as the book awards now seem too often a bad joke, given the odd choices and the nearly complete absence of consensus as to where excellence lies. Although Matthew Arnold (and others) long ago decried the lowering of cultural standards, the present situation goes far beyond what he or any of the older critics could have imagined.

The art of serious reading is something like the art of serious writing, an exacting endeavor that demands years of turning discipline into a pleasure, a steady self-training in preserving the solitary habit on into adulthood. Surely the only worthwhile motive for such an eccentric pursuit has to be love, love as a disciplined passion. Some fifty years ago, in 1947, E. M. Forster considered the relationship between the critic and the artist in his essay "On the *Raison d'Être* of Criticism in the Arts." He concluded that though criticism might help the artist in two small ways—in providing him with "good company," and in helping him "over details, niggling details, minutiae of style"—there remained a gulf between criticism and creativity. Yet there was one saving point. "The only activity which can establish such a *raison d'être* is love. However cautiously, with whatever reservations, after whatever purifications, we must come back to love. That alone raises us to the co-operation with the artist which is the sole reason for our aesthetic pilgrimage. That alone promises spiritual parity." Critics today could do worse than to read Forster's lucid essays, and to heed him here, about the nature of the partnership.

Or have we come now to the end of the era of the serious reader? Truthfully, all signs would point in that direction. Undergraduates in good colleges such as Dartmouth, where I teach, have read very little, and will read less when they leave school. Computer screens are replacing the printed page for many students, literature hours giving way to hours of cybertalk. The lure and ease of screenwriting frequently absorb the careers of young talented writers. Libraries more and more are giving up on the world of books and stack-browsing for an electronic world of computer programs, discs, and video terminals. English professors are more intrigued with learning the new version of Windows or showing the latest Jane Austen movie than with rereading Austen or Hardy. "Literary" journalists inform us how boring are the great masters of the twentieth century. Although these are but a collection of random impressions, they suggest an obvious path.

So what are the dwindling few who are still hooked on the old archaic habit left with? In the early part of the century and at age thirty-four, in his essay "Of Reading" Proust offered this: "The indolent mind can obtain nothing from pure solitude since it is incapable of setting its creativity in motion. But the loftiest conversation, the most pressing advice, would be of absolutely no use to it, since they cannot produce directly this original activity. What is necessary, then, is an intervention which, while coming from another takes place in our innermost selves, which is indeed the impetus of another mind, but received in the midst of solitude. Now we have seen that this was precisely the definition of reading, and that it fitted reading only."

What hope and belief in the innermost self! What solace (and energy exchange) in solitude! But are these values relevant any longer? For the ragtag army that still travels to the music of books, splendid, serious books, the answer is yes. But the far greater majority of this citizenry heeds a different, simpler tune, and is headed in a very different direction, where the play and power of written words count for little. Post-literate, video-literate, and pre-literate, the new majority constitutes the expanding future, giddy with gigabytes, heady with an Arriflex, high on rappers' lyrics. Moreover, if the innermost self can't be shown on the wide silver screen or revealed on the Internet, then does it really exist?

In the new "downloaded" world, is there room for reflection, solitude, interior literary intervention? For the subtle responses of a well-tuned reader to a novel radiant with literary imagination, irony, ambiguity, or one combative with vital negative energy? Room for literary complexity or wit, a Proustian/Joycean frequency so ravishing to the ears of a devoted reader, so "boring" to the journalist? Are not these qualities the very enemy of the forces that rule the day now—oversimplicity, fashion, political cant, and moral piety? And yet the serious reader, along with his counterpart the serious novelist, is being defined as the odd man out.

At precisely the moment when literature may be of the most use for intelligent citizens in our society, as a spiritual guide to the secular perplexed and a lighthouse for complex inner truth, it seems to be fading. For never before has a society been so firebombed by noise and distraction, so drowned in information and illusion. All the more need for truth telling, clarity, reflective quiet, the pleasures and challenges of literary reading.

And no matter how hard anyone on the Internet strives to recreate literature for the wired age, it will be a long, long while before the likes of a Joyce or Bellow produces a *Ulysses* or *Herzog* on a Web site.

W. E. Kennick

Who Needs Literary Theory?

There are moments when it is impossible not to feel that
literary criticism has got out of hand.

Anthony Powell

A critic ought to trust his own nose, like the hunting dog,
and if he lets any kind of theory or principle distract him
from that, he is not doing his work.

William Empson

I WAS BORN too late to be aware of the famous exchange in the pages of
Scrutiny between René Wellek and F. R. Leavis in 1937, but when, some
fifteen years later and as a young teacher of philosophy interested in aesthetics, I caught up with it, I remember being all on Leavis's side. Why
should he feel obliged to state his "assumptions [as a critic] more explicitly and defend them systematically"? Why should a critic be expected to
do this any more than a mathematician or a lawyer or a painter or a tennis player? Leavis was right to decline Wellek's invitation: "I am not a
philosopher," and "Literary criticism and philosophy seem to me to be
quite distinct and different kinds of disciplines." They are distinct and different kinds of disciplines, and there is no reason why Leavis should have
felt constrained to become a philosopher in addition to being a literary
critic.

The literary theorists, however, see it differently. According to them
the systematic defense of one's assumptions as a critic—which is to say,
literary theory—is not something *de trop* but *de rigueur*. How so? Three
lines of reasoning, all unsound, are given in answer to this question: the

Only Reasonable Alternative Argument, the Theory and Practice Argument, and the Nature of Literature Argument.

1. *The Only Reasonable Alternative.* The only reasonable alternative to a theory-based criticism is unbridled subjectivism, literary chit-chat, dilettantism, a liberal humanist approach to literature, or genteel amateurism (the name of Sir Walter Raleigh, the Oxford professor, not the Elizabethan courtier, is ominously mentioned). Of course, we are all opposed to mere chitchat and the rest of this farrago of despicable alternatives. Therefore, a theory-based criticism is all that is left to us.

The argument is formally valid but unsound. The first premise is patently false. The only alternative to theory-based criticism is not amateurish chitchat about books. The very existence of 'anti-theoretical' critics like T. S. Eliot, F. R. Leavis, and Lionel Trilling, or, in our own day, Helen Vendler, Hugh Kenner, and William H. Pritchard, gives the lie to the major premise of this argument. By no stretch of the imagination, in the light of no theory, can these critics reasonably be branded amateurish dilettantes.

2. *Theory and Practice.* In a nutshell, practical criticism is, tautologically, a practice, and every practice presupposes a theory. *Ergo* . . . Conceding, if only for the sake of argument, that a practice is conceivable only in relation to a set of assumptions (that is, granting the major premise of the argument), still the conclusion drawn does not follow; it is a non sequitur. Not every set of assumptions amounts to a theory. To think otherwise is to use the word 'theory' in a Pickwickian way. In *Doing What Comes Naturally* (1989) Stanley Fish puts the point this way: "Am I following or enacting a theory when I stop for a red light, or use my American Express card, or rise to speak at a conference? Are you now furiously theorizing as you sit reading what I have to say? . . . Clearly it is possible to answer yes to all these questions, but just as clearly that answer will render the notion of 'theory' . . . trivial." As Christopher Ricks points out in his *Essays in Appreciation,* to employ certain principles (Fish calls them rules of thumb) in critical practice is not *eo ipso* to invoke or apply a theory; and, to his credit, Wellek in his letter to Leavis clearly recognizes this distinction, for he isolates half a dozen or so principles that Leavis employed in *Revaluation* and calls for a theoretical defense of these. So the argument from practice to theory is, flatly, invalid.

A variant of it, however, might be—and Wellek may have had something of this sort in mind—that every practice or its assumed set of principles calls for or requires theoretical justification or defense. But this is simply false. Playing tennis or painting pictures calls for no theoretical defense at all. Can one even imagine such a defense? Most activities are justified on what are loosely called 'pragmatic', not theoretical, grounds. And the same goes for principles. One principle I employ in teaching philosophy is to try not to talk over the heads of my students; and the justification for it is simply that not to do so would be to undercut the larger effort of getting them to understand philosophy. The Theory and Practice Argument is therefore a total washout.

3. *The Nature of Literature.* Some proponents of theory hold that it is impossible for critics and students of literature not to have a literary theory. Terry Eagleton in his *Literary Theory* (1983) writes "without some kind of theory, however unreflective and implicit, we would not know what a 'literary work' was in the first place." The very term 'literature', it would appear, is, as some philosophers would say, 'theory-laden': without a theory or definition of literature it is impossible to pick out or identify works of literature. How so? Well, literature is not something "eternally given and immutable" (Is anything? And could it possibly help if it were?); it is "not a stable, well-defined entity," "not an unchanging object"; it "does not exist in the way insects do"; literature in the modern sense of the word is "an historically recent phenomenon: it was invented sometime around the turn of the eighteenth [nineteenth?] century"; "in eighteenth-century England, the concept of literature was not confined as it sometimes is today to 'creative' or 'imaginative' writing"; and so on. In short, literature is not what is sometimes called a natural kind and so needs to be defined or theoretically characterized.

At this point the argument usually stops. But not for Eagleton. He proceeds to examine several attempts to define literature, finds all of them wanting (as well he might, but for the wrong reasons), and concludes that literature does not exist "as a distinct, bounded object of knowledge," that "literature is an illusion"—and hence that "literary theory is an illusion too." Would that theory were so easily disposed of!

But all of this is a tissue of sophistry. Consider first Eagleton's idea that "literature is a recent historical invention." This is false; literature is at least as old as Homer. To appreciate this point, consider the question "Are numbers a recent historical invention?" According to Aristotle and Euclid a number is a multitude, plurality, or aggregate composed of units; hence the smallest number is 2. Zero and 1 are not numbers. (This view was also, incidentally, embraced by Husserl in his *Philosophie der Arithmetik* of 1891.) Are so-called irrational numbers numbers? Michael Stifel in his

Arithmetica Integra of 1544 says no: "That cannot be called a true number which is of such a nature as to lack precision. . . . Therefore, just as an infinite number is not a number, so an irrational number is a not a true number." And most mathematicians in the sixteenth and seventeenth centuries, for instance Pascal, denied that negative numbers are true numbers and regarded the subtraction of 4 from 0 as nonsense.

Were Aristotle and Euclid, Stifel and Pascal simply mistaken? No. Given what was meant by a number—and not just what they idiosyncratically meant by 'number'—0, ∞, $\sqrt{2}$, π, and -7 were not, and are not, numbers; given what we mean by 'number' they are.

But the fact that what we mean by 'number' is of relatively recent origin does not mean that numbers are of relatively recent origin. What we mean by a number has not changed (it makes no sense even to think of it as having changed, as Plato knew); but what we mean by 'number' has changed. And the same holds for literature: our concept of literature dates from around 1750, when 'literature' became the name of one of the fine arts.[1] But that does not mean that literature, as we understand the word, did not exist prior to 1750 or that it was invented around that date. Shakespeare did not have our notion of literature, and he could not even have thought of himself as producing literature (in our sense, obviously), that is, producing plays that properly belong in the same class as Tintoretto's *Christ before Pilot*, Michelangelo's *Moses*, Andrea Palladio's *Villa Rotonda*, and Claudio Monteverdi's *La favola d'Orfeo*. But this does not mean that his plays were not literature when he wrote them, any more than the fact that our notion of a white blood cell, a leukocyte, is of recent origin means that the ancient Egyptians did not have white blood cells.

Second, can literature be defined? That depends on what you mean by a definition. If you have in mind a list of those properties that all and only works of literature have in common and that constitute the logically necessary and sufficient conditions of something's being a work of literature—as being the brother of either of one's parents is what all and only uncles have in common and constitutes the necessary and sufficient conditions of being one's uncle—then the answer is no. But this is in no way peculiar to literature. As just about everybody knows, Wittgenstein pointed out that game cannot be so defined either. And neither can furniture. Words such as 'game', 'furniture', 'literature', and a host of others, unlike 'uncle', 'circle', or 'hexapod', were not introduced into the language, and are not taught to us, by means of definitions in the sense here understood. As in the case of games, we are taught what furniture is or what lit-

erature is by having sample works of furniture or of literature pointed out
to us and described, that is, by a process sometimes called 'denotative
definition' to mark it off from the kind here under scrutiny. What is literature? Well, the poems of Homer and Virgil, of Milton and Wordsworth,
the plays of Sophocles and Racine, of Shakespeare and Beckett, the novels
of Proust and George Eliot, of Dostoyevsky and Trollope; these and
things like them are called 'literature', whereas other things—and here
you can write your own list, for you know it as well as I do—are not called
'literature'. And if you know what is and is not called literature, and also
know what are the borderline cases (A blanket chest is a piece of furniture,
but is a coffin?), in short, if you know how to apply the word 'literature' as
everybody else applies it, including the theorists—for oddly, although
they disagree with one another about everything else, they don't disagree
about this!—and if you have a first-hand acquaintance with some works of
literature, then you know what literature is as well as it can be known.
And if Wittgenstein is right in saying that "*Essence* is expressed by grammar" and "Grammar tells what kind of object anything is," then you also
thereby know the 'timeless essence' or 'eternally given and immutable nature' of literature too.

Since literature is not defined in terms of a conjunction of logically
necessary and sufficient conditions (by what in some circles would be
called a theory of literature), it is relatively easy, as it is with proposed
definitions of art in aesthetics, to show that putative definitions of literature, of which there are many, are inadequate; and Eagleton has a picnic
showing their inadequacy in the first chapter of his *Literary Theory*. But
'literature' is not a theory-laden term; it is a perfectly ordinary term like
'furniture' or 'art' or 'religion', and to show that it has no adequate definition of the sort here under discussion is not, Eagleton to the contrary, to
show that literature is an illusion. Only the most 'logocentric' of theorists
could think otherwise. Hence, the argument for theory from the nature of
literature collapses.

A variant of it, put forward by Jefferson and Robey in their *Modern Literary Theory* (1982), is also a shambles. They hold, not that we all need a literary theory to recognize a work of literature in the first place, but that the
"academic study of literature" or *"literary scholarship"* needs such a theory.
They have the odd idea that a demand "can reasonably be made of any academic discipline: that it should provide an adequate definition of its subject-matter," and they are under the impression that "almost every other
academic discipline can say in exact general terms what its subject-matter

is." Where these people have been I cannot imagine. I can think of few demands less reasonable than the demand that philosophy, for one, should provide an adequate definition of its subject-matter! When it comes to defining its subject-matter philosophy comes forth with such gems as "Philosophy is human thought become self-conscious" (Simon Blackburn), "Philosophy is thinking about thinking" (Lord Quinton), "To philosophize is to ask 'Why are there essents rather than nothing?'" (Heidegger), "Philosophy . . . is a voluntary living amid ice and mountain heights" (Nietzsche). There are thousands of such definitions of philosophy, all of them absolutely worthless for the purposes Jefferson and Robey have in mind. I have been teaching philosophy for over forty years and have never tried to define the subject for my students, other than by example, and I do not believe I have been derelict in my duty. Students learn what philosophy is in the one way worth learning it, namely, by engaging with it at first hand. And surely that is the best way to learn what literature is too. The discipline of literary studies that Armstrong and Robey have in mind—which I find distinctly uninviting—may need a theory of literature, but the study and criticism of literature has no such need.

So far I have been proceeding as if it were perfectly clear to everyone what a literary theory is—or, indeed, what a theory is. Literary theorists beg this question, to their intellectual peril as we shall see.

First, theories come in all logical sizes, as it were: a theory may be about an individual person, place, or thing; about some but not all members of a class; or about all members of a class. Literary theories are, or purport to be, universal: they are meant to cover all of literature—or, as in the case of narratology or a theory of tragedy, all of a certain genre of literature. So much, I think, is clear. What is unclear is the purported relation between a general theory of literature and individual works of literature and their criticism.

Individual works of literature stand to a quasi-scientific theory as individual fruit flies, peas, or white rats stand to genetic theory; they are just evidence or data. To a quasi-philosophical theory, they are merely instances or examples. In either case, it is the theory that counts—that is privileged or hegemonized, as theorists like to say. The structuralist literary theorist Tzvetan Todorov puts the point this way in his *Poétique*: "the individual text is simply the means by which one can describe the properties of literature in general. . . . [E]ach work is regarded only as the manifestation of a far more general abstract structure, of which it is only one of the many possible incarnations." This is diametrically opposed to the approach of practical criticism (the only kind of criticism pertinent to this discussion), for which the individual work is all-important.

Stanley Fish, however, sees the relation between theory and criticism in a somewhat different light. He accepts a definition of theory according to which it is an attempt to govern the interpretation of particular works by appealing to an account of interpretation in general (what E. D. Hirsch calls a "general hermeneutics"). Such an account of interpretation in general is not, as Fish sees it, the sort of thing one finds in Annette Barnes's *On Interpretation*, however, but the provision of a general rule or algorithm, similar to the rule for standard multiplication, such that any two or more critics employing the rule must come up with the very same interpretation. For reasons we need not go into, Fish rightly finds this to be a logically impossible goal; and hence finds theory in this sense to be impossible too, and thus to have no consequences for critical practice. But theory is obviously not impossible, because it is actual: *ab esse ad posse valet consequentia;* hence, there must be something amiss with Fish's definition of theory. If his point is that the notion of interpretation does not entail any literary theory, that no theory can have exclusive rights to interpretation, it is a point well taken; for it raises the interesting question whether, and how, a literary theory does, or even can, have consequences for practical criticism.

As a statement or set of statements in the indicative or assertoric mode, no theory entails anything with respect to critical practice. This is simply an instance of the well-known principle attributed to Hume that 'Is' does not imply 'Ought'. And so Stanley Fish is right when he says: "theory is not consequential [for practice] even when the practitioner is himself a theorist. Indeed, the practitioner may cease to be a theorist or may awake one morning (as I predict we all will) to find that theory has passed from the scene and still continue his life's work without ever missing a beat." Any literary theory is compatible with a practical criticism that is not theory driven, that is, that does not consist in the application of theory. But, although theory does not entail practice, it can be applied; which leaves us with the question of *which* theory to apply.

Like philosophy, literary theory presents us with an *embarras de richesses:* there are more theories than anyone knows what to do with. In *Beyond Deconstruction* (1985) Howard Felperin expresses the embarrassment in this way: "In so far as theory turns out to be only so many theories . . . the claim to authority of any particular theory must be so limited and relative as to amount to hardly more than a rhetorical gesture."

Should a reader wish to avail herself of a literary theory to guide her critical practice, how is she meant to choose from the various formalist (several kinds, including the New Criticism), structuralist, Freudian (at least four kinds), Marxist (at least five kinds), and poststructuralist theories at her disposal? There is no super-theory to appeal to, and, unless she is willing—which most theorists are not, although there are some pitiful attempts at this in the manuals, for instance in *Modern Literary Theory*—to commit herself to a philosophical vetting of the alternatives, she appears to be left with simply picking something that appeals to her, for whatever reason. Unless, of course, she wishes to adopt them all—or as many as strike her fancy. But is that possible?

Realizing that "modern literary theory is anything but monolithic" but "consists of a multiplicity of competing theories," Jefferson and Robey are of the opinion that these theories "frequently contradict one another"; that they do not "simply relate to different aspects of the subject, and can therefore all be added together to form a single comprehensive vision." But other theorists are not convinced of this. Eagleton holds that "a psychoanalytical reading of [*Sons and Lovers*] need not be an alternative to a social [read 'Marxist'] interpretation of it," which implies that at least some psychoanalytic and some Marxist theories are logically compatible. And although literary theories are simply not stated with sufficient clarity for us to decide this simple logical issue with confidence, I am inclined not only to agree with Eagleton but to extend his generosity to all literary theories: they are logically compatible with one another, and, although I cannot, for largely aesthetic reasons, imagine them all being added together to form "a single comprehensive vision," I see no logical obstacle to someone's taking his cue from Marx's famous description, in *The German Ideology*, of life under communism: being a formalist today and a Marxist tomorrow, or a New Critic in the morning, a Freudian in the afternoon, a structuralist in the evening, and a deconstructionist after dinner—and all of this without contradicting himself or making the least alteration in his practice as a literary critic.

One reason for my confidence in the compatibility of alternative literary theories lies in the fact that most of them (structuralist, Freudian, Marxist, deconstructionist) are not specifically addressed to literature to begin with but are applications to literature of more global theories having to do with diverse but coexistent phenomena, such as language, social history, and abnormal psychology. To try to find logical incompatibility between such enterprises would be like trying to find it between, say, the atomic theory, the theory of evolution, and the heliocentric theory.

Further, the very fact that a literary theory is just a special application or case of a larger theory, frequently, if not always, shifts attention from the work to the pathology or depravity (sexism, racism, homophobia, anti-Semitism . . .) of the author, and leads to the treating of literary works as something in addition to or other than works of literature; as simply 'texts' in structuralist and deconstructionist theories, something on all fours with a bank statement, a bus ticket, a telephone directory, a birth certificate, and anything else written—or even unwritten, if you are an adept of the metaphysics of *archi-écriture*—including itself;[2] or as just a sign or symptom of the workings of the author's Unconscious, in some versions of psychoanalytic theory; or as merely an expression of the author's personal 'ideology' or that of her class, in some versions of Marxist theory.[3] As a result, literary interpretation becomes something analogous to medical diagnosis, and this preoccupation with the genesis—psychological, political, historical, economic, ideological—of the work carries over into fruitless speculation about the causes of readers' responses. But criticism, unlike medicine, is not interested in causes and effects. The causes of a reader's responses—boredom, confusion, exhilaration, you name it—are of no more interest to a critic than they are to a mathematician or a chemist. That I am always reminded of a great-uncle and great-aunt on my mother's side by Dickens's Joe and Mrs. Joe Gargery is a reader's response to *Great Expectations* that doubtless has its causes, but this response is of no interest to anyone, including me, and the same goes for any other response conceived as an effect. In criticism, as elsewhere, people tend to confuse reasons and causes. Both explain (which is the source of the confusion), but there are important differences between them. Briefly, reasons justify, causes at best excuse; reasons are given, causes are discovered; reasons are good or bad, causes are not. Only reasons are of interest in criticism.

One of the staples of literary theory is the idea that every 'text' is susceptible to more than one interpretation; which often leads to the view that the 'meaning' of any text is indeterminate and that the reader has to supply a meaning, thereby being the real creator of the literary work. But the basic premise that every text cries out for interpretation is mistaken. Most of the time, in reading and in conversation, we are not interpreting. To say that we are and must be is self-defeating. For any interpretation is itself a 'text' that either does or does not require interpretation. If it does, then its interpretation also requires an interpretation, and the result is a vicious infinite regress. If it does not require interpretation, then the initial principle is false. Take your pick. The idea that whenever we are confronted with a 'text' we have to interpret it, because it *can* mean something other than what we take it to mean, is like that kind of philosophical skepticism that holds that because we can be in doubt we are in doubt. But Wittgenstein has put this error to rest: that we can *imagine* a doubt is not to say we are in doubt (*Philosophical Investigations* #84). Likewise, because it is possible for us to imagine a 'text' having a meaning other than the one we take it to have does not mean that we are interpreting that text.

And what does interpreting a work of literature have to do with meaning anyhow? The usual view is taken to be truistic: that's just what interpretation is, saying what a text means. But this, I think, is a mistake. In Chapter 21 of Trollope's *The Bertrams* we read: "I trust that Miss Todd, umquhile of the valley of Jehosophat . . . ." What does 'umquhile' mean? This is answered by a dictionary definition of the word. In reading Chapter 1 of the same author's *The Way We Live Now* we read *Nullius addictus jurare in verba magistri.* What does this mean? We answer by giving a translation. In *King Lear,* II.iv, Lear says, "If only to go warm were gorgeous, / Why, nature needs not what thou gorgeous wear'st, / Which scarcely keeps thee warm." What does he mean? We answer by giving a paraphrase. About parts of literary works, these questions—and others, having to do with ambiguity, metaphor, and the like, that can be easily devised—make sense. But, although 'meaning' has many meanings, when you ask for the meaning of a whole work the sense of the term seems to vanish. What is the meaning of the *Iliad,* or of *Middlemarch?* What is one asking for? What are we meant to answer? How does one finish such sentences as "The meaning of the *Iliad* is . . . ," "The meaning of *Middlemarch* is . . . "? These questions might be about the *point* of a work—Is it a satire? a ghost story? a love poem? a condemnation of superstition?—and that too could be called its meaning, and answers to such questions would be interpretations. But beyond that, which is where we are, what is it that anyone can be asking for when he asks for the 'meaning' of a whole work? I have no idea. Moreover, I think the question is rarely if ever asked; the idea that an interpretation of a literary work is an account of its meaning is, I suspect, a critical fiction. In describing the teaching of Mansfield Forbes at Cambridge during the first quarter of this century, D. H. Hard-ing wrote: "He took us with him into a poem . . . while he worked out the most effective rhythms and phrasings, changes of tempo, pitch of voice— all stemming from and adding to one's grasp of what the poem was doing." This, although it does not tell us in any interesting detail what interpretation is, strikes me as a more authentic description of interpretation—an account of what the poem is doing—than that of interpretation as an account of what the poem means. (It is also closer to what we count as interpretation in music.)

Whether literary theory is science, philosophy, or some *tertium quid* is sometimes raised. Some literary theorists (formalists, structuralists, Marxists, and Freudians come to mind) have claimed scientific standing for their work. Such claims, however, are at least questionable and turn to some extent on what we think of a scientific theory as being. Although this is a matter of some dispute among scientists and philosophers of science, no literary theory, I think, will satisfy any moderately rigorous notion of scientific theory, such as that embodied in the hypothetico-deductive model, or meet even more relaxed empirical conditions of testability and self-correction that any theory claiming scientific standing must surely meet. Marxist theory may be *Wissenschaft* but it is not science, and psychoanalytic theory, which Freud thought of as exactly analogous to physics, has been shown by Popper, Wittgenstein, Crews, Grünbaum, and others to be nothing of the kind. Although some literary theories may aspire to science, this is an aspiration none of them has met.

Literary theorists also tend to be of two minds about whether what they do is philosophy. Some wag has said that literary theory is just the practice of philosophy without a license; and there is something to this. Theorists usually have little or no training in philosophy to speak of, and some of them have very odd ideas of what philosophy is. Philosophy, to be sure, is a house of many mansions, and all sorts of intellectual endeavors are called philosophy; so that if literary theory is expelled from science it would not be entirely inappropriate to welcome it to philosophy; or to see it, as Felperin does, as occupying some *terrain vague* between science and philosophy, as a new mode of discourse falling "between the compartmentalizations of the classical disciplines." But all of this speculation is academic in the bad sense, and the reason for it is not hard to find and goes to the root of the matter. I have said that literary theorists beg the question of what literary theory is, which is really the question of to what question(s) literary theory is meant to be the answer. Until this problem is solved, literary theory may be a source of amusement or a living for those so inclined, but it will fall foul of the great Kant's warning: "To know what questions may reasonably be asked is already a great and necessary proof of sagacity and insight. For if a question is absurd in itself and calls for an answer where none is required, it not only brings shame on the propounder of the question, but may betray an incautious listener into absurd answers, thus presenting, as the ancients said, the ludicrous spectacle of one man milking a he-goat and the other holding a sieve underneath."[4]

Notes

1. The best non-tendentious account of this that I know of is given by Paul Oskar Kristeller in his "The Modern System of the Arts" that appeared in the *Journal of the History of Ideas* in 1951 and 1952. It can be found reprinted in his *Renaissance Thought and the Arts* and, without its 278 footnotes, in the second edition of my *Art and Philosophy*.

2. That structuralist and deconstructionist theories are themselves 'texts' and hence apply to themselves is often conveniently forgotten. But, alas, if you try to apply Derrida's or Lacan's theory of texts to itself, it self-destructs—or, shall we say, self-deconstructs. Derrida's text itself—his grammatology, as well as his *Of Grammatology*—becomes the plaything of *différance*, radically and irremediably indeterminate, undercutting itself; and, given Lacan's vertiginous idea that every word is a Freudian slip, every word of Lacan is a Freudian slip, and he is saying nothing.

3. That all literature is political or ideological, that it expresses an agenda [*sic*] of the author or of some group or class to which the author belongs, is an idea often found in literary theory. But it is either vacuous, because such words as 'political' and 'ideological' are tendentiously used in such a way that it makes no sense to say that a work of literature is non-political or non-ideological (in which case, to say that it is political is also to say nothing informative), or it is manifestly false. As Freud said, a cigar is sometimes just a cigar; and a poem is sometimes just a poem, too.

4. I am told by those in a position to know that the rage for theory has abated, and, if that is so, this essay may have the appearance of flogging a dead horse. That is as may be. I have no interest in academic fashions or politics, but only in logic.

Patricia Meyer Spacks

Reading Dr. Johnson

A Confession

I AM A PROFESSOR of English and I love my profession. To say that now is unfashionable, both because current discourse tends to focus on what's wrong with the profession and because it seems rather tasteless to proclaim one's pleasure in a set of activities that many talented young people these days would like to engage in too but find no opportunity to enjoy. Still, it's true: I love my profession.

The ground of my profession is reading, which proliferates into writing and teaching. Reading both focuses my endeavors and instructs me in the nature of my work, however I conceive that work. I want to illustrate these assertions by concentrating, rather lengthily, on ten words of Samuel Johnson's—by way of introduction to a confession of faith in the profession of English at this historical moment.

First, my ten words, seven of them single syllables, from the end of a long sentence in Johnson's "Preface to Shakespeare" (1765): *"the mind can only repose on the stability of truth."*[1] What makes this assertion so moving, at least to me? Let me surmise, first by removing the words temporarily from their immediate verbal context in order to focus on some of their larger imaginative functions.

"The mind can only repose on the stability of truth." At first sight, this may seem a rather complacent observation about an orderly system in which truth remains single, stable, and graspable by the human mind. In fact, the clause delineates not actuality but conceptual possibility. Although it posits equivalence between "stability" and "truth," it holds forth no promise that any particular mind will ever attain that stability for which it implicitly longs.

Conspicuously lacking in mental repose, Johnson himself led a life of self-reproach. His prayers and meditations show him blaming himself for laziness, for late sleeping, for insufficient attentiveness to religious duties. He confessed to Boswell his lifelong tendency to depression. He worried about going mad. His moral essays, like much of his poetry, insist that desire always exceeds the possibility of satisfaction. Both his direct and indirect revelations of his psychic condition suggest painful unrest rather than equilibrium.

Equilibrium, though, is what he speaks for. At the emphatic midpoint of the Johnsonian assertion, the verb *repose* has the poignancy of the contrary-to-fact. One can imagine other possible valuable mental actions: the mind might *strive*, say, or *grow*. It performs such actions more easily than it can repose. The superficially more modest notion of rest articulates an ideal remote from human actuality, challenging the value of ordinary notions of energy and expansion. From the perspective of repose, energy that asserts itself by constant activity becomes mere distraction. Repose, in the immediate context, implies serenity rather than mere quiescence, an achievement rather than a passive state: the peace that passeth understanding. The ambiguous placement of *only*—has the mind no alternative to repose, given the presence of truth? Or is truth the only place the mind can repose?—challenges the reader to ponder the conceivable conditions for repose as well as the imagined nature of the experience.

The special quality of the mind's repose depends on the stability that enables it. As the statement's single four-syllable word, the term itself acquires emphasis, intensified by its rolling iambic rhythm. The state of being it designates—solidity, permanence—opposes the flux of human experience. And this solidity depends on association with truth, truth all alone, without an article, not *a* truth or *the* truth, not the truth of accumulated facts, but universal, absolute truth, awe-inspiring in its permanence.

If the verb *repose* has the force of metaphor, evoking the physicality and steadiness of rest even while grasping it as action rather than passive state, the three nouns (*mind, stability, truth*), richly implicated with one another, draw on the different energies of abstraction—energies that eighteenth-century prose forces you to respect even if you feel uncomfortable with the abstract. A mind belonging to no one; stability independent of the physical; ungraspable truth—these vast generalizations organize the utterance. Their authority extends to the assertion as a whole, implicitly claiming its status as a fragment of larger truth.

This collection of fairly obvious facts and associations only begins to account for the power of Johnson's utterance taken in isolation. I have emphasized relatively self-evident aspects of the clause and of the attitudes it conveys. The confidence implicit in the simple vocabulary, the magnitude of the ideas condensed into the abstractions, the promise of peace held forth: all contribute to emotional effect. Yet they also appear easily vulnerable to late-twentieth-century debunking. How can we believe in peace? If psychic peace is indeed attainable, doesn't it necessarily depend on selfish and dangerous exclusions? Such large ideas as those Johnson traffics in surely imply the ignoring of difficult small facts. Absolute truth, many now believe, must constitute an absolute fiction.

To some extent, the line's immediate context counteracts such objection by locating abstractions in a literary rather than a metaphysical situation. "Truth," in Johnson's rendition, belongs to Shakespeare and contrasts with "wonder," which lesser writers readily arouse in desiring readers. Wonder is easier than truth, to invent and to accept. But it lacks staying power. "The irregular combinations of fanciful invention may delight awhile by that novelty of which the common satiety of life sends us all in quest; but the pleasures of sudden wonder are soon exhausted, and the mind can only repose on the stability of truth" ("Preface," 61–62). All of us, Johnson points out, seek excitement to compensate for the tedium of ordinary existence. Truth, inexhaustible, alone provides satisfaction, in contrast with wonder's brief stimulation. A great writer who, like Shakespeare, functions as "the poet of nature; the poet that holds up to his readers a faithful mirror of manners and of life" (62)—such a writer provides bits of ultimate truth. He makes stability available to his readers. The urgency of Johnson's assertion about truth comes from his desire both to make high claims for Shakespeare and to promulgate general wisdom himself.

The context, then, reveals that Johnson's words bear on actualities of reading and writing, as well as on the realm of the ideal. They specify both Shakespeare's effects on readers—pleasure, repose—and their cause: the dramatist's access to profound generalizations about human life. Nor do the words evoke only positive suggestions. The statement acquires force from the faith it embraces but also from what it consciously rejects. Boldly and insistently, Johnson here repudiates both mere fancy and mere specificity in favor of moral deduction.

The paragraph that ends with the clause that I have quoted three times already begins, famously, "Nothing can please many, and please long, but just representations of general nature" (61). In other words, meditation on the value of abstraction and generalization supplies the immediate setting for Johnson's abstractions. His first explanation for Shakespeare's continuing power draws on the dramatist's alleged commitment to the universal. Shakespeare, Johnson explains, does not concern himself with customs, attitudes, or behaviors that mark particular times and places. Instead the playwright dwells on thoughts and feelings that all will recognize because all have shared them. For this reason, Shakespeare's plays have survived his death by a century and a half. For this reason, they will long continue to please.

The literary critic's forms of representation differ from the dramatist's, but critics too must choose, Johnson manifestly believes, between ephemeral and lasting statement. The particular, as Johnson's discussion of Shakespeare makes clear, presents itself more readily to the mind. We all live through and in particularities. The philosopher pondering eternal truth feels the scratch of his shirt collar; the sculptor creating her masterpiece dimly notices her desire for coffee. They can choose to ignore scratch and thirst, to reject the burden of specificities, but the choice demands at least a minor act of will.

To posit stability entails a major act of will. Johnson claims it less as fact than as ideal, the ideal implied by the actuality of its opposite. The note of wistfulness in the evocation of mind resting on truth stems partly from the assertion's theoretical nature, its defiance of all experience—or, perhaps more accurately, its reformulation of experience so as tacitly to acknowledge the instability of mental process by imagining the consequences of attaining the unattainable. Shakespeare provides a version of the ideal, yet the terms summarizing the dramatist's moral achievement can only remind the reader of longings unfulfillable by any writer, any piece of writing. Johnson's phrasing acknowledges his assertion's counterfactual nature. "The mind *can* only repose"—not "the mind only reposes" or "the mind *will* only repose." The mind has been constructed, this formulation suggests, so as to seek its satisfaction in rest, but with no guarantee of satisfaction.

In order to imagine repose, Johnson conjures up generalized mind empty of content. Deprived not only of race, class, and gender, but even of location, it exists in a philosophic void. The notion of truth likewise lacks content and depends on the lack. Any specific truth must risk refutation. The theoretical concept of universal truth remains as irrefutable as it is unprovable.

Reliance on such generalizations, devoid of all contingency, generates the assurance and grandeur of Johnson's apothegm. But the statement of relationship among abstractions also registers the tension of its bareness. Exclusion requires effort. Johnson's commitment to the truth of generalization, the commitment he honors in his praise of Shakespeare, demands of him strenuous excisions. The pared-down assertion of the mind's capacity to rest on truth reflects determined rejection of doubt. To move from the desperate self-castigation of his own mind to the large idea of "the mind," to bridge the huge gap between even generalized mind and the vastness of "truth" by means of the notion of repose: these mental actions entail conceptual energy and epistemological faith. Johnson's particular mind perhaps shares with the larger idea of "the mind" nothing more than the tendency to motion and the longing for rest hinted in his statement, a slender basis for hopeful generalization. Yet Johnson insists on generalizing, since, as his account of Shakespeare indicates, he values the capacity to convey large truths. He knows from painful experience how such accidents as class, temperament, and gender actually determine many of the mind's operations: his letters, his prayers, and his intimate conversation as reported by Boswell tell us as much. But he also believes in community across time and space, the notion of community inherent in the idea of generalization. In refining and enlarging his categories, Johnson demonstrates in action the commitment he defends in his critique of Shakespeare and suggests its arduousness.

I would maintain, then, that a sense of the stress of generalization and abstraction informs Johnson's utterance, constituting another aspect of the statement's emotional claim. As his praise of Shakespeare indicates, Johnson considers the preclusion of particularity a triumph—one that he achieves more obviously, to twentieth-century eyes, than does Shakespeare. His pronouncement about the mind implies intellectual as well as emotional challenge to us, his successors. Taken seriously, it questions our allegiance to contingencies and particularities, to divisive individuality and its rewards and miseries, as well as to the particular kinds of generality, the verbal identity politics, we use to explain ourselves. (I allude to our current habit of interpreting in terms of such favored generalizations as race, class, and gender—generalizations that come readily to our minds and lips, with none of the tension I have claimed for Johnson.)

Yet if Johnson's arduous abstractions can raise questions about modern habits of thought and feeling, it is equally true that our habits of mind challenge his. I have claimed thus far that the assertion about the mind accretes emotional power by the spareness of its diction, the weight of its single metaphor, and the force and tension of its abstractions. Power inheres also, though, in historical particularities. To consider Johnson's assertion and his vocabulary in the context of his predecessors and contemporaries and in relation to other words of his own clarifies unstated assumptions and further sources of the statement's energy, although such consideration depends on attitudes and procedures quite different from Johnson's own.

We might begin with *truth*, which appears in Johnson's line where one would expect the more inclusive term, *goodness*. Boswell's account of his great mentor makes it apparent that the concept of truth had intense personal meaning for Johnson. There is, for instance, the famous story about how Johnson retreated to the attic when he wanted to be undisturbed, because he wouldn't allow his servant to say he was not at home if he really was: the servant might thus get the habit of lying. Over and over, Boswell reports, Johnson recurred to the importance of scrupulosity about fact. "It is more from carelessness about truth than from intentional lying," he said, "that there is so much falsehood in the world."[2] His friends all knew of and depended on the sage's absolute veracity, and he recommended it to them.

Such an idea of truth, however, refers only to factuality. The clause that I have been brooding about concerns an abstraction with lingering associations to the realm of the spiritual. About this kind of truth, Boswell suggests, Johnson in fact felt troubling doubts. When others asked him how to ascertain religious truth, he responded, more than once, that martyrdom supplied the only test of certainty. Buddhists and Christians alike might believe themselves in possession of the truth. Their willingness to endure martyrdom for it would indicate its power. If this explanation seems less than logical, the fact hints Johnson's anxiety as well as his honesty. He cannot rest even on the truth of revelation. Indeed—and this is, of course, the important point—he cannot rest anywhere.

In a letter to his friend Bennet Langton, written in 1758, Johnson reveals his uncertainty in terms strikingly close to those of the line from the "Preface to Shakespeare": "Let us endeavour to see things as they are, and then enquire whether we ought to complain. Whether to see life as it is will give us much consolation I know not, but the consolation which is drawn from truth, if any there be, is solid and durable, that which may be derived from errour must be like its original fallacious and fugitive."[3] Truth, in Johnson's imagining here, provides "consolation" rather than "repose"—but provides that only dubiously, since "if any there be" emphatically qualifies the idea of consolation. Truth, more dependable than error, implicitly represents the divine rather than the diabolic: that's as far as Johnson is willing to go. His observations reveal the moral heroism of his effort to "see things as they are," an enterprise from which, he here makes clear, he anticipates no necessary reward.

The discrepancy in tone and substance between the letter and the "Preface to Shakespeare" partly reflects Johnson's sense of the difference between personal and public utterance. Believing ardently in the writer's responsibility to try to make the world better, he considered his public writing an opportunity for moral instruction, not a venue for the expression of private doubt. The "Preface to Shakespeare" does not invite readers to make comparisons with what its author says elsewhere. Yet contextual awareness of Johnson's personal writing corroborates the syntactical hint of uncertainty in the stated possibility of repose, reminds one of Johnson's consciousness that truth remains difficult to attain and to know, and helps locate the tensions that energize the public statement.

Mind, apparently a more transparent locution than *truth*, conveys comparably dense and ambiguous import. By designating the mind's resting place as truth, Johnson staked out his position in a debate about mental process that had persisted for centuries. To go over some familiar ground: Plato and Aristotle believed that a cosmic order, in which human beings necessarily participate, governs the universe. The human task is to understand our place and as much as possible of the system we inhabit, humbly accepting the necessary limits of our knowledge. Self-knowledge, part of the recommended awareness, entails coming to comprehend the human nature that all men and women share.

Seventeenth-century empiricists challenged these propositions. By the middle of the eighteenth century, David Hume had carried their emphasis on the importance of sense impressions to its logical conclusion, maintaining that the mind lacks the capacity even to establish the independent existence of anything outside itself. Like Locke and Berkeley before him, thought exemplifies the shift of interest from ontology to epistemology that marked the development of British empiricism. Johnson wrote at a moment when emphasis on human understanding rather than cosmic systems preoccupied most philosophers. His assertion that the mind bears some affinity to truth allies him with the past, implying a belief in order and reality independent of human perception. By saying that the mind reposes on something outside itself, Johnson takes a controversial position.

Repose as an ideal has its own history. A little over a century before Johnson, the Anglican divine George Herbert wrote his great poem, "The Pulley," a meditation on rest. It opens with a creation myth. "When God at first made man, / Having a glasse of blessings standing by," the deity bestowed His blessings one by one: beauty, strength, wisdom, honor, and so on.[4] As He prepares to offer the final blessing, rest, He decides after all to withhold it, knowing that, given repose, man would "adore My gifts in stead of Me." So God promises restlessness as the human condition, saying of man,

> Let him be rich and wearie, that at least,
> If goodnesse leade him not, yet wearinesse
> May tosse him to My breast. (lines 18–20, p. 144)

Herbert's sense of the human situation corresponds to Johnson's—with the striking difference that Johnson does not place the issue of repose in a theological context. (In his private prayers and meditations, though, he writes of "the act of prayer as a reposal of myself upon God.") Like Johnson's formulation, Herbert's lyric acknowledges the always unfulfilled human yearning for quiescence, but it provides a resolution less entirely counterfactual, more immediately comforting. Given the existence and the presence of a personalized deity, human possibility enlarges. And Herbert's version of deity employs reassuringly human logic, displays recognizably human motivation. The elaborate fable about how "rest" acquired its importance for salvation rationalizes the mystery of humankind's situation.

Abundant evidence testifies to Johnson's devout Christianity, but in thinking about the mind—or at least in thinking about it in connection with Shakespeare—he apparently found Christianity no help. One might consider "truth" in its ultimate, absolute sense to be a form of the divine, but Johnson here suggests nothing of the sort. Divinity as truth, in any case, would provide less comfort than does Herbert's deity, who can be designated by a personal pronoun and who consciously plans for the welfare of His creation. The confidence of the seventeenth-century poem makes more apparent Johnson's lack of immediate certainty. If not goodness, weariness: one way or another, according to Herbert, human beings will probably unite themselves with God. The mind may never actually repose on truth.

The enterprise of a lyric poem by definition must differ from that of a single clause in an extended prose argument, so a comparison between the two may seem relatively pointless, except inasmuch as it calls attention to historical differences in the certainty of religious faith. Yet the distance between Herbert's rhetoric and Johnson's also helps clarify the sources of the prose writer's effectiveness. Herbert relies on interlocking but oddly connected figures—primarily the metaphor of the pulley in the title, never directly alluded to in the text, and the elaborated personification that creates the fable—to draw readers into the poem. Johnson elsewhere in his "Preface" loads every rift with metaphor, characterizing *Othello*, for instance, as "the vigorous and vivacious offspring of observation impregnated by genius," or providing in a single short paragraph detailed images of a garden, a forest, a cabinet of rarities, and a mine of gold and diamonds ("Preface," 84). He thus allures his readers and generates authority by displaying his powers. To employ a simple vocabulary, a reduced cadence, and a single shadowy metaphor for an important statement involves deliberate choice. Herbert's complex effect depends on figural interplay. Johnson's refusal to use comparable resources allows him an emphasis that appears derived from the bareness of hard-won conviction.

Johnson's specific historical situation, although it does not overtly influence his formulation, is worth considering too. England after 1763, when the Seven Years' War came to an end with the Peace of Paris, displayed unusual political and social uncertainty. Linda Colley summarizes:

> To those used to being at the centre of things, . . . but also to those below them, the prospects in 1763 were exhilarating but also frighteningly wide open. Indeed, it is not too much to say that from this point on until the American Revolution and beyond, the British were in the grip of collective agoraphobia, captivated by, but also adrift and at odds in a vast empire abroad and a new political world at home which few of them properly

understood. It was a time of raised expectations, disorientation and anxiety in which demands for change on the one hand, and denunciations of change on the other, came from the peripheries of the political nation, from the peripheries of Great Britain itself and from the peripheries of the empire as well. At home, John Wilkes and his supporters launched a turbulent campaign for old English liberties and new English rights, while English patriots more generally felt themselves under threat from Scottish ambition and Scottish constructions of Great Britain. Abroad, those American colonists whom many Englishmen and women had been accustomed to viewing as mirror images of themselves, rejected both the authority of the British Parliament and in the end their own residual British identity.[5]

Boswell details Johnson's mental implication in such issues—his detestation of Wilkes, both for the unrest the political agitator created and for Wilkes's challenges to the royal family, and his insistence that the American colonists had no right to dissatisfaction. As an upholder of established hierarchies, Johnson hated and feared threats to the order of things. And such threats abounded during the period in which he wrote the "Preface to Shakespeare," partly as a consequence of the great enlargement of the British Empire effected by the Peace of Paris.

Johnson wrote, then, at a historical moment when many perceived widespread menaces to the stability of the political and social order. In such a context, the metaphysical solidity of universal truth would seem at once particularly inaccessible and especially desirable. The claim of universality for Shakespeare, already perceived as a national monument, would hold political as well as literary force. Even Colley's condensed account suggests the national turbulence against which, perhaps, Johnson posited the psychic power of truth.

He posited that power against internal turbulence as well. Consider this characteristic fragment of one of his "meditations," written on 21 April 1764:

> My indolence, since my last reception of the Sacrament, has sunk into grosser sluggishness, and my dissipation spread into wilder negligence. My thoughts have been clouded with sensuality, and, except that from the beginning of this year I have in some measure forborn excess of Strong Drink my appetites have predominated over my reason. A kind of strange oblivion has overspread me, so that I know not what has become of the last year, and perceive that incidents and intelligence pass over me without leaving any impression.[6]

"Dissipation," in the eighteenth-century sense, implies frivolity, scattering of energies, rather than dissoluteness. Johnson accuses himself here not of corruption but of lack of focus and discipline—lack, in other words, of *stability*. The unattainable repose on truth that he imagines would answer both personal and national needs.

Nothing that Johnson wrote in the clause I am considering or in the paragraph that contains it speaks directly of the national or of his personal situation. He acknowledges no controversy over "mind," no history for the idea of "repose," no private relevance for "truth." I may appear to have gone far afield from my original purpose of ascertaining how ten words by Samuel Johnson have accreted so much emotional power for me, far afield, even, from what Johnson wrote, in my suggestions. Yet what one knows always helps determine how one reads—as what one knows and experiences helps determine how one writes. Johnson's omissions and inclusions reveal convictions and purposes. My ability to "read" omissions as well as inclusions allows me to be enlightened and moved. The power of Johnson's words depends on the density of their incorporations, some of which I have tried to specify.

The richest component of that density, to my mind, is the aspect of opposition in Johnson's prose, revealed only by investigation of what isn't there. As W. K. Wimsatt long ago demonstrated, Johnson speaks consistently of conflict, his metaphorical structures reiterating his view that human life invariably entails struggle.[7] "I will be conquered, I will not capitulate," he said, succumbing to multiple fatal ailments (*Life*, 1358). The words I have been considering do not overtly allude to the battle of existence, but their large context—personal, historical, philosophic—reminds us that they are hard won. Johnson's apparently calm promise of stability confronts desperate instabilities. His statement moves me by hinting the doubt and anxiety that it defies and by surmounting all obstacles to declare in form and content the possibility of universal assertion: assertion that through its generalizing energy insists on the presence and the power of human community despite all diversities of history and geography. It challenges my forms of discouragement by refuting its own.

I have performed a little exercise in reading, a sample of what I call "my work." My observations about Johnson's ten words reveal my private and personal form of engagement. My engagement is public as well, of course, but it begins with solitary pleasure and solitary effort. Like everything I read, Johnson's clause has personal meanings for me, some of which I shall specify. Every week in Charlottesville, I have lunch with a colleague whose professional attention focuses on Romantic poetry, and we argue.

One day, a year or so ago, I began our lunch by quoting Johnson's words and inquiring whether my friend didn't find them deeply affecting. He readily agreed about their power, but when we talked about what the words actually meant, we turned out—as usual—to disagree. Both of us thought that the statement did not suggest any actual repose of the mind —only the imagining of such repose. Beyond that, the Romanticist thought Johnson's dictum essentially optimistic, in that it opened the possibility for a quest with a constantly receding goal, the quest itself supplying value. I saw it as pessimistic, suggesting, as Johnson so often suggests, the impossibility of satisfaction. My colleague read the statement, I thought, from a nineteenth-century point of view: that made it sound different. My impulse to comment publicly about these words, then, stems partly from this unresolved private discussion, which made me realize that for me the strength of Johnson's assertion derives partly from historical particularities not obviously at issue.

Vaguer forces also impelled me to ponder Johnson's statement. Some of them I wouldn't be able to locate clearly enough to specify. I know, though, that I was feeling irritated about newspaper reports of attacks that alleged a disregard for "values" among scholars and teachers of the humanities. It seemed to me that in my classroom and in my writing, ethical and moral issues held an important place. I also thought that "values" were not such a simple matter as some of their defenders suggested. Johnson in his praise for truth conveys the complexity of the human relation to such glorious abstractions as "truth." I urgently wanted to say that.

Such causal explanations do not exhaust the reasons for my current meditations. I list them, though, in order at least to hint that my concept of "my work" involves bringing together various sorts of impulse quite divergent from any notion of simple, unified professional trajectory. If I call what I have written here part of "my work" for other reasons than the fact that I have written it, I thus claim that such work draws together scholarship, collegiality, conversation, and newspaper reading.

Most importantly, reading Johnson's prose reminds me what reading does. Those ten words move me and instruct me. They thus fulfill the classical criteria for literature, the criteria Johnson himself accepted. I have been holding forth about how they move me, but the matter of instruction is at least equally important—if slightly embarrassing in a postmodern context. I'll say it boldly, though: Johnson reminds me, by his practice, even in a sentence fragment, and by what he says, that what I aspire to do in my own writing is to articulate truth. Not "truth" in the large, universal sense: only fragments. But not error either. He reminds me too that as a writer I believe in and rely on various kinds of community. In small ways and large, he helps me do my work, and he helps me believe in it.

My work may at any given moment consist only of thinking, or it might involve talking or, for that matter, listening. It happens in the classroom or on an airplane, in study or kitchen or lecture hall. It assumes shifting shapes, and it always starts with reading. It necessarily draws on many resources beyond the immediate contents of my mind and depends on many people. I do not write or think alone.

One set of actualities on which I draw for my work can be labeled "the profession." Presumably because I recently served as an officer of the Modern Language Association, I get asked often to talk about "the state of the profession." Usually I respond to such requests by discussing the job crisis, the diminished opportunities for advancement and security that too much of the time strike me as defining our collective professional situation these days. But in fact our profession involves more than jobs.

To profess English, or aspire to profess it, entails systems of ideas as well as of employment. Our profession's operative intellectual schemes have proliferated wildly in recent years, bringing with them kinds of debate that often cross the line of civility. Conspicuous contempt for adherents of opposed doctrines has characterized some who espoused the newest thing, whatever that thing might be. As a consequence, those whose intellectual commitments belong to even a quite proximate past often feel discredited by those who declare themselves on the cutting edge—and correspondingly resentful. Indeed, I cannot remember and I have not heard about a period in which resentment flourished so widely and so publicly as it does now. To call the current intellectual climate one of mutual suspicion understates the case.

Yet such a description fails to do justice to the positive consequences of that proliferation of doctrines I mentioned. If I had tried twenty years ago to articulate the force of Johnson's comment about the mind and truth, my conclusions would have sounded different because the questions that occurred to me would have been different—simpler, I think, less rich. I myself have never declared allegiance to structuralism, poststructuralism, Marxism, new historicism, or any other of the multiplying -isms that have thrived among literary critics in the past few decades. But all of them have enabled me to grasp critical issues in new ways.

If Johnson, like the other authors whose writing I read, helps me do my work, so does the profession in which I participate. Recent modes of interpretation, however ahistorical in approach, constitute ways to make the past accessible. They provide principles of understanding that allow inhabitants of the late twentieth century to comprehend the actions of other minds as relevant to their own. Johnson read Shakespeare and found corroboration for his belief in the value of the generalized over the particular. I read Johnson and find evidence of intellectual and psychological conflict. The past speaks to us in the terms we need, as it spoke to Johnson in his terms, and new critical methods have helped us locate our understanding.

It's not that I like everything that has happened in the profession. I think it's always a mistake to feel superior to the past, and some of the doctrines now current encourage false superiority. Not all modes of interpretation have equal value. Some strike me as inherently reductive, some seem simply uninteresting. Some desperately distort the words of the past to serve the needs of the present. And I deplore the atmosphere of incivility, the degree to which many have lost sight of common purpose among those who teach and study the written word. In my darker moments, I too see the profession as dangerously divided and sadly unable to speak effectively for itself. At all times, I see economic and employment actualities as invidious in direct and indirect ways to serious intellectual activity.

But I also see evidence of fruitful energies. The invigorated intellectual debates of the last quarter century have forced many of us to think anew about what is at stake in our acts of reading and writing and to become self-conscious about our intellectual choices. A new eclecticism is abroad in the land, as many among us work to incorporate fresh ways of understanding. We grow, always, by means of community—community marked not by unanimity but by diversity. Our operative communities include the immediate institutional community of students and teachers, the larger community that we call "the profession," and the literary community, existing through history, that sustained Johnson. These communities depend on one another, and we depend on them—but not only for support. As Johnson challenges our assumptions, so also do, and should, our students and our teachers. And so do the other members of the profession, vividly declaring their separate and often conflicting convictions. I have moved from the first person singular to the first person plural pronoun, from *I* to *we*. That is my act of faith. I know that the three communities I have mentioned enable me to do my own work; I believe that they enable us all: enable us to think responsibly and creatively and perhaps, perhaps, even to approach more closely to truth.

Notes

1. "Preface to Shakespeare" (1765), *Johnson on Shakespeare*, ed. Arthur Sherbo, *The Yale Edition of the Works of Samuel Johnson*, vol. 7 (New Haven: Yale University Press, 1968), 62. Subsequent references will be incorporated in the text.

2. James Boswell, *Life of Johnson* (1791), ed. R. W. Chapman (Oxford: Oxford University Press, 1970), 899. Subsequent references will be incorporated in the text.

3. *The Letters of Samuel Johnson*, ed. Bruce Redford (Princeton: Princeton University Press, 1992), 1:167.

4. 1–2. *The Poems of George Herbert*, ed. A. B. Grosart (London: Oxford University Press, 1907), 144.

5. *Britons: Forging the Nation 1707–1837* (New Haven: Yale University Press, 1992), 105.

6. *Diaries, Prayers, and Annals*, ed. E. L. McAdam, Jr., *The Yale Edition of the Works of Samuel Johnson*, vol. 1 (New Haven: Yale University Press, 1958), 77–78.

7. *The Prose Style of Samuel Johnson* (1972) (Hamden, Conn.: Archon Books, 1991), *passim*.

Paul Alpers

Leavis Today

I WAS PROMPTED to write about Leavis on this occasion, partly because
he has been so important a critic for Bill Pritchard and partly because
trying to interest graduate students in him has prompted me to wonder
about his currency and that of other great critics of the middle decades of
this century. But there was also a coincidence too striking to resist. About
the time I received a copy of *English Papers*, but before I had read it, I par-
ticipated in a local colloquium that addressed the question, "What Are
'Traditional' Scholars Doing Now?" I began my remarks by saying that I
do not think of myself primarily as a scholar, because my scholarly knowledge has been acquired in the interests of answering critical and interpretive questions. I went on to say that despite this distinction, the critic, no
less than the scholar, must have what Eliot called "a highly developed
sense of fact." As an example of this critical power, I cited Leavis's observation of "the way in which the stress is put on 'Did' and the intonation
controlled" in the first lines of Donne's "The Good Morrow":

> I wonder by my troth, what thou, and I
> Did, till we loved?

A week or so later, I discovered, reading *English Papers*, that this very passage, from "The Line of Wit" (the first chapter of *Revaluation*), was one of

the memorable moments in Bill's discovery of Leavis. Bill cites the preceding paragraph, in which Leavis quotes the whole first stanza of "The Good Morrow" and says that when we come to it, in *The Oxford Book of Seventeenth-Century Verse*, "we cease reading as students, or as connoisseurs of anthology pieces, and read on as we read the living." That sentence, Bill reports, "made a particular impact on me"—as it did on me, probably a few years later. In what follows, I want to reflect on the ways in which Leavis was an important critic for Bill and me and our contemporaries; I also want to ask whether we can expect students and younger colleagues to read him today, "as we read the living."

The first thing to say is that this is about Leavis in America, both then and now. In England, despite the sense his writings give of being embattled and marginalized, he achieved the cultural centrality to which he aspired. The ranks of secondary-school English masters were and still are filled with his disciples and the students of disciples. In the pages of *The Times Literary Supplement*, not always friendly to Leavis, one still finds him invoked as a critic who matters. Leavis, as he himself might have put it, is indisputably "there," because he changed—and is recognized as having changed—the character of literary study in England. There might be considerable objection to what Terry Eagleton says in his account of "The Rise of English," but the point is that no American, no matter how much an admirer of Leavis, would speak as Eagleton does:

> Whatever the "failure" or "success" of *Scrutiny*, however one might argue the toss between the anti-Leavisian prejudice of the literary establishment and the waspishness of the *Scrutiny* movement itself, the fact remains that English students in England today are "Leavisites" whether they know it or not, irremediably altered by that historic intervention. There is no more need to be a card-carrying Leavisite today than there is to be a card-carrying Copernican: that current has entered the bloodstream of English studies in England as Copernicus reshaped our astronomical beliefs.[1]

If for English critics Leavis has been an inescapable presence, Americans, it seems, have been able to take him or leave him. A good many, as I've discovered in recent conversations, chose to leave him—mainly because of the tone of his writings and what is perceived as his dogmatism. Others had little opportunity to make up their minds. Leavis, I am told, was scarcely mentioned in the Yale Department of English, certainly the country's most distinguished in the '50s and '60s, just as there is not a word about him in Wimsatt and Brooks's *Literary Criticism: A Short His-*

tory. There is conflicting testimony about the degree to which Leavis mattered as a critic in Canada and the United States. But we can take as symptomatic Stanley Edgar Hyman's *The Armed Vision* (1948), the book which, we are told, introduced the young Pritchard to the excitements of literary criticism. Hyman devotes whole chapters to Richards and Empson, as well as to several American critics, but Leavis gets only a nod, along with the remark that his and *Scrutiny's* work is not well known in the United States. In the same year, Eric Bentley edited a volume, *The Importance of Scrutiny*, expressly to overcome American ignorance of Leavis and his journal.

My conscious obligation to Leavis comes under two heads, one surprising, the other not. But before I was aware of his influence, I had felt it in Reuben Brower's teaching, particularly in the seminar on Pope in which Bill Pritchard and I met. Brower had studied with Leavis and thanks him, in *The Fields of Light*, for introducing him to "practical criticism." What he particularly learned is suggested by Richard Poirier's account of his own indebtedness to Leavis, who was his tutor at Downing College, and to Brower, with whom he taught (as Bill and I did) in Harvard's Humanities 6. The lesson of these masters, in Poirier's account, is "the dramatic use of language"—"the way words and sentences 'talk to each other,' the way they undo and reconstitute each other beyond the grasp of critical interpretations that look for unity and order."[2] This puts Poirier's own spin on the idea—"imaginative design" was a watchword for Brower, and Leavis was deeply committed to the idea that works of literature are complex orderings of experience—but it certainly brings out what was to be learned in Brower's classroom. He was wonderful at revealing shifts of tone and the play of different registers of language, as when he discussed the callow youth's Grand Tour in *Dunciad* IV and dwelt (in a moment I particularly remember from the Pope seminar) on the representation of

> happy Convents, bosom'd deep in vines,
> Where slumber Abbots, purple as their wines. (301–2)

Brower made us see that there is more than mockery here. The scene of natural bounty is not only contrasted with monastic indolence but also (to use a Leavisian term) realizes it. The resonances between the images and sounds of "bosom'd," "slumber," and "purple" bring these avatars of dullness to life and at the same time imply an ironic critique. The sense of positive ordering (aesthetic felicity intimating the values of a culture), is focused in "happy," which should remind the reader versed in georgic poetry that the Latin word *laetus* means both "happy" and "fertile." Brower had learned to read this way from Leavis, as he would have been the first to acknowledge. But I learned it from Brower, not only in his seminar but also in the splendid analysis of the Epistle to Burlington in *The Fields of Light*. Hence when I read Leavis's chapter on Pope, which I can now see represents what he taught Brower, it seemed not a "revaluation" but what I already knew.

I was certainly aware of Leavis: apart from Brower and Poirier, he was an important critic for Bill and for others in his circle of former Amherst students, who were the peers from whom I learned most in graduate school. But at the same time he was not a critic who mattered a great deal to me; indeed I remember being somewhat resistant to him. The critical books I most admired—the ones that had the most intellectual and moral force and that most revealed what the enterprise of literary interpretation could be—were Trilling's *The Liberal Imagination*, Jarrell's *Poetry and the Age*, Empson's *Some Versions of Pastoral*, Auerbach's *Mimesis*, and Pound's *Letters*. What I found compelling in each of these books could have led me to admiring Leavis. There was, on one side, Empson's and Auerbach's ability to elicit human significance from detailed literary analysis, and on another, Trilling's confidence that aesthetic intelligence both enables one to think about democratic society and culture and provides some distance from them. Pound and Jarrell were inspiriting because they combined a feisty and combative love of poetry with antagonism to middlebrow culture. I've come to feel somewhat abashed at the pleasure I took in Jarrell's mockery of ordinary folk, not to mention Pound's abusiveness, but they spoke powerfully to me of what had brought me to graduate school (rather than medical school, where I had thought I was headed—with, it seemed, half my classmates—when I graduated from college). The change in my plans and ambitions was due, as I but dimly realized, to a classic American experience. A year in Europe after college had made me aware of cultures older and richer, more accepting of human realities, and more committed to aesthetic and intellectual life than Eisenhower's and McCarthy's America. "Mass civilization and minority culture" was thus very much on my mind, even though I did not know the pamphlet of that title Leavis had written. Leavis, indeed, might have filled any of the needs these other critics did, but it was probably because of them that he did not seem necessary to me. Not being American, his brooding on culture and society meant less to me than Trilling's, and his acerbity cheered me less than Jarrell's extravagant wit. In the matter of most immediate concern, he was not going to be of any help to me in writing a dissertation on *The Faerie Queene.*

Leavis, however, eventually gave me something these other critics could not—an example of forceful and intelligent resistance to inert and conventional valuations in the teaching and academic interpretation of literature. Pound, Jarrell, and even Empson had no use for professors' views on literature and the arts, and neither did my other maverick heroes, Shaw, Orwell, and Edmund Wilson. But I was hoping to be a professor, and I was going to have to find my voice and establish my independence in the world of learned journals and academic criticism. Of all the forthright, witty, combative voices to which I was so susceptible, Leavis alone took the universities' valuations seriously (though *Scrutiny* was insistently not an academic journal). Trilling, to be sure, took teaching and university life—at least *his* university's life—very seriously. But the "we" for whom he professed to speak in his writing was the New York intelligentsia, and his acts of revaluation were undertaken with it in mind. "Manners, Morals, and the Novel," one of the essays I most admired (it spoke to my Europhilia), was addressed to certain misconceptions, as he saw them, in the American mind and the culture of democracy. Leavis spoke of things that were, if not nearer to my heart, then closer to home.

The first piece of Leavis's that spoke decisively to me was the opening chapter of *The Great Tradition*. I had first read the nineteenth-century novel in a Harvard course in which the books were lined up, from *Emma* to *The Mayor of Casterbridge*, as if all were "classics" and as if each book and each author were of equivalent worth. The course exemplified the undiscriminating eclecticism that troubled Bill Pritchard when he began his studies at Harvard. As it happens, Bill's account of Leavis's importance for him as a graduate student—the strong valuations that gave a clear idea of which authors were significant and which were not—leads him to reflect on what he failed to see at the time: "In some ways Harvard English turned out to be right: for a young scholar-critic it was as important—perhaps *more* important—to be catholic in one's taste, to try to enter into as many different sorts of literary experience as one could manage, rather than become too exclusive and prematurely severe." I was a product of Harvard English, which no doubt helps explain some of my resistance to Leavis, but I welcomed the counter-force of the opening sentence of *The Great Tradition:* "The great English novelists are Jane Austen, George Eliot, Henry James and Joseph Conrad—to stop for the moment at that comparatively safe point in history." It was not the specific valuations that followed that mattered to me, though I loved the demolition of Meredith. I had written my undergraduate honors thesis on Fielding, whose candor and generosity (splendidly praised by Empson in a later essay on *Tom Jones*) made him another one of my heroes. But somehow I didn't mind being told that Jane Austen's distinction makes one "feel that life isn't long enough to permit of one's giving much time to Fielding." What mattered was Leavis's insistence that "in the field of fiction some challenging discriminations are very much called for."

This challenge to judgment based on pertinent analysis was one way, the unsurprising way, in which Leavis made a difference to me. I felt it when *The Common Pursuit* appeared in paperback, and I read "The Irony of Swift." The scrupulous account of the negative intensity of Swift's writing seemed to me to speak far more truthfully about his disturbing power than the pious invocations of Reason I was used to hearing in Harvard classrooms. The famous essay on *Othello*, "Diabolic Intellect and the Noble Hero," was similarly clarifying. The view it aimed to correct was not one I particularly associated with Harvard English. But I recognized that the focus of Leavis's critique—the attempt to explain the tragedy solely by Iago's machinations—was something I had either uncritically accepted or had merely distrusted, when put in the form of calling Iago's actions "conventional." I thought I understood *Othello* less well than any other of the tragedies, but I had no way of acting on my dissatisfaction. Leavis enabled me to think productively about the play, by shifting the question to what makes Othello responsive to Iago's suggestions. Seen this way, the essay is a forerunner of some of the most searching recent studies of *Othello*, which has succeeded *Hamlet* and then *Lear* (central for my generation) as, in the era of gender studies and postcolonial awareness, the definitive Shakespearean tragedy. Leavis's essay also made a difference in the theater, where it decisively influenced major productions of *Othello*—most notably, Olivier's at the Old Vic, but also RSC productions by Peter Hall, Trevor Nunn, and John Barton.[3] At the same time, few of Leavis's essays have prompted so much opposition, and disagreements with it can be found in very recent studies.[4] Yet I do not think it is an essay that we now read "as we read the living." Leavis's interpretation is as much a piece of character criticism as Bradley's—this is, indeed, what made it fruitful for Olivier—and we could say, with some antagonists, that his account of Othello's character is as partial (in the opposite direction) as Bradley's.

More broadly, no student of the play will be satisfied by referring its anxieties and turbulence solely to the "obtuse and brutal egotism" that underlies the hero's noble conception of himself.

The general effect of Leavis's criticism on me was, as I have said, unsurprising. But my major specific debt to him may seem very odd. In the early '60s, the publication of Christopher Ricks's *Milton's Grand Style* and the fact that I was teaching my first course on Milton led me back to the notorious chapter in *Revaluation* on "Milton's Verse." Ricks's book was a brilliant and, so far as critical politics went, extremely effective reply to the disparaging criticisms of *Paradise Lost* by Eliot, Leavis, and A. J. A. Waldock. But at the same time, Ricks did not see that Leavis's fundamental objection to Milton's verse—that "the medium calls pervasively for a kind of attention, compels an attitude towards itself, that is incompatible with sharp, concrete realization"—points to its essential strength. With his strong bias for the dramatic and the concretely realized, Leavis could not see the possibilities of the style he described; nor could Ricks, who shares Leavis's bias, and who therefore answered him on his own grounds (by demonstrating, for example, the dramatic force and concentration of Satan's speeches). His answer was therefore all the more effective, but it did not, in my view, go far enough. The sign of this limitation was that Ricks did not mention, much less discuss, the description of Eden (*PL* 4.233–47), which was precisely the passage Leavis had singled out as representing the vices of Milton's style. Ricks presumably felt he could not defend this passage, but it seemed to me that it had to be justified if Leavis was to be adequately answered. In undertaking this justification, I thought the most helpful single tip was what Leavis had conceived as a devastating critique—that the poet "exhibits a feeling *for* words rather than a capacity for feeling *through* words." In the present context, I will have to leave the matter there and refer any interested reader to the essay I wrote, which was both a defense of Milton and a defense of Leavis.[5] (It was also, in effect, a tribute to Humanities 6, for I had first worked out an account of the description of Eden in preparing one of the exercises in which we guided students through a particular scene or passage.) I sometimes wonder whether any other critic as committed to Spenser and Milton as I am feels similarly grateful for Leavis's essay—and for the essays ("Mr. Eliot and Milton" and "In Defence of Milton," both in *The Common Pursuit*) in which he later stood his ground. Yet odd as this particular instance may seem, what made these essays challenging and enabling for me was Leavis's central virtues as a critic—the sense of fact, as Eliot called it, and (in Leavisian lingo) the capacity for closely relevant analysis and argument.

The question remains whether today's students can learn from Leavis as Bill and I did. This is the question to which my title refers, and I want to approach it by considering the way some of his American contemporaries praised him. With their perhaps simplified but not unfounded notions of the New Criticism, students today might be pleased to discover Leavis's insistence that "one of the virtues of literary studies is that they lead constantly outside themselves."[6] But this aspect of Leavis's program probably never had its due effect. In a review of the 1964 reissue of *Scrutiny*, Brower praised its scope in its early years: "What surprised readers early and late was that Leavis and his colleagues insisted on adding to th[e] conventional list of creative writers the historian, the philosopher, the sociologist, the anthropologist, in short all writers who are engaged in the business of evaluating and shaping the world in which we live."[7] Brower goes on to contrast what Americans are used to as the "explication" of texts with "the characteristic explorations of Leavis and his colleagues." But he then recognizes the problem of learning from the example of *Scrutiny*. If the strengths of the journal's contributors are "an awareness of the complexities of actual situations past or present" and its educational program recognizes that "one must think locally and particularly to think and act effectively" (304–5), then there is an inherent difficulty in translating not only the educational program but even Leavisian critical practice to this country.

On these shores, Leavis always mattered most as, in Francis Fergusson's words, "the very model of the accomplished literary critic in English." In so describing him, Fergusson means that he writes "in a fine, civilized, essayistic and conversational style, based on taste and the perception of literary values," and therefore that reading him "could hardly fail to sharpen one's enjoyment and promote the development of accurate insight."[8] Despite the old-fashioned terms, students today, in my experience, understand and can value what they mark out. Nevertheless, they are unlikely to agree that he is an exemplary critic—not only because of the brusque judgments and broad assertions that dominate some of his writings, but also because his critical strengths are embedded in a particular sense of literary tradition. In what is perhaps the most interesting cis-Atlantic defense of him, Marshall (then H. M.) McLuhan argued on his behalf against the rhetorical criticism of Richards, Empson, and

Burke.[9] McLuhan calls these critics "rhetorical" because their attention is on the relation between speaker and audience. For this reason, he argues, they pay attention to any kind of writing, and therefore give no help in evaluating poems or even in recognizing that poems are poems. Leavis, on the other hand, is always aware of poems as internally organized and coherent. McLuhan contrasts Burke's account of Clifford Odets's *Golden Boy* (where he is right to say that the issue of literary value is bypassed) with Leavis's exegesis of a passage from *Macbeth* (II.vi, lines which include "the temple-haunting martlet"): "There are a dozen points in this analysis where a rhetorical exegesis would have led us down exciting semantic and synecdochal vistas at the cost of missing the way in which the fusion of the elements occurred and is significant for the play as a whole" (275). Leavis's analysis cannot seem as fresh and challenging as when it appeared, more than sixty years ago, in *How to Teach Reading* (a pamphlet responding to Pound's *How to Read*).[10] But it could be current in the way the best of Bradley is current, and McLuhan's praise suggests the way it speaks to our present debates about critical practice: those synecdochal vistas are a dime a dozen these days.

Leavis begins to appear dated, however, when McLuhan connects the refinement of his sensibility and the purity of his critical attention to Eliot's view that works of art "form an ideal order among themselves, which is modified by the introduction of the new (the really new) work of art among them." Leavis often expressed his indebtedness to this idea of tradition, according to which, in McLuhan's words, "the entire literature of Europe is to be viewed as a single emergent work of art, having a dramatic principle of its own" (272). This is a particularly American version of the ideal order of art (no hint here of the claims about *English* traditions that pervade Leavis's criticism), and it calls to mind New Critical ideology as much as Leavisian sensibility. But what McLuhan says is essentially right. Writing twenty years later, Brower said:

> It is the quality of attention elicited by Leavis and the major *Scrutiny* critics that is worth insisting on again: an almost tactile and sinuous response to the working of language, the most searching inquiry into the literary experience, but with a mind pressing toward the evaluation of the kind of life implied for the individual and society, not forgetting that any estimate must be tempered by direct experience of the tradition of civilized life in England and in Europe. (311)

Describing his response to Leavis's teaching and to *Scrutiny* when he was in Cambridge in the early thirties, Brower says, "The most remarkable thing for many of us was to find works of earlier writers treated with this immediacy of concern and works by contemporaries explored with an equally vivid sense of their relation to a living past" (307). But he also was aware that "no American, even in the thirties, could speak with *Scrutiny's* assurance of '*the* tradition'" (313). How, then, can any student today share this sense of poetry and its past, which so clearly belongs to a phase of English and American modernism?

I recently asked two graduate students for their thoughts about "The Line of Wit," which I had assigned in a course on Renaissance lyric. Each was struck by, as one put it, "the way Leavis wrote about Donne et al. as if they were living, breathing writers." They truly found him impressive, but perhaps in no other way than Arnold or Ruskin is impressive. On their testimony, today's students should know Leavis at least in the sense of understanding what he was about. But can he still be a critic who makes a difference to them, as Empson and Burke sometimes do? If so, it will be on the basis of something that emerged in what one of these students wrote in response to my inquiry. In a long commentary, both deeply appreciative and acutely critical, she noted Leavis's distinction, in his "utterly persuasive assessment of Dryden," between the poet's actual community, for which Dryden (he argues) too entirely wrote, and the "predominantly ideal" community which Ben Jonson always had in mind. The "imagined community" (a Leavisian phrase from a later essay) seemed to her a particularly felicitous or appropriate way to speak of what Leavis usually called tradition. So it seems to me also, for, as I have already suggested, we cannot commend Leavis to our students in the name of "tradition" as he meant it. I was struck by the coincidence between my student's comment and Dan Jacobson's account of his gratitude for Leavis's criticism when he left South Africa, where he could not "feel that I was part of any of the groups to which the country belonged":

> Here I was in England, . . . with which I had no direct connection. . . . And here was Dr. Leavis, in prose that reached again and again to the very heart of particular literary works, implicitly proposing an ideal community: a community that could be realized (if anywhere) only inside my own head, but that nevertheless felt more like a real community than any other I could imagine myself joining.[11]

Jacobson's sense of his situation may not be unlike that of many students today. What writings of Leavis can we recommend to them that will suggest that they belong to a community of readers? My own choice would be the three essays to which Leavis gave the overall title "Judgment and Analysis." These essays appeared in *Scrutiny* after Leavis published *Education and the University* (1943), and they give a full view of the means by which he proposed, in the chapter on "Literary Studies," to make the practice of criticism "a discipline of intelligence and sensibility."[12] There is something ironic in singling out these essays. When they appeared in *Scrutiny*, they were said to constitute parts of a book. The book was never completed, and the reason appears to be that the essays are too exclusively concerned with "practical criticism"—a label Leavis acknowledged as appropriate for what he did, but which he resisted, since it seemed to exclude the larger educational and cultural ambitions implicit in his practice. Nevertheless, I think these are the essays in which readers today can most readily discover what he has to offer. Re-reading "The Line of Wit" and wondering (again) why it did not "take" in my graduate courses on Renaissance lyric, I was struck by how little developed analysis it actually offers—how little there is even of the kind of precise observation I cited as exemplary at the beginning of this essay. Its treatment of Carew's "Know Celia (since thou art so proud)" is characteristic. Leavis says, absolutely rightly, that it is "a more distinguished achievement" than is commonly recognized and that "it has in its light grace a remarkable strength." His powers of discrimination are nowhere more evident than in his recognizing Carew's distinction, and his presentation of this poem leads to one of his most perceptive emphases as a historian of English poetry—the argument that behind the wit of poets like Carew lies not only Donne's achievement but Ben Jonson's. But Leavis's commendation of Carew's poem consists entirely of asserting that it is "immeasurably finer" than any apparently similar poems by the rakish gallants of Restoration England. At the end of the essay, he turns to these poets and says that they are inferior because they "lack the positive fineness, the implicit subtlety, examined above in Carew." But these qualities were not *examined* at all: they were simply instanced, alleged to exist in the quoted poem. Again, I think Leavis entirely right in his assessment; but I can understand why my students (and not a few of my contemporaries) were turned off.

Francis Fergusson had complained, of the four essays devoted to Shakespeare in *The Common Pursuit*, that "in all of them he stops at the very point where I should like to see him continue, as though something in his conception of criticism, or even in his style, resisted further investigation." The critical practice of "The Line of Wit" must have had some-

thing to do with Eliot's way of using telling quotations and pregnant remarks. But the essays on "Judgment and Analysis" are entirely different.
They move patiently and attentively over various poems, continually returning (for the purposes of fuller explanation) both to the details that
Leavis has claimed are most telling and to the terms and judgments that
he means these analyses to advance. They thus give today's reader—who
will not come to Leavis knowing (or burdened by) the once conventional
views that were often the starting point for his revaluations—a sense of
why and how he arrives at particular judgments. The reason for the distinctiveness and (for the purpose I have in mind) the superiority of these
essays is that they are closer to Leavis's pedagogical practice than any
other of his writings. Pairs of poems are examined in turn, in order to elu-
cidate reasons for preferring one to the other or to clarify critical terms
and ways of working (the second essay, for example, is directed against
naive notions of "image"). The manner of the essays is very much that of
the classroom. Leavis moves from point to point, discusses a revealing detail, sometimes returns to it, says we have come this far and now let's look
at something else. He justifiably speaks, at the end of the first essay, of "the
exploratory path we have pursued." These essays enable you to see why
Thom Gunn says that Leavis's lectures "helped teach me to write, better
than any creative-writing class could have":

> His insistence on the realized, being the life of poetry, was exactly what I
> needed. His perceptions about language and verse movement in discussing
> the first lines of "Burnt Norton," Wordsworth's "Surprised by joy," or "If it
> were done when 'tis done," for example—by going directly to the texture
> of poetry, by showing how the reader's halting and attentive voice is an
> equivalent to the poet's act of exploration, by risking close scrutiny that
> entered into the terms of creation—brought me right to the hearth of my
> own activity.[13]

Many of Leavis's students speak of his extraordinary gifts as a reader: one
says, "he seemed to be intent on allowing the poet's words and rhythms to
speak through him, as it were."[14] Some passages in "Judgment and Analysis," with their consciousness of words on a page as cues for performance,
seem to bring us close to what one heard in the lecture room.

One other aspect of Leavis's critical practice is distinctively revealed in
these essays. He liked to say that "the form of a judgment is 'This is so,
isn't it?,' the question asking for confirmation that the thing *is* so, but prepared for an answer in the form, 'Yes, but—,' the 'but' standing for correc-

tions, refinements, precisions, amplifications."[15] But one frequently feels, in reading his criticism, that if challenged he would not stay for an answer. As for his teaching, L. C. Knights observes:

> The critic, he used to say, puts his judgements in the form "this is so, is it not?"; and he certainly hoped to provoke a "response" to his "challenge." But he did not realize the moral weight that he commanded—especially in relation to young minds fresh from school—that made "No, it is not" virtually impossible as a response to his question.[16]

The essays on "Judgment and Analysis" may be, in this respect, fortunately free of the conditions of the lecture room or the seminar. For as Leavis's analyses and arguments exist on the page, there is not only plenty to disagree with but room implicitly provided for one's disagreement. The essays extend the invitation which he claimed was always there partly because they mention what other readers have thought about these poems, but mainly by their fullness and clarity about the grounds of his judgments. If you disagree (as I don't) with the disparaging comparison of Shelley's "Music, when soft voices die" to Blake's "The Sick Rose," or if you disagree (as I do) with his dismissal of Wordsworth's "It is a beauteous evening, calm and free," the very example of his critical practice enables you to say, "I think not." These essays put on full display his recommended method of finding a detail that will reveal the character and distinction of a poem. (His admiring review of *Seven Types of Ambiguity* singled out the great and hilarious passage in which Empson says a critic looks for "a good place to scratch.")[17] There is a superb page on the adjective "smokeless" ("All bright and glittering in the smokeless air") with which Leavis argues for the superiority of "Composed upon Westminster Bridge" to "It is a beauteous evening." Analysis and judgment so exemplified both challenge and encourage you to find, in the poem you value, details that, when their life is discerned, can lead you to make a case for the life of the poem.

If these three essays enable today's student to understand the terms and bases of Leavis's judgments, it is not only in the sense that they might seek to understand Dr. Johnson's or Hazlitt's or Arnold's judgments. Leavis may or may not come to figure (again I speak from an American standpoint) as a critic of similar historical importance. But there is a broader sense in which these essays show a major critic at work. Their fullness and unspecialized clarity make them unusually valuable examples of critical analysis as both a practice of modernist criticism and a mode of teaching. Though aspects of them are dated (as when Leavis introduces the comparison of Lawrence's "Piano" to "Tears, idle tears" by speaking of "emotional hygiene"), their candor and grasp of the specific can give any student or teacher something to emulate. Every generation has to reinvent the terms on which it values literature, and for our students these terms are not the same as Bill's and mine, any more than they can be Leavis's. And yet as the existence of this volume testifies, students in Bill's classroom (as, one trusts, in the classrooms of many others of our generation) have acquired a sense of why literature matters and why it is absorbingly interesting. What I would claim for the essays on "Judgment and Analysis" is that students can see in them, more fully than anywhere else, what it meant to Leavis to read a poet "as we read the living." To the extent that they come to grasp his critical force and intelligence, they will read him too—even if they cannot share his tastes and protocols—as they read the living.

Notes

1. *Literary Theory: An Introduction* (Minneapolis: University of Minnesota Press, 1983), 31.

2. *Poetry and Pragmatism* (Cambridge: Harvard University Press, 1992), 190.

3. James E. Fisher, "Olivier and the Realistic *Othello*," *Literature/Film Quarterly* 1 (1973): 322; Barbara Hodgdon, "The Critic, the Poor Player, Prince Hamlet, and the Lady in the Dark," in *Shakespeare Reread*, ed. Russ McDonald (Ithaca: Cornell University Press, 1994), 260, 264.

4. For recent criticism, see Barbara Hodgdon's essay, cited above, and Graham Bradshaw, *Misrepresentations: Shakespeare and the Materialists* (Ithaca: Cornell University Press, 1993), 20–23, 190–93.

5. "The Milton Controversy," in *Twentieth-Century Literature in Retrospect* (Harvard English Studies 2), ed. Reuben A. Brower (Cambridge: Harvard University Press, 1971), 269–98.

6. *Education and the University* (London: Chatto & Windus, "new edition," 1948), 35.

7. "Scrutiny: Revolution from Within," *Partisan Review* 31 (1964): 301. Later page references will be parenthetical in the text. Elsewhere in this review-article, Brower discusses Leavis's effect on him when he was a student in Cambridge in the early '30s.

8. *Literary Landmarks* (New Brunswick: Rutgers University Press, 1975), 132. This essay is a review of *The Common Pursuit*, originally published in *Partisan Review* 20 (1953): 232–35.

9. "Poetic vs. Rhetorical Exegesis: The Case for Leavis against Richards and Empson," *Sewanee Review* 52 (1944): 266–76.

10. It is reprinted in *Education and the University* (above, n. 6). The passage from *Macbeth* is discussed on pp. 122–24.

11. *American Scholar* (Spring 1985), 222.

12. The essays appeared in *Scrutiny* as follows: "Thought and Emotional Quality" (13 [1945]: 53–71), "Imagery and Movement" (13 [1945]: 119–34), "Reality and Sincerity" (19 [1952–53]: 90–98). They were reprinted in *A Selection from Scrutiny*, ed. F. R. Leavis, 2 vols. (Cambridge: Cambridge University Press, 1968), 1:211–57, and in F. R. Leavis, *The Living Principle* (New York: Oxford University Press, 1975), 71–134. In this latter volume, there are some additions and modifications (notably pp. 93–106) which reflect Leavis's later preoccupations with, to use the book's subtitle, "'English' as a discipline of thought." In my view, these additions diminish the effectiveness of the original essays. In *F. R. Leavis: A Life in Criticism* (London: Allen Lane, 1995), Ian MacKillop commends these essays and gives some interesting details about their place in Leavis's work and his own regard for them (182).

13. Thom Gunn, *The Occasions of Poetry* (San Francisco: North Point Press, 1985), 170. Gunn's essay was originally published in *My Cambridge*, ed. Ronald Hayman (London: Robson, 1977).

14. Frank Whitehead, in Denys Thompson, ed., *The Leavises: Recollections and Impressions* (Cambridge: Cambridge University Press, 1984), 142. References by others to Leavis's brilliance as a reader can be found on pp. 86, 111.

15. *The Living Principle*, 35.

16. In *The Leavises*, 79.

17. *Seven Types of Ambiguity*, 3d ed. (London: Chatto & Windus, 1953), 9. Leavis's review (1931) is reprinted in a posthumous collection, *Valuation in Criticism and Other Essays*, ed. G. Singh (Cambridge: Cambridge University Press, 1986), 26–28. Leavis's best account of the method of putting one's finger on a telling detail is in *Education and the University*, 74–78. This discussion leads into an analysis of "If it were done when 'tis done" that must resemble what Thom Gunn heard in Leavis's lectures.

III

READINGS
Criticism in Practice

David Ferry

Notes on "Translating" the Gilgamesh Epic

from David Ferry, Gilgamesh: A New Rendering in English Verse,
Tablet IX *(Farrar, Straus and Giroux, 1993):*

Gilgamesh wandered in the wilderness
grieving over the death of Enkidu

and weeping saying: "Enkidu has died.
Must I die too? Must Gilgamesh be like that?"

Gilgamesh felt the fear of it in his belly.
He said to himself that he would seek the son

of Ubartutu, Utnapishtim, he,
the only one of men by means of whom

he might find out how death could be avoided.
He said to himself that he would hasten to him,

the dangers of the journey notwithstanding.
. . .

At night in the mountain passes there were lions,
and Gilgamesh was afraid, and entered afraid

into the moonlit mountain passes, praying
to Sin the moon god: "Hear my prayer and save me

as I enter into the passes where there are lions!"
At night when he lay down to sleep there were

confusions of dreams and in the dreams confusions
of noises, confusions of swords, daggers, axes.

199

An adversary gloried over him
in struggle, and in the dream who knows who won?
. . .
Gilgamesh came to the mountain called Mashu,
whose great twin heads look one way and the other.
. . .
Terror in the body of Gilgamesh
seized hold of him from within and held him there

in terror. But then, in terror, he went forward.
Then the Male Dragon Being said to him:

"Who is it dares come here? Why have you journeyed
through fearful wilderness, making your way through dangers

to come to this mountain no mortal has ever come to?"
Gilgamesh answered, his body seized in terror:

"I come to seek the father, Utnapishtim,
who was admitted to the company

of gods, who granted him eternal life.
I come to seek the answer to the question

that I must ask concerning life and death."
The Scorpion Monster Being said to him:

"No mortal has ever journeyed through the mountain.
This is the path of the sun's journey by night.

Lightless the sun utterly lightless goes
from the setting to the rising through the mountain.

This is the path of the sun, utterly dark,
twelve leagues of darkness through, utterly lightless.

No mortal would ever be able to go this way."
Gilgamesh said, his body seized in terror:

"This is the way that Gilgamesh must go,
weeping and fearful, struggling to keep breathing,

whether in heat or cold, companionless.
Open the gate to the entrance into the mountain."

Monster Husband and Wife murmured together.
Then the Male Twin Monster said to Gilgamesh:

"The gate to the entrance into the mountain is open.
May Gilgamesh in safety make the journey."

After the Scorpion Dragon Being spoke,
Gilgamesh went to the entrance into the mountain

and entered the darkness alone, without a companion.
By the time he reached the end of the first league

the darkness was total, nothing behind or before.
He made his way, companionless, to the end

of the second league. Utterly lightless, black.
There was nothing behind or before, nothing at all.

Only, the blackness pressed in upon his body.
He felt his blind way through the mountain tunnel,

struggling for breath, through the third league, alone,
and companionless through the fourth, making his way,

and struggling for every breath, to the end of the fifth,
in the absolute dark, nothing behind or before,

the weight of the blackness pressing in upon him.
Weeping and fearful he journeyed a sixth league,

and, blind, to the end of the seventh league, alone,
without a companion, seeing nothing at all,

weeping and fearful, struggling to keep breathing.
At the end of the eighth league he cried aloud

and tried to cry out something against the pressure
of blackness: "Two people, who are companions, they . . . !"

There was nothing behind or before him in the darkness;
utterly lightless, the way of the sun's night journey.

He struggled to breathe, trying to breathe the darkness.
He was weeping and fearful, alone, without a companion.

Just then, at the end of the ninth league, just once
the rough tongue of the North Wind licked at his face.

It was like the tongue of a wild bull or a lion.
He struggled on through darkness, trying to breathe.

The darkness pressed in upon him, both nothing and something.
After he struggled, blind, his companionless way

through eleven leagues of the darkness, nothing at all
and something, ahead of him, a league ahead

a little light, a grayness, began to show.
Weeping and fearful, struggling to keep breathing,

he made his way through the last league of the journey,
twelve leagues in the darkness, alone, companionless,

weeping and fearful, struggling to keep breathing,
he made his way and finally struggled out free

into the morning air and the morning sunlight.

The diffident quotes (Notes on "Translating") are because I don't read Babylonian and so was dependent, in my rendering of the Gilgamesh poem, on several scholarly word-for-word translations, mainly "The Epic of Gilgamesh," by E. A. Speiser in *Ancient Near Eastern Texts Relating to the Old Testament* (Princeton University Press, 1969), and two more recent works, *Gilgamesh*, by John Gardner and John Maier (Vintage, 1985) and *The Epic of Gilgamesh*, by Maureen Gallery Kovacs (Stanford University Press, 1989). I also consulted the excellent free prose version by B. K. Sandars, *The Epic of Gilgamesh* (Penguin, 1972). My commitment, of course, was different from theirs. Theirs was to the closest philological accuracy possible, acknowledging always the condition of the tablets as we have them; mine was, while trying earnestly to be as faithful as possible to the scholars' translations, to make a continuous metrical poem. Time after time I was confronted with two problems: the tablets on which the Gilgamesh poem was found are often extremely fragmentary; there are many places where the word-for-word translators disagree—that is, where their own particular word choices imply somewhat different readings of the passage in question. These were problems but also opportunities, and I found that the obligations to make choices, where the text is fragmentary or where the scholars differ, throws a particularly vivid light on the "translator's" conception of the nature of the text, its principles of organization.

For me the principal feature of the literary organization of the Gilgamesh is its resonance, episode to episode, expression to expression, backwards and forwards, driven by the intensely concentrated energies of the poem. I'd like to document this resonance by commenting on several places in Tablet IX of the poem where I had to make choices either to bridge egregious gaps or to follow one scholar rather than others. Of course I don't know whether these choices between scholars were "right" or "wrong" (and I'll indicate a couple of places where my uncertainty is acute), but I do know that they were almost always made to bring out my sense of this intensive resonance.

Here is the story leading up to Tablet IX: Gilgamesh was the king of Sumerian Uruk, so radiantly powerful and intimidating that his people called for a double to be created by the gods to contend with him and bring him under control. The gods created the wild man Enkidu, who ran with and was one with the wild beasts, and who, having been humanized by being seduced by Shamhat the temple-prostitute, went to Uruk to challenge Gilgamesh. They wrestled and Gilgamesh won and the two became, as it were, brothers, comrades in the heroic adventure of killing Huwawa the Demon Guardian of the Cedar Forest. This deed was offensive to the goddess Ishtar, whose servant Huwawa was. Nevertheless, when Gilgamesh came home from this adventure and washed up and dressed in clean clothes, he was so beautiful that Ishtar tried to seduce him. Gilgamesh knew what had happened to her previous lovers, human, animal, and divine, and so he refused her. Incensed, Ishtar got permission from her father Anu to send down the Bull of Heaven upon Gilgamesh and Enkidu. Gilgamesh and Enkidu killed the Bull of Heaven and Enkidu threw its haunch insultingly at the outraged goddess. The gods in council then decreed that one of these two, Gilgamesh and Enkidu, must die, and Enkidu was chosen. The death of Enkidu brought home to the grief-stricken Gilgamesh the actuality of his own mortality. He therefore desperately set out to discover from Utnapishtim, the Babylonia Noah, who was granted immortality because he survived the Great Flood, how he, Gilgamesh, could avoid death.

Here again is the opening passage of Tablet IX:

> Gilgamesh wandered in the wilderness
> grieving over the death of Enkidu
>
> and weeping saying: "Enkidu has died.
> Must I die too? Must Gilgamesh be like that?"

Gilgamesh felt the fear of it in his belly.
He said to himself that he would seek the son

of Ubartutu, Utnapishtim, he,
the only one of men by means of whom

he might find out how death could be avoided.
He said to himself that he would hasten to him,

the dangers of the journey notwithstanding.

The first time the expression I've rendered as "fear in his belly" occurs in
the poem is in Tablet I, where a hunter sees the wild man Enkidu:

One day a hunter came to a watering place
and *saw* the Wild Man Enkidu; he stood expressionless,

astonished; then with his silent dogs he went
home to his father's house, fear in his belly.

His face was as one estranged from what he knows.

It is an uncanny compelling moment, so early in the poem. The hunter is
staring astonished across the gap that separate human beings, with their
awareness of mortality, from the rest of creation, and he's at that moment
disoriented from himself and momentarily from his culture. The three
scholarly word-for-word translations I worked from make clearer than I
did, perhaps, here in Tablet I, how this encounter is proleptic for Gilgamesh's wandering and his desperate quest as Tablet IX begins to tell
about it. Speiser says, "His face was like that of a wayfarer from afar," Kovacs, "His face was like one who had made a long journey," and Gardner
and Maier, "His face was like that of one who travels a long road." My own
rendering concentrates on his disorientation but my intention, like the
translators', was to make the resonant connection with Gilgamesh, who
is, until the end, estranged from his acceptance of his mortality, but finally
accepts it and returns to his home. He is, in the end, "the one who knew
the most of all men know; / who made the journey; heartbroken; reconciled." The hunters' disorientation at the sight of Enkidu among his fellow
wild creatures, about to be "born" as a mortal human being, both anticipates and is a figure for Gilgamesh's disorientation caused by Enkidu's
death. A strange moment indeed, and I tried to emphasize its strangeness
by the juxtaposition of the extreme simplicity of "fear in his belly" and the
complex grammar of "His face was as one estranged from what he knows."

The fear in the hunter's belly is simple, in one way, the visceral fear of wild creatures; but it is also something else, not fully realizable for the reader when first encountered.

The hunter is himself an agent of the consequences of this moment. He goes home to his father, who sends him to Gilgamesh, who sends him back with the temple prostitute to humanize Enkidu, and the whole chain of circumstances is set in motion that leads to Enkidu's death and to Gilgamesh's setting out, dressed as a Wild Man, on his fruitless quest for immortality.

The word-for-word translations that I relied on provide different versions of the line "Gilgamesh felt the fear of it in his belly," when it occurs again, in Tablet IX. Speiser, for example, has "woe has entered his belly," Gardner and Maier, "sorrow came into [his] belly," and Kovacs, more abstractly, "deep sadness penetrated [his] core." In all of them, as in my rendering, the phrases, or phrases like them, become formulaic in the poem, expressive in their repetition as in Tablet X Gilgamesh tells and retells his story. I chose "fear in his belly" because I had used it about the hunter in Tablet I and I wanted to keep it simple, and easily adaptable to repetition in the various circumstances of its subsequent utterance. It also seemed to me that this simpler expression, characterizing Gilgamesh's state of mind after the death of Enkidu, was closer to the bone, more elemental, less human, less already-thought-through, than "sorrow" or "deep sadness" or even "woe." "Fear in his belly" seemed as much a thing of the body as of the mind. Gilgamesh's experience of his friend's mortality is horribly physical, as he sits beside the body for days and days. Over and over, estranged from what he knows and beginning to have a new knowledge, as he tells his story, he says obsessively: "I saw the worm drop out of Enkidu's nose. // Must I die too? Must I too be like that?"

I chose "fear in his belly," rather than "woe," "sorrow," or "sadness," for another reason, its place in the poem's vocabulary of its attitude toward the heroic. Gilgamesh encounters lions in the mountain passes, and Scorpion Monster Beings, and on his desperate futile journey he goes through the tunnel the sun goes through at night, and crosses the sea and the waters of death. His epic quest to allay his own anxiety is put in the terms of heroic adventure. But it is one of the thrilling things about this ancient poem, developed in a culture whose art often seems brutally oblivious to pity and brutally admiring of invincible confident heroes, that it recognizes, and pities, the vulnerability of this hero and his companion. These giant men are often terrified, often bewildered: "Then Gilgamesh saw the face of Huwawa the demon / and fled from the face, hiding himself away, . . . / Then Enkidu saw the face of Huwawa the demon / and fled from the face, hiding himself away, . . . Gilgamesh, weeping, cried out to the god Shamash: 'Protect us as we pass through fearfulness.'" And their heroism often consists in their going ahead in spite of, and indeed because of, their terror: "Then Gilgamesh was afraid, and Enkidu / was afraid, and they entered into the Forest, afraid." I tried to render this in a syntactical echoing pattern: "Gilgamesh was afraid, and entered afraid / into the moonlit mountain passes, praying," and, later in the Tablet, when he approaches the Twin Monster Scorpion Beings whose shimmering is death to see: "Terror in the body of Gilgamesh / seized hold of him from within and held him there / In terror. But then, in terror, he went forward."

The word "confusions" itself I borrowed from the Sandars version, where Gilgamesh, in the Cedar Forest episode, says to Enkidu his companion, also recounting a dream: "The sleep that the gods sent me is broken. Ah, my friend, what a dream I have had! Terror and confusion . . ." (pp. 77-78). The battle with Huwawa is full of confusion, and so is the text, broken and fragmented at that point, just as it is at this point in Tablet IX. This is the way the Tablet IX passage reads, for example, in Gardner and Maier's translation:

> Gilgamesh takes up the axe in his hand;
> he drew the weapon from his belt
> and like an arrow he fell among them.
>
> He struck . . . smashing them,
> . . . enjoying it.
> He threw . . .
> He guarded . . .
> Second . . .
> He lifted . . .

So the word "confusion," generalized as it is, was a kind of private joke for me about the condition of the text, and it was convenient for me in making my way across this gap in it. But it was also a very rich word for me in my interpretation of this poem, and I would argue that the choice of it is true to the poem's interpretation of itself, for one way to talk about the story of Gilgamesh is to say that it is the story of his confusion on the subject of the consequences of pride, of heroism, of the denial of mortality. When he returns to Uruk at the end of the poem, disabused of his hopes of defeating death, the confusion is at last dispelled.

At this point I had to choose between two scholarly readings, both powerful. Speiser and Kovacs put this confused heroic encounter *inside* Gilgamesh's dream. I read their translations as saying that he awakened from his dream remembering, in an excited, frightened way, the battle that took place in that dream. The Gardner and Maier translation, saying "though he lay down to sleep, the dream did not come," posits that Gilgamesh asked for a predictive dream and didn't get it and had to go on through dangers without it. In their reading Gilgamesh must go forward stripped naked of the foreknowledge, for good or ill, that dream-omens can give. Without the comfort of this foreknowledge, and without the companionship of Enkidu, he seems more and more alone. But I chose to follow Speiser and Kovacs here because the choice seemed to make this episode at the beginning of Tablet IX enter more directly, as a kindred experience, into the chain of dreadfully ambiguous dreams Gilgamesh had on his way to the encounter with Huwawa, dreams of a mountain falling on them, a rain of fire and ashes, a struggle with a monstrous or divine bull. Enkidu endearingly interpreted the dream, every time, as foretelling good fortune —"There were other dreams that disturbed the sleep of the king, / night after night as they journeyed to the Forest, // And Enkidu always said they were fortunate." And in a way they *were* fortunate, foretelling the glorious victory over Huwawa, and after that over the Bull of Heaven, but they foretell also the death of Enkidu and the subsequent anguish and humiliation of Gilgamesh. It isn't just that the dreams are portents. Dramatically the dream-recounting and dream-interpreting are a site of the enacting of the companionship of these two, and therefore foretell the companionless grief of Gilgamesh as he goes through the tunnel the sun travels through at night, in quest of life.

Those dreams on the mountainside echo backward to Gilgamesh's dream of a fallen meteorite, and his mother's interpretation of the dream, in Tablet I, as a dream of the coming of Enkidu into his life.

> "The star you were drawn to as if drawn to a woman,
>
> is the strong companion, powerful as a star,
> the meteorite of the heavens, a gift of the gods.
>
> That you were drawn to it as if drawn to a woman
> means that this companion will not forsake you.
>
> He will protect and guard you with his life.
> This is the fortunate meaning of your dream."

Thus the friendship and their heroic achievements have the fated, foretold approval of the gods, and the death of Enkidu is fated too. And the dreams echo forward, so to speak, to Enkidu's dreams in Tablet VII: "I dreamed that the gods were offended and held a council, / . . . 'They have killed the Bull of Heaven // and killed Huwawa. One of them must die'"; and the dream, just before his death, "of the man with a lion head, and the paws of a lion too, / but the nails were talons, the talons of an eagle," come to conduct him to the place where Ereshkigal the Queen of the Underworld waits to greet him. The dreams are dreams, occurrences in the inner lives of human beings, and they are riddling portents, messages from the gods; they are events in the ongoing implacable narrative, and powerful dramatizations commenting on those events.

In the next episode of Tablet IX Gilgamesh arrives at the tunnel and, having received permission from the Scorpion Guardian Beings, enters into it. The tunnel episode itself, at least as we have it in its fragmented condition, is extremely repetitive. For example, from the Speiser translation:

> When five leagues he had attained,
> Dense is the darkness and light there is none;
> He can see nothing ahead or behind.
> When six leagues he had attained,
> Dense is the darkness and light there is none;
> He can see nothing ahead or behind.
> When seven leagues he had attained,
> Dense is the darkness and light there is none;
> He can see nothing ahead or behind.
> Eight leagues he has traveled and he cries out.
> Dense is the darkness and light there is none;
> He can see nothing ahead or behind.
> Nine leagues he has traveled . . .

I knew that this extreme repetitiveness would be very difficult to render without monotony, without the passage becoming something of a dead spot. At least it seemed so to me when I read the word-for-word translations. I felt called upon to produce a narrative and rhythmical pattern that was less unvarying and yet would still represent the serial ordeal of Gilgamesh making his way through what seemed an endless darkness. Speiser's translation provided a clue. At the seventh league the wording hasn't changed, but at the eighth he "cries out." What is it he cries out, and to whom? Previously in the poem the two personages cried out to are

Shamash the sun god (for his help in the fight with Huwawa) and Enkidu (for encouragement and help in the same fight; and also, in a bereaved cry, when Enkidu has just died). Either choice has its power. Going through the tunnel Gilgamesh in darkness longs for the light, and Shamash, who has been his protector god throughout the poem, is the god of light. Indeed, in a much earlier, Old Babylonian, version of this passage, Shamash apparently speaks to Gilgamesh during this night journey. To my mind, though, the other choice was better, richer in the possibilities of its resonant echoing of things Gilgamesh and Enkidu had said to one another in the days of their heroic deeds, and echoing also what Enkidu had said on his deathbed. And it seemed advantageous to me to intensify the loneliness of Gilgamesh, without the companionship of Enkidu, and, without any idea of the hovering sponsorship of Shamash, at least until the end of the journey, when he begins to see the light of day and then comes out into it. Furthermore, the interpolations of these phrases permitted me to vary somewhat the rhythms and syntax of the clauses describing the stages of his journey:

> Weeping and fearful he journeyed a sixth league,
>
> and, blind, to the end of the seventh league, alone,
> without a companion, seeing nothing at all,
>
> weeping and fearful, struggling to keep breathing.
> At the end of the eighth league he cried aloud
>
> and tried to cry out something against the pressure
> of blackness: "Two people, who are companions, they . . . !"
>
> There was nothing behind or before him in the darkness;
> utterly lightless, the way of the sun's night journey.
>
> He struggled to breathe, trying to breathe the darkness.
> He was weeping and fearful, alone, without a companion.
>
> Just then, at the end of the ninth league, just once
> the rough tongue of the North Wind licked at his face.
>
> It was like the tongue of a wild bull or a lion.
> He struggled on through darkness, trying to breathe.

At the ninth stage of his journey Speiser says the North Wind "fanned" his face, Gardner and Maier say it "bit into" and Kovacs says it "licked at"

his face. "Licked at" was physically more vivid for me as I read it, given the
fetid closeness of the blackness in the tunnel, and at the same time less decisive than "bit," therefore more suitable to his only being at the end of the
ninth league. "Licked at" reminded me, and I wanted it to remind the
reader, of the horrible embraces, the wrestlings with, the reeking foul
closeness of the Bull of Heaven, which in Tablet VI the gods, at the behest
of the indignant goddess Ishtar, had sent down to punish Gilgamesh and
Enkidu for their impudence in killing the Demon Guardian of the Cedar
Forest and (in Gilgamesh's case) for rejecting her advances:

> . . . For the third time the Bull of Heaven bellowed
> and Uruk shook; and Enkidu fought the Bull
>
> and took hold of the Bull by the horns and the great bull head
> thrashed over him and the reeking bull slobber poured
>
> over his face and Enkidu fought the Bull
> and the foul tail of the Bull brushed over his face
>
> and Enkidu wrestled and Enkidu cried out
> to Gilgamesh: "The life of man is short,
>
> let us contend with the Bull of Heaven, and win,"
> and Gilgamesh fought, and fighting the Bull they cried:
>
> "Two people, companions, they can prevail together,"
> and Enkidu seized the Bull by the reeking tail
>
> and Gilgamesh thrust his sword with the skill of a butcher
> between the shoulders and horns, and they killed the Bull.
>
> They tore out the great bull heart and offered the heart
> to Shamash, bowing before the god, two brothers.
>
> After the battle the two sat down and rested.

I also wanted the reader to be reminded of one of the dreams Gilgamesh
had on the mountain, in Tablet IV, when he and Enkidu were preparing to
confront Huwawa the Demon Guardian of the Cedar Forest. It is a night-
mare that Enkidu interprets otherwise.

> Enkidu, born in the wilderness, made a shelter.
> The two of them sheltered themselves against the wind.
>
> After a time the oblivion of sleep
> poured in upon the king. He fell asleep,

but at midnight suddenly woke up, disturbed,
and said to the companion, Enkidu:

"Did you call out to me in the night? Was it you
that touched me? Was it a god went through the camp?

In the dream I had, a great bull head was thrashing
over my body in glory, and bellowing

over me, me helpless on the ground; the breath
of the bull snout breathed on me; the bellowing

bull noise shook the earth and broke it open;
the choking dust rose up and filled the dream.

Then one brought water to me in my dream."
"The dream you dreamed tonight is fortunate.

The bull you dreamed of in your dream is not
the demon enemy guardian of the Forest.

The bull is Shamash. The wrestling is his blessing.
The one who brought you water is your father."

In one way the dream is a dream of blessing and in another it is a night-mare. Gilgamesh and Enkidu survive the encounter and are indeed victorious over him (or it), and Gilgamesh goes on, after the death of Enkidu, to be our representative and make his heroic and quixotic journey in quest of protection against death. He becomes our representative too in learning his mortal lesson and finally accepting it. But the victory over Huwawa is an offence against Ishtar and other divine beings, and so is the victory in Tablet VI over the Bull of Heaven. Taken together they bring about the death of Enkidu, who, after the Bull of Heaven was killed, had thrown its haunch insultingly at the goddess Ishtar. So Enkidu's interpretation of the dream is pitifully, wrenchingly, complex in its rightness and wrongness.

If the wind licking at his face like a bull in the tunnel passage is a fatherly blessing, it is equivocally so. It signals Gilgamesh's safe passage through the tunnel on his heroic journey to seek immortality; but this is a journey that will end in failure. When the serpent steals the plant called How-the-Old-Man-Once-Again-Becomes-Young-Man, Gilgamesh says,

"What shall I do? The journey has gone for nothing.
For whom has my heart's blood been spent? For whom?

For the serpent who has taken away the plant.
I descended into the waters to find the plant

and what I found was a sign telling me to
abandon the journey and what it was I sought for."

But it is this failure that leads Gilgamesh at last to accept his condition of mortality. The end of the poem echoes the beginning, in which it was said of him that "he knew the most of all men know." He returned to his city, "heartbroken; reconciled," no longer estranged from what he knows.

Peter R. Pouncey

Plutarch on the Sign of Socrates[1]

IN 1870, A HANDSOME EDITION of Plutarch's collected works was produced, five volumes of Essays (the *Moralia*) and five volumes of Lives.[2]
Emerson wrote an introduction to the Essays, and used part of it to track
Plutarch's influence in Europe—in France, from Amyot's translations
through Rabelais, Montaigne, Voltaire, and Rousseau; in England, from
North, through Shakespeare, Bacon, and Dryden. With the tradition safely
established behind him, Emerson advances on the text and judgment:

> He [Plutarch] is . . . a repertory for those who want the story without
> searching for it at first hand—a compend [*sic*] of all accepted traditions.
> And all this without any supreme intellectual gifts. He is not a profound
> mind. . . . But if he had not the highest powers, he was yet a man of rare
> gifts. He had that universal sympathy with genius which makes all its vic-
> tories his own; though he never used verse, he had many qualities of the
> poet in the power of his imagination, the speed of his mental associations,
> and his sharp, objective eyes. (Introduction, xi)

Sneaky praise, but condescending just the same. The tone is common
among scholars of Plutarch, and unfair. He is more than the compend of

all accepted traditions, the prolix antiquarian, safely and virtuously unengaged in the problems of his day, writing moderate judgments from his country silence. In what follows I hope to show, from a small corner of his writing, that he is no passive receiver and transmitter of the tradition he inherits, but capable of reimagining it in strenuous and interesting ways.

A word first about his life. We have only approximate dates for it, c.50–c.120, from Claudius to Hadrian, but though he knew prominent Romans and dedicated works to some of them, by his own choice he let most of the business of empire pass him by. It was enough to know their history. He was born and spent most of his days in a prosperous family in Chaeronea, a village in Boeotia famous for his country's defeat. It was there in 338 B.C.E. that Philip of Macedon and his eighteen-year-old son Alexander crushed Boeotia's leading city Thebes with its allies from Athens; you can still visit the Lion Monument to the Sacred Band of Thebes, killed on a single day almost to a man by Alexander's cavalry. Plutarch was educated in Athens, and traveled a little, certainly to Egypt, perhaps twice to Rome, but always returned to Chaeronea. From there he could see Mount Parnassus, on whose slopes was the oracle of Delphi, still numinous in decline as it is today in its ruins. Plutarch became the chief administrator *(epimeletes)* at Delphi in his later years, where we see him preserving the traditions, and grateful for renewed interest from the latest Roman Emperor, Hadrian. The whole life seems to have been one of piety, in its fullest sense, expressed in reading, writing, and remembering.

Plutarch's essay "On the Sign of Socrates" is a work of surprising, planned disjointedness. It sets out to be an account of how a group of conspirators reclaim Thebes from tyranny and the Spartan occupation in December of 379 B.C.E., though, as the title conveys, a large piece of emphasis falls elsewhere. The actual historical event is a high-water mark in the chronicles of Boeotia, in contrast to the Battle of Chaeronea; it led directly to the brief hegemony of Thebes over the Greek world. The essay is written in the form of a dialogue within a dialogue, and does record, excitingly and in detail, the stirring events of the liberation, in the words of one of the participants, Caphisias, to an interested group of contemporary Athenians. As the plot matures and the hour of its execution approaches, the reader is drawn into the anxieties and suspense of the conspirators, between the false and genuine alarms, and the comings and goings of participants and strangers, as they wait for their moment. How do they spend the time? They spend it, with interruptions from the door opening for new arrivals and developments, on a philosophic debate between those privy to the conspiracy as to what the real nature of Socrates' *daimon* was. The allusion is to the famous passage in the *Apology* (31d) where Socrates tells the court that he has had "a divine or spiritual experience" *(theion ti kai daimonion)*, and defines it as a "voice, beginning in his childhood, which when it occurs, always stops him from doing something he is about to do, but never urges him on." Twenty years after Socrates' death, the conspirators, waiting for nightfall to liberate their city, settle down to discuss the nature of this cautionary voice, and how it operated. The argument begins with short specifics and anecdotes, and then is handed to a senior figure, the veteran Simmias, nursing a wounded leg, and therefore *hors de combat;* we are told that he had traveled widely, including at least once with Plato, and had a great store of exotic information. When the floor is yielded to Simmias, the give and take of argument smooths itself to an expansive monologue on the role of spirit, and of separate spirits, in the life of humans; and finally, still in the words of Simmias, the discussion passes the bounds of reason and is raised to a cosmic myth of great beauty, on the world-after-death and the cycles of existence. At the end of the myth and after a short endorsement of its truth by Theanor, the conspirators finally launch themselves into action against the leaders of the tyranny and achieve total success.[3]

The presence of Simmias the Theban sends us back (perhaps with some prompting!) to Plato's *Phaedo,* in which he is one of the two main discussants with Socrates about the immortality of the soul. Once we have made the association, we see further parallels—the *Phaedo,* like Plutarch's essay, is a dialogue within a dialogue, the discussion takes place as the participants count down to an ominous event (the death of Socrates), and the dialogue ends on an elevated note with a myth about the world-after-death and the cycles of existence. Is this a case of the Old Derivative rehashing the Master's material with a nationalist spin, substituting the triumph of Thebes for the loss to Athens of Socrates? The simple answer is "no" (this has to be a short paper).

Plutarch's essay is structurally more ambitious than Plato's. In the *Phaedo,* the scene in the prison is set at the outset, Socrates' relaxed acceptance of the prospect of death is established, and then the dialogue on immortality proceeds without interruption until the sad denouement. But Plutarch complicates his situation by interweaving the debate on the *daimon* with practical developments in the conspiracy; he is a master storyteller, but in this case he must see to it that the suspense of his exciting story does not sag among the philosophic exchanges. It is not clear to me that he is at every point successful in avoiding this pitfall. But it becomes clear why he wants to take the risk.

Caphisias begins his story with a message from young exiles privy to the plot: they will come to the city for the action that night. Whose house should they come to? Charon bravely and forthrightly volunteers his. The first scene seems to be set in the street, which gives Plutarch the chance to introduce some more of the characters on both sides. We hear of Caphisias's brother, Epaminondas (a great figure in later Theban history and privy to this plot, but not active in it, because of his scruple against killing civilians without a trial), Theocritus, a soothsayer, Galaxidorus, and Phyllidas, secretary to the board of tyrants but a conspirator against them. Of the tyrants themselves, we hear of the Thebans Archias and Leontiades, and of Lysanoridas, the commander of the Spartan garrison that keeps them in power. Plutarch has Archias take Theocritus aside and question him—the first note of suspense: What are they talking about? Is Archias interrogating him about the conspiracy? It turns out he wants Theocritus's professional opinion: there have been bad omens for the Spartans because they have disturbed Alcmena's tomb.

The conspirators come to the haven of Simmias's house. More of them are introduced, and we will not follow all the twists and turns between them. The passage is linked to what we have just read by the mention of the Stranger, who turns out to be Theanor, a pious and wealthy Pythagorean from Italy on a pilgrimage to the grave of Lysis, a former leader of his sect. Plutarch, a lover of pairs or doublets (in everything from phrasing to large themes; he wrote the *Parallel Lives*, after all), has played off Spartan graverobbers against pious respecters of the dead, with a great deal of arcane archaeology buried among them.

At this point, the plainspoken Galaxidorus delivers some asperities against all this mumbo jumbo. Thank God for Socrates, who brought philosophy down to earth and grounded it on reason. Theocritus rises to this challenge to his profession: "What then are we to make of Socrates' *daimonion* (sign from heaven)? Was it a lie?" The principal subject of our essay is introduced and instances are given of Socrates' premonitions, both on amusing and serious occasions. The thought that his "sign" may have been conveyed to him by a sneeze is both defended and disparaged, and then Plutarch ends this more trivial part of his debate with the arrival of Epaminondas and his guest Theanor.

The essay now takes a long and seemingly irrelevant detour. Theanor tells how the *daimonion* of Lysis had communicated in a dream to his sect in Italy that he was dead, and how he had been sent to perform the final rites and perhaps take the body home. This is all right as far as it goes, but we then have an almost interminable debate (nearly seven pages in the Greek) between Theanor and Epaminondas on the question of whether a benefactor has an obligation to accept a gift of gratitude from the one he has benefited. Epaminondas has attended to Lysis in his exile lovingly and piously, and Theanor wants to reward him for it; Epaminondas has refused the gift. We shall explore Plutarch's thinking behind this digression below.

The question of true gratitude has barely been laid to rest when there are new and agitated arrivals. Phyllidas comes in, dragging a reluctant Hippostheneidas, whom we have not met before; he is presented as the weak link in the conspiracy. He has taken it on himself to send a message to the young exiles they are expecting that night, not to come. It is too dangerous. Even if they kill Archias and Leontiades, they will not be able to dispose of the Spartan garrison in the citadel. Furthermore a friend of his, Hypatodorus, reported a worrying dream about Charon and his house: the house was straining, apparently in labor, and Charon and his people were anxiously praying in it, in a confused and inaudible sort of way, when it burst into fire. The blaze of flame extended through the city, but only smoke reached the citadel.

Charon is about to reply to this, but Theocritus the soothsayer intervenes with some damage control of his own: he is greatly encouraged by the dream, and finds it wholly favorable. The blaze of light spreading through the city from Charon's pregnant house indicates the success of the conspiracy when they take it public; the fact that only smoke reaches the citadel must mean that the Spartans are totally in the dark about what is happening.

And, it turns out, there is more tangible reassurance at the door: Chlidon, the messenger sent to warn off the exiles, the man with the fastest mount in Thebes, never left. He had had an argument with his wife about his horse's bridle, which she had lent to a neighbor, and he was too upset to go. The message was never taken. But the episode had been unsettling. Plutarch skilfully sketches the shift in emotions among the conspirators from initial disappointment at the cancellation of their plans, back to renewed anxiety at the realization that now their course is set and they have no choice but to follow through. Phyllidas leaves to prepare for the party he is throwing for Archias, at which he will get him drunk and ready for the liberators.

Into this unsettled mood of nervous preoccupation, old Simmias, who, we remember, had been with Socrates when he died, calmly takes up the question of the *daimonion* again. Let us have no talk of sneezes. Really what we need to understand is the way spirit communes with spirit. Our minds are constantly agitated and darkened by the crassness of the world and its business, and by our appetites, and our hearing is muffled by their constant dinning in our ears. Simmias gives us some of the physics of hearing: the air is disturbed by the explosive sounds of speech, and the shock-waves of so many voices press upon our ear confusingly. For most mortals, it is only when they sleep and dream that their spirits are lulled enough to hear the voice of other spirits, human or otherwise, speaking to them. But there are some few like Socrates, who, by constant discipline and restraint and attention to the claims of spirit, have hushed the busy world and possess their souls in peace. To them the spirit speaks directly, and they can hear.

> In truth, we become aware of each other's thoughts, when they speak to us, as though groping in the dark. But the thoughts of spirits illumine spiritual souls by simple light, and have no need of words or phrases, which men must use as symbols with each other and so are left looking only at like-nesses and images of what is meant. (589B–C)

We should not be surprised at this capacity of spirit to move our souls directly, unmediated by sound or air. Even in the physical world things can be made surprisingly responsive to the gentlest touch—a large ship can be turned by the movement of a small tiller, and a potter's wheel can be so balanced that it will be set spinning by the lightest touch of a fingertip (588F). Just so, inside our bodies, our spirits instruct our limbs to carry out our will: but how much more immediate and direct must be the touch, when insubstantial spirits move upon our souls? Simmias feels he has done all he can by reasoned argument to account for the work of Socrates' *daimon*. He alludes with some diffidence to the myth of Timarchus of Chaeronea,[+] as though this might not be appropriate for such an audience, but Theocritus immediately insists that he tell it: "for Myth, even if it falls short of rigor, still finds its way to touch the truth" (589F). Simmias proceeds. It seems that Timarchus, a young disciple of Socrates, was so preoccupied with his master's "sign" that he determined to get to the bottom of it. He went down into the crypt of Trophonius (a Boeotian oracle), and after being down for two nights and given up for dead, he came up again radiant on the next morning, and told what had happened to him.

He had lain down and gone to sleep, but was suddenly aware of a crash and a mighty blow to the head, so that the seams of his skull sprung apart, and his soul escaped. It mounted joyfully, conscious of a new expansiveness and freedom, "like a sail billowing out before the wind" (590B). This is what he saw:

> He saw islands glowing with a soft fire exchanging colors as they moved among each other like a dye catching different tints from the shifting light. The islands seemed countless in number, and enormous in size, but not all equal, though all circular in shape and all spinning. He had the impression that the air around them was sounding a soft vibrant chord on a high note caught from their rotation, the gentle sound in perfect harmony with the smoothness of their motions. (ibid.)

But that was not all:

> Looking down, he saw the funnel of a chasm, . . . monstrously frightening and deep, which was not at rest, but churning with agitated waves and currents. Out of it he heard a welter of bellows and groans of living creatures, countless cries of infants and sobs of men and women, an uproar from every kind of torment reaching dimly upwards from out of the far depths. . . . And after a pause, someone spoke to him unseen: "Timarchus, what do you want to know?" And he said: "Everything. For what is there not to wonder at?" (590F–591A)

The unseen voice goes on to explain the workings of this cosmic structure. The individual points of light that Timarchus can see are the souls or demons stripped of their bodies. But some of them are faltering both in the clear persistence of their light and the steadiness of their movements. These are the souls who carry still an admixture of their earthly passions from their previous life; they hover near the lip of the chasm, and though they may struggle to stay in the upper air, they will be sucked down again into the dark for rebirth in the world below. (It is interesting that though this underworld is called Hades, Timarchus understands that it is the Earth.) There are other more fortunate souls, few in number, whose light soars steadily and clearly into the upper air; they are now purified souls and their Sisyphean cycle of death and rebirth is over.

It is worth looking at this last description of the chasm a little more closely, to point up some of the differences between Plato's and Plutarch's handling of the scene. Plato has Socrates give us elaborate details of *geography:* among all the chasms of the earth, there is indeed one that is deepest (Plato, *Phd.* 111e–112a) into which rivers flow. There are four principal rivers, which sweep the souls of the dead from their tuck in the earth's surface (which is where human life is spent) down towards Tartarus (this deepest chasm). The four rivers are Oceanus, Acheron, Pyriphlegethon (molten), and Cocytus. The sinuosities of these rivers, and their relationships to each other, are elaborated (Plato, *Phd.* 112e–113c), and so is some of the freight of souls they carry. The incurably evil are swept by Cocytus forever into Tartarus; those with lesser sins may petition those they offended in their lives for forgiveness, and when it is granted they may start to rise towards rebirth. All of this is narrated with limpid factuality.

Plutarch's cosmology is elaborate and geometrically measured, but it dispenses with the rivers. Instead it concentrates them all into the Styx, the great chasm, path, or "river" of darkness formed by the earth's shadow, which rises towards the Moon. The passage quoted above describes the chasm in a scene of great torment, worthy of Dante's *Inferno*. The churning waves of darkness carry upwards the billowing sounds of grief from every kind of creature, not only humans. "For we know that the whole creation groaneth and travaileth in pain together until now" (St. Paul, *Rom.* 8.22). The pagan but deeply religious Plutarch engages this scene with a wonderfully rich vocabulary, whose very sounds carry the note of sorrow (in Greek, both -u and -ou are pronounced as English "oo"): *akouesthai murias men orugas kai stenagmous zoon. . . . psophous de pantodapous kai thorubous ek bathous porrothen amudrous anapempomenous*—the ear is under a barrage of long "o's" and "oo's" through the whole passage (twenty-three "oo's" alone in under seven lines!). This rhetorical insistence forces the reader's engagement with the picture. The words alone voice constant agitation and struggle.

But Plutarch lightens these lugubrious scenes and sounds with his insistence on the role of attendant spirits *(daimones)*, who supervise the progress of the souls through their ordeals of purification and illumination. The voice that speaks to young Timarchus is not a god's voice, but a *daimon*'s, and it explains to him: "With the higher realms we have little to do—they belong to the gods" (591A). This is not the place for a theological or metaphysical exegesis on the grades of spiritual being; we will not land far afield if we chart Plutarch's position on these matters along the line of successors to Plato, running with some idiosyncratic curves through Posidonius (c.135–51 B.C.E.) on the way to Plotinus (205–270 A.D.).[5] There is a growing intellectual preoccupation over this period: to strip the gods of their often disedifying anthropomorphic antics and attributes, and arrive at the conception of a spiritual divinity so pure and refined that it need not, indeed must not, engage with the management of the cosmos at all. Once you have achieved that, you have then created the need for other intermediary spirits, to serve as guardian, or other, angels to engage the creation and work the God's will.[6]

Plutarch takes this idea and gives it a very dynamic charge. When Simmias finishes his myth and falls silent, Theanor endorses his argument and embellishes it. He describes the sympathetic role of the *daimones* in surveying and supporting the ordeal of human souls. They are like people standing on the beach, who come to the help of swimmers struggling through the surf to make it to the shore; or they are like former athletes themselves, who in retirement serve as trainers and coaches holding the next generation to the discipline and highest standards of their sport. We might take these similes and consider them extensions of Timarchus's myth—and there is a straight continuity in the thought. Looking further back, we also pick up the allusion to Epaminondas's argument for refusing to accept Theanor's lavish gift for having looked after Lysis. He is proud of his poverty; he speaks more than once as though he is an athlete in training for the highest prize (the prize of virtue, which means having a head clear of the corrupting fog of appetite and greed). One needs to *exercise* true *discipline* (*askesis*—584E–F, 585A, etc.) when perfectly legitimate opportunities arise, if one is going to be strong and clear-sighted with the insidious approaches of corruption. Epaminondas, who had been accused by Theocritus of "dodging" the action for all his high-flown philosophy, is feelingly vindicated by Simmias after this argument. "Epaminondas is great," he said, "great!" (585D). And Theanor adds his own praise, when he says that Epaminondas's care of Lysis was perfect to the last detail, right down to the proper (secret) rituals of burial, and concluded that he must have used the same *daimon* as his guide in life:

> "For countless are the paths of human life, but few the ones where spirits serve as guides." With these words, he looked at Epaminondas attentively, as though to contemplate anew his nature and essence. (586A)[7]

Suddenly now, the patterns of Plutarch's essay start to emerge. The treatment of the two perfect (each in his own way) sons of Polymnis point the way for us. Our narrator Caphisias, who is teased by his friends in the dialogue for his athleticism and love of wrestling (by Phyllidas at 577B; Epaminondas at 583D) is a leader of a conspiracy to free his country from tyranny. He has trained himself for his role. But in Plutarch's mind, Epaminondas's training to free his mind from the tyranny of false appetite is exactly parallel and equally practical. Once the tyrants are killed,

Epaminondas joins his brother and rallies the citizens to the cause (598C–D). The Spartan garrison withdraws without further bloodshed, so his principles remain intact. For Plutarch, the pursuit of true virtue is always practical and always socially beneficial, and it also takes courage, just as much as fighting a political oppressor. There are only two "friendly" casualties in this essay. One is Cephisodorus, who is killed in the night attack on the tyrant Leontiades, and dies happy that he has freed his country; the other is Timarchus, the young teller of the myth, who goes down, apparently into the grave, but returns with a partially liberating vision for his friends, and then dies three months later. The whole world of human action is a dark and threatening place, in which we make gains only by stern resolve.

Even if we do not accept the dramatic success of these elaborately drawn parallels, I think we can see some of the reasoning that led Plutarch to his structure of interwoven action and debate. It is more than a display of philosophic "cool" by practical men before their desperate venture; to search for the truth is just another kind of *agon* attended by its own hazards.

But why do I call Timarchus's vision "partially liberating"? I think the phrase can be understood best in contrast to the tenor of Plato's myth in the *Phaedo.* There the myth is told on the firm premise that Socrates is reaching the end, that it is a final end, that he is leaving a tainted world behind, with every sign of pleasure, and going to a better place. There is, then, a kind of serenity, and no agitation, in the dialogue that moves to the quiet repose of his death. Plutarch's argument, and the pictures he paints in his myth, do not offer the same reassurance. He cannot say when the arduous cycles of death and rebirth are finished, except that it can only occur when the last traces of contamination from the world have been purged: there is more energy in Plutarch's account, because he observes, and stresses, the human lot as one of persistent, ongoing struggle (the *agon*), on the earth below and also on the very doorstep of heaven. There is nothing very liberating about that; but I call Timarchus's myth *partially* liberating, because of the insistence it makes that our passage through this world and into the next is attended at every step by unseen but helpful spirits, who send us signs amid the murky confusion about the way to go, or not to go, and occasionally smooth our path with unexpected happenings. The whole world, up to the grave and after it, is charged with spirit. I would suggest that Plutarch's belief in this world of strenuous spiritual interactions carries us on to ground relatively untrodden by scholars over

the centuries—the ground of private devotion, on which philosophic reasoning, the careful performance of ritual, and a kind of religious curiosity
to discover practices and beliefs far afield are all joined to, and put in the
service of, a spiritual yearning to make sense of one's life.

There is, in fact, some serious infighting, and some apologetics, that
Plutarch puts to work in this dialogue in support of his religious beliefs,
and uses as a further binding agent between the active and philosophic
parts of the essay. The interior current of this argument may be summa-
rized as follows. In the practical world, where confusing developments
break fast upon us, and we must make decisions with limited intelligence,
we find ourselves seeking information from every quarter, and we train
ourselves to *read the signs.* Some of the signs are quite straightforward—
messages are sent (the exiles will come to Thebes tonight) or not sent
(Hippostheneides' message not to come) or sent but not read (the message
sent to the carousing tyrant Archias giving full details about the conspiracy, but not read by him: It's serious, the messenger told him; "Serious is
for tomorrow," said Archias, putting the message under his pillow un-
read—596F). Some signs are harder to read: what does it mean when
Archias calls Theocritus to him on the street, or sends guards to summon
Charon to his house at the end of Simmias's exposition (594E ff.)? We seek
signs from the ground (what do the contents of Alcmena's grave have to
tell us, whether we're Spartans or conspirators), and from the sky (the encouraging flash of lightning on the right, without thunder, when the
muffled exiles enter the city in the cold twilight—594E). We read the
signs sent when we are awake and when we are asleep. It might be argued
that one should not confuse signs of fact with signs of superstition. But of
course Plutarch will not allow a distinction between the two; his own
epistemology can accommodate every kind of prophetic revelation of the
future, just as well as an old document can tell us the past. The outspoken
Galaxidorus makes the comparison explicit:

> If an illiterate person, who did not even know what writing was, saw letters
> on a page, few in number and insignificant in shape, he would not believe
> that a literate man could actually read out of these shapes the story of great
> wars, which befell people in the past, the founding of cities and the suffer-
> ings of kings. No, he would say some spirit *(daimonion ti)* was reporting and
> narrating all these things to this historian. We would have a pleasant laugh
> at the ignorance of such a fellow. But consider whether we are not in the
> same position. Because we are ignorant of the powers of prophecy and how
> they come to bear on the future, we are naively angry and incredulous that

someone of a particular kind of intelligence can reveal from such things something that is hidden from us. (582A–B)

I am not sure that Galaxidorus's logic holds up under close scrutiny, but Plutarch accepts whole-heartedly the conclusion: it is no more extraordinary to be able to read signs of the future here and there in this uncertain world, than it is to be able to recapture human experience in the past from the records that earlier generations have left us. As Timarchus says, "What is there not to wonder at?"

It is a long way from Chaeronea to Amherst, and still further from a credulous age to an agnostic one, and it is more than nineteen centuries from Plutarch's birth to 1958, when Professor Pritchard began to teach. Across such a divide, it is good to salute the continuities: there is still a master who considers it important to read the signs in a text with attention, and to train the ear to hear the voice.

Notes

1. The only readily accessible edition of Plutarch's *De genio Socratis* is the Loeb Classical Library, *Plutarch's Moralia*, vol. VII, edited and well translated by Phillip H. De Lacy and Benedict Einarsen (Cambridge: Harvard University Press, 1984). The standard Greek text in the Teubner edition (*Plutarchus Moralia*, Vol III, ed. Paton, Pohlenz, Sieveking [Leipzig, 1972]) is already out of print. In this paper, the translations of all texts are my own. The best general introduction to Plutarch and his work is D. A. Russell's *Plutarch*, in Duckworth's Classical Life and Letters series (London, 1972).

2. *Plutarchus. Essays and Miscellanies*, edited by A. H. Clough and William W. Goodwin, with an introduction by Ralph Waldo Emerson, published by Simpkins, Marshall, Hamilton, and Kent (London, 1870). Joel Porte chose not to include the piece in his selection of Emerson's essays for the Library of America—a pity, I think. But he does mention it in his chronology.

3. For reasons of space this is only a bare-bones summary. Other details are mentioned in the body of the text.

4. Plutarch uses myths in other essays, but it is hard to avoid the impression that he takes a particular pride of authorship in this one. The fictional Timarchus of Chaeronea seems to invite an assumption of the author's identity with him, taking his name "upscale," from wealth *(ploutos)* to honor *(time)*. Alternatively, it could be a pleasant hybrid of a name, linking his own with his wife's, Timoxena, implying perhaps that they shared the same hopes and fantasies.

5. For Posidonius, see Karl Reinhardt, *Poseidonios* (Munich: Beck, 1921). For Posidonius's influence on Plutarch, including this essay, see 464 ff. For a very liter-

ate translation of the complicated thought of Plotinus, one would still recommend Stephen MacKenna, *Plotinus. The Enneads* (London: Medici Society, 1917–1930; Rev. ed., 1956).

6. There are plenty of allusions in Plato to this role of the *daimones* as guardian angels over human lives and concerns (see *Symposium,* 203A, etc.), but Plutarch prefers to send us back to his native poet Hesiod (eighth century), *Works and Days,* 121–23:

> The Earth covered this race—
>
> And now they are called holy spirits *(daimones)* upon the land,
>
> Good to men, and scourges of evil, the guardians of us mortals . . . .

7. It is interesting that in this dialogue Plutarch "saves" the personality of Epaminondas exclusively for philosophy. To his contemporary readers, Epaminondas would be the Theban man of action *par excellence,* the hero who, by his defeat of Sparta at the Battle of Leuctra in 371, brought the hegemony of Greece to Thebes. But it is precisely Plutarch's point that the two lives, so far from being opposed to each other, involve exactly the same struggle, the same courage, and the same excellence.

Neil Hertz

Voices of Two or Three
Different Natures

THE ISSUES THAT I'd like to take up in this paper may be rapidly engaged by juxtaposing two quotations that sound surprisingly alike,
although they were set down one hundred and fifty years apart. One is
from the Fifth Book of *The Prelude* (1805)—some famous lines in which
Wordsworth is paying tribute to what he calls "the great Nature that exists in works / Of mighty Poets":

> Visionary Power
> Attends upon the motions of the winds
> Embodied in the mystery of words.
> There darkness makes abode, and all the host
> Of shadowy things do work their changes there,
> As in a mansion like their proper home;
> Even forms and substances are circumfused
> By that transparent veil with light divine;
> And through the turnings intricate of Verse,
> Present themselves as objects recognis'd,
> In flashes, and with a glory scarce their own.

226

The other is from Merleau-Ponty's 1952 essay "Indirect Language and the Voices of Silence":

> Language does not *presuppose* its table of correspondence; it unveils its secrets itself. It teaches them to every child who comes into the world. It is entirely a "monstration." Its opaqueness, its obstinate reference to itself, and its turning and folding back upon itself are precisely what make it a mental power; for it in turn becomes something like a universe, and it is capable of lodging things themselves in this universe—after it has transformed them into their meaning.

There is no reason to suppose that Merleau-Ponty had read Wordsworth (or vice versa!), yet they seem to have independently arrived at strikingly similar figures for whatever it is about language—its capacity? its "power"? —that allows "things themselves" to be "lodged" within its folds. But we should note at once an important difference: Merleau-Ponty is considering language as it is (inescapably) available to "every child who comes into the world"; Wordsworth is celebrating the "turnings intricate of Verse," and not just any verse, but that to be found in "works of mighty Poets." Taken together, in their likeness and difference, the passages speak of the region I shall be concerned with in these pages, a discursive field where distinctions between ordinary and extraordinary manifestations of language are sometimes sharpened, sometimes blurred.

My title refers to a line in another poem of Wordsworth's, some quatrains called "Yes, it was the mountain Echo," which spell out, rather too flatly, this same distinction. The difference between language as it is ordinarily employed or encountered and its more extraordinary exemplifications, a displaced version of the older distinction between what is profane and what is sacred, is a central articulation of Romantic and post-Romantic poetics. The opposition may take on a variety of thematic guises—as the difference between prose and poetry, between instrumental and literary, empirical and transcendental uses of language, between human speech and the Voice of Nature, between speech and silence, between verbal and musical expression, between intelligible and hermetic utterances. Here it appears as the difference between the cry of a bird and its echo:

> Yes, it was the mountain Echo,
> Solitary, clear, profound,
> Answering to the shouting Cuckoo,
> Giving to her sound for sound!

Unsolicited reply
To a babbling wanderer sent;
Like her ordinary cry,
Like—but oh, how different!

Hears not also mortal Life?
Hear not we, unthinking Creatures!
Slaves of folly, love, or strife—
Voices of two different natures?

Have not *we* too?—yes, we have
Answers, and we know not whence;
Echoes from beyond the grave,
Recognised intelligence!

Such rebounds our inward ear
Catches sometimes from afar—
Listen, ponder, hold them dear;
For of God,—of God they are.

Readers of Wordsworth know that privileged Voice: it resonates through-out his poetry, as "the voice of mountain torrents" heard by the Boy of Winander; or as the "ghostly language of the ancient earth"; or as the strangely transformed speech of the old man in "Resolution and Independence," whose "voice to me" (the poet says) "was like a stream / Scarce heard; nor word from word could I divide"; or, in another poem of bird-song, as the voice of the cuckoo itself. Indeed, to read "Yes, it was the mountain Echo" along with the earlier and better known lyric, "To the Cuckoo," is to realize that it is not the content of the message or the na-ture of the medium that turns an ordinary sound into an extraordinary communication, but rather its location in a structural opposition: the same Cuckoo that, calling from the woods, is "No bird, but an invisible thing, / A voice, a mystery" in the earlier poem will be demoted to a "babbling wanderer" when the listener catches its cry—"solitary, clear, profound"—echoing off the face of the mountain.

Uncommon, authentic influxes of this sort cannot serve as models for the production of poetry, but they do function, within the poems, as em-blems of the penetrative force that poetry may aspire to. Hence, one might expect the same binary opposition—between the ordinary and the extra-ordinary—to hold true when Wordsworth is considering his own poetic practice. That is frequently the case, but at an intriguing point in *The Pre-*

lude, what one finds instead is a *three*fold distinction among producers of language: there are, first, men in urban society—adept participants in what Wordsworth disdainfully calls "the talking world,"

> men adroit
> In speech and for communion with the world
> Accomplish'd, minds whose faculties are then
> Most active when they are most eloquent
> And elevated most when most admired.

The last two lines suspend the characteristic run of Wordsworth's blank verse to fold over on themselves for the space of a chiasm *(active/eloquent . . . elevated/admired),* miming an Augustan couplet while turning its satirical bite back on these adroit speakers and linking them to a rhetorical practice Wordsworth would condemn in the Preface to the *Lyrical Ballads.* The poet then goes on to contrast these worldly types with the articulate countrymen in whose speech he had found that "plainer and more emphatic language" (in the words of the Preface) on which he would base his own:

> Men may be found of other mold than these,
> Who are their own upholders, to themselves
> Encouragement, and energy and will,
> Expressing liveliest thoughts in lively words
> As native passion dictates.

So far, so good: these lines reproduce the contrast familiar to readers of the Preface, not between ordinary language and poetry but rather between a debased and an authentic (but still nonliterary) speech, a distinction that anticipates a similar opposition in Merleau-Ponty between "empirical" and "creative" uses of language. Given the clarity of the contrast, and the strength of Wordsworth's investment in choosing the language of "native passion" as a model for his own poetic speech, it is puzzling to find him adding to his list yet a third category of speaker—although "speaker," as you will see, is not quite the right term:

> Others, too,
> There are among the walks of homely life
> Still higher, men for contemplation framed,
> Shy, and unpractis'd in the strife of phrase,
> Meek men, whose very souls perhaps would sink

Beneath them, summon'd to such intercourse:
Theirs is the language of the heavens, the power,
The thought, the image, and the silent joy;
Words are but under-agents in their souls;
When they are grasping with their greatest strength
They do not breathe among them.

Who are these meek and silent men, and what are they doing here, in a section of *The Prelude* devoted to Wordsworth's hopes for his poetry? They are at once tokens of the poet's humility and signs of the scale of his ambition: for Wordsworth is celebrating the muteness of rustic interiority in the high declamatory idiom of *Paradise Lost.* To call these "homely" figures "men for contemplation framed" is to echo Milton's description of Adam before the Fall: "For contemplation he and valor formed"; and to describe them as first sinking beneath the weight of verbal exchange then rising to "breathe" in a region of "silent joy" above that "strife of phrase," indeed, above words altogether, is to set them in a cosmic space that Wordsworth elsewhere prays to Milton's Muse for the power to enter:

Urania, I shall need
Thy guidance, or a greater Muse, if such
Descend to earth or dwell in highest heaven!
For I must tread on shadowy ground, must sink
Deep—and, aloft ascending, breathe in worlds
To which the heaven of heavens is but a veil.

We are suddenly no longer dealing with an invidious sociology of language, one that would have us distinguish "good" (rural) from "bad" (urban) speakers, but rather with an allegory of poetry as Adamic speech, that is, as originary discourse. And we should note that a negative moment—a moment not of "encouragement, and energy and will," but of sinking and silence, of self-loss—would seem to play an essential part in this narrative of a wished-for movement back to the sources of poetic power.

We may still wonder why the initial twofold distinction wasn't good enough, why it seemed necessary to Wordsworth to ground his poetic practice in something still more extraordinary than "liveliest thoughts in lively words." To say that he was an idealist, engaged in the Romantic project of naturalizing a sacred poetics while not abandoning its transcendental possibilities, may sound like a plausible bit of literary history. In fact it doesn't get us very far, precisely because it presumes that we occupy a position sufficiently distant from that of the Romantics to allow us to objectify and define the particular ways in which poets like Wordsworth may have been mystified. That's hardly the case, as a look at a more recent instance will make clear.

Maurice Merleau-Ponty's "Indirect Language and the Voices of Silence" was written in part as a response to the long essays André Malraux was publishing in the late 1940s on the psychology of art, essays that were brought together in the volume *Les Voix du Silence (The Voices of Silence)* in 1951. Malraux's title of course alludes to the mute expressiveness of painting and sculpture, an "ordinary" or empirical silence, but it would confer on that silence some of the pathos of time past, of the ways in which art puts us in touch with dead masters and with vanished civilizations. Merleau-Ponty, while admiring much in Malraux's work, finds such pathos suspect, and would detach his own reflections from what he calls that "philosophy of the individual or of death which, with its nostalgic inclination towards civilizations based on the sacred, is at the forefront of [Malraux's] thought." His own evocation of "silence" emerges in a manner that is at once both more matter-of-fact than Malraux's and, in its own way, more surprising, for it occurs in a discussion not of the visual arts but of language.

The central thirty pages of Merleau-Ponty's essay are concerned with painting—with its relation to perception, to the body's location in the world, to the gestures that bring the painter into touch with the world and to the history that shapes those gestures and in turn is created by them—but because he is interested in more general questions of expressiveness, and because he would correct Malraux's account of the relation of painting to language, Merleau-Ponty begins with a rapid summary of "what we have learned from Saussure" about language acquisition and verbal signification. "With the first phonemic oppositions," he writes, paraphrasing Saussure, "the child is initiated to the lateral liaison of sign to sign as the foundation of the ultimate relation of sign to meaning." Because of this lateral relation, because language is not a matching-up of individual signs to the things in the world that they mean, Merleau-Ponty goes on, "meaning appears only at the intersection and as it were [*comme*] in the interval between words." I note the "as it were" because Merleau-Ponty himself is here casually drawing attention to his figure of speech, just as he will a page later in the declaration that gives his essay its title: "Now if we rid our minds of the idea that our language is the translation or cipher of some *original text*, we shall see that the idea of *complete* expression is nonsensical, and that all language is indirect or allusive—that is, if you wish [*si l'on veut*], silence."

"Language as silence!" we might be tempted to exclaim, and thus align a bit too hastily Merleau-Ponty's account with Wordsworth's celebration of those meek men who speak—"as it were"—"the language of the heavens, the . . . thought, the image, and the silent joy," in whose Adamic souls "words are but under-agents." If we *did* so exclaim, we might be making a big mistake. For Merleau-Ponty intends to be talking about something *perfectly ordinary*, the mundane process of signification—meaning emerging in the intervals between words—to be found across the board, not just in the privileged speech-acts of poets and peasants. This said, the figure of silence will nevertheless recur in his essay in more intriguing ways. I want to look closely at its several occurrences, and that will require some lengthy quotations.

> The empirical use of already established language should be distinguished from its creative use. Empirical language can only be the result of creative language. Speech in the sense of empirical language—that is, the opportune recollection of a pre-established sign—is not speech in respect to authentic language. It is, as Mallarmé said, the worn coin placed silently in my hand. True speech [*la parole vraie*], on the contrary—speech which signifies, which finally renders *"l'absente de tous bouquets"* present and frees the meaning captive in the thing—is only silence in respect to empirical usage, for it does not go so far as to become a common name [*elle ne va pas jusqu'au nom commun*].

I'm not sure I understand that last phrase, or that its translation is accurate, although the general purport of the sentence is clear enough, once the distinction between "empirical" and "creative" uses of language is acknowledged. What is worth noting, however, is that this evocation of silence occurs in a slightly different context. Now it is not *all* language that can be thought of as, "if you wish, silence," but rather "authentic language," "true speech," language when it is employed creatively, not when spoken by rote.

A page later, elaborating an analogy between the painter's hand hesitating among possibilities and the way "truly expressive speech . . . gropes around a significative intention," Merleau-Ponty thickens up the texture of this rhetoric of silence. "If we want to do justice to expressive speech," he writes, "we must consider speech before it is spoken, the background of silence which does not cease to surround it and without which it is nothing."

Or to put the matter another way [he continues], we must uncover the threads of silence that speech is mixed together with. In already acquired expressions there is a direct meaning which corresponds point for point to figures, forms, and established words. Apparently there are no gaps or expressive silences here. But the meaning of expressions which are in the process of being accomplished cannot be of this sort: it is a lateral or oblique meaning which runs between the words. It is another way of shaking the linguistic or narrative apparatus [*l'appareil du langage ou du récit*] in order to tear a new sound from it. If we want to understand language as an originating operation, we must pretend to have never spoken, submit language to a reduction without which it would once more escape us by referring us to what it signifies for us, *look* at it as deaf people look at those who are speaking . . . .

Here the stress is on silence's presence at the genesis of speech: "expressions . . . in the process of being accomplished," "language as an originating operation." In an earlier study of expression, a chapter of his great work *Phenomenology of Perception* (1945), Merleau-Ponty had given some instances of originary speech (*la parole originaire*): "the speech of the infant pronouncing his first word, of the lover discovering his feelings, of the 'first man who ever spoke,' [and] of the writer or philosopher who awakens the primordial experience covered over by tradition." It is noteworthy that allusions to that "first man," to the historical or Adamic origins of language, would seem to have dropped out of this later discussion, perhaps in order to contrast his own resolutely non-metaphysical treatment of expressiveness with the pathos implicit in Malraux's writings. Still, while Merleau-Ponty would insist on a continuity between more and less mundane uses of language, doesn't the figure of silence, as it operates in *his* language, lend a flickering sense of mystery and privilege to his evocations of what counts as "originary"?

There is something else to remark in that paragraph, as well: the introduction of the notion of narrative *(récit)*. In its immediate context, it wouldn't seem to be particularly pertinent—simply referring to the "linguistic apparatus" would do if what is under consideration is "language as an originating operation." In the larger context of the entire essay, however, this first allusion to yet another mode of expression—not language in general, not vividly inventive speech, but narrative —prepares the way for an analogy Merleau-Ponty will later set down between painting and novels as comparable "voices of silence."

"Like a painting a novel expresses tacitly," he writes. And, as an example, he offers this astonishingly beautiful and apt reading of a moment in Stendhal's *The Red and the Black*.

Like a painting, a novel expresses tacitly. Its subject, like that of a painting, can be related [*raconté*]. But Julien Sorel's trip to Verrières and his attempt to kill Mme de Rênal after he has learned that she has betrayed him are not as important as that silence, that dream-like journey, that unthinking certitude, and that eternal resolution which follow the news. Now these things are nowhere *said*. There is no need of a "Julien thought" or a "Julien wished." In order to express them, Stendhal had only to insinuate himself into Julien and make objects, obstacles, means, and hazards appear before our eyes with the swiftness of the journey. He has only to decide to narrate in one page instead of five. That brevity, that unusual proportion of things omitted to things said, is not even the result of a *choice*. Consulting his own sensitivity to others, Stendhal suddenly found an imaginary body for Julien which was more agile than his own body. As if in a second life, he made the trip to Verrières according to a cadence of cold passion which itself decided what was visible and what was invisible, what was to be said and what was to remain unspoken. The desire to kill [*la volonté de mort*] is thus not in the words at all. It is between them, in the hollows of space, time, and signification they mark out, as movement at the cinema is between the immobile images which follow one another.

This is a narrative about a narrative, a passionate reenacting of what is in fact not a page but two sentences in Stendhal, the brief paragraph that carries Julien from the Hôtel de la Mole in Paris to Verrières in the Franche-Comté. Here it is, in its entirety:

> Julien had set off for Verrières. On this rapid journey, he was unable to write to Mathilde [de la Mole] as he had intended, his hand traced nothing more than illegible marks on the paper [*sa main ne formait sur le papier que des traits illisibles*].

Merleau-Ponty is remembering those illegible marks, the tracing that obliquely expresses a journey across France, and remembering them, obliquely, as silence. As such, his paraphrase provides a telling supplement to his earlier discussion of the workings of originary speech. For what we now find occupying the intervals between words is no longer called their "meaning" or simply a background of interstitial "silence" but rather a silence that speaks of *"la volonté de mort."* The English translator's rendering of that as "the desire to kill" doesn't catch the ambiguity of the phrase: it is at once Julien's wish to kill and his wish to die; more literally and more abstractly it is "the will to death."

I would read this as the same "death" that Merleau-Ponty had distanced himself from in his earlier disavowal of Malraux's brand of pathos, "death" reemerging here not in the argument of his essay but indirectly, in the mini-narrative he chose as illustrative. As such, by introducing the sacrifice implicit in Julien's journey, Merleau-Ponty has moved his account of originary speech not exactly in Malraux's direction—there is still much that separates them—but a little closer to those lines of Wordsworth's I quoted earlier, where Adamic figures gain access to "the language of the heavens" only by way of a sacrificial sinking.

Both Wordsworth and Merleau-Ponty are seeking language adequate to their sense of language's power, of "language as an originating operation," in Merleau-Ponty's phrase. Neither would restrict the designation of "originary discourse" to works of literature alone: both acknowledge that vivid and inventive speech can be heard elsewhere. Yet we have found each of them sketching a brief, allegorical narrative in which a moment of silence and self-loss is linked to the achievement of this verbal power, even though more ordinary instances of that power would seem to be functions of a speaker's "encouragement, and energy and will." Why might this be so? What might account for such dramatic evocations of sacrifice, or for such fluctuations in what one could call the level of pathos of the language in which this questioning of language is engaged?

A look at an essay by a contemporary of Merleau-Ponty's may prove useful here. In 1964, Maurice Blanchot published an article in the *Nouvelle Revue Française* entitled "La Voix narrative (le 'il', le neutre)"—it has been translated as "The Narrative Voice (the 'he,' the neuter)" and appears in a collection of Blanchot's essays called *The Gaze of Orpheus*. English-speaking readers soon realize that Blanchot is using the expression "the narrative voice" in an unaccustomed fashion: he is not referring to the voice of a story's narrator—*that* he calls "the narrating voice" *(la voix narratrice)*. He is in fact elaborating a contrast similar to that between the voice of the cuckoo and its echo in Wordsworth, or between empirical and originary language in Merleau-Ponty. Narrative voice, in this usage, is something much closer to that silence Merleau-Ponty "hears" in Stendhal's pages: in a sentence that may very well be consciously echoing Merleau-Ponty's 1952 essay, Blanchot characterizes this voice as "tacit" and adds that "it attracts language obliquely, indirectly and within this attraction—that of oblique speech—allows the neuter [*le neutre*] to speak." "The narrative voice," he goes on, "carries the neuter."

What Blanchot means by "the neuter" or, as it is sometimes rendered, "the neutral," is not immediately perspicuous, but the notion is so central to his understanding of language and literature, and so pertinent to the issues I have been concerned with in this paper, that it is worth attempting to come to terms with it, in however summary a fashion.

"In the narrative form," Blanchot writes, "we hear—and always as though in addition to other things—something indeterminate speaking, something that the evolution of this form outlines, isolates, so that it gradually becomes manifest, though in a deceptive way." That "something indeterminate" is the narrative voice, its indeterminacy a function of its odd and recalcitrant neutrality, and, in Blanchot's rapid account of the evolution of narrative—from ancient epic through Cervantes and Flaubert to Thomas Mann, Kafka, and Marguerite Duras—it is Kafka who is credited with making this oddness manifest, bringing it into saliency, or, to shift metaphors, steeping his works in it. Blanchot had, in 1949, cited Kafka's dictum that literary language involved the movement from "I" to "he," which meant not that narratives could no longer use the first person, but rather that when the first person entered the space of storytelling, as narrator or character, it bracketed its engagement with "life," leaving behind its primary relation to such things as "encouragement, and energy and will." In Kafka's stories, Blanchot writes,

> the bearers of speech, the subjects of the action—who used to take the place of characters—fall into a relationship of nonidentification with themselves: something happens to them, something they cannot recapture except by relinquishing their power to say "I," and what happens to them has always happened already: they can only account for it indirectly, as self-forgetfulness, the forgetfulness that introduces them into the present without memory that is the present of narrating speech.

Two things are worth remarking about this self-forgetfulness: first, that, although it is being described at work quite locally—as befalling those "bearers of speech" to be found in Kafka's narratives—it is revealing, Blanchot would insist, of that "present without memory" to be found in *all* "narrating speech." The *stories* one tells may engage the fullest resources of memory, move linearly through time or, in modernist fashion, play several temporalities off against each other; the *telling* of them nevertheless unfolds in a uniform narrative present. Kafka has simply made it easier for us to notice this; that is his distinction.

The second point is that this "fall" into self-forgetfulness does not sound exactly like a sacrifice. Blanchot's account of what goes on in Kafka feels blander, blanker than the scenarios I've been tracing in Wordsworth and Merleau-Ponty, the sinking of those tongue-tied Adamic countrymen, the will-to-death of Julien Sorel. Blanchot's writing is not without its own violent or lugubrious moments, but he would have us read such lurid figures, wherever they are encountered, as vivid, delusively rewarding disguises of a form of "relinquishment" at once harder to characterize and more commonplace than notions like that of "sacrifice" would suggest. In the final paragraph of his essay he links this neutralization of narrative subjectivity to a more general suspension of "the attributive structure of language, that relationship to being, implicit or explicit, that is immediately posed in our languages as soon as something is said."

> It has often been remarked [he continues]—by philosophers, linguists, political commentators—that nothing can be denied that has not already been posed beforehand. To put it another way, all language begins by articulating, and in articulating it affirms. But it could be that telling (writing) [*raconter (écrire)*] is drawing language into a possibility of saying that would say without saying being and still without denying it either—or, more clearly, too clearly, that it is establishing the center of gravity of speech elsewhere, where speaking is not a matter of affirming being nor of needing negation [*for example, I would add, the negation inherent in sacrificial scenarios—NH*] in order to suspend the work of being, the work that ordinarily occurs in every form of expression.

Note that Blanchot is here no longer talking just about Kafka, or just about storytelling, or just about literature, or just about writing-in-general, but rather about what experimental writing like Kafka's can reveal about the relations among speakers, their languages and the world. Like Wordsworth and Merleau-Ponty, he is making a case for literature, but not by rendering it irrelevant to more ordinary uses of language.

Blanchot's characteristic manner, an odd combination of tentativeness ("But it could be . . . ") and plangent affirmation, can seem maddeningly disingenuous, but that may be no more than his way of recording, willy-nilly, the fluctuations in the level of pathos I drew attention to earlier in Wordsworth's and Merleau-Ponty's writing. Blanchot implies as much when he concludes his essay by noting that we tend to confuse what he has been calling the narrative voice "with the oblique voice of unhappiness or the oblique voice of madness."

I would like to conclude, in turn, with a final instance of contrasting voices, one that I hope will clarify the pertinence of Blanchot's categories for understanding all three of these discussions of what is originary and what is ordinary about language.

In 1843, many years after he had written "Yes, it was the mountain

Echo," Wordsworth added a note to the poem, dictated, along with many others, to an admiring reader:

> Town-end. 1805. The echo came from Nab-Scar, when I was walking on the opposite side of Rydal Mere. I will here mention, for my dear Sister's sake, that, while she was sitting alone one day high up on this part of Loughrigg Fell, she was so affected by the voice of the Cuckoo heard from the crags at some distance that she could not suppress a wish to have a stone inscribed with her name among the rocks from which the sound proceeded. On my return home from my walk I recited these verses to Mary, who was then confined with her son Thomas, who died in his 7th year, as is recorded on his head-stone in Grasmere Church-yard.

This is an old man's reminiscence, nostalgically meticulous in its naming of places and times, in its anchoring of this moment of composition in an emotionally laden family scene. Dorothy Wordsworth, still living but long since withdrawn into a private world, is honored for the wish she could not suppress, to symbolically locate her name, her self, at the source of William's Voice, as her words had often been, indeed, the literal source of William's own. Thematic elements begin to cluster in Wordsworth's mind. Echo and inscription come together: both require the resistance of stone to materialize. Then one stone recalls another. The happy recital of the newly created poem joins with the happy expectancy of birth: William's walking produced these verses, Mary's confinement will produce Thomas. But there would seem to have been, unbeknownst to them at the time, a price to be paid for this particular access to language, a price that will fall due seven years later when Thomas dies. Quietly, adding one thing to another, the *narrating* voice traces this sacrificial scenario, an unhappiness recollected in tranquillity. But if we seek an instance of *narrative* voice, we can find it not in the memory of sacrifice and creation, but "behind" or alongside that, in its present telling, made beautifully manifest in the run of that last sentence, audible in the pauses that define its phrasing: *On my return home from my walk* [pause] *I recited these verses to Mary* [pause] *who was then confined with her son Thomas* [pause] *who died in his 7th year* [pause] *as is recorded on his head-stone* [pause] *in Grasmere Church-yard.*

In introducing "Yes, it was the mountain Echo" earlier, I remarked that it seemed to me to present "rather too flatly" the distinction between the empirical and the transcendental: its "Voices of two different natures" were too confidently named as, on the one hand, the mortal voices of "folly, love, or strife," on the other, the voices that come "of God." In 1843,

Wordsworth returns to that distinction in subtler, less schematic terms and offers—in a rambling narrative that, to echo Merleau-Ponty on Stendhal, was probably "not even the result of a *choice*"—a more revealing and persuasive insight into the unmysterious—but nonetheless difficult to account for—articulation of language in its most ordinary and its most extraordinary manifestations.

Bibliographical Notes

William Wordsworth: The passages discussed from *The (1805) Prelude* are in Book 5, lines 619 ff. ("Visionary Power . . .") and Book 12, lines 255 ff. (". . . men adroit"); the prayer to Urania is from the Prospectus to *The Recluse* in "Home at Grasmere." "To the Cuckoo" (1802) and "Yes, it was the mountain Echo" (1806), along with the 1843 Fenwick notes, may be found in any edition of his complete *Poetical Works.*

Maurice Merleau-Ponty: Passages from the essay "Indirect Language and the Voices of Silence" (1952) are translated by Richard C. McCleary in *Signs* (Evanston, Ill.: Northwestern University Press, 1964; *Signes* was published in 1960); in the earlier passage from *Phénoménologie de la perception* (1945) the translation is mine.

Stendhal: Julien Sorel's journey to Verrières is recorded in Book Two, Chapter 35 of *The Red and the Black. Le Rouge et le Noir* first appeared in 1830. Translation mine.

Maurice Blanchot: Passages from "The Narrative Voice (the 'he,' the neuter)" (1964) are translated by Lydia Davis in *The Gaze of Orpheus* (Barrytown, N.Y.: Station Hill Press, 1981). The essay will also be found, along with other explorations of "the neuter," in *The Infinite Conversation* (1993), a translation of *L'Entretien infini* (1969).

Francis Murphy

Poor Strether

IN THE FALL of the academic year 1995–96 I joined the staff of English 3 ("Reading and Criticism") at Amherst as a one-time visitor from Smith. The assigned reading included poems by Billy Collins, George Herbert, and James Merrill, two plays by Shakespeare, and the prose of Jane Smiley and Henry James. Working with Bill Pritchard, Dick Cody, David Sofield, and Howell Chickering was a unique opportunity to learn much from attentive readers. Monday morning the mailbox was always full of communications from the four of them, mostly helpful exercises aimed at getting good class discussion and lively papers out of the students. One morning late in the semester we heard from Bill that he had spent Sunday in bed finishing *The Ambassadors* ("Very good place to read the book," he decided), paying particular attention to those chapters in which Strether "heads into the country and finds not quite what he expected to find." Bill wondered if James's attitude toward Strether changed (as has been argued) in these chapters, and if James was harder on Strether than he had been earlier. He decided that his class would take up the question of James's treatment of Strether both early and late, and that their papers would try to come to terms with "what if anything" we are "supposed to be feeling, thinking, doing about our hero." I thought it might be useful to try the assignment myself and see what I could come up with.

≈

Anyone familiar with *The Ambassadors* will recall that just exactly what common household article comes off the production line of the "big brave bouncing business" in Woollett, Massachusetts, is never identified; all that we know is that business is thriving, and that if properly advertised and the market cornered, as expected, the Newsomes and Pococks will be very rich indeed. Strether refuses to identify the article not because it is unmentionable—"we constantly talk of it" he says—but because now that he is abroad it seems too trivial to name: "Right here therefore, with everything so grand—!" "It's a false note?" Miss Gostrey asks, and Strether replies, "Sadly. It's vulgar." And it is the vulgar which Strether has now determined to eschew. For our ambassador has two assignments in his portfolio. One concerns Mrs. Newsome—he will bring home the "wicked" heir to promote Woollett's thriving industry; the other is deeply personal, one for which he has been biding his time: the chance to escape the vulgar and at last worship in "the temple of taste" that he had long "dreamed of raising up." For what is so conspicuously missing from the New England review which Strether edits, the green-covered journal that the unmentioned but not unmentionable article underwrites, is any "tribute to letters." Instead, it is a "mere rich kernel" of economics, politics, and ethics, and as such a "specious shell," which has displaced Strether's first love, represented in the novel by those "stale and soiled" lemon-colored volumes which he purchased in Paris "in the sixties" and which, left unbound, have turned "sallow" like the paint on the temple door. Contrary to received opinion, *The Ambassadors* does not attempt to chart Strether's gradual conversion to the virtues of Europe. The famous opening paragraph alerts us to the fact that our editor is overjoyed ("not wholly disconcerted" is a more polite way of putting it) to find Waymarsh's sour countenance missing as he sets foot for the second time on foreign soil, prepared to be governed by new principles. Between the truly vulgar Pococks and a man of "uncontrolled perception," who would not side with Strether? But from very early on in the novel James treats Strether as a comic figure, one whose unleashed enthusiasm for Europe takes our breath away. Strether is not a careful judge of what he sees and he is happy in his ignorance. That is why, at the beginning of Book II, Maria Gostrey has to remind him that the London theater where he finds himself in her company is no less vulgar than Woollett itself:

> "But surely not vulgarer than this." Then on his wondering as she herself had done: "Than everything about us." She seemed a trifle irritated. "What do you take this for?"
>
> "Why for—comparatively—divine."
>
> "This dreadful London theatre? It's impossible, if you really want to know."
>
> "Oh then," laughed Strether, "I *don't* really want to know!"

Off and running, and blissful in his unknowing, Strether is hard to keep up with, speaking French "out quite loud," enjoying a candle-lit dinner (with rose-colored shades) in the company of a woman whose dress is cut down, and whose antique jewelry ("he was rather complacently sure it was antique") calls attention to her naked throat, a far cry from Mrs. Newsome, who wears a lace ruff and looks like Queen Elizabeth. He assumes the painter's eye and, rather than open letters from home, watches figures in a park "compose" themselves while "the cup of his impressions seemed truly to overflow." He's energized and no longer "fagged-out," and to deny him these few pleasures, James insists, would be churlish given the "dreadful cheerful sociable solitude" of his life, the death of his young wife and his remorse for his little boy. Impressionism is in the air, and Paris hangs before him like a "vast bright Babylon," an "iridescent object" in which "parts were not to be discriminated nor differences comfortably marked." But the reference to Babylon is a reminder that things are not as "adorable" as Strether assumes. How appropriate, then, that he should proceed from the Luxembourg gardens to Chad's apartment and find himself looking "up and up" at the "distinguished front" and "rejoicing to think that he might reach" these heights, the house itself being "admirably built" and of a quality which fairly "sprang" on him: "the fine relation of part to part and space to space," aided "by the presence of ornament as positive as it was discreet, and by the complexion of the stone, a cold fair grey warmed and polished a little by life." Strether finds himself challenged to live up to the architecture; for this New Englander is sure that a beautifully proportioned edifice must mirror a beautifully proportioned soul. Giddy with expectation, Strether reduces everything to a choice between Waymarsh and the aesthetic. He crosses the street to enter the apartment, "leaving Waymarsh out." But Waymarsh reappears in the novel shortly after

Strether's visit to Chad's "lovely home," and he never sounds more foolish than when he informs the Connecticut lawyer that he had "looked around" the apartment and did not beat a retreat: "I saw, in fine; and—I don't know what to call it—I sniffed. It's a detail, but it's as if there were something—something very good—to sniff." Waymarsh has moral putrification in mind: "Do you mean a smell? What of?" he crudely inquires. This is a scene worth reading aloud as Strether, once again, asserts his ignorance, at first self-satisfiedly and then exultantly, full of superiority for his tolerance of what he does not know, and his expanding Bohemianism:

> "Do you mean a smell? What of?"
>
> "A charming scent. But I don't know."
>
> Waymarsh gave an indifferent grunt. "Does he live there with a woman?"
>
> "I don't know."
>
> Waymarsh waited an instant more, than resumed. "Has he taken her off with him?"
>
> "And will he bring her back?"—Strether fell into the enquiry. But he wound it up as before. "I don't know."
>
> The way he wound it up, accompanied as this was with another drop back, another degustation of the Léoville, another wipe of his moustache and another good word for [the waiter] François, seemed to produce in his companion a slight irritation. "Then what the devil do you know?"
>
> "Well," said Strether almost gaily, "I guess I don't know anything!"

Any character as smug as this in his unknowing is ripe for a fall, and James treats Strether with a considerable degree of levity in the first third of the novel, at the same time that his fondness for him is readily apparent. But perhaps no moment has thrown readers more off the scent (to continue the metaphor) of James's irony than the famous scene in Gloriani's garden (Book V) when Strether, overwhelmed by a sense of regret for opportunities lost, tells Little Bilham to "Live all you can." It was these words of William Dean Howells, repeated to James by Jonathan Sturges, that first moved the novelist to conceive of "a little situation" ripe with narrative possibilities. How can anyone fail to be other than moved by an account of an older man "in the evening, as it were, of life" who, as James puts it in his October 31, 1898 notebook entry, "hasn't 'lived,' hasn't at all, in the sense of sensations, passions, impulses, pleasures—and to whom, in the presence of some great human spectacle, some great organization for the Immediate, the agreeable, for curiosity, and experiment and perception, for Enjoyment, in a word, becomes, *sur la fin*, or toward it, sorrowfully aware" of it. James seems to respond to the plight of this figure in a deeply personal way, but he rejects the idea that his character might be a novelist—too worldly wise and experienced for James's purpose. Nor would a lawyer, a journalist, or a physician do—much too jaded, much too involved in the "complications and turpitudes and general vitality of mankind." Even a college professor, James adds, would "imply some knowledge of the lives of the young." And so he settles upon the "Editor of a Magazine"—"not at all of a newspaper"—because who could edit a newspaper and be ignorant of life's horrors? Strether is one of the last in a long line of James's naifs who know little of the world, and more importantly, know little of themselves. Taking Strether's prescription to "Live" out of context makes it as sentimental a cliché as Polonius's advice to his son: "to thine own self be true." For in Gloriani's garden, teeming with social and moral complications, Strether has no idea of just how ambiguous life may be, although Chad's response to Strether's question of whether Madame de Vionnet and her daughter are French—"Yes. That is no!"—should alert him to the fact that life's winding path is often strewn with mines. Strether hardly needs, as he puts it, to remind himself "of his odious suspicion of any form of beauty." Rather, the opposite is true. He longs for the artist's life without knowing anything about how artists, with their *"femmes du monde,"* live. Gloriani's face is, paradoxically, "like an open letter in a foreign tongue," and although the painter offers only a few welcoming phrases, Strether feels like a schoolboy who has come through a difficult examination. He finds himself looking at a kind of sun-god, Gloriani is all "penetrating radiance," and he has the "consciousness of opening to it, for the happy instant, all the windows of his mind." What Strether is so in awe of is Gloriani's "deep human expertness" and "the terrible life" behind it, at the same time that he is ignorant of Gloriani's history. Strether sees in Gloriani a man who has transformed life into art, and in Strether's quiet hours he rehearsed what he sensed was "the deepest intellectual sounding to which he had ever been exposed," speaking about it, however, to no one because he "couldn't have spoken without appearing to talk nonsense. Was what it had told him or what it had asked him the greater of the mysteries? Was it the most special flare, unequalled, supreme, of the aesthetic torch, lighting that wondrous world for ever, or was it above all the long straight shaft sunk by a personal acuteness that life has seasoned to steel?" Strether fails to comprehend the aggressive nature of this final metaphor and how incompatible it is with the idea of harmonious pastoral that any scene set in a garden anticipates. But from the very beginning we know that Gloriani's "rococo" garden is no "happy rural seat of various view." Gloriani's garden is a recessed garden, disorienting in its unexpected locale, and a "chamber of state" where social distinctions are upheld, not relaxed, as Strether learns, much to his chagrin, on not being introduced to the "Duchesse," an exclusionary note, which, we are informed without a trace of irony on Strether's part, is "false to the Woollett scale and Woollett humanity."

To the degree that Strether is willfully ignorant—"you're not a person to whom it's easy to tell things you don't want to know" Little Bilham says—Strether bears the full brunt of James's irony. But, of course, the novel is more complicated than this; for what makes Strether ultimately a figure suitable for comedy but not full-blown mockery is his innocence. Deep down, for James, he is worth more than these others because he is less worldly-wise, less cynical, more capable of being wounded. And that is why, just before his great outpouring, James leaves him entirely alone, protesting that he really does not feel snubbed when by a "trick of three words" a gentleman takes all his company away and he is left looking at four receding backs, troubled in spite of his protests by "the want of ceremony with which he had just been used." Strether's operatic moment, however, is not meant to be judged too harshly. It takes place in this stifling setting precisely because it asserts a moment of deep unguarded feeling and because one would have to have a heart of stone not to be moved by Strether's grief at opportunities lost.

After Strether's great moment in Gloriani's garden James never treats him as a purely comic figure again. His magnanimousness toward Madame de Vionnet, his willingness to "save" her, precludes this. Then too, the world in which he is moving seems less vital, more studied than we had supposed, something suggested at first by the calculated placement of "the great *Revue*" by Chad in Madame de Vionnet's apartment, an effort to provide a modern touch, a prop somewhat at odds with the First Empire decor in a room in which every object spoke of "intense little preferences and sharp little exclusions, a deep suspicion of the vulgar and a personal view of the right," all exuding an air of "supreme respectability." We learn all this at the very moment when our information about Madame de Vionnet's history expands: the fact that she remains and will remain (given her Catholicism) married to a man who may or may not be a brute; the fact that she loves Chad more than he loves her and that Chad is now bored and is anxious to depart; the fact that her past is muddy (she is not compared to "various and multifold" Cleopatra for nothing); and last, but not least in Strether's mind, her too calculating efforts to arrange her daughter's life. He asks Madame de Vionnet not to ask Jeanne if she loves Chad, "don't touch her. Don't know—don't want to know. And moreover—yes—you *won't*." But when she accedes he feels trapped and goes from thinking of himself as her savior to thinking of himself as her crucified victim:

> "As a favour to you?"
> "Well—since you ask me."
> "Anything, everything you ask," she smiled. . . .
> The sound of it lingered with him, making him fairly feel as if he had been tripped up and had a fall. In the very act of arranging with her for his independence he had, under pressure from a particular perception, inconsistently, quite stupidly, committed himself, and with her subtlety sensitive on the spot to an advantage, she had driven in by a single word a little golden nail, the sharp intention of which he signally felt.

James enlists our sympathy for Strether in other ways. Chad seems slicker, shallower, colder; it's he who becomes the comic figure—"But I want to see Mother." "Remember how long it is since I've seen Mother." What had once seemed glamorous about him to Strether now seems merely facile: "There he was in all the pleasant morning freshness of it—strong and sleek and gay, easy and fragrant and fathomless, with happy health in his color and pleasant silver in his thick young hair, and the right word for everything on his lips that his clear brownness caused to show as red." What James is doing is distancing Strether from his European connections in the novel just moments before the ambassadors from Woollett arrive. His intention is to isolate Strether, to leave him disappointed in the Europeans but appalled by the inflexible and rude ugly Americans. "Let yourself, on the contrary, go—in all agreeable directions. These are precious hours—at our age they mayn't recur. . . . Live up to Mrs. Pocock," he tells Waymarsh in a parody of his urgings to Little Bilham, adopting a new, uncharacteristic tone of mockery, and not at all unhappy toward the end of Book XI to find himself alone, with time on his hands, and Paris empty. James has thus far artfully, some might say shamelessly, turned the tide of our affections toward Strether after treating him earlier so comically. But *The Ambassadors* is not, in the end, a novel about a man who is the victim of the insensitivity of others.

Some of the greatest moments in James's fiction occur when his most anxious characters—I'm thinking of Isabel Archer in Rome and Olive Chancellor on Cape Cod—rethink the choices they have made and the lives they have led and learn something about themselves in the process.

James observes in *The Bostonians* that "These hours of backward clearness come to all men and women, once at least, when they read the past in the light of the present, with the reasons of things, like unobserved finger-posts, protruding where they never saw them before. The journey behind them is mapped out and figured, with its false steps, its wrong observations, all its infatuated, deluded geography." The end result of the extraordinarily painterly and theatrical details of the scene on the river, the culmination of all the talk in the novel about art and life, finds Strether alone in his room thinking about what it was in that "cool special green" setting that "they had to put a face upon," "blinking it all round," to carry their supper off and get them back to Paris without a scene, without "violence" to their friendship. It's the sexual intimacy, of course, between Chad and Madame de Vionnet, and the fact that they have hidden something from him is not what finally shocks Strether: it's knowing that they feel that he is someone from whom these facts must be hidden, someone who has to be lied to because he needs to be protected, like a little girl clothing her doll's nakedness, from this basic fact of human experience.

> It was the quantity of make-believe involved and so vividly exemplified that most disagreed with his spiritual stomach. He moved, however, from the consideration of that quantity—to say nothing of the consciousness of that organ—back to the other feature of the show, the deep, deep truth of the intimacy revealed. That was what, in his vain vigil, he oftenest reverted to: intimacy, at such a point, was *like* that—and what in the world else would one have wished it to be like? It was all very well for him to feel the pity of its being so much like lying; he almost blushed, in the dark, for the way he had dressed the possibility in vagueness, as a little girl might have dressed her doll. He had made them—and by no fault of their own—momentarily pull it for him, the possibility, out of this vagueness; and must he not therefore take it now as they had had simply, with whatever thin attenuations, to give it to him? The very question, it may be added, made him feel lonely and cold.

Strether has to acknowledge to himself that others have taken him as a product of a stifling Woollett morality and that he has done nothing to discourage this view. A husband and father, was he not once a lover, too?

The novel has moved from the broadly comic to the melodramatic and from there to the meditative and ruminative. In the end, Book XII, laughter reasserts itself, but in a bittersweet mode, what Frye called ironic comedy, a world in which, alas, there are no illusions, a place where, as Strether observes, "they were no worse than he, in short, and he no worse than they—if, queerly enough, no better . . . ." In a novel which often speaks of tone, this concluding book tries to get the tone of farewell just right. These last five chapters are difficult for many readers; all present Strether when he is most in control, and in his insistence on leaving, his blunt confession that he is "done" with Madame de Vionnet and expects nothing much from "just Chad," critics have argued that Strether represents the New England provincial in his most Puritanical, life-denying guise. But from the beginning of the novel James anticipates his return. Europe by the end of the novel does not offer a practical alternative to Strether; it is a world of moral ambiguity, a world of snobbery, a world where there are too many arranged everythings, a world where the aesthetic principle turns out to rationalize and disguise disorder. But Strether is no mere child of Woollett either. What he will not do is require that "somebody" pay "something somewhere and somehow." What may be his most New England trait is his renunciation of every fireside. "Renunciation," Emily Dickinson noted, "is a piercing virtue." Ian Watt, in perhaps the most famous essay ever written on *The Ambassadors*, said that in the very last sentence of the novel's *first* paragraph "We don't, in the end, see Strether's probing hesitations mainly as an ironic indication by James of mankind's general muddlement; we find it, increasingly, a touching example of how, despite all their inevitable incongruities and shortcomings, human ties remain only, but still, human." Isn't this the note we also hear in the very last volley in the novel between Maria Gostrey and Strether, where James's affection for Strether is so clearly apparent?

"It isn't so much your *being* 'right'—it's your horrible sharp eye for what makes you so."

"Oh but you're just as bad yourself. You can't resist me when I point that out."

She sighed it at last all comically, all tragically, away. "I can't indeed resist you."

"Then there we are!" said Strether.

Anne Ferry

Frost's "Land of *The Golden Treasury*"

WILLIAM PRITCHARD'S *Frost: A Literary Life Reconsidered* begins its reconsidering by quoting one of the well-known verbal dodges typical of Frost's responses to questions about choices in his life and art:

> I must have been asked once years ago what I was doing in England, and I had forgotten what I was doing. . . . I said to somebody—I saw it in print somewhere—that I said I had come to the land of *The Golden Treasury.* That's what I went for.[1]

The fairy-tale language of this explanation is one form of evasiveness; another is the offer in the next sentence of an alternative, matchingly fanciful, explanation: "that I went to live under thatch." What Pritchard sees in this mischievous guessing game is Frost exercising "play of mind" by which his experience "must be imagined and successively reimagined" so as to be "sufficient unto the needs" of his poetry.

The corollary point to be discussed here is that this instance of Frost's reconsidering of his own life in 1956, at the age of eighty-two, is perfectly continuous with his imagining of it in the early years as he was writing the poems of *A Boy's Will*, published in 1913 in England soon after he brought his family to live there. The act of weaving his experience into a myth, and the very form and matter of this particular myth of himself having sailed the seas and "come to the land of *The Golden Treasury*" (rather like Keats's traveler among "the realms of gold" in the sonnet Frost could read in the anthology) illustrate the seamlessness of his life-long imagining. The endurance of Palgrave's book as a focus for Frost's mythologizing in his writings and sayings from the 1890s into his last years seems to be at once the reflection and the cause of its special power to nourish his literary life. Tracing some of its recurrences, we can watch Frost turning fact into myth, and myth into material he could use: in making poems and in making a space for himself as a poet. Frost's early reading of *The Golden Treasury* was one of the most important things that happened to him in his literary life. The book was a shaping influence on his poetry at its beginnings in a remarkable variety of ways, and through all his life it was his chief instrument in measuring his distance from modernism. Beyond that, *The Golden Treasury* embodied what he understood poetic tradition to be, and by that embodying helped Frost to imagine a place for his poems in it. His encounter with it was an event in the history of modern poetry and in the history of modern criticism.

Halcyon days!

Some early matters of fact are that Frost in a letter of 1906 told of having discovered and bought a copy of Palgrave's alluringly titled anthology in 1892, and of "neglecting my studies" at Dartmouth to bask in its radiance "(Halcyon days!)."[2] In a letter of 1904 he listed as his "favorites" poems by Keats, Shelley, Tennyson, and Browning, and "Besides these I am fond of the whole collection of Palgrave's."[3] The same range of taste was displayed on the shelves of a parlor bookcase in the Frosts' house during these years: "Poe, Coleridge, Tennyson, Matthew Arnold, Jean Ingelow, Palgrave's *Golden Treasury*, and the *Songs of Shakespeare*."[4] Frost's own children learned poems by heart from this store, while his pupils in English I at Pinkerton Academy were more systematically required to memorize "Twenty poems from the Golden Treasury; basis of subsequent study of the history of English literature."[5] Then in a letter written soon after leaving "*New* England" for "Old England" or Palgrave country, Frost described where he settled with his family in what his wife approved as "a dear little cottage," not literally thatched but at least vine-covered:[6]

> Here we are between high hedges of laurel and red-osier dogwood, within a mile or two of where Milton finished Paradise Lost on the one hand and a

mile or two of where Grey lies buried on the other. . . . If there is any virtue in Location—but don't think I think there is. I know where the poetry must come from if it comes.[7]

Between Wordsworthian hedgerows, between Milton and Gray, within seeing distance of the "lights" of Shakespeare's "London town," Frost imagined himself in a pastoral world mapped like *The Golden Treasury*, which Palgrave in its preface compares to a "landscape" measured out in "Books of Shakespeare, Milton, Gray, and Wordsworth."

a water spout
Frost in his youthful work celebrated Palgrave's claim in his preface that "Poetry gives treasures 'more golden than gold'": the poems in *A Boy's Will* are suffused with the golden pastoral diction that is everywhere the mark of the taste reflected in the anthology. So are other poems Frost wrote in this preparatory period but never included in his collected editions, where we come across "Gold flowers," "autumn gold," "golden autumn," "fainter gold behind the golden stars." The poems Frost winnowed from the "loose-leaf heap" of work he brought to England are all in the lyric forms allowed by Palgrave's rules for inclusion among what his full title calls *The Best Songs and Lyrical Poems in the English Language*: sonnets, odes, ballads, songs, elegiac poems.[8]

Much of Frost's early work shows that he had not only immersed himself in the diction and forms preferred in *The Golden Treasury*, but had deeply explored the poems in it by early writers it seems he met first there alongside many of his favorite nineteenth-century poets: Spenser, Shakespeare in sonnets, Herrick, Marvell, and Milton, particularly in "Lycidas," where an end note of Palgrave's says the conventions of classical pastoral "are exhibited more magnificently . . . than in any other pastoral." When, as so often in the public performances of Frost's later life, he dismissed academic study of poems, he seems to have been contrasting it in his mind with his adventure of "discovering on my own Palgrave's *Golden Treasury*" and privately reveling in its riches: "Goodness' sakes, the beauty of those poems at the top of everything," a metaphor of heights, of the summit that he used often for Palgrave's book, "is that some of them must be in your nature, you know, in your head. You can't hear them without their catching on to you without being studied."[9] The "Location" where he knew his poetry must come from was this internalized "land of *The Golden Treasury*."

In an interview with Richard Poirier in 1960, Frost, having caught his questioner "trying to trace" his "line of preference" among poets, ducked the question with a remembrance of his explorations in Palgrave's treasure trove:

> Oh, I read 'em all. One of my points of departure is an anthology. I find a poet I admire, and I think, well, there must be a lot to that. Some old one— Shirley, for instance, "The glories of our blood and state"—that sort of splendid poem. I go looking for more. [10]

Of all the selections in the anthology, this poem (along with Herrick's "To Daffodils") came to mind most often in Frost's letters and talks about poetry, lovingly remembered as if he still pictured it as he had first seen it on the page: "Now at the head of that it says in the Palgrave, if I remember rightly . . . 'Death the Leveller.'"[11]

Traces of Frost having assimilated particular poems in the anthology are everywhere in *A Boy's Will*, and take various forms. "Rose Pogonias" is itself a kind of anthology of effects borrowed from Palgrave's choices among poems by Herrick, Vaughan, and Marvell, with some remembrances of Keats's "To Autumn." In the later lines of "Waiting—Afield at Dusk," the "stubble field" and the progression of natural sounds catalogued by present participles more particularly evoke "To Autumn," with some reminders of Collins's "Ode to Evening." "Stars" owes the line "When wintry winds do blow" to one in a song by Shakespeare, "When all the winds doth blow." The sonnet "The Vantage Point" sets up its structure in the first line, "If tired of trees I seek again mankind," on the model of Shakespeare's sonnet "Tired with all these, for restful death I cry," but reverses the direction of the argument, pivoting on the playful rhyming substitution of "trees" for "these." In the last poem of the volume, "Reluctance," as the youthful poet moves "Out through the fields and the woods," the hopeful mood and simplified pastoral diction of that line call up the closing line of "Lycidas," where the young shepherd-poet moves "Tomorrow to fresh woods, and pastures new."[12]

Two instances of Frost's assimilations from *The Golden Treasury* constitute what might more precisely be called answer-poems. "Asking for Roses," dropped by Frost from the collected editions of his poems, includes a stanza rewriting Herrick's smilingly admonitory *carpe diem* song. That poem was given a title by Palgrave, "Counsel to Girls," which, like Frost's stanza, tries for Herrick's lightness of touch:

> "A word with you, that of the singer recalling—
>   Old Herrick: a saying that every maid knows is

A flower unplucked is but left to the falling,
And nothing is gained by not gathering roses."

More radical and surprising is the response to Shelley's "Ode to the West Wind" in Frost's "To the Thawing Wind," listed in a letter of 1913 among poems he thought "almost or quite as perfect" as "My November Guest."[13] This is the volume's only poem of apostrophe—"Come with rain, O loud Southwester"—compressing into six couplets and a closing triplet its response to Shelley's long stanzaic ode with its opening apostrophe—"O wild West Wind, thou breath of Autumn's being." The more layered relation to its source of this answer-poem may have to do with the fact that in "To the Thawing Wind" the youthful lover is for the first time explicit about being a poet, when he implores the wind to burst the walls of his self-enclosure: "Scatter poems on the floor; / Turn the poet out of door." The allusions to Shelley's importunate "Drive my dead thoughts . . . / Like withered leaves," "Scatter . . . / my words among mankind" are at once tributes and distancing sounds of the new poet's different voice: his imperatives, acknowledging Shelley's double meaning of "leaves," turn into an amused evocation of domestic untidiness.

There is nothing particularly surprising about this lavish appropriation in Frost's early poems, as he may well have known when he was writing them, and certainly recognized in amused retrospect when in 1925 he contributed the introduction to an anthology of "Dartmouth Verse":

> No one given to looking under-ground in spring can have failed to notice how a bean starts its growth from the seed. Now the manner of a poet's germination is less like that of a bean in the ground than of a waterspout at sea. He has to begin as a cloud of all the other poets he ever read.[14]

Still, what is remarkable about these traces of Frost's reading in his early poems is their being concentrated and focused by one book, which guided him by its own selective presentation of poets and poems.

the worn book of old-golden song

In Frost's arrangement of *A Boy's Will* as it was originally published, the poem at the very center of the first and longest by far of its three parts is "Flower-Gathering." He rarely if ever read or commented on it in his public performances, a reticence perhaps deliberately matched to the curious silences in the poem itself, but he did include it among his recommendations to William Braithwaite in 1915 of the best poems he and other friends should read in *A Boy's Will*.[15] Its importance here is that it is the first of several poems in the volume that go beyond assimilations from Palgrave's choices to use the book of *The Golden Treasury* itself as a focus for Frost's concerns about making his own poems, and about making a place for himself in poetic tradition.

In the first arrangement of *A Boy's Will*, the introduction of the lover as a poet in "To the Thawing Wind" is followed by "A Prayer in Spring." This is headed by the gloss "He discovers that the greatness of love lies not in forward looking thoughts," which is then linked to the gloss of the next poem, "Flower-Gathering": "nor yet in any spur it may be to ambition." In this grouping, love-making and verse-making come together, or pull apart, a pattern in Frost's work discussed extensively by Poirier.[16] The point to begin the related argument here is that the title "Flower-Gathering" is a translation into English of the literal meaning of *anthology* from its Greek root *anthos (flower)* + *legein (to gather)*, and that this title introduces the first poem in *A Boy's Will* to use Palgrave's gathering of poems as a metaphor. Here, besides being a love-offering, the gathering of flowers makes a figure for the poem itself, for the other verses of the poet-lover, and for all poetry.

The first stanza of "Flower-Gathering" tells a ballad-like story of how the youth, having left his beloved "in the morning glow," then returns "in the gloaming, / Gaunt and dusty gray with roaming," to be met by her unreadable silence: "Are you dumb because you know me not, / Or dumb because you know?" These unanswered questions raise their own questions about her silence and his inward separation from her: "because you know me not" as a poet to be taken seriously? "because you know" me to be a poet spurred to be a great poet by ambition that will keep me separate from you? Her silence is then marked by the space between the stanzas, and during it, as we learn from the second stanza, the lover holds out the bunch of flowers he has gathered for his beloved, which it seems she does not take, perhaps turns away not to see?

> All for me? And not a question
> For the faded flowers gay
> That could take me from beside you
> For the ages of a day?
> They are yours and be the measure

Of their worth for you to treasure,
The measure of the little while
That I've been long away.

Here his reassurance to the beloved raises more unanswered questions, not all of them about her unreadable silence. Offering what he has spent the day away from her to gather, he says simply "They are yours," but what follows is not simply said. The explicit meaning intended for her seems to be that her treasuring of the gift will be the measure of its worth, but there are suggestions of meanings tugging in other directions in the insistent associations of "measure," "measure" with poems, of "treasure" and "Flower-Gathering" with Palgrave's anthology. These tensions seem to deflect the explicit meaning: there are suggestions that the poems are "treasure" in their own "worth" by virtue of their "measure." And though they are "faded flowers gay," once "gay" but "faded" now because he has picked and carried them home to her, he does not apologize for them. In a sense he takes away their fadedness, gives them back their "gay" freshness by his archaic poetical word order (called "straddled adjectives" by Pound) describing them. Poirier, reading nearby poems in the volume concerned with the connections "between sexual love and poetic making," says the poems are "the stranger for not showing much acknowledgement of their strangeness," as if the two kinds of making "were so naturally, so instinctively identified as not to call for comment." Besides that strangeness in "Flower-Gathering," there is another kind that seems to surround the association, verging on identification, of the poem and others in *A Boy's Will* with the selections in *The Golden Treasury*. Unacknowledged in the poem is the possibility that these "flowers gay" are not "faded" because they have been gathered, but because they are the work of poets no longer living, so not responsive to the coming together, or pulling apart, of sexual and literary creation, which is the experience pressing its demands on the young lover's poetic making.

Frost originally placed "Waiting—Afield at Dusk" three poems after "Flower-Gathering," with "Rose Pogonias" and "Asking for Roses"—both to do with gathering flowers—in between. "Waiting" is glossed "He arrives at the turn of the year," predicting some turn in the poet-lover's inner direction. As in "Flower-Gathering," the lovers are separated, but here she is the "one absent," and he is left "alone" in "my secret place" to dream on nature's changing lights; more especially on the motions and

sounds of the nighthawks, the bat, and the swallow. Then, last in this catalogue of things in nature, joined simply by another "And" almost as if it
were one among them, comes another source of sound to dream on:

> And on the worn book of old-golden song,
> I brought not here to read, it seems, but hold
> And freshen in this air of withering sweetness.

This book is certainly Palgrave's gathering of poems, here not faded from
having been picked, but lovingly "worn" with handling which has rubbed
it to a soft "old-golden" burnish. This poet has brought it "not to read, it
seems, but hold" in his hand—but *hold* perhaps also with a slight trace of
the biblical sense of *to keep, to treasure*—not needing to gather anything
from it, not wholly preoccupied in dreaming on it, "But on the memory of
one absent most, / For whom these lines when they shall greet her eye."
The poem is achieved, made out of what the poet's senses have gathered
from natural sights and sounds into the "secret place" where he holds his
beloved in "memory"; and those imaginative resources have the power to
"freshen" the "book of old-golden song." The fullness and ease of the
poem's articulation makes a turn away from the strangely spare or cramped
manner of "Flower-Gathering," and that new direction seems to be focused
by the poet's power to "hold" and "freshen" the "old-golden song" from
within his own treasury of immediate and remembered experience.

The gloss of "Mowing," second from the end of the poems in Part I, announces another phase of the poet's growth: "He takes up life simply with
the small tasks." Looking back in 1925, Frost may have suggested how he
thought of this change of direction when he spoke of "Mowing" as his first
"talk-song," a departure from "old-golden song."[17] The mower-poet, listening to the sound of the scythe he used "to make" the hay, was unsure
what it was it did in "fact" whisper—whether about the sun's heat or the
silence—but he was certain what it was not. "It was no dream of the gift
of idle hours," what the poem "Waiting" could be said to be, "Or easy gold
at the hand of fay or elf," which suggests Frost might have been hearing
in his head lines he had read in *The Golden Treasury*, for instance about the
"faery child" in her "elfin grot" in Keats's "La Belle Dame Sans Merci."
Certainly the seductive power of these lines for the mower-poet, and for
Frost, is felt as it is held off: "easy gold" is not rejected but resisted. Behind the mower, Frost refigures himself as a poet: he no longer imagines
making poems as flower-gathering; he holds the "long scythe" as the instrument of his making, and not the "old-golden book of song."

In a public performance in 1958, Frost traced the course of his literary

life to "Mowing," which he had said as early as 1914 was the best poem in
A Boy's Will.[18]

> There, way back very early, this little one. . . . Now you see that one line in
> there. . . . "The fact is the sweetest dream that labor knows." That had a lot
> to do with my career. . . . The fact . . . not getting up fanciful things. I had
> no business to mention fay and elf in it. I always feel sorry about that.[19]

This reconsidering says a lot about why, after *A Boy's Will,* none of Frost's
books came as close to being like "a cloud of all the other poets he ever
read," or to imagining *The Golden Treasury* as a mythical place where his
poems were to come from.

Even so, there is one much later and very beautiful poem, suggestively
titled "Time Out," where it may be that *The Golden Treasury* is present,
somewhere not far below the surface, as a metaphor for poetry. The poem
is about—to state it most simply—an experience of reading. It is a sonnet,
a form Frost closely associated with Palgrave's book, and it strictly follows the Shakespearean rhyme scheme, not usual among Frost's sonnets.
In *A Witness Tree* of 1942, Frost placed this sonnet only two poems before
"The Lost Follower," described by Pritchard as "a crisply argued, ironic
tribute to a fellow poet who gave his soul to politics."[20] "The Lost Follower" begins:

> As I have known them passionate and fine
> The gold for which they leave the golden line
> Of lyric is a golden light divine

misguiding them to seek the "Golden Age" in "state-manipulated pelf, /
Or politics of Ghibelline or Guelph" instead of "right beside you book-like
on a shelf."

This poem seems to be a kind of gloss on "Time Out," which celebrates
a "pause" when the speaker in the sonnet escaped to a place above the
clamor of "cause and sect"; a place where nature and poetry come together
as metaphors for each other. He tells how he climbed a mountain that part
way up he discovered to have the same slant as "a book held up before his
eyes / (And was a text albeit done in plant)," like the "lovely leaves" we
"may read" in Herrick's "To Blossoms," one of Palgrave's choices. This
pastoral high place is described in "the golden line / Of lyric":

> Dwarf cornel, gold-thread, and maianthemum,
> He followingly fingered as he read,
> The flowers fading on the seed to come.

But what signified most to the climber was the angle the mountain gave to his seeing:

> The same for reading as it was for thought,
> So different from the hard and level stare
> Of enemies defied and battles fought.

He had climbed above party rancor and strife to a halcyon sphere freshened and calmed by the "obstinately gentle air / That may be clamored at by cause and sect, / But it will have its moment to reflect." Frost might have been listening to what seems to press against the explicit meaning of "Time Out" when, in a talk of 1956, he expanded on "what I think is the height of it all for me? I might sum it up in the word *Golden Treasury*— lyric poetry. A book almost without animus; all up in the spirit of high poetry, a book all the way up in the high guesses."[21]

the legacy of Tennyson

Frost's praises lifted *The Golden Treasury* to a summit beyond the reach of rancorous opinion, while at the same time he was entirely aware of its actual situation as a focus of modernists' attacks against nineteenth-century poetry and criticism. Pound, as always, led the fight, and Frost, as characteristically, made sly counterattacks, using praises of Palgrave for the purpose.

Pound's intemperate opinion of *The Golden Treasury*—"that stinking sugar teat Palgrave"—was well-publicized, by him and by others.[22] Yeats in a letter to Lady Gregory of 1928 joked about it as if it had been declared by manifesto to be of public importance:

> He has most of Maud Gonne's opinions (political and economic) about the world in general. . . . The chief difference is that he hates Palgrave's *Golden Treasury* as she does the Free State Government, and thinks even worse of its editor than she does of President Cosgrave.[23]

Even when Pound did not mention "that doddard Palgrave" by name, he repeatedly defined his own critical positions by their opposition to all that *The Golden Treasury* stood for in the opinion of its admiring public, still growing when the Oxford Press brought out in 1931 an edition expanded into a fifth book by Laurence Binyon.[24] In 1915 in Pound's preface to *Poetical Works of Lionel Johnson* he wrote:

> I think I have been chosen to write this Preface largely because I am known to hold theories which some people think new, and which several people

know to be hostile to much that hitherto has been accepted as "classic" in English poetry; that is to say, I reverence Dante and Villon and Catullus; for Milton and Victorianism . . . I have different degrees of antipathy or even contempt.[25]

In letters of this period, when Frost's first two books were being published in England, Pound called his own "*new* work. . . . absolutely the *last* obsequies of the Victorian period," which he identified with the poetry and influence of Palgrave's friend and chief adviser on the choice of entries in *The Golden Treasury:* "no hindside-beforeness, no straddled adjectives (as 'addled mosses dank'), no Tennysonianness of speech."[26]

Frost's letters in this period describe his initial uneasiness hardening into resentment at Pound's patronizing patronage, and all through his later correspondence, conversations, and public performances he never stopped feeling pressed to distance his poems and critical opinions from Pound's. In this effort he enlisted on his side *The Golden Treasury* and all its multiple associations, in a variety of counter-moves to Pound's game of demonizing Palgrave.

In Frost's more general ways of praising the anthology, he identified his own taste in poetry with Palgrave's, and this implies the larger dimension of his difference with Pound. In a talk on "Attitudes toward Poetry" in 1960 he said:

> Thinking of Tennyson again—he helped to make the most of a gem of a little book of poetry the world's ever seen—lyric poetry—Palgrave's *Golden Treasury.* It was his choices—a good part of it. It's beautiful—it's the top of the far of English literature. [27]

Three weeks later Frost continued these remarks about Tennyson's shaping influence on the unity of taste in the selection of entries: "And it gets violated all the time. People are always putting in more poems, calling it Palgrave's," a desecration of the book "like throwing away Tennyson. It's the legacy of Tennyson."[28]

In more detailed comments scattered through his work, Frost used the anthology to counter specific positions associated with what he sometimes called "the new Movement" of which "Ezra Pound was the Prime Mover," or "Imagism" and "He was the first Imagist too," or "the free-verse people" and "Ezra Pound used to say that you've got to get all the meter out of it—extirpate the meter." Carrying *The Golden Treasury* as his shield (Frost once praised a student for making the metaphor "He is the kind that wounds with his shield"), he went to battle against Pound, most particularly over issues about poetry to do with obscurity, and with the values of using visual imagery, meter, and rhyme.[29]

Frost's commentary about poetry over the years includes many sly observations that there "have been works lately to surpass all records for hardness," where his term is a practical, workmanlike substitute for what he considered buzz-words like *obscurity* or *difficulty*.[30] To a discussion of the impenetrability of the ancient Eleusinian mysteries, "the real mysteries," he added as if parenthetically, "And that's so with some people's poetry."[31] The celebration of difficulty as a criterion for poems that should be taken seriously Frost saw as the danger of "the general critical approach," of too complicated interpretive readings that at once over-value and exaggerate or even manufacture difficulty. By contrast, "the anthology," meaning chiefly Palgrave's but also the genre of poetry book, "is the best form of criticism": "I was told when I was young, let the anthologies alone. You might as well say, let all opinion in poetry alone, for the anthology is the best of all opinionation. It is a good form of criticism, just because it is pure example."[32]

Without acknowledging the target of the maneuver, he more particularly used the absence of footnotes in *The Golden Treasury* (overlooking, perhaps for the purposes of his argument, the notes at the end of the book) to challenge the worth of obscurity in poetry: "Most of you are teachers. What would you do with the Palgrave? It was published without a single note, if I'm not mistaken. . . . And what is there to be said about poetry like that?"[33] In another talk he marshaled the support to his side—and Palgrave's—of Emerson, Henry Dana (probably meaning Charles Anderson Dana), and Oliver Goldsmith, all makers of anthologies: "There've been anthologizing right down. Taking the top of poetry—interesting—there isn't anything in any of them that needs a note when you get up to that height of poetry."[34]

Paradoxically, the omission of notes was related for Frost to Palgrave's—and other anthologists'—addition of simple titles to untitled entries, or substitution of more explicitly explanatory titles for those already given. Both these decisions about how to present the poem to the reader seemed to Frost to be expressions of his own sense that poems should not be treated as mysteries inaccessible to the uninitiated. Referring to one of his most treasured examples from *The Golden Treasury*, Shirley's "The glories of our blood and state," he praised its explanatory title, "Death the Leveller": "Palgrave just added that—a smart addition."[35]

Elsewhere, after reciting Shakespeare's sonnet "They that have power to hurt and will do none," he slipped it into his attack on obscurity, saying it "always has had my great admiration. But lately someone told me it is considered one of the great puzzles." Then approving Palgrave's dubious title for it, "Life without Passion," he concluded blandly, "That's my idea of it. But it's supposed to be controversial."[36] The titles regularly supplied by Palgrave and other anthologists are more like Frost's own apparently simple, declarative titles than like Pound's often elusively allusive titles, often untranslated from European languages.

Though Frost was less critical of Pound's imagist insistence "on clearer sharper less muddled half realized images (chiefly eye images)," he still felt the need to stake out his different interest: "Strange with all their modernity and psychology they didnt have more to say about ear images," or what he more often called "sentence-sounds," his own prerequisite for what makes a good poem.[37] On this issue he characteristically defended himself with examples from Palgrave's book. He declared in a letter of 1915: "The sentence is everything—the sentence well imagined. See the beautiful sentences in a thing like Wordsworth's To Sleep or Herrick's To Daffodils. . . . We will prove it out of the Golden Treasury some day."[38] In a letter of 1918 he made the same point with the same supporting example, that the roots of every good poem are "well within the colloquial as I use the word. And so is all the lyric in Palgrave's Treasury. Consider Herrick's To Daffodils."

Frost took a more strenuous poke at Pound in his essay "The Constant Symbol" of 1946. This time the target was his program as a "free-verser" to liberate poetry from meter—in Pound's idiom "the god damn iambic"—and from lyric forms constrained by fixed lineation and rhyme, an idea Frost enjoyed saying would make writing poems like playing tennis with the net down.[39] In the essay Frost pictured the poet playing a different game, jump rope (elsewhere it is hopscotch, and the poet-player is Pope writing "Ode on Solitude," the only one of his poems chosen by Palgrave).[40] The rope skipper enters into the game "to make the most of his opportunities," which are the choices of: "two meters, strict iambic and loose iambic"; "any length of line up to six feet"; and "an assortment of line lengths for any shape of stanza, like Herrick in 'To Daffodils.'"[41]

The entries in *The Golden Treasury* that Frost returned to all his writing life in defining his poems and poetics, often in their differences from Pound's, are beautifully true to his own preferences in lyric forms: "my love of neatness, of a little poem, you know, the rhymes of it and the little bits."[42] His chosen examples are equally representative of Palgrave's commitment to meter, rhyme, and the lyric: the rules he explained in the preface to his anthology excluded "Blank verse and the ten-syllable couplet . . . as alien from what is commonly understood by Song, and rarely conforming to Lyric conditions in treatment."

Short stanzaic poems like Shirley's and Pope's and Herrick's, sonnets like Shakespeare's and Wordsworth's, and those of Frost's favorite poems that he often affectionately called the "little ones" ("Stopping by Woods on a Snowy Evening" and "Mowing," for example) are described by an extended metaphor in a talk of 1958: "I have a little ivory box . . . a couple of inches—a little box with a slide cover, carved, and in two layers of pieces and they fitted together—a little puzzle. . . . they're very like a poem to me . . . and the poem is the box."[43] Not only particular favorites among Palgrave's choices were used by Frost as representations of his ideal poem. He even made such a figure out of the book of *The Golden Treasury* itself: "It's a pretty little sonnet of a book"; "And I wouldn't have that book violated any more than I'd have one of Shakespeare's sonnets violated."[44]

the English anthology

In the interview of 1960 quoted earlier, Poirier, denying Frost's accusation that he had been "trying to trace" the poet to his sources, tried again by asking what Frost would say to the fact that "Eliot and Pound seem to many people to be writing in a tradition that's very different from yours." Frost's answer is much more importantly revealing than its playful naughtiness pretends:

> Pound seemed to me very like a troubadour. . . . I never touched that. I don't know Old French. I don't like foreign languages that I haven't had. . . . I like to say dreadful, unpleasant things about Dante. Pound, though, he's supposed to know Old French.[45]

Asked next if Pound was a good linguist, Frost repeated what a teacher once told him about Pound's performance in a college Latin course: that he "never knew the difference between a declension and a conjugation." While delighting in his own mischief, Frost characteristically used it here to hint at essentially the same answer about his different understanding of poetic tradition from Pound's that he had given in 1942 in the "Preface to Poems in 'This Is My Best.'" There his sense of profound difference between himself and Pound, though unmentioned, seems as usual to be somewhere behind Frost's way of placing himself as a poet:

> It would be hard to gather biography from poems of mine except as they were all written by the same person, out of the same general region north of Boston, and out of the same books, a few Greek and Latin, practically no others in any other tongue than our own.[46]

This unspoken contrast with Pound's Europeanism expresses Frost's sense of belonging to the classic tradition of English poetry and his appreciation of its continuity, for which Palgrave's anthology was to him both an actual embodiment and a metaphor. He seems to have been imagining the tradition of poetry in English as *The Golden Treasury* hypostatized when, in the course of praising Gerard Manley Hopkins, he spoke of a poet's immortality: "A very fine poet, and one of our poets. There'll always be some of him in the anthology, speaking of him that way—[in] the English Anthology."[47] He seems also to have been picturing poems of his own inscribed forever among the pages of such a book when he made a wish for his own poetic immortality: "The utmost of ambition is to lodge a few poems where they will be hard to get rid of, a few irreducible bits."[48]

Notes

1. Reginald Cook, *Robert Frost: A Living Voice* (Amherst: University of Massachusetts Press, 1974), 109–10; William Pritchard, *Frost: A Literary Life Reconsidered* (New York: Oxford University Press, 1984), 3.

2. Robert Frost, *Selected Letters of Robert Frost*, ed. Lawrance Thompson (New York: Holt, Rinehart and Winston, 1964), 37. In 1960 Frost described to the audience at one of his talks the copy "that fell into my lap" of one of the earliest editions of *The Golden Treasury* (Cook, *Robert Frost*, 159), but it was his practice to bring a modern edition to refer to, as he often did, on such occasions. In this essay all quotations from *The Golden Treasury* are from the annotated edition made by Christopher Ricks (London: Penguin, 1991), which includes all the poems in the first edition of 1861, and all the additions through the last revision by Palgrave of 1891.

3. Frost, *Selected Letters*, 20.

4. Lawrance Thompson, *Robert Frost: The Early Years 1874–1915* (New York: Holt, Rinehart and Winston, 1966), 304.

5. Ibid., 347.

6. Robert Frost, *Collected Poems, Prose, & Plays*, ed. Richard Poirier and Mark Richardson (New York: Library of America, 1995), 686; Frost, *Selected Letters*, 54.

7. Frost, *Selected Letters* 52.

8. Frost, *Collected Poems*, 874; 503, 511, 514. All other quotations of Frost's poems are from this edition but not referenced in notes because they can be located in its table of contents listing poems by volume and title.

9. Elizabeth Sergeant, *Robert Frost: The Trial by Existence* (New York: Holt, Rinehart and Winston, 1960), 28; Cook, *Robert Frost*, 243.

10. Frost, *Collected Poems*, 881, 879.

11. Cook, *Robert Frost*, 58.

12. For a discussion of "Lycidas" as a shaping influence on *A Boy's Will* see Anne Ferry, *The Title to the Poem* (Stanford: Stanford University Press, 1996), 25, 27, 28–29.

13. Frost, *Selected Letters*, 76–77.

14. Frost, *Collected Poems*, 709.

15. Ibid., 684.

16. Richard Poirier, *Robert Frost: The Work of Knowing* (New York: Oxford University Press, 1977), especially 62–72. In discussing poems in *A Boy's Will*, Poirier points out some of the allusions to choices in *The Golden Treasury* that are expanded on here.

17. Sergeant, *Robert Frost*, 423.

18. Frost, *Selected Letters*, 141.

19. Cook, *Robert Frost*, 123. "Spoils of the Dead" with its "faeries" was omitted from collected editions.

20. Pritchard, *Frost*, 239.

21. Cook, *Robert Frost*, 109.

22. Ezra Pound, *Ezra Pound: Letters to Ibbotson, 1935–1952*, ed. Vittoria Mondolfo and Margaret Hurley (Orono: University of Maine, 1979), 24.

23. W. B. Yeats, *The Letters of W. B. Yeats*, ed. Allan Wade (London: Rupert Hart-Davis, 1954), 739.

24. Ezra Pound, *Literary Essays of Ezra Pound*, ed. T. S. Eliot (New York: New Directions, 1968), 18.

25. Ibid., 362.

26. Ezra Pound, *The Letters of Ezra Pound 1907–1941*, ed. D. D. Paige (New York: Harcourt, Brace, 1950), 23, 49.

27. Cook, *Robert Frost*, 144.

28. Ibid., 159.

29. Frost, *Collected Poems*, 734–35, 690, 856.

30. Ibid., 786.

31. Cook, *Robert Frost*, 39.

32. Frost, *Collected Poems*, 768–69.

33. Cook, *Robert Frost*, 46.

34. Ibid., 58.

35. Ibid. Palgrave himself probably found this song in an anthology he acknowledged having consulted, Robert Bell's *Songs from the Dramatists*, first published in 1854, where the poem is given the title "The Equality of the Grave."

36. Ibid., 156.

37. Frost, *Collected Poems*, 734.

38. William Evans, *Robert Frost and Sidney Cox* (Hanover, N. H.: University Press of New England, 1981), 61.

39. Pound, *Letters 1907–1941*, 260.

40. Sergeant, *Robert Frost*, 410–11; Cook, *Robert Frost*, 146–47.

41. Frost, *Collected Poems*, 788.

42. Cook, *Robert Frost*, 122.

43. Ibid.

44. Ibid., 159.

45. Frost, *Collected Poems*, 881.

46. Ibid., 783.

47. Cook, *Robert Frost*, 63.

48. Frost, *Collected Poems*, 744.

Christopher Benfey

"The Wife of Eli Whitney"

Jarrell and Dickinson

1

WILLIAM H. PRITCHARD's account of Randall Jarrell's death raises the possibility that the last written words of Jarrell that we have may be his notes on Emily Dickinson's poetry, scrawled on the flyleaves and margins of Thomas H. Johnson's edition of 1955. When Jarrell checked into the Hand House of the University of North Carolina's medical school at Chapel Hill, during the fall of 1964, for physical therapy on his injured right wrist, he brought along with him, according to Pritchard,

> a copy of [Elizabeth] Bishop's new book of poems, *Questions of Travel*, which he planned to review, and the Johnson three-volume edition of Emily Dickinson's poetry . . . about which he also hoped to write. On Monday evening, October 11, he talked on the phone to his wife, requesting a heavy wool sports jacket and leather gloves for walking in the early evening.[1]

Three days later, walking back to the hospital along a highway, he was struck and killed by an oncoming car.

Jarrell had been mulling over an essay on Dickinson for over a decade. In the preface to *Poetry and the Age* (1953), he wrote: "Several of the American poets I like most—Eliot and Dickinson for instance—I've never written about; I mean to write about them later."[2] He seemed to feel no urgency. Jarrell wrote some of his best criticism in defense of writers he felt were unfairly slighted or neglected—thus the assessments of Christina Stead and Robert Frost, and the famous Whitman essay, in Pritchard's view, "a lively provoking of New Critics like Ransom and Tate and Blackmur who had avoided dealing with Whitman's poetry."[3] Whitman needed an advocate during the 1950s; Dickinson and Eliot did not. Everyone read them and wrote about them and mostly praised them. "During the past thirty or forty years," Jarrell remarked in 1962, "Eliot has been so much the most famous and influential of American poets that it seems almost absurd to write about him, especially when everybody else already has: when all of you can read me your own articles about Eliot, would it have really been worth while to write you mine?"[4]

Neither was Dickinson neglected. Precisely those critics that Pritchard mentions as avoiding Whitman—Ransom, Tate, and Blackmur—wrote handsome tributes to Dickinson's poetry, as though, if a choice must be made, Dickinson served as a better precursor of modern American poetry than the "disgraceful" (Dickinson's word for what she had heard of his poetry) Whitman. Tate, in his pioneering essay on Dickinson in 1932, when he could still complain that "Miss Dickinson's poetry has not been widely read," described her as "a deep mind writing from a deep culture," untouched by "the rising plutocracy of the East."[5] Never mind that Dickinson's father and brother, both treasurers of Amherst College, did their damnedest to join that plutocracy.

Blackmur's essay, which Tate judged "one of the great critical essays of our time," was also in Dickinson's favor, but with some sharp qualifications. Although gifted with a "natural aptitude for language," Dickinson, Blackmur claimed, "never knew anything about the craft of verse well enough to exemplify it, let alone revolt from it."[6] For these critics, Dickinson's appeal lay not in her innovations or her "rebellion," but rather in her conformity to "deep" traditions, as opposed to the wayward and experimental Whitman. She "triumphed," as Roy Harvey Pearce once explained, "because at some points she acknowledged the restraining orthodoxy of her milieu."[7]

The generation of the New Critics had learned their Dickinson from the cleaned-up versions of Thomas Higginson and Mabel Loomis Todd.

The 1955 publication of all the extant poems and their variants, with Dickinson's spelling and punctuation and alternative word choices restored, introduced a new and more "modern" Dickinson, a poet of open-endedness ("Choosing Not Choosing," as Sharon Cameron has character-ized her in a recent book) and experiment. This new Dickinson had a profound impact on some of the poets who came of age during the 1950s, including John Berryman—who shifted allegiances from Whitman (the inspiration for the form of the *Dream Songs*) to Dickinson (the formal model for his later poems in *Love and Fame* and after)—and Jarrell.

When I spoke to Mary Jarrell, around 1980 as I recall, about her hus-band's relation to Dickinson, she encouraged me to borrow his three-vol-ume set of Dickinson's poems—the bound galleys for the 1955 edition; he seemed not to own the finished volumes.[8] The poems were heavily under-lined, the margins often crammed with notes, and the endpapers covered with Jarrell's close handwriting. Marginalia such as "write about" and "quote this" suggested that he was on the way to an essay, and Mary Jar-rell confirmed that at the time of his death Jarrell was working on the essay. The ideas I assembled at that time (and wrote up for an independent study under Professor Warner Berthoff at Harvard) are the basis for what follows.

2

The notes on the flyleaves do not in themselves make consistently exhila-rating or coherent reading. Each remark, enclosed by semicolons, rarely has any relation to what precedes or follows it. Jarrell was still far from a finished essay, or even from a draft. The best we can do is to provide a plausible context—drawn from Jarrell's published essays and poems, and from Pritchard's narrative of his life—for these notes on Dickinson, and perhaps catch some intimations of what would, in a finished Jarrell essay, be much more concisely and elegantly expressed.

Jarrell's wide-ranging cultural curiosity is on display in the notes, such as his suggestion that Dickinson's "Humphrey-like qualities make her good for modern dancers to love and mirror." Humphrey I take it is the choreographer Doris Humphrey (1895–1958), author of *The Art of Mak-ing Dances*, whose emphasis on technique and abstract movement helped free modern dance from its earlier reliance on folklore and mythology. Jarrell may have discerned a kindred allegiance to abstract form and technical rigor in Dickinson's work. Of course it was Humphrey's contemporary, Martha Graham, who actually choreographed a dance—"Letter to the World" (1940)—explicitly based on Dickinson's poetry and life.

In a less arcane vein, several notes indicate Jarrell's interest in Dickinson as an investigator of the human mind. Jarrell's friend Adrienne Rich has called Dickinson "a great psychologist" and *"the* American poet whose work consisted in exploring states of psychic extremity."[9] Jarrell, exhibiting his college training in experimental psychology at Vanderbilt, tells himself to "relate [Dickinson] to all the introspective psychologists of the time, Ebbinghaus with nonsense syllables—she's often a scientific observer of processes." (Hermann Ebbinghaus [1850–1909] conducted pioneering research on the nature of memory, among other subjects.) Then Jarrell laments that "many of her observations [are] so acute you wish she'd had the Great World, Bad World to observe too"—a remark fairly close to early insinuations, by William Carlos Williams and Conrad Aiken among others, that Dickinson's experience of "the world"—meaning the world of *men*—was rather limited.

Such strictures are countered in Adrienne Rich's observation that "like every great psychologist, [Dickinson] began with the material she had at hand: herself."[10] Jarrell, on a similar note, reminds himself to "Talk about how it feels to be as she was, how many of [the] things she says come directly from that—the most personal, almost, of poets—herself her absorbing, inescapable subject" (something she shared, by the way, with Ebbinghaus's self-directed studies).

And yet Jarrell is quick to note that Dickinson's condition often parallels our own: she's "good at accurately observed things about how we think and feel, live our life." Many of the poems, Jarrell felt, though "not good as poetry [are] still interesting as life, her life, or as observing statements about living." In this "queer direct kind of autobiography," Jarrell noted that "so many" of the poems are "interesting not exactly as separate works of art but as really well done entries in [a] diary."

Jarrell is groping for a way to read the poetry whole, as a body of work, in which even the weaker poems have their place. Jarrell never dodged the question of value, though, and much of his thinking about Dickinson has to do with trying to "sort out," in J. V. Cunningham's phrase, the daunting miscellany of her work. In almost all Jarrell's essays on poetry, a prominent place is reserved for a list of the poet's best poems, and often a second list of runners-up. On the fly-leaf of the first Dickinson volume Jarrell has a list of twenty entries headed "Best Poems," and opposite it a shorter list, presumably of poems "almost as good." Some of the poems in the "best" list have been relegated by arrows to the second list; one of these demoted poems, the popular riddle in verse "A narrow Fellow in the Grass" (Johnson 986), is also crossed out.[11]

There are few surprises in the first of Jarrell's lists. Most of the entries are from the canon of the New Critics, poems like "Further in Summer than the Birds" (1068, a favorite of Yvor Winters), "Because I could not stop for Death" (712, "one of the most perfect poems in English," in Tate's view), and "I heard a Fly buzz" (465). These poems had been on Jarrell's mind for some time. He once confessed that he preferred the version of the fly poem edited by Higginson and published in the 1890s to the 1955 "restored" version. And he had suggested to a poetry class, circa 1960, that the opening lines of "Because I could not stop" were like someone saying, "We have a nice hotel room. The girl, myself, and the Sphinx."[12] These three poems and three others are underlined twice, the others in the "best" list only once. My guess is that Jarrell thought these six poems particularly fine, the best of the best.

The three other "best of the best" poems, while not exactly obscure, are not nearly as well known as the first three. Most readers are familiar with "After great pain, a formal feeling comes" (341), the first three words of which comprise the title to a psychoanalytic biography of Dickinson, and with "I felt a Funeral, in my Brain" (280), which the great German critic Leo Spitzer once claimed was a naturalistic account of a migraine ("And mourners to and fro / Kept treading, treading . . ."). The third, "Twas like a Maelstrom, with a notch" (414), is hardly an anthology piece.

These three poems, especially the last two, are strikingly similar to one another in theme. Since Jarrell planned in his essay to "say what subjects her best poems are about," it is worth trying to identify the subjects of these poems. In all three poems Dickinson describes a numbing or stiffening of human faculties.

> After great pain, a formal feeling comes—
> The Nerves sit ceremonious, like Tombs—
> The stiff Heart questions was it He, that bore,
> And Yesterday, or Centuries before? (341)

> And when they all were seated,
> A Service, like a Drum—
> Kept Beating—beating—till I thought
> My Mind was going numb— (280)

> And not a Sinew—stirred—could help,
> And sense was setting numb— (414)

In all three poems there is also a moment of release from this numbness and stiffening:

> This is the Hour of Lead—
> Remembered, if outlived,
> As Freezing persons, recollect the Snow—
> First—Chill—then Stupor—then the letting go— (341)

> And then a Plank in Reason, broke,
> And I dropped down, and down— (280)

> And you dropt, lost,
> When something broke—
> And let you from a Dream— (414)

Everyone knows that death was one of Dickinson's great subjects. These poems (like Jarrell's ball turret gunner poem) attempt to find words for what dying might feel like. But they are also poems about the stiffening of the imagination, about having a mind of winter. As Adrienne Rich interprets "After great pain": "For the poet, the terror is precisely in those periods of psychic death, when even the possibility of work is negated; her occupation's gone."[13]

During the period of his most intense involvement with Dickinson's poetry, Jarrell was experiencing prolonged depression and creative dearth —"as if the real Jarrell," as Pritchard puts it, "had gone away somewhere." These poems of Dickinson, with their imagery of freezing and paralysis and final release, may have had a special, personal meaning for Jarrell.

Throughout his career, Jarrell had been drawn to this scenario, as though to something both attractive and feared, and in some of his finest poems. One thinks of the polar fantasy of "90 North," in Pritchard's view "the strongest early intimation of Jarrell's distinctiveness as a poet,"[14] the frozen fur of the ball turret gunner, and the "cold made-up face" of the dead friend in "Next Day." It is hard not to think, also, of the wool jacket and gloves Jarrell requested a couple days before his death. "Randall," wrote Ransom in the memorial volume, "had a great flair for the poetry of desperation."[15]

3

One of the challenges Randall Jarrell set for himself in his projected essay on Emily Dickinson was to find the proper literary context for reading her work. What tradition did her poems belong to? How was she like and unlike other poets? Jarrell began his 1962 lecture "Fifty Years of American Poetry" with the following assessment:

> In 1910 American poetry was a bare sight. We were not, like Canada or New Zealand, a province without a national poetry of its own. There had been good American poets—but how few, and already how far in the past! Whitman and Dickinson, the two greatest and most decidedly American, seemed to owe both their greatness and their Americanness to their own entire originality and eccentricity.[16]

Later in the same lecture, discussing poetry written by women, Jarrell judged Elizabeth Bishop and Marianne Moore the "best women poets since Emily Dickinson."[17] Had Jarrell lived to write an essay on Dickinson, we might expect him to focus on the two aspects of her poetry and person implied in these passages from the "Fifty Years" lecture: first, the extent to which her poems are distinctively American; and second, the degree to which her poetry is part of a women's tradition in poetry. For a moment in the notes the two aspects merge: "exag/ everything—*Am. hyperbole*, fem. hyperbole, the exaggeration of [inserted: "all by herself"] loudly suffering introspection." The unfortunate sexism of the twinned hyperboles should not diminish the descriptive force of that fine last phrase, "loudly suffering introspection."

A phrase running through much of Jarrell's criticism is his attempt to define what it means to be American, especially an American poet. He liked to quote Henry James's remark—the final line of Marianne Moore's "New York"—that America provides "accessibility to experience."[18] Not, however, Jarrell added, experience of the rest of the world. If Yeats called Keats "a schoolboy . . . with face and nose pressed to a sweet-shop window," "we Americans," Jarrell noted, "stand with our noses pressed against the window of the world."[19] Jarrell, who had lamented Dickinson's exclusion from the "Great World, Bad World," found this outsider's view of the world pervasive in Dickinson's poetry: "Child's geography-book feel about continents, mountains also abstract feel of world as made up of sea, land, etc."

It is too bad that Jarrell, who was reading Elizabeth Bishop's *Questions of Travel* even as he reread Dickinson, did not live long enough to see her *Geography III*, which opens with an epigraph from a "child's geography-book . . . about continents, mountains . . . etc." There was a missed opportunity to draw a rich comparison here between the imaginary traveler in Amherst and the traveler between Brazil and Nova Scotia. Instead, Jarrell falls back on another sexist comparison. Dickinson's "frigid, unimaginative use of Cordillera, Appenine [*sic*], etc." reminded him of the "lady reporter in James"—Henrietta Stackpole in *The Portrait of a Lady*, I assume. If Jarrell's use of "frigid" recalls what earlier critics had sometimes implied about Dickinson's erotic life, it also returns us to the theme of freezing and numbness that so attracted him in her poetry.

Among the American aspects of Dickinson's poetry, Jarrell included her use of abstractions—words as big as "cordillera," to be sure, but presumably used more imaginatively and less frigidly. He praises her "good use of abstract words that continues in Pound, Moore, Stevens," and calls this practice "characteristic of American poetry, which has a more abstract see-through line than English." "Abstractions," he wrote in the margin of poem 963:

> A nearness to Tremendousness—
> An Agony procures—
> Affliction ranges Boundlessness—
> Vicinity to Laws
>
> Contentment's quiet Suburb—
> Affliction cannot stay
> In Acres—It's Location
> Is Illocality—

and in the notes he wrote of this poem: "'A nearness to tremendousness' shows use of abstractions at most concentrated—these leading to Marianne Moore, very American somehow."

Jarrell was surely aware that this conjunction of the American and the abstract had a long foreground in cultural commentary. Tocqueville had noticed in the United States a tendency towards abstract formulations. "Democratic nations are passionately addicted to generic terms and abstract expressions," he maintained, "because these modes of speech enlarge thought and assist the operations of the mind by enabling it to include many objects in a small compass."[20] Commenting on Dickinson's "An ignorance a Sunset / Confer upon the Eye— / Of Territory—

Color— / Circumference— Decay—" (552), a poem syntactically and the-
matically similar to "A nearness to Tremendousness," Jarrell seems almost to paraphrase Tocqueville: "Rhetoric likes a bare canvas—or rather,
a big blank wall—Life, Death, Eternity—all intensive absolutes which
justify everything, preclude nothing, don't hold you down; cramp your
style, make petty specific demands."

There is a tension never fully resolved in Jarrell's criticism between the
abstract formulations of modern art which he accepted (see his poem "The
Old and the New Masters") in Williams, Moore, and the early Stevens—
"their reproduction of things, in its empirical gaiety, its clear abstract
refinement of presentation, has something peculiarly and paradoxically
American about it"[21]—and the abstract monotony of "philosophical" poetry. The key word in the quote is probably "things," though a later assessment of Williams drops even the things. Williams, Jarrell observed,
"loves abstractions for their own sake and makes accomplished, characteristic, inveterate use of them, exactly as if they were sensations or emotions."[22] Santayana's defense of philosophical poetry, and of Dante in
particular, relies on this premise. "The life of theory is not less human or
less emotional than the life of sense," Santayana argued; "it is more typically human and more keenly emotional." Hence, "philosophy, when a poet
is not mindless, enters inevitably into his poetry, since it has entered into
his life; or rather, the detail of things and the detail of ideas pass equally
into his verse."[23]

At the risk of pushing these rarified reflections even farther, it is worth
noting that a leaning towards abstract formulation was in Jarrell's critical
framework (and in Modernist polemic in general—"no ideas but in things")
a leaning towards philosophy, pernicious he felt to poetry. It was Santayana's disciple, Wallace Stevens, who most consistently drew Jarrell's
censure in this regard. "As a poet Stevens has every gift but the dramatic,"
Jarrell—a persistently "dramatic" poet himself—maintained. "It is the
lack of immediate contact with lives that hurts his poetry more than anything else, and that has made it easier and easier for him to abstract, to
philosophize."[24]

During the period in which he was reading Dickinson seriously, Jarrell
had been reading Wallace Stevens aloud to his wife.[25] A comparison between the two poets and their reliance on abstraction would therefore
seem likely in a finished essay. Jarrell's attention to Dickinson's abstractions seems largely a question of rhetoric, of abstractions as interesting
pieces of language and sound; the issue of the relation of the abstractions

in her poems to specific philosophical ideas never arises in his notes. It was perhaps Dickinson's skill in juxtaposing abstract and concrete words ("Contentment's quiet Suburb") that Jarrell most admired. He had praised Auden's device of placing abstract words against a concrete ground (the opposite of the orator's usual tactic); now he noted in Dickinson's poetry "polysyllables here and there in setting of monosyllables," and, more specifically, "polysyllabic abstractions joined by monosyllables and the verb *to be*." An example might be: "In Acres—It's Location / Is Illocality."

Dickinson's playful use of abstractions and slang reminded Jarrell of E. E. Cummings: "American-ness; beginning of many characteristics of Am. poetry—like Cummings, Moore—slang or such—abstractions—etc." Jarrell heard Cummings in lines like "I leaned upon the Awe— / I lingered with Before—" (609). Next to the lines, "But Sunrise stopped upon the place / And fastened it in Dawn" (1053), he wrote, "Cummings manipulation, false specificness." In the phrase "yellow noise" Jarrell detected a "Cummings-y use of words as transferable counters," and of "Shame is the shawl of Pink" (1412) he commented, "pink[,] like many other words, becomes an absolute quality capable of being used anywhere for anything (this in Cummings)."

Jarrell's favorite word for Dickinson's verbal experiments was "operations." He suggested that "her rhetoric" was often "obtained by operations like those in symbolic logic," noting that the word "overtakelessness" (1691) was "made by negation + *ness*, a shame no further operation possible." Such devices led Jarrell to call Dickinson "the wife of Eli Whitney," and, in a gloss to "Hope is a strange invention— / A Patent of the Heart" (1392), to marvel at "her yankee mechanical ingenuity." In Jarrell's view, Dickinson had constructed "a rhetoric that, easily or with effort, can do up anything."

4

Dickinson was a distinctively American poet for Jarrell, and a central one. But she was also a woman poet. Jarrell was aware of the patronizing force of the phrase as many critics (including himself) used it during the 1950s. "I have read that several people think So-and-So the greatest living woman poet," he wrote; "anybody would dislike applying so clumsy a phrase to Miss Moore—but surely she is."[26] In the "Fifty Years" speech, Jarrell made a distinction between what he called a "feminine" tradition in

American poetry, and another tradition of American women poets which he had no name for:

> Earlier in this century there was a tradition of feminine verse—roughly, an Elizabeth Barrett Browning tradition—which produced many frankly romantic and poetic poems, most of them about love or nature. Elinor Wylie was the most crystalline and superficially metaphysical of these writers, and Edna St. Vincent Millay the most powerful and most popular. . . . Millay seems to me at her best in a comparatively quiet and unpretentious poem like "The Return"; two later poets in this tradition, Leonie Adams and Louise Bogan, have produced . . . poems more delicately beautiful than any of Millay's or Wylie's.[27]

Jarrell refers to this feminine tradition in the Dickinson notes: "the feminine way from E. B. B. on."

Jarrell felt that Dickinson belonged to another tradition of women poets, one that rejected the gender restrictions implied by "femininity." The passage from the "Fifty Years" speech continues: "I have already written of two poets in a very different tradition, Marianne Moore and Elizabeth Bishop, who seem to me the best woman poets since Emily Dickinson."[28]

Marianne Moore is the poet to whom Jarrell most often compares Dickinson in the notes. He wrote "m. m." next to these lines from "The Robin is a Gabriel" (1483):

> He has the punctuality
> Of the New England Farmer—
> The same oblique integrity,
> A Vista vastly warmer—

A poem like Moore's "Propriety" (of which Jarrell commented, "if ever a poem was perfect 'Propriety' is") suddenly seems thoroughly Dickinsonian, a "definition poem" to place beside Dickinson's inventive definitions.[29] Moore follows Dickinson's practice of taking an airy abstraction and concretizing it: "'Hope' is the thing with feathers . . ." (254); "'Crisis is a Hair . . ." (889).

That Dickinson, like Moore, escaped from a narrowly defined notion of feminine propriety in her poetry was confirmed, for Jarrell, in her attempts to assume a male persona or voice. He reminded himself to "Notice change in versions" of poem 446, from "I showed her Heights she never saw—" to "I showed *him* Heights. . . ." Jarrell took a special interest in the two versions of poem 49—"Going to Him! Happy letter!" and "Going—

to—Her!"—a poem in which Dickinson seems playfully aware of her own strategies: "Tell Him—I only said the Syntax— / And left the Verb and the pronoun out—." Jarrell wrote beside these lines, "quote," and added, "talk about 'him-her' versions—seemed to her pity something so intense couldn't be used for both."

Of course, neither of these poems necessarily implies a change in the sex of the speaker. A woman can show heights and send happy letters to another woman. What Jarrell detected in Dickinson's shifting pronouns was a parallel to his own experiments in assuming the voice of a woman, "altering," as Mary Jarrell once noted, "the gender of his feelings."[30] "The Face" was an early attempt, where Jarrell amended his first version, "Not good anymore, not handsome—," to "Not good anymore, not beautiful."[31] Later, more ambitious poems like "The Woman at the Washington Zoo" and "Next Day" extended Jarrell's sympathetic appropriation of women's voices. When he wrote in the margin of the following poem,

> Her sweet Weight on my Heart at Night
> Has scarcely deigned to lie—
> When, stirring, for Belief's delight,
> My bride had slipped away— (518),

"made dramatic monologue for him; the complications of the process," Jarrell knew from experience what these complications were.

5

Let us venture, then, a summary of what might have been the major points of Jarrell's essay on Emily Dickinson. To the extent that we can reconstruct his assessment of her work, Dickinson was a profound explorer of the human psyche, who took her own mental processes as her subject. Jarrell was particularly drawn to those poems of "psychic extremity" (Adrienne Rich's phrase) in which Dickinson recorded the numbing and stiffening of the imaginative faculties.

Such psychic investigations required a new language, and Dickinson was, in Jarrell's account, a restless experimenter and inventor with the raw materials of poetry. She tinkered with the pieces of language most available in America—abstractions and slang—and gave them new and arresting settings in her poems. Her neologisms and wrenched syntax produced a rhetoric that could "do up anything." Rejecting the strictures of "feminine" verse, she used ambiguous pronouns to shift the sex of her speakers. Dickinson's bold ways with language had analogues in other art forms, as well as in science and logic. Along with Whitman, she had pretty much singlehandedly invented American poetry. Later poets as diverse as William Carlos Williams, Marianne Moore, E. E. Cummings, Wallace Stevens, and Ezra Pound seemed to have emerged from Emily Dickinson's overcoat, or rather from her clean white dress.

Notes

1. William H. Pritchard, *Randall Jarrell: A Literary Life* (New York: Farrar, Straus, 1990), 295.

2. Jarrell, *Poetry and the Age* (New York: Vintage Books, 1953), vi.

3. Pritchard, *Randall Jarrell*, 214.

4. Jarrell, *The Third Book of Criticism* (New York: Farrar, Straus, 1971), 314.

5. For Tate's views, see "Emily Dickinson," in *The Man of Letters in the Modern World: Selected Essays, 1928–1955* (Cleveland: Meridian, 1955), 211, 215–16, 221, 224.

6. For the Tate judgment see his review article, "The Poet and Her Biographer," in *The Kenyon Review* 1 (Spring 1939): 203. For Blackmur, "Emily Dickinson: Notes on Prejudice and Fact," in *Language as Gesture* (New York: Harcourt, Brace, 1952), 28.

7. I have been unable to locate this quote in Pearce's *The Continuity of American Poetry* (Princeton: Princeton University Press, 1961).

8. Jarrell's papers and books are in the library of the University of North Carolina at Greensboro.

9. Adrienne Rich, "Vesuvius at Home: The Power of Emily Dickinson," in *Parnassus: Poetry in Review* 5 (1976): 67.

10. Rich, 67.

11. The list of Best Poems includes: 49, 280, 289, 341, 414, 465, 510, 520, 615, 712, 1068, 1100, 1147, 1540, 1732, 1749 (and, out of order, and presumably added after another read-through of the poems), 348, 258, 640. Relegated to the second list are: 376, 1078, 1670. The second list includes: 130, 303, 389, 528, 561, 579, 664, 745, 754, 812, 1072, 1075, 1084, 1593. The poem numbers refer to *The Poems of Emily Dickinson*, 3 volumes, edited by Thomas H. Johnson (Cambridge: Harvard University Press, 1955).

William Pritchard, with whom I shared an earlier version of this essay, has called Jarrell's list-making his "way of talking back to Dickinson." Looking over the Dickinson criticism of the past few decades, Pritchard comments, in a lecture called "Talking Back to Emily Dickinson," that he "would welcome more subjectivity, more list-makings by individual readers of the fine and not-so fine poems. This might help in sharpening appreciation and making criticism of her less a sacred act of homage." Jarrell was fascinated by lists as form, and as rhetorical device. Thus, on a passage in Whitman's "Song of Myself" ("The pure contralto sings in the organ loft . . ."), Jarrell comments, "It is only a list—but what a list!" (*Poetry and the Age*, 109). After making a list of Auden's use of various rhetorical devices, he adds: "This collection of lists must by now have suggested a generalization to the reader: that in his later poems Auden depends to an extraordinary extent on *devices*. I could now add to my lists the device of—lists; but I will leave to the reader the pleasure of discovering that Auden not only imitates Joyce, Whitman, *et cetera*, but even parodies a list of Chaucer's" (*The Third Book of Criticism*, 145).

12. Pritchard, *Randall Jarrell*, 278.

13. Rich, "Vesuvius at Home," 70.

14. Pritchard, 290, 81.

15. John Crowe Ransom, "The Rugged Way of Genius," in *Randall Jarrell: 1914–1965*, edited by Robert Lowell, Peter Taylor, and Robert Penn Warren (New York: Farrar, Straus, 1967), 160.

16. Jarrell, *Third Book of Criticism*, 295. On this speech, which Pritchard calls "an astonishing performance" and "the end of the line for Jarrell as a critic of modern poets," see Pritchard, 283 ff.

17. *Third Book of Criticism*, 329.

18. *Poetry and the Age*, 217.

19. *Third Book*, 70. The Yeats passage is in his "Ego Dominus Tuus."

20. Alexis de Tocqueville, *Democracy in America*, edited by Phillips Bradley, vol. 2 (New York: Vintage, 1945), 73.

21. *Poetry and the Age*, 217.

22. *Third Book of Criticism*, 310.

23. Santayana, *Three Philosophical Poets* (New York: Doubleday Anchor, 1938), 114.

24. *Poetry and the Age*, 128.

25. Pritchard, *Randall Jarrell*, 294.

26. *Poetry and the Age*, 166.

27. *Third Book of Criticism*, 329–30. Jarrell was, perhaps unconsciously, echoing Ransom in his praise for Millay's "The Return." Ransom wrote, "the poem of all of Miss Millay's work I like best is *The Return*. This is almost effortless, like the grave speech of a woman with beautiful intonations of a voice which she does not raise." See *The World's Body* (Baton Rouge: Louisiana State University Press, 1968), 108. The Millay poem is frankly Audenesque—"Earth does not understand her child, / Who from the loud gregarious town / Returns, depleted and defiled . . ."—and would have appealed to Jarrell in that regard.

28. *Third Book of Criticism*, 330.

29. *Poetry and the Age*, 186.

30. Mary Jarrell, "Ideas and Poems," *Parnassus* 5 (1976): 218.

31. For more on Jarrell's use of female personae see Christopher Benfey, "The Woman in the Mirror: John Berryman and Randall Jarrell," in *Recovering Berryman: Essays on a Poet*, edited by Richard J. Kelly and Alan K. Lathrop (Ann Arbor: University of Michigan Press, 1993), 153–68.

Christopher Ricks

The Lesson

HARD TO DECIDE what would be most apt as celebration of Bill Pritchard, given all that he has given us all: range of delight, diversity of enterprise, such felicities, alive within an assiduity always loving.

Something of Johnson, for the author of *Lives of the Modern Poets*, and something of modern poetry. Some closeness of reading. A point of principle. Positive praise, nowt nasal. Something at once American and English. Amherst College. An Amherst poet? And Frost had better show his quizzical phiz. Something, too, of Amherst's traditional understanding that there exists literature outside the English language. What should they know of English who only English know?

So here, in honor of William H. Pritchard, is an account of why store, more than store, is to be set by David Ferry's "The Lesson,"[1] from the Latin of Samuel Johnson:

> *In Rivum a Mola Stoana Lichfeldiæ diffluentem*
>
> Errat adhuc vitreus per prata virentia rivus,
>   Quo toties lavi membra tenella puer;
> Hic delusa rudi frustrabar brachia motu,
>   Dum docuit blanda voce natare pater.
> Fecerunt rami latebras, tenebrisque diurnis

280

Pendula secretas abdidit arbor aquas.
Nunc veteres duris periêre securibus umbræ,
    Longinquisque oculis nuda lavacra patent.
Lympha tamen cursus agit indefessa perennis,
    Tectaque qua fluxit, nunc et aperta fluit.
Quid ferat externi velox, quid deterat ætas,
    Tu quoque securus res age, Nise, tuas.

The Lesson
    —from the Latin of Samuel Johnson

The stream still flows through the meadow grass,
as clear as it was when I used to go in swimming,
not good at it at all, while my father's voice
gently called out through the light of the shadowy glade,
trying to help me learn. The branches hung down low
over those waters made secret by their shadows.
My arms flailed in a childlike helpless way.

And now the sharp blade of the axe of time
has utterly cut away that tangle of shadows.
The naked waters are open to the sky now
and the stream still flows through the meadow grass.

Matthew Arnold, in his unmatched essay "The Study of Poetry," formulated a principle precise and passionate: "The superior character of truth and seriousness, in the matter and substance of the best poetry, is inseparable from the superiority of diction and movement marking its style and manner. The two superiorities are closely related, and are in steadfast proportion one to the other." (Inseparable, not indistinguishable.) It is the movement of Ferry's poem, of his poems, that is especially of note. His transitions are masterly, but then translation partakes of transition. His rhythms and cadences are at once tentative and firm, always with an entire respect for the integrity of the poem he is translating, manifesting itself anew in the integrity of the poem he creates.

"In Rivum a Mola Stoana Lichfeldiæ diffluentem": the traditional thing is to judge neo-Latin poetry guilty until it is proven innocent. Johnson himself knew that neo-Latin poetry by the English was seldom of the best: "The pretensions of the English to the reputation of writing Latin founded not so much on the specimens . . . which they have produced, as on the quantity of talent diffused through the country" (from William

Windham's *Diary*). But Johnson put in a good word for this exercise of talents, within praise of one of his masters: "Pope had sought for images and sentiments in a region not known to have been explored by many other of the English writers; he had consulted the modern writers of Latin poetry, a class of authors whom Boileau endeavoured to bring into contempt, and who are too generally neglected" (*The Lives of the English Poets*, "Pope"). The contempt into which Boileau endeavored to bring modern Latin poetry, Richard Porson vented. "For all modern Greek and Latin poetry he had the profoundest contempt. When Herbert published the *Musæ Etonensis*, Porson said, after looking over one of the volumes, 'Here is trash, fit only to be put behind the fire'" (*Porsoniana*, in Samuel Rogers's *Table Talk*).

Latin poems written by speakers of Latin are one thing, a thing for us distant and difficult enough. Latin poems written posthumously, written centuries after Latin became what we call a dead language: these press anew the old question of whether it has been left to us ever truly to appreciate Latin (or Greek) poetry.

Robert Frost was Johnsonianly robust. He insisted not that we have little chance of ever being inward enough with the ancient languages but that we have no chance.

> The living part of a poem is the intonation entangled somehow in the syntax idiom and meaning of a sentence. It is only there for those who have heard it previously in conversation. It is not for us in any Greek or Latin poem because our ears have not been filled with the tones of Greek and Roman talk. It is the most volatile and at the same time important part of poetry. It goes and the language becomes a dead language the poetry dead poetry.... When men no longer know the intonation on which we string our words they will fall back on what I may call the absolute length of our syllables which is the length we would give them in passages that meant nothing. The psychologist can actually measure this with a what-do-you-call-it. English poetry would then be read as Latin poetry is now read and as of course Latin poetry was never read by Romans. (letter to Sidney Cox, 19 January 1914)

Critics of the classics may be great in proportion as they recognize that there is an irreducible truth in what Frost says.

What then of Latin poetry that was never written by Romans?

A neo-Latin poem is written in a language unheard conversationally. Oratorically, it may be heard, even in this country and this century. I felt a twinge of Oxonian pride a few years ago, during the sesquicentennial celebrations at Boston University, when the Vice-Chancellor of Oxford University was among those in the procession of kindly tributes. "When you invited us," he intoned to the President of Boston University, "you said that we might if we wished speak in a language other than English. I assume that you meant Latin." Whereupon he uttered ceremonial Latin, being then so good as to translate it into English, British English.

There are paradoxes about dead languages in themselves: if truly dead, how can they still be alive in ceremony, as well as alive to those who can still read, with deep delight, great classical literature? There is a further contrariety when someone living in our world, our language, turns to such a language tellingly.

Let me turn to "The Lesson."

> The stream still flows through the meadow grass,

As soon as we reach a verb, and this is soon, we hear the subdued oxymoron of moment and movement in "still flows." This has something of T. S. Eliot's sense of a world—like that of Ferry's translation—of light and shadows.

> daylight
> Investing form with lucid stillness
> Turning shadow into transient beauty
> With slow rotation suggesting permanence
> ("Burnt Norton" III)

"As a Chinese jar still / Moves perpetually in its stillness" ("Burnt Norton" V): Eliot anticipated Ferry as to the simultaneity of mobility and immobility in the word "still." "The stream still flows." Still waters run deep.

When Ferry first published his poem in *Raritan* (Spring 1986), the first line ran, not "through the meadow grass," but "through the meadow-grass"; I take it that the later gentle expatiation of what had been a compound noun ("meadowgrass" consonantally thickened, *wgr*, at its middle), this one word then becoming in revision relaxedly and expansively two words, was effected so as the better to go with the flow. The line now becomes all monosyllables except for the apt expanse of "meadow"; the trisyllabic "meadowgrass" had been perhaps a touch coagulated.

The words "through the meadow grass" flow through the poem, concluding both its first and its last line. But the last line is not in toto the first line, being it in toto and more, given the modest modification of the syntax and rhythm which prefixes the closing line with "And." Not, now,

"The stream still flows through the meadow grass," but "and the stream still flows through the meadow grass." This realizes something which both is and is not the same, even as the rhythm and cadence of a stream change from moment to moment, within its enduring flow. The stream has modulated itself; you don't step twice into the same stream of the line.

One flow is that of the stream that is translation; Ferry's stream of consciousness, and not only because of the stream of time, is Johnson's and yet not. "How like the former, and almost the same" (Dryden, *Aeneis*, vi.1195): Ferry, whose Horace is now establishing him in the line of great translators from the Latin, gives us something at once repeated and other, even as his conclusion gently calls out, through the light of the poem, to its opening. How fittingly, too, the final line—"and the stream still flows through the meadow grass"—takes up not only the opening line, extendedly revisited, but also, from a few lines earlier, the starting anew with "And": "And now the sharp blade of the axe of time."

The internal nature of memory, and the nature at once internal and external of the entirely fluid: these ask on occasion the conjunction of an external rhyme with an internal one. So it is that, at the end of its line, "the shadowy glade" is later threatened (but is not in the end lopped) by "the sharp blade of the axe of time." It is not only the rhyme *glade/blade*, and not only the thick alliteration *shadowy/sharp*, but the syntax "the [adjective] [noun]," which prompts our readerly memory within this poem devoted to a writer's memory and everyone's memory.

Over time, the time taken and given by the poem, "shadowy" is both cut back and expanded to "shadows": cut back, in that it is axed from three to two syllables; expanded, in that an epithet comes to take on the substantiality that is a noun—and a plural noun at that, and a plural noun repeated. Twice a line ends in shadows: "over those waters made secret by their shadows," foreshadowing "has utterly cut away that tangle of shadows." In the actual landscape, yes, the trees have been cut away; in the landscape of memory, no, for there the shadows of the shadowy glade have all the continuing haunting life of shades. There is a comfort, despite the sense of loss, when a line comes to repose again upon the darkened noun followed with a period:

over those waters made secret by their shadows.
. . . . .
has utterly cut away that tangle of shadows.

Such a memorious shadowing is at one with the way "way" has come back in this next sentence (not the next line, discreetly), to be heard in "away": "a childlike helpless way," "Has utterly cut away" (as if the word "away" were a sad contraction of the entire phrase "*a childlike helpless way*"). This last effect is then deepened by the double internal rhyme, not just of "*utterly cut*" but of "*utterly cut away*." There the reduction of the trisyllabic "utterly" to the monosyllabic "cut" does itself feel like the cutting of something away.

Johnson himself delighted in such truly sound effects.

> Should Reason guide thee with her brightest Ray,
> And pour on misty Doubt resistless Day;
> (The Vanity of Human Wishes, 145–46)

The alliterating monosyllables *Doubt* and *Day* may meet as equals, equipollent, but how dextrously the trisyllabic "res*ist*less Day" triumphs, irresistibly, over the disyllabic "m*ist*y Doubt."

The chastened realization of the cutting away owes something to another small crucial change that Ferry made to the poem after periodical publication. In *Raritan*, there was this flowing on:

> The branches hung down low
> Over those waters made secret by their shadows.
> My arms flailed in a childlike helpless way.
> And now the sharp blade of the axe of time
> Has utterly cut away that tangle of shadows.

In *Dwelling Places*, the sequence is open ("open to the sky now"), is cut and opened up, there upon the page:

> The branches hung down low
> over those waters made secret by their shadows.
> My arms flailed in a childlike helpless way.
>
> And now the sharp blade of the axe of time
> has utterly cut away that tangle of shadows.

The risk of such a cutting enactment, with two successive lines cut from one another, is that the severance will not so much dramatize as melodramatize the timely utterance of "And now." What saves Ferry's lines from melodrama is not only the chastened sobriety of manner and movement but the quiet assurance with which "And now" is duly succeeded by "now / and," a chiasmus that operates across a chasm both of lines traversed and of a line-ending crossed:

286 ≈ *Christopher Ricks*

> The naked waters are open to the sky now
> and the stream still flows through the meadow grass.

There the first line ends with no insistence on an ending (there is no end to the natural world and one's memories of it, however much the Binsey poplars or the *lauriers* may have been cut), and this is achieved by the successive openness of sound: "The naked waters are open to the sky now," with both *sky* and *now* ending open-mouthed, no termination of sound and then no punctuation at the line-ending, only the naked space. (Completely, or rather incompletely, different from the sibilants that close the first and last lines of the poem: "grass.") This so evoking the open is Wordsworthian; there was no end to how much Wordsworth could strangely utter by stationing *sky* at the line-ending:

> Oh! at that time,
> While on the perilous ridge I hung alone,
> With what strange utterance did the loud dry wind
> Blow through my ears! the sky seem'd not a sky
> Of earth, and with what motion mov'd the clouds!
>
> > (*The Prelude*, i, 346–50)

Ferry shares with Wordsworth a gratitude for the ample flexibility of so modest a word as "it."

> The stream still flows through the meadow grass,
> as clear as it was when I used to go in swimming,
> not good at it at all,

We are to take the measure of the simple power of "it." I can imagine a misguided critic deprecating the recurrence of "it" there, especially with the change of referent, the first "it" being the stream and the second swimming. Clumsy in Ferry? Not at all, but attentive to clumsiness and meant to call an honest ungainliness to mind (as, again, often in Wordsworth), and aware of the precariousness of gait which precludes flowing swimmingly through those dental endings: "not good at it at all." The sequence "at it at" is a challenge to the prejudice in favor of the fluent, the flowing, the overvaluing good Surrey and the undervaluing great Wyatt.

"Not good at it at all." I am reminded of Ezra Pound's objecting to one of the greatest openings to a poem even of Eliot's:

> Here I am, an old man in a dry month,
> Being read to by a boy, waiting for rain.
>
> > ("Gerontion")

Pound underlined in the manuscript: "<u>Being read to by</u> a <u>b</u>oy"; he wrote in the margin "? <u>to by</u>"; and he wrote above Eliot's opening words, entries one below the other: "b—b—b / <u>B</u> <u>d</u> + <u>b</u> <u>b</u> / consonants, / & two prepositions" (Eliot, *Inventions of the March Hare* [1996], 351). Eliot stuck to his heaved cutlass.

As the poem rounds the bend into the ensuing line—

> not good at it at all, while my father's voice
> gently called out through the light of the shadowy glade,

—the inverted foot, "gently" but strikingly at the head of the line, is the opposite of how such an inversion of stress is often employed. The accents are not those, say, of Milton, swinging round the corner with a vengeance:

> And over them triumphant Death his Dart
> Shook, but delaid to strike, though oft invok'd
>
> > (*Paradise Lost*, xi, 488–89)

—but instead the milder accents of gentleness's power. There is a related effect in the gentle calling out of a line that is undulatingly hypermetrical, a line with two further syllables at ease with any elision that we might fluidly practice. Not, say, "gently called through the light of the shady glade," but "gently called *out* through the light of the shad*ow*y glade." It would have been so easy to take out the word "out," to reduce the line to the expected.

The idiom "not good at it at all" is markedly unJohnsonian, and not only because of anachronism. A crux for the translator must be this: what do you do about translating a poem that could have been written in English had the English-speaking author wished? This is a particular form of translation; it is a very special case, but it must connect with the more usual and more general case, of asking how, say, Baudelaire would have written such-and-such in English. Johnson, after all, could perfectly well have written this poem in English if he had wanted to; it is not only that he wrote so many fine poems in English, but that he even wrote in English about swimming—though he was to change the word "Swim" to "Roll":

> Must helpless Man, in Ignorance sedate,
> Swim darkling down the Current of his fate?
>
> > (*The Vanity of Human Wishes*, 345–46)

(Was Johnson's "helpless" here of help to Ferry when it came to his "helpless"?) The second line of this, the text of 1749, became in 1755: "Roll darkling down the Torrent of his fate?"—*Swim* having perhaps suggested too great a control over the element when immersion was destructive. Johnson, in his physical strength, enjoyed such control in swimming; he became a powerful audacious swimmer, his father's tender lesson having taken and stayed.

Ferry's translation is radically unJohnsonian, and this as a consequence of the fact that Johnson chose not to write a poem in Johnsonian English—since he chose not to write it in English at all. Ferry does not in any way go for a Johnsonian manner, whether that of Johnson's poetry, or prose on the page or in conversation. "Not good at it at all" is unmisgivingly distant from any way in which Johnson would have been good at putting it. The odd effect, since Johnson has so marked a character as a stylist, whether in poetry or prose, is of a kind of foreignness when the poem is put back (or rather *not* put *back*) into English. For on this occasion what the translator has to do is make it sound as if it were in a vernacular that is not Johnson's; Johnson's eschewal is being respected and honored.

The process at work is complicated; the lines that issue from the process are simple and direct.

One way of catching Ferry's success, of letting his success catch the light, is to compare what others make of Johnson's Latin here. There is the verse translation by John Wain:

> Here, as a boy, I bathed
> my tender limbs, unskilled, frustrated, while
> [. . .]

The movement has the wrong kind of clumsiness, an alien gawkiness that makes it feel, with its Latinate deposits, like Johnson on a bad day. The translation by J. P. Sullivan in the Penguin edition of Johnson's poems is straight prose: "wherein as a boy I so often bathed my tender limbs; here I frustrated my deluded arms with unpractised movements, while . . ." But should even the unpracticed be quite that unlimber? The sequence, though true to the words of the original, is not true to its spirit. And something similar goes for the verbal ineptitude, which cannot be justified by invoking physical ineptitude (the fallacy of imitative form . . .), when the Yale edition by E. L. McAdam offers the following: "where so often as a boy I bathed my young body. Here I was frustrated by the awkward movement of my arms playing me false when . . ."

To Johnson, the Latin language offered the decency of distance and decorum. Not being his language, it offered a chance of creating a poem that both was and was not exactly *his*. It provided, as in his great poem on completing the Dictionary, a *cordon sanitaire* between himself and the blurting of personal feeling or (the Romantic failing) "self-expression." To speak directly of his father he needed indirection, something other than his mother tongue. He could be the more personal when he was not being nakedly so. Leave it to waters to be naked.

To write in Latin was to temper the personally moving with historic impersonality. Being himself was sometimes to mean being someone other than the known public man Johnson. He did not publish the poem, which was written late in life; it appeared three years after his death.

His father had given him these swimming lessons, never to be forgotten either in memory or as skill. At the very end of his life, at the age of seventy-five in November 1784, Johnson remembered how he had taught himself a lesson, a lesson that involved his father and the element of water.

> To Mr. Henry White, a young clergyman, with whom he now formed an intimacy, so as to talk to him with great freedom, he mentioned that he could not in general accuse himself of having been an undutiful son. "Once, indeed, (said he,) I was disobedient; I refused to attend my father to Uttoxeter-market. Pride was the source of that refusal, and the remembrance of it was painful. A few years ago, I desired to atone for this fault; I went to Uttoxeter in very bad weather, and stood for a considerable time bareheaded in the rain, on the spot where my father's stall used to stand. In contrition I stood, and I hope the penance was expiatory."

It is a moving and justly famous moment in Boswell: Johnson, years on, standing in the rain, its waters absolving him. Bareheaded.

> "I am a man,
> More sinn'd against, than sinning."
>
> "Alack, bareheaded?"

Johnson, bareheaded in "very bad weather," knew that he was, in this matter, a man more sinning than sinned against.

The memory of his disobedience to his father may be arched against the memory of his obedience to his father's tender lesson. Ferry catches this happiness of relation in the lovely loving sequence "trying to help me learn":

> when I used to go in swimming,
> not good at it at all, while my father's voice
> gently called out through the light of the shadowy glade,
> trying to help me learn.

The delicacy of this comes from the fact that "trying to help me" constitutes a unit in itself, a unit of sense: "trying to help me" *and*—one learns this in the reading, in the flow—"trying to help me learn." Further, much more evocative than would have been the protracted stiffness of "trying to help me to learn," where the formal phrasing would have been the opposite of the informal rueful gaucherie of "not good at it at all."

When Ferry first published the poem, it had no title, or rather it had as a title what would ordinarily look more like a subtitle: "Adapted from the Latin of Samuel Johnson." There was a propriety in this, a self-abnegation by the translator that might itself be a lesson to translators. But even better than propriety is grace, and in *Dwelling Places* the poem gained its due title:

The Lesson

—from the Latin of Samuel Johnson

The poem is, in Ferry's translation, one of the great evocations of what a true lesson is, of what education is, of what it is to educe. Ferry dropped the last two lines of Johnson's poem, where the lesson feels too admonitorily that of a dominie: "You also, Nisus, heedless of what swift time brings from outside or what it wears away, do what is yours to do." Perhaps time has worn away our amenability to so moralizing a destination for the poem. Certainly Ferry judged it best to do what is his to do.

"The Lesson," as poem, as translation, at once educational and educative, is a lesson in love. As is the lifework of the man in whose honor this book is gathered.

Notes

1. *Dwelling Places* (Chicago: University of Chicago Press, 1993). Reprinted by permission of the publisher.

David Sofield

Richard Wilbur's "Lying"

R[ICHARD]{.small} W[ILBUR]{.small}'S in no sense lying when he offers a critic advice
that in his own essays he has largely taken. "I think the main thing to
do in criticism is to tell somebody else who might be about to read what
you've just read what you see in it and what he might miss if he read with
a little less care or experience than you have read with. It's mostly a matter of appreciative mediation." More pointedly, "I'm not in the least disposed to impose archetypal, Freudian or other patterns on the poems we
read. In general my attitude about criticism and about teaching is that you
look at the thing and see what it wants you to say about it."[1] Though he
might shy at "mediation" and prefer "listen to" to "look at," these are sentences William Pritchard, who has reviewed many of Wilbur's books,
could have written. Their modesty, programmatic flexibility, intentional
linking of criticism and teaching, and focus on a poem as the kind of
"thing" it is name elements of "Amherst English" as some have practiced
it since the late 1930s when Wilbur was a student at the College. In his
generation, and well beyond Amherst, many poets who also write criticism
have invoked such apparent common sense. No one should be surprised

that their poems ask to be read with whatever "care" one can summon. They were written to repay it.

There are lies and lies, surely, and the poem will make distinctions. It begins with something of a truism about lying and ends in a determinative truth. In the interest of quickening a dull moment, a fib is allowable.

> To claim, at a dead party, to have spotted a grackle,
> When in fact you haven't of late, can do no harm.

A pair of long and loose pentameters, but indeed a pair: in the absence of rhyme and strict meter, this couplet in its moderately elaborated syntax, full stop, and medial pause begins to construct an idiom at the same time conversational and artificial. It stays there a moment, as the next four lines are in their larger rhythms also couplets but ones that begin to contract metrically to what the ear has been anticipating, the frequently enjambed and only slightly relaxed blank verse that Wilbur has employed in half a dozen of his longer poems from the writing of "Walking to Sleep" in the mid-1960s. Like Robert Frost, Wilbur has called iambic pentameter "the most variable meter in English" and "the best in which to build large verse-masses." In 1993 he remarked, "In 'Lying' I used a rather Miltonic blank verse. I hope that my paragraphs of verse are as muscular as his."[2]

> Your reputation for saying things of interest
> Will not be marred, if you hasten to other topics,
> Nor will the delicate web of human trust
> Be ruptured by that airy fabrication.

"Your" and "you": the three principal longer poems of Wilbur's maturity are distinct, among other ways in their moving chronologically from straightforward second-person ("Walking to Sleep") to first-person-singular ("The Mind-Reader," who announces that "it makes no difference that my lies are bald") and back to an altered, putative second-person narration. Despite the presence of a very generalized "you" in the first ten lines (only) and the occasional "we," "our," and "us" thereafter, the poem's narrative manners are chiefly those of third-person telling. Reviewing Wilbur's *New and Collected Poems*, William Logan puts it well. "For a poet secure in the self, the authorial 'I' can be an intrusion. The 'I' is what lies behind the lines, not in front of them: For such a poet, the personality is incarnate in language, in the intimate operation of the words, not insinuated as a dramatic character."[3] The sparely used and somewhat distant "we" will allow Wilbur to allow himself the nobility of speech with which "Lying" brilliantly concludes.

Milton and Frost have been the pervasive models: Wilbur's poems written in the measure of "Lying" marry Milton's impressive Latinity in rhythm, diction, and allusiveness and Frost's cunningly offhanded north-of-Boston talking voice. Wilbur's recent response to the question "Whose poems have you read most often during your life?" was: "Milton's. Robert Frost's. And a vast list of others."[4] The vocabulary of the lines just quoted—reputation, delicate, ruptured, fabrication—is that of a poet who taught a Milton course for decades and in 1966 published a useful essay on "L'Allegro" and "Il Penseroso." A third and in certain ways more remote predecessor than Milton has to be the poet who most thoroughly absorbed his example. In "Tintern Abbey" Wordsworth may be said to have made possible the kind of long meditative poem in blank verse that "Lying" is.[5]

Grackles (Latin: *graculus*) are common in western Massachusetts, where this poem like many others of his is set. To claim to have spotted one would hardly be striking, as the poem will acknowledge in a few lines: not every so often but "each morning brings to light . . . grass and grackles." The third and fourth lines, then, wittily suggest that one had best move the conversation elsewhere. The poem's first analogy puts Wilbur in familiar territory: in a work that will make the very largest claims for the good lying that poetry is and for metaphor as its most fundamental component, the figure is modest. It is a "web" of trust that knits together even the dullest cocktail parties. "I would agree with Stevens," Wilbur has said, "that the central thing in poetry is metaphor. I'd agree with Mr. Aristotle that the specific gift is for metaphor."[6]

The party picks up. As the next lines overrun their ends and the language grows tauter, a guest "may," for a second, "enjoy" the small thrill of having been bad. At a dead party one amuses oneself as one can.

> Later, however, talking with toxic zest
> Of golf, or taxes, or the rest of it
> Where the beaked ladle plies the chuckling ice,
> You may enjoy a chill of severance, hearing
> Above your head the shrug of unreal wings.

In his own brief comments on "Lying" Wilbur writes: "a high subject, unless perhaps one is writing a hymn [and 'A Christmas Hymn' is faithful unto his word⌉, should not be approached with remorseless nobility, and this poem has its comic elements. . . . Comedy is serious; it is the voice of balance; and its presence in a serious poem is a test and earnest of its earnestness."[7] One poet's earnestness plainly is not another's. The un-Wordsworthian comedy at hand is not serious in itself; it resides in the heightened anticipation inherent in ending a line, "talking with . . . zest"—picking up "interest" for the poem's only clear end rhyme in a small sea of consonantal half-rhyming—and then deflating the subject of that talk by starting the next line, "Of golf, or taxes." "Taxes" reminds the ear that it has just registered both "toxic," the adjective elided a moment ago, and "talking." In spirit and technique the wit is rather like that of Pope or Molière, whom Wilbur had been translating for years, in the silliness of entertaining enthusiastic talk about golf and taxes. Yes, people do talk that way, but the tennis-playing Wilbur is clear on which sport is preferable.[8] "Or the rest of it" is, as it should be, dismissive, but then a line that Pope would have included happily in "The Rape of the Lock"—"Where the beaked ladle plies the chuckling ice"—may redeem the whole party. The two visually and aurally specific epithets are neoclassical; the surprising and surprisingly modest verb snaps the line to attention. This resourcefulness, the results of which seem effortless but are not, Wilbur has exhibited for so long that one takes it for granted. Since among his peers perhaps only James Merrill is capable of a similar radiance, one shouldn't, and one reason one shouldn't is that, like getting a forehand slice right, getting a line right can involve trial and error. The first draft of this line reads, "Where the glass ladle breaks the chuckling ice"; the next and last turns verb to adjective, "breaks" to (remembering the grackle?) "beaked," then supplies the suave "plies."[9]

It was Frost himself—he liked to think he was a capable baseball and tennis player—who famously drew the analogy between writing and sport. The whole passage is to the point here, as it will be later when "Lying" turns to speak metaphorically of metaphor. "I look at a poem as a performance. I look on the poet as a man of prowess, just like an athlete. . . . The whole thing is performance and prowess and feats of association. Why don't critics talk about those things—what a feat it was to turn that that way, and what a feat it was to remember that, to be reminded of that by this. . . . Scoring. You've got to score." Aware of these words, Wilbur significantly extends them: "I don't think a poem is a message. It's a kind of performance; it's a kind of machine of feeling which other people can use."[10] Like a good performer, the poem moves on with a shrug, albeit one "of unreal wings." Why unreal? Presumably because there is only a notional grackle hovering. Or might the imagined wings be those of the master-liar Satan, unimpressed by the lie trivial? He will be powerfully evoked presently.

The next five lines, in a declarative voice not infrequent in Wilbur's work, define boredom, palpable as that is at a dead party. The passage hinges on a pair of oxymorons, the second more astringent than the first: boredom is "a dull / Impatience" or "a fierce velleity." A more critical point is scored, though, in the productive ambiguity of what follows. "In the strict sense, of course, / We invent nothing." In a sense not strict, we make up a story about a grackle, but grackles exist independent of our fabrications. The poem will spell this out. What then do we invent? Nothing, the idea of nothing: no one (or One) else invents nothing, we party-goers and poets do, though poem and poet doubt the wisdom of our doing so.[11] What we also and more importantly do is "merely" bear "witness"

> To what each morning brings again to light:
> Gold crosses, cornices, astonishment
> Of panes, the turbine-vent which natural law
> Spins on the grill-end of the diner's roof,
> Then grass and grackles or, at the end of town
> In sheen-swept pastureland, the horse's neck
> Clothed with its usual thunder, and the stones
> Beginning now to tug their shadows in
> And track the air with glitter. All these things
> Are there before us; there before we look
> Or fail to look; . . .

Moving with something like Miltonic muscularity—the adroitly handled list, the steady iambs varied by initial trochees, a spondee, and an anapest, the dominant enjambing, the considerable expansion and contraction of phrase-lengths, the ear-perfect alliteration Wilbur has always provided, the quick shift in diction from the conversational to the freshly seen "sheen-swept pastureland," followed by a lightly altered, resonant quotation from the Metaphorist who asks Job (39.19) whether the latter has "clothed" the horse's neck with "thunder"—these lines create not just what is to be seen but also an empathic intelligence that shows us how to see it. As critics used to say, the lines and the things they name are *there*, in this case perhaps in compensation for someone's saying he saw what he hadn't seen. Indeed, they are "there before us; there before we look / Or fail to look." Comprehensively "before," as the word moves from space to time as unassumingly as words move. In an interview published shortly after "Lying" appeared in the *New Yorker* in January 1983 Wilbur said, tactfully: "The world is sufficient before I ever trouble myself to say so. It's not raw material waiting for the artistic kiss of life to revive it."[12] Fair enough, and it is worth recognizing that throughout this passage Wilbur has knowingly refused the gorgeous language that some have thought limits as well as defines his first books. "Sheen-swept" to the contrary, he relinquishes here what Christopher Ricks, referring to Geoffrey Hill's own avoidance, has termed a "glazing art sense." The echoes sounded by these lines—how consciously may always be in question—include Bishop's description of "stones" that "pulled" their "shadows . . . in" in "The End of March" and, less expectedly, Larkin's thrush "astonishing the brickwork" in "Coming."[13]

For a moment "nothing" returns. It too is there before us, to be "seen" or not. Curiously, the line terms it "that most rare conception," then promptly demystifies it as no more than "something missed," for instance the water that was once in a well but now does no less than "assail the cliffs of Labrador"—natural law still and always at work. Properly understood, Nothing is not a phenomenon or fact; it is in fact a conception. "Lying," then, reworks "'A World without Objects Is a Sensible Emptiness'" (1950), and in doing so declines what one critic writing about the earlier poem has called "an undeniable attraction to this emptiness."[14] As Wilbur's poems have always insisted, what are not conceptual are "The cells and heavens of a given world," the ones that "galled the arch-negator." The first jottings for "Lying," a handful of prose sentences, happen to occur at the bottom of a draft of the poem "Shad-Time." That poem details and by detailing celebrates the particulars of spring, and like "Lying" and others it stages the great dialectic of nothing ("great fields of emptiness," the metaphor nearly making those voids substantial rural commonplaces) versus the natural world that, following Milton, he thinks of as made for us. One could speculate that part of the impulse to write "Lying," the title of which was there from the start, lay in that opposition. The first independent draft page contains a version of the poem's four opening lines densely surrounded by such marginalia as "Roland" and "shame the devil" (so in the beginning is our end) and "New Yorker Nov 28 126–8." The 1977 issue thus dated and paged contains these sentences from one of Hannah Arendt's widely read installments on "Thinking." To "the philosopher everything present is absent because something actually absent [a grackle? a squirrel?] is present to the mind." You possess the "elementary ability to . . . have present *before* [emphases hers] (and not just *in*) your mind what is physically absent. The ability to create *in* your mind fictive entities, such as the . . . centaur . . . ." The centaur Chiron, perhaps.[15]

Two intelligent critics of the poem flatly state that Wilbur's arch-negator is Goethe's Mephistopheles, citing "Ich bin der Geist, der stets verneint!"[16] Mephistopheles denies and negates, it is true, but in *Faust* he is not termed—in a Miltonic coinage, as if Wilbur were for a moment Milton finding another hyphenated-invective epithet for Satan—the arch-negator. It seems a needless stretch when one of Goethe's own sources is so close to hand. Milton's Satan at this point becomes a character in "Lying," so pronouncedly that Wilbur does what he does nowhere else, quotes another text verbatim and in italics. Wilbur's Milton's Satan "drifted . . . / In a *black mist low creeping*" through Eden. If the poet projects himself to that degree, why not call the arch-enemy, the arch-felon, the arch-fiend, the arch-foe also the arch-negator? There are indications that Wilbur takes Milton's Satan at least as gravely as Milton does: "I think I knew from the beginning that Milton's Satan would get into my poem, because the illusory aesthetic of which I've been speaking is ultimately Satanic. Satan, in his insanity, sets himself up as a rival to the Creator."[17] As experienced readers of Wilbur might have expected, he was thinking also of another writer, Poe, and there are a couple of marginalia naming him. In 1975 Wilbur remarked that "Poe's subject matter became the depicted process of negating this world, and his more exciting techniques are techniques of erasure, of explosion, of uncreation."[18] Tellingly, the first draft of the line has "great negator"; it must have taken an instant for Wilbur to realize that he could dare the (literary) identification.

What the arch-negator in "Lying" does is "to probe with intellectual sight" a reenvisioned Eden that partially appropriates Milton's. Like us he may feel a touch disadvantaged by having fewer than "the bee's twelve thousand eyes." "Intellectual sight" may have puzzled more than one reader, but it appears that in choosing the adjective Wilbur was thinking as much of Poe as of Milton. Because the first draft reads "angelic sight," one might recall his 1982 essay "Poe and the Art of Suggestion," where Wilbur writes that "throughout his early work . . . Poe argues that intellectual knowledge is not fit for man in the earthly condition of his soul," but that angels have always possessed it.[19] Wilbur's Satanic verses, which for an instant remind us of the "total eclipse" mentioned ten lines back, conclude as vatically as Milton's: Satan

> drifted through the bar-like boles of Eden
> In a *black mist low creeping*, dragging down
> And darkening with moody self-absorption
> What, when he left it, lifted and, if seen
> From the sun's vantage, seethed with vaulting hues.[20]

Four consecutive lines ending in *n* (with another half-dozen nasals along the way) provide some of the elevation here, as do the enjambments, the alliterative *b*'s giving way to the heavier *d*'s, and the two exquisite pararhymes, "left it, lifted" and "seen / From the sun's." The double reference of "it" (mist and Eden), the final line's two puns, the obvious one in "sun's vantage" nearly obscuring the two senses of "vaulting" (leaping and overarching, both descriptive of a rainbow, as the black mist turns into one), and the semi-ecstatic "seethed" do the rest. Such effects are not without risk in an age accustomed to styles prosaic or whimsical, styles flat though hardly final. One imagines Wilbur feeling emboldened by the example of his friend Elizabeth Bishop in "Over 2000 Illustrations" and "At the Fishhouses," among other poems that when they need to put modest conversational tones aside.

Wilbur returns to his immediately. Giving Satan at least minimal due, the next lines read, "Closer to making than the deftest fraud / Is seeing how the catbird's tail was made." It's the deft opposite of fraud, this stylish formulation: closer to "making" than making something up is is seeing how something already made (by the Maker) has been made. A no less stylish transition—"lighter still" than the catbird's spine—introduces one of the most dazzling and indelible figures in Wilbur's work. A second "seeing" shows us

> How the shucked tunic of an onion, brushed
> To one side on a backlit chopping board
> And rocked by trifling currents, prints and prints
> Its bright, ribbed shadow like a flapping sail.

These lines endow the slightest of things one encounters in an ordinary day, a single layer of onion peel, with notable presence. Strong *k*'s anchor the lines, "board" echoes "brushed," "rocked by trifling" is (raising "fierce velleity" to a higher power) memorably oxymoronic, the strong, emphatically doubled verb "prints" leads to adjectives that make the shadow instantly precise in "bright, ribbed," and the simple simile "like a flapping sail" shifts scale dramatically. A peel printing its bright shadow is, moreover, like and unlike the stones that, having tugged their shadows in, "track the air with glitter." Frost would call this performing, as who would not?[21]

If we invent nothing, paradoxically we "invent" similitudes, which in Wilbur's sense of things is how we achieve the verisimilitude that matters.[22] The poem says this directly, despite morning's having brought to light many things not seen through metaphor. "Odd that a thing is most itself when likened." The casual phrasing only makes the assertion itself more persuasive. One might read all of Wilbur's work as a sustained effort to earn this claim. The subtext here, muted until the poem's penultimate line, Wilbur has repeated in interviews. A succinct version reads, "If anything may be compared to anything else, the ground of the comparison is apt to be divine."[23] A short run of illustrative likenings follows the declaration, ending in this:

> And in the barnyard near the sawdust-pile
> Some great thing is tormented. Either it is
> A tarp torn loose and in the groaning wind
> Now puffed, now flattened, or a hip-shot beast
> Which tries again, and once again, to rise.

Across Dodwells Road in Cummington the speaker sees what has to be put in terms themselves richly metaphorical. We do not have, a given A is like B and thus we discover more about A, and perhaps B as well, but rather an A ("some great thing") that has to be (not be *like*) B or C. Being unable to distinguish between them, though, means that at least to the distant eye they are after all and to that degree similar. And then within B, the possible tarp, "now puffed, now flattened" recalls the onion's "tunic" that was, astonishingly, like a sail. It is, though, the second possibility, a struggling, tormented beast, that the poem requires at this point. The lines are present, among other reasons, to contradict categorically Randall Jarrell's too-clever complaint: Wilbur "obsessively sees, and shows, the bright underside of every dark thing." Not this time. If, as Wilbur has said he believes, "the ultimate character of things is comely and good," he also knows that sometimes it cannot be thus described or felt. And although he holds with Milton that divinity brings good from evil, no good comes to a crippled animal. It would normally be put away. In print Wilbur has called the animal a "big Holstein with a hopelessly dislocated hip";[24] in a manuscript note it was first "a stallion with a splintered leg [who] struggles to rise." In rendering the beast as well as the black mist lifting Wilbur strikingly adapts these talismanic lines from Adam and Eve's morning hymn: "Ye mists and exhalations that now rise . . . In honour to the world's great author rise . . . Rising or falling still advance His praise."[25] Eden is not a village in the Berkshires, but, in both, sunlight makes visible much—cornices, a turbine-vent, a catbird, a rainbow—to be grateful for.

Still, no further praise may be advanced or gratitude spoken until a necessary question is asked. "What, though for pain there is no other word, / Finds pleasure in the cruellest simile?"[26] That for pain there has already been another word, "panes," only sharpens the point. Within the poem we have survived the Satanic threat, but now we are in touch with a harsh condition of existence itself. Wilbur has spoken of and to it often. "Poetry, to be vital, does seem to need a periodic acquaintance with the threat of chaos." Recalling Frost's "momentary stay against confusion," and perhaps Henry Adams's phrase in *The Education* (a central text in Wilbur's Amherst), "running order through chaos," Wilbur presciently wrote this in 1948: "It is the province of poems to make some order in the world, but poets can't afford to forget that there is a reality of things which survives all orders great and small. Things *are*. The cow is there. No poetry can have any strength unless it continually bashes itself against the reality of things." Twenty years on: "I like the world to resist my ordering of it, so that I can feel it is real and that I'm honoring its reality." Notwithstanding a horse's thundermane and Milton and metaphor and, soon, Chiron and Roland, poets may be assured of the world's continued resistance. Given, then, a beast's irredeemable suffering, what in addition to representing pain is the poet's task? "One of the jobs of poetry is to make the unbearable bearable, not by falsehood but by clear, precise confrontation."[27]

He confronts it, or begins to, by returning to the catbird, left balancing on a spray of shrub itself nominally imitative, mock-orange. As grey catbirds do, it sings, some "grey of morning," in the pure metaphor that is mimicry. By this point "Lying" is itself coming to sound like the best song a catbird has sung for some time. A scale of simulations and associations—from direct quotation to imitation to allusion and echoing—has been building. The originals can be listed chronologically: *Job*, Milton, Pope, Poe, Frost, Bishop, Jarrell, and Larkin (with Wordsworth and Moore contributing less specifically) so far, *Genesis*, the *Chanson de Roland*, and more Milton to come. No doubt there are others. A line that could have been written by Frost, "It is something in us like the catbird's song," now ramifies into "a chant / Of the first springs," season and source alike, a chant that, as the conclusion in a huge and final Miltonic sentence flows forth,[28]

> is tributary
> To the great lies told with the eyes half-shut
> That have the truth in view: the tale of Chiron
> Who, with sage head, wild heart, and planted hoof
> Instructed brute Achilles in the lyre,
> Or of the garden where we first mislaid
> Simplicity of wish and will, forgetting
> Out of what cognate splendor all things came
> To take their scattering names; and nonetheless
> That matter of a baggage-train surprised
> By a few Gascons in the Pyrenees
> Which, having worked three centuries and more
> In the dark caves of France, poured out at last
> The blood of Roland, who to Charles his king
> And to the dove that hatched the dove-tailed world
> Was faithful unto death, and shamed the Devil.

The lines perform their own chant, primarily through the unstoppable motion enacted in ten consecutive enjambments. Milton rarely goes so far. But the full internal rhyme "lies ... eyes" contributes, along with three audible pairs of rhymes composed of terminal words that find echoes in the middles of the next lines: "came ... names," "Pyrenees ... centuries," "more ... poured." The driving iambs lift the voice, yet are modulated by four pyrrhic-spondee line-beginnings and three unstressed line-endings. The pun is fully operative: a catbird's song can pay tribute to the epic (en)chantings that tell us who we are and, as springs contribute waters to larger bodies, its singing embellishes an early hour. Two of our best poets are on record praising such flight in Wilbur, Anthony Hecht finding in the poem's climax "nobility [of] utterance" and Brad Leithauser specifying an "elevated grandness" that the poet commands when he wants.[29]

Having located its birds, bushes, barnyards, and diners in New England, with a brief excursion to Labrador and a longer one to prelapsarian Eden, the poem extends its geography to Greece and Roncevaux. The first great lie having the truth in view has Chiron—himself a transmutation of God's horse in *Job*—instructing the young Achilles in the lyre. In antiquity the only primary literary texts that come at all close to Wilbur's two and a half lines are Ovid's *Ars Amatoria* 1.11–12 and his *Fasti* 5.385–86, and their treatments are even briefer. In the first Chiron "puerum cithara perfecit Achillem / atque animos placida contudit arte feros." Mozley and Goold translate: Chiron "made the boy Achilles accomplished on the lyre, and by his peaceful art subdued those savage passions," while Molly Myerowitz renders "animos . . . feros" as "savage heart."[30] "Lying" gives the heart to Chiron and terms it "wild," nicely straddling thereby his half-human, half-horse being and placing that heart spatially between the "sage head" of a man and, in a quiet metaphor, the "planted hoof" of a beast. In draft this passage begins, "the tale of how / Chiron, in whom all natures were combined," and in his précis Wilbur calls centaurs, not disapprovingly, "combinative monsters." In a letter (deposited in Frost Library) to a *New Yorker* editor he further states that "the Chiron story says that we must partake of the harmony of all creation." Chiron of course teaches Achilles harmony as well as melody, but these glosses may suggest that the contracted passage as we have it tries to carry more than it can, namely the harmonious combining of "all natures"—human, animal, and in the figure, vegetal.

The poem's *Genesis* myth needs little annotation. Having mislaid simplicity of wish and will has got us where, as we've been told, we are lost in fierce velleities and stalled wishes. "Cognate" is one of perhaps four words in the long poem that we might not encounter in, say, a decent newspaper.[31] Since we're in Eden not long after the creation, Wilbur must mean us to take it in the Latin root sense of "related by birth." That leads neatly to "scattering names," dispersing because the Fall both scatters the namers and their progeny and subjects us to new experiences that in turn require names. We need and get a "nonetheless": despite the original sin, the tale of Charlemagne's nephew can set us back on track.

Roland's heroic death, sung in the *Chanson*, precisely expresses simplicity of will. His example is what "we" need in order to confront boredom, the sight of a tormented and by definition innocent animal, and that Satan who is to be answered less by theology than by moral action. In his heedless military courage Roland emulates brute Achilles himself, and he does so because he is faithful. In this he atones for the title character in "The Agent" (1969), "a pure impostor / Faithless to everything." Roland is faithful unto, to the very point of, death, and faithful to death itself, sufficiently so—the poem's range is enormous—as to put to rest a dead party. Michelson writes of "one of Wilbur's enduring themes, that a way we can make sense of our timeless condition is to be intensely aware of the here and now."[32] Maybe so. But in "Lying" our eyes are finally on the there and then of Roland in the Pyrenees in 778. Wilbur recently reflected on finding him. "I'm sure that when the idea of using the Roland story . . . came to me, of course it didn't come to me as, 'Hey, I think I'll use the Roland story,' but it came as a feeling that there was also a potentiality in Roland and the idea of Roland that could pull the whole poem together and say what I had been moving toward." He then speaks of a jazz player's "good improvising horn"—Roland's Olivant reconditioned? the sultry horn a grayfly winds in "Lycidas"?—and continues, "if you can possibly find a way which gestures to every note you've already sounded, then you think, 'Well, I can really finish this thing.' Roland's story, and the images of blood and wine and caves and all of that, the long sleep of the Roland story, presented me with a way to wind it all up and say it all, at least by implication."[33]

Roland was present, as noted, in the first jottings, along with one who didn't find her place in the poem, Dulcinea. The attraction to her occurred by means of a luminous paragraph of Michael Wood's; Wilbur reminded himself in a margin to see "André" and then "Wood on Tartuffe."[34] Quixote, Wood writes, "rebukes a group of merchants for refusing to say that Dulcinea is the most beautiful woman in the world without first seeing her: 'if I were to show her to you, what merit would there be in your confessing a truth so self-evident? The important thing is for you, without seeing her, to believe . . . that truth.'" He concludes, "Cervantes . . . offers a definition of faith, perfectly correct and perfectly ludicrous." Roland's faithfulness is another matter. It is to Charles and, in a provocative grammatical equivalence, to the Holy Spirit, who "hatched the dovetailed world." That is, the catbird-tailed one we've seen and heard.

This next-to-last line of the poem was not in the typescript offered to the *New Yorker* in the spring of 1981. In response to editorial queries about the conclusion, Wilbur wrote a new line. Two attempts precede the line as we now have it: "And to the dove that brooded on the world" (with "waste" as alternative to "world"), "And to the dovetailed bird that hatched the world." The last step, then, was to form the definitive joint, dovetailing "dove-tailed" into the world. In both draft and submitted typescript, though, he adopted the usual orthography, "dovetailed," and the magazine so printed it. He also responded positively to a suggestion that he place a dash after "Pyrenees," thus breaking the run of run-on lines in half. When collecting the poem he returned to the unpunctuated line-end, apparently having decided that the referent of "which" ("matter") is clearer without the dash than with; he also inserted the hyphen, a shard of the lost dash, in "dove-tailed," thus articulating the word's own parts, perhaps in order to remind us of the catbird's tail that tells a tale no less than does its song.[35] Hatching the world, the dove hatches a songbird that can incorporate into its everyday music something like pigeon coos and cat cries. And it sings "of its own accord," free will and catbird chording at once. The dove itself is unquestionably Milton's. Flexing, he invokes the Spirit in a complicated, Hermetic metaphor:

> O Spirit, that . . .
>
>   . . . from the first
> Wast present, and with mighty wings outspread
> Dove-like sat'st brooding on the vast Abyss
> And mad'st it pregnant. . . .

In an extended passage of much feeling Wilbur's allusion intensifies it. Thirty years ago he wrote, "The fact is that we are not always divided in spirit and that we sometimes yield utterly to a feeling or idea." Jarrell's other reservation, that in his poems Wilbur "never goes far enough," would seem to be answered here, as would James Breslin, who has it that Wilbur writes "a poetry that seldom challenges his readers—or itself."[36]

    Again it is metaphor that does the work. "Lying" is a poem in which punch as it were becomes well water that (no longer as it were) becomes a part of the north Atlantic, then mist, a river vitrified by cold, and the first springs, all informing a wine that matures for more than three centuries. When that wine finally pours out in the great *Chanson*, it does so as "The blood of Roland." In the poem's own terms, this ultimate metaphor—the blood of hemorrhagic death becoming the transubstantiated wine that is blood—is nearly blasphemous. An aesthetic imperative, then, can on occasion subordinate others that normally would prevail. One honors the honesty.

    Back between the covers of the *New and Collected* there are some last things to note. All this healthy literary lying seems to have been in part prompted by Wilde's "The Decay of Lying": "The only form of lying that is absolutely beyond reproach is lying for its own sake, and the highest development of this is . . . lying in Art." Pencilling another phrase from the dialogue on both the "Shad-Time" sheet and the first manuscript page, "he . . . falls into careless habits of accuracy," Wilbur proceeds to be carefully and habitually accurate.[37] Further, Roland joins and culminates (for now) a varied roster of iconic hero-figures who end some of the longer poems: Prospero, forgiving and forgiven, in "Castles and Distances"; the "Walking Man" sculpture, a quasi-heroic Everyman, in "Giacometti"; Saint Francis, envisioning bliss, in "A Baroque Wall-Fountain in the Villa Sciarra"; and Vishnu, his dreaming sleep untroubled, in "Walking to Sleep." Pritchard in his review of the *New and Collected* names five poems from *Walking to Sleep* and *The Mind-Reader* that "express exemplary moral attitudes."[38] So does "Lying," but with a difference. It takes moral stands, but does so mainly by presenting three exemplars at their work, performing: a poet-like catbird that by proclaiming "its many kin" tells us the world is one; Chiron, who civilizes Achilles; and Roland, whose faithfulness enacts the very truth that—as Harry Hotspur, whose foolhardy valor mocks Achilles and Roland both, proverbially puts it—shames the devil.

Finally, they all give way to another bird. Wilbur's aviary is coming to rival Frost's and Wordsworth's. He assumes a reader who would want "Lying" to be followed by no more, or less, than a self-ironic quatrain.[39] From grackle to catbird to dove to thrush, neither Larkin's evening nor Hardy's or Frost's (in "Come In") darkling ones.

On Having Mis-identified a Wild Flower

A thrush, because I'd been wrong,
Burst rightly into song
In a world not vague, not lonely,
Not governed by me only.

Game, thrush. Still, no mis-identification occurs in sensing clove in basil; rather, one's taste is refined. The progressive image of a rocking onion peel, a flapping sail, a puffed then flattened tarp, and a hip-shot Holstein rising and falling does more than refine taste—it engages, it enlarges, the heart. Roland, all but transubstantiated by the *Chanson*, tells us how to act, whether we have been in combat, like Richard Wilbur, or not. If we fall short of Roland, or even the perfectly intuitive catbird, we remain faithful to death. Like others in the *New and Collected*, this agile, ambitious, wholly realized poem, a teachable poem that teaches, remains a thing of this world. It lies its way into a truth or two.

Notes

1. Hal May and James G. Lesnick, eds., *Contemporary Authors*, New Revision Series Vol. 29 (1990), 455, and William Butts, ed., *Conversations with Richard Wilbur* (Jackson: University Press of Mississippi, 1990), 119. Wilbur may be the most often interviewed writer in the language, a function of his generosity, one suspects, as well as of how long he has been publishing. To quote some of Wilbur's thoughts about poets and poetry, including his own, is deliberately to place "Lying" in the context of what is now a fifty-year career.

2. The quotations: Butts, 119; Richard Wilbur, *The Catbird's Song: Prose Pieces 1963–1995* [hereafter *CS*] (New York: Harcourt, Brace, 1997), 140; and Jewel Spears Brooker, "A Conversation with Richard Wilbur," *Christianity and Literature* 42 (1993): 524. Wilbur elaborates on Milton's muscularity in "Richard Wilbur: An Interview by Steve Kronen," *APR: American Poetry Review* (May–June 1991): 48. Before "Walking to Sleep" Wilbur's few blank verse poems were all under forty lines and some were set up in would-be stanzas.

3. William Logan, "Richard Wilbur's Civil Tongue," *Parnassus* 21 (1993): 102.

4. "*Babel* Interview—Richard Wilbur," *Babel* 8 (1994): 30. Also: "I'm very glad that Eliot changed his mind about John Milton. Because when people ask me what poet of another time I might like to be, I know that's the answer. I'm very devoted to Milton except for *Paradise Regained*, which I can't stomach" (Kronen, 47).

5. Wilbur states that reading certain Wordsworth poems is akin to "revisiting beloved houses in which I've lived. . . . What Coleridge, Wordsworth, and Emerson suppose about the relations of mind, God, and nature are part of my inheritance and lexicon. As is Frost's critique of those suppositions" (Brooker, 529). Trained at Amherst to admire the bright ironies of Donne, Herbert, and Marvell, Wilbur has persistently rejected the egotistical sublime. Even in high school, he has said, "I found much of [Wordsworth] damnably earnest, and still do" (Butts, 89).

6. Kronen, 53. Wilbur is also remembering his Frost. At the time Wilbur was coming to know him in Cambridge, Frost stated: "There are many other things I have found myself saying about poetry, but the chiefest of these is that . . . poetry is made of metaphor" ("The Constant Symbol," published October 1946). Frost left Amherst in 1938 (the year Wilbur arrived as a student), but what he called "education by metaphor" left a mark on its classrooms, in particular those of Theodore Baird and Armour Craig. See Robin Varnum's *Fencing with Words: A History of Writing Instruction at Amherst College during the Era of Theodore Baird, 1938–1966* (Urbana, Ill.: National Council of Teachers of English, 1996), 45 ff., and Pritchard's review of it in *Raritan* 16 (Winter 1997): 143 ff. It was Craig, for nearly thirty years Baird's main support in freshman English, who first exemplified strong and imaginative reading to both Wilbur and Pritchard.

7. *CS*, 140.

8. "I like to live out here in the country and lead a fairly physical life—play a lot of tennis" (Butts, 181; also 118).

9. The manuscripts of "Lying" are in the Robert Frost Library at Amherst College. I thank Richard Wilbur for permission to quote from them and John Lancaster for aid in the archives. When Wilbur recently wrote of Merrill's having "a style that

could consume all material whatever," he could have been speaking of what he attempts in "Lying." See *JM: A Remembrance* (New York: Academy of American Poets, 1996), 88.

10. Frost in George Plimpton, ed., *Writers at Work: The "Paris Review" Interviews*, Second Series (New York: Viking, 1965), 30, 32, and Wilbur in Butts, 200. Pritchard has repeatedly quoted Frost on performance, commenting in *English Papers: A Teaching Life* (Saint Paul, Minn.: Graywolf Press, 1995) that those remarks "were never far from my mind" (163).

11. Did Satan, who had read his *Lear*, reinvent Nothing? The word comes to him four times in *Paradise Lost*. He'd also read Theseus's poetics in *A Midsummer Night's Dream*: "as imagination bodies forth / The forms of things unknown, the poet's pen / Turns them to shapes and gives to airy nothing / A local habitation and a name."

12. Aidan C. Mathews, "Writers and Wrongs: An Interview with W. D. Snodgrass and Richard Wilbur," *The Crane Bag* 7 (1983): 125. In an essay on Tennyson's "Ulysses" Wilbur also calls "enlightened" Adam's words to Raphael: "to know / That which before us lies in daily life, / Is the prime Wisdom" (*CS*, 100–101).

13. It was Pritchard who heard tones that link Wilbur and Larkin. See *Playing It by Ear* (Amherst: University of Massachusetts Press, 1994), 73.

14. John Gery, "The Sensible Emptiness in Three Poems by Richard Wilbur," *Essays in Literature* 16 (1989): 116.

15. Another recently published text may have been somewhere in Wilbur's (pre-?)conscious. George Steiner's *After Babel: Aspects of Language and Translation* (New York: Oxford University Press, 1975) has a chapter on what he calls "the creativity of falsehood." "Full humanity only begins with a reply stating 'the thing which is not' [Gulliver's Houyhnhnm-Master's phrase]: i.e., 'the water-hole is a hundred yards to my left' when it is actually fifty yards to my right. . . . 'the water-hole is dry.' . . . The series of possible false answers . . . is crucial both to human liberty and to the genius of language" (223).

16. Clara Claiborne Park, "Called to Praise: Richard Wilbur's Brilliant Positive," *Christianity and Literature* 42 (1993): 554, and Rodney Stenning Edgecombe, *A Reader's Guide to the Poetry of Richard Wilbur* (Tuscaloosa: University of Alabama Press, 1995), 142.

17. *CS*, 139–40.

18. Butts, 151. He would have remembered, too, his phrase in "Cottage Street, 1953" for Sylvia Plath, who in her last poems stated her own "brilliant negative."

19. *CS*, 10.

20. In a manuscript page containing a précis of the poem's argument Wilbur writes: "Satan, changing, could but take the given form of mist and fog"—given, not invented by him.

21. Another way of approaching these lines and others is implicit in a recent interview. "I . . . felt a natural affinity for [Marianne Moore's] kind of . . . close observation, for poetry that acknowledges the importance of things however small, poetry that aims to fuse moral and other thought with the creatures of this world" (Paul Mariani, "A Conversation with Richard Wilbur," *Image* no. 12 [Winter 1995–96]: 58). Creatures and, at least for Wilbur (and Frost), plant life.

22. Wyatt Prunty, who asserts that "line for line, Wilbur is one of the most re-

warding poets of the twentieth century," has some thoughtful paragraphs on Wilbur's similitudes in *"Fallen from the Symboled World": Precedents for the New Formalism* (New York and Oxford: Oxford University Press, 1990), 247–58.

23. Butts, 25. Of "Lying" itself Wilbur has said, "the poem assumes that the essential poetic act is the discovery of resemblance, the making of metaphor, and that, the world being one thing, all metaphor tends toward the truth" (*CS*, 140).

24. Jarrell in Wendy Salinger, ed., *Richard Wilbur's Creation* (Ann Arbor: University of Michigan Press, 1983), 85; Wilbur in Butts, 190, and *CS*, 141.

25. "What art needs to do, as Milton said, is to reflect how all things 'Rising and falling, still advance His praise,' and in the process to make a full acknowledgement of fallen-ness, doubt, and death" (Butts, 121). In *The Figure of Echo: A Mode of Allusion in Milton and After* John Hollander comes to Milton's lines from another angle. His instructive book and Wilbur's poem appear to have been written at the same moment, neither alluding to the other.

26. Bruce Michelson shrewdly connects Wilbur's lines to Jarrell's annihilating conclusion of "90 North": "nothing comes from nothing, / The darkness from the darkness. Pain comes from the darkness / And we call it wisdom. It is pain." (*Wilbur's Poetry* [Amherst: University of Massachusetts Press, 1991], 210.)

27. The four quotations: Stanley Kunitz, ed., *Twentieth Century Authors*, First Supplement (New York: Wilson, 1955), 1080; Richard Wilbur, *Responses: Prose Pieces, 1953–1976* (New York: Harcourt Brace Jovanovich, 1976), 217; Butts, 51, 194.

28. Wilbur has said of "Lying": "everything in that poem is trying to say something very hard. . . . it is a sort of torrential poem" and yet "the poem is . . . simply saying throughout that . . . every likening we might make is justified because everything belongs to one creation" (Kronen, 53). This torrent begins, we remember, with a mere ladle of punch. One could argue that the poem's marked if subtle transitions, its orderly lists, its expansive yet rigorous syntax, and its blank verse pacing make it feel like something other than a torrent.

29. Anthony Hecht, "Master of Metaphor: The Achievement of Richard Wilbur," *New Republic*, 16 May 1988, 32, and Salinger, 287.

30. Loeb Classical Library (Cambridge and London, 1979), 13, and *Ovid's Games of Love* (Detroit: Wayne State University Press, 1985), 44. The only other classical literary text Wilbur could have been working from is the first set of *Imagines* (Philostratus, *Imagines* [LCL, 1931], 135–37). See the *Lexicon Iconographicum Mythologiae Classicae* (Zurich and Munich: Artemis, 1981–), vol. 1, pt. 2, pp. 242–43, for visual representations, four of which Wilbur could have seen in Rome and Pompeii.

31. The others are "velleity," "boles," and "cullet," as Wilbur's poems go, a deliberately meager crop. Some time ago he set out to chasten the vocabulary that once won him much praise and blame. "I have a general impression that I've grown plainer, that to some extent as Yeats said, I've withered into the truth" (Kronen, 53).

32. Michelson, 53. This fine book does, strangely, call "Lying" "a burst of angst" (202). Even when Wilbur evokes Satan and the Fall, those words seem misjudged.

33. "On Formalism, Translation, and Beloved Books of Childhood," *Black Warrior Review* 22 (1996): 156. Again one wonders if sentences from Steiner's *After Babel* had lodged somewhere. "There is a myth of hand-to-hand encounter . . . which we

come across in almost every known language . . . two men meet at a narrow place . . . they fight . . . each of the two discloses his name to the other—'I am Roland' . . ." (225). And Browning's "Childe Roland" begins, "My first thought was, he lied in every word."

34. Michael Wood in *New York Review of Books*, 8 December 1977, 47. Wilbur's Amherst and Harvard friend the poet André du Bouchet is cited as a primary instigator of the poem by virtue of having Wildely theorized lying thus: "On one occasion André observed that it would be a pure creative act to announce that one had seen a squirrel in front of the Fogg Museum, if one had *not* seen a squirrel there; one would thus harmlessly and disinterestedly introduce into the minds of one's friends a squirrel which had never existed" (*CS*, 138). Inventive, one might say.

35. In reprinting "Lying" in *CS* Wilbur changes his mind a third time, reinstating the dash after "Pyrenees"; he also returns to the unhyphenated "dovetailed." He leaves untouched the fifteen other alterations of the *New Yorker* text in the *New and Collected*, where Milton's words become italicized, "gray" becomes "grey," and hyphens are added, dashes deleted, commas, colons, and periods reassigned, usually in the interest of more fluid rhythms. The present essay quotes all poems from the *New and Collected*.

36. Wilbur in *Responses*, 122, Jarrell in Salinger, 48–49, Breslin in *From Modern to Contemporary: American Poetry, 1945-1965* (Chicago: University of Chicago Press, 1984), 36. The line in question puts the poem further into the hands of Wilbur's Christian appreciators, a group on the evidence more concerned with theme-hunting than with alertness to what Yeats once called intimacies of expression. In his letter to the *New Yorker* editor Wilbur writes, "I did not wish to be thumpingly Christian in this poem." Michelson concludes his sensible discussion of the matter this way: "to read too much into the religious vocabulary of his poems is, I think, to reduce and confine his achievement unfairly, and portray his vision as more bounded and safe than it is" (99).

37. *Complete Works of Oscar Wilde*, intr. Vyvyan Holland (New York: Perennial Library, 1989), 990, 973, and, somewhere behind the poem's unignorable "snow upon the rose," this: "Nature . . . can . . . send the snow upon the ripe cornfield" (982).

38. *Boston Globe*, 24 April 1988.

39. Ordering the pieces in *CS*, Wilbur places "Some Notes on 'Lying'" directly after "Milton's 'L'Allegro' and 'Il Penseroso.'" Like those paired poems Wilbur's is meditative-descriptive, allusive, long-sentenced, and "sportfull" (thus Florio's *Dictionary* for "allegro") as well as pensive. It leaves Milton's five birds unborrowed.

Contributors

Paul Alpers is Class of 1942 Professor of English at the University of California, Berkeley. He is the author of books on Spenser's *Faerie Queene* and Virgil's Eclogues, and, most recently, of *What Is Pastoral?* (University of Chicago Press).

Christopher Benfey teaches American literature at Mount Holyoke College. He is the author of *Emily Dickinson and the Problem of Others* (1984), *The Double Life of Stephen Crane* (1992), and *Degas in New Orleans* (1997). He is a regular contributor to *The New Republic* and the online magazine *Slate.*

Howell Chickering holds the G. Armour Craig Chair of Language and Literature at Amherst College. He is the author of *Beowulf: A Dual-Language Edition* (Anchor Books, 1977, 1990) and co-editor, with Thomas H. Seiler, of *The Study of Chivalry: Resources and Approaches* (Medieval Institute Publications, 1988) and, with Margaret Switten, of *The Medieval Lyric* (Mount Holyoke College, 1989).

Rand Richards Cooper, Amherst '80, is the author of *The Last to Go* (Harcourt Brace Jovanovich) and *Big As Life* (The Dial Press). He has taught at Amherst and at Emerson colleges; his writing has appeared in *Harper's*, *The Atlantic*, and many other magazines. He lives in Hartford, Connecticut.

Helen Deutsch, Amherst '82, teaches English literature at UCLA. She is the author of *Resemblance and Disgrace: Alexander Pope and the Deformation of Culture* (Harvard University Press, 1996), and a translator of Augustan Latin poetry. She is currently pondering a book on Samuel Johnson and the mind-body problem.

Joseph Epstein is the editor of *The Norton Book of Personal Essays.* His most recent book is *Life Sentences,* a collection of literary essays, also published by W. W. Norton.

Anne Ferry's books include *The "Inward" Language, The Art of Naming,* and *The Title to the Poem* (Stanford, 1996). She is now writing a book about anthologies of poetry.

David Ferry, Amherst '46, is Sophie Chantal Professor, Emeritus, at Wellesley College. His most recent books are *Gilgamesh: A New Rendering in English Verse* (Farrar Straus & Giroux, 1992); *Dwelling Places: Poems and Translations* (University of Chicago Press, 1993), and *The Odes of Horace: A Translation* (Farrar Straus & Giroux, 1997).

Neil Hertz teaches in the Humanities Center at Johns Hopkins University. He is the author of *The End of the Line: Essays on Psychoanalysis and the Sublime* and is completing a book on George Eliot. He met Bill Pritchard years ago at Amherst College, of all places.

W. E. Kennick is G. Henry Whitcomb Professor Emeritus of Philosophy at Amherst College. A graduate of Oberlin College (B.A., 1945) and Cornell University (Ph.D., 1952), he has taught at Amherst for over forty years, specializing in history of philosophy, aesthetics, metaphysics, and Wittgenstein. He is the editor/author of *Art and Philosophy* (St. Martin's Press, 1964, 1979).

Alan Lelchuk is the author of six novels, among them *American Mischief, Miriam at 34,* and, most recently, *Brooklyn Boy* and *Playing the Game.* He has taught at Brandeis and at Amherst College, where he was Visiting Writer from 1982 to 1984. He currently teaches at Dartmouth.

Frank Lentricchia's recent books include two novels, *Johnny Critelli* and *The Knifeman,* and a memoir, *The Edge of Night.* Readers of this volume may recall that he is also the author of *After the New Criticism* and *Criticism* *and Social Change*. He teaches at Duke University, where he is Katherine Everett Gilbert Professor of Literature.

Francis Murphy teaches at Smith College and along with Bill Pritchard is a co-editor of *The Norton Anthology of American Literature*.

Fred Pfeil, Amherst '71, is most recently the author of *White Guys: Studies in Postmodern Domination and Difference* (Verso, 1995) and *What They Tell You to Forget* (Pushcart Press, 1996), a collection of shorter fiction. He also teaches English and American studies at Trinity College, in Hartford, Connecticut.

Peter R. Pouncey is Fobes Professor of Greek at Amherst. He was dean of Columbia College and professor of classics at Columbia, and wrote *The Necessities of War: A Study of Thucydides' Pessimism*, which won the University's Lionel Trilling Award. From 1984 to 1994 he was president of Amherst.

Will Pritchard, youngest son of William H. and Marietta Pritchard, is a graduate student in English at the University of Chicago. He is finishing his dissertation, which is entitled "Outward Appearances: The Display of Women in Restoration London."

Christopher Ricks teaches at Boston University, and is a member of the Association of Literary Scholars and Critics.

Roger Sale taught with Bill Pritchard at Amherst, 1958–62, and since then at the University of Washington. He is the author of two books about Seattle, one about composition, and some others about books. He hopes, when it is just about time to retire, to finish a book about teaching.

David Sofield is Samuel Williston Professor of English at Amherst College, where he teaches seventeenth- and twentieth-century poetry and creative writing. His poems and essays have appeared in *The New Yorker*, *The New Republic*, *The New Criterion*, *Poetry*, and *America*.

Patricia Meyer Spacks, Edgar Shannon Professor of English at the University of Virginia, is author most recently of *Boredom: The Literary His-*

tory of a State of Mind. She is currently writing a study of privacy in eighteenth- and nineteenth-century England.

Herbert F. Tucker, Amherst '71, teaches English at the University of Virginia. He is the author of *Browning's Beginnings* (1980) and *Tennyson and the Doom of Romanticism* (1988), and the editor of *Critical Essays on Alfred Lord Tennyson* (1993) and the forthcoming *Blackwell Companion to Victorian Literature and Culture.* He is also associate editor of *New Literary History.*

Helen Vendler, A. Kingsley Porter University Professor at Harvard, is the author of books on Yeats, Keats, Herbert, and Stevens. Harvard University Press published *The Art of Shakespeare's Sonnets* in 1997, and Harper-Collins will publish, in its Modern Masters series, her *Seamus Heaney* (1998). She writes frequently on contemporary poetry.

William Youngren (Amherst '53, Ph.D. Harvard) has taught at M.I.T., Smith, and (since 1971) Boston College. His publications include *Semantics, Linguistics, and Criticism* and several articles on neoclassical literary theory, as well as essays on and reviews of music and records in *The Atlantic, Fanfare,* and other magazines. He is at present completing a doctoral dissertation in musicology for Brandeis, on the songs of C. P. E. Bach, and a book called *Generality and the Poetic Image.* He is also collaborating with Igor Kipnis on a biography of the great Russian basso Alexander Kipnis. Now and then he plays jazz piano.

Index